Lecture Notes in Computer Scien

T0237749

Commenced Publication in 1973
Founding and Former Series Editors:
Gerhard Goos, Juris Hartmanis, and Jan van Leeuwen

Steve Dunne   Bill Stoddart (Eds.)

Unifying Theories of Programming

First International Symposium, UTP 2006
Walworth Castle, County Durham, UK
February 5-7, 2006
Revised Selected Papers

Springer

Volume Editors

Steve Dunne
Bill Stoddart
University of Teesside
School of Computing
Borough Road, Middlesbrough, TS1 3BA, UK
E-mail: {s.e.dunne,w.j.stoddart}@tees.ac.uk

The cover illustration represents Walworth Castle, County Durham, UK

Library of Congress Control Number: 2006926663

CR Subject Classification (1998): F.1, D.3, D.1, D.2, D.4

LNCS Sublibrary: SL 1 – Theoretical Computer Science and General Issues

ISSN 0302-9743
ISBN-10 3-540-34750-X Springer Berlin Heidelberg New York
ISBN-13 978-3-540-34750-7 Springer Berlin Heidelberg New York

Springer is a part of Springer Science+Business Media

springer.com

Printed in Germany

Typesetting: Camera-ready by author, data conversion by Scientific Publishing Services, Chennai, India
Printed on acid-free paper SPIN: 11768173 06/3142 5 4 3 2 1 0

Preface

A number of formal notations and theories have now emerged and proved themselves effective as tools for the practising software engineer. Within these theories we see a number of common themes, such as abstraction, refinement, choice, termination, feasibility, concurrency and communication. The commonality of such themes opens perspectives for unifying theories, an activity which can increase our ability to use existing methods and notations, to recognise their limitations, and to extend and generalise them. Based on the pioneering work on unifying theories of programming of Tony Hoare and He Jifeng, which itself acknowledges the influence of Eric Hehner's seminal ideas on predicative programming, the aims of this first UTP symposium are to reaffirm the significance of the ongoing UTP project, to encourage efforts to advance it by providing a focus for the sharing of results by those already actively contributing, and to raise awareness of the benefits of unifying theoretical frameworks among the wider computer science and software engineering communities.

We are extremely fortunate in having secured the participation of such a formidable panel of invited speakers as Ian Hayes, He Jifeng, Rick Hehner, Tony Hoare, Jeff Sanders and Jim Woodcock, who truly comprise the leading lights in the development and ongoing exploitation of the unifying theories of programming.

I'm pleased to express my appreciation for the sterling efforts of all members of the UTP 2006 programme committee, and also those of the additional reviewers, in reviewing all the submitted papers so conscientiously. I must express my particular appreciation to my Teesside colleagues Bill Stoddart and Frank Zeyda who supported me unfailingly in my role as Program Chair in many practical ways. Indeed, Frank's technical prowess in developing and maintaining the symposium's various websites proved absolutely invaluable. I'm also grateful for the sensible advice I invariably obtained from my good friend Andy Galloway of the University of York who was always willing to act as a discreet sounding board on various aspects of the organisation of the symposium.

Finally, I must of course thank all the sponsors of the symposium, but here I should particularly acknowledge the generous financial support of the University of Teesside's School of Computing, whose willingness and readiness to underwrite this symposium from the outset were in large part instrumental in its coming about at all.

February 2006 Steve Dunne

Organisation

Programme Committee

Steve Dunne (University of Teesside) [**chair**]
Bernhard Aichernig (UNU-IIST, Macau)
Didier Bert (LSR-IMAG, Grenoble)
Jonathan Bowen (London South Bank University)
Andrew Butterfield (Trinity College Dublin)
Ana Cavalcanti (University of York)
Yifeng Chen (Durham University)
Colin Fidge (Queensland University of Technology)
Andy Galloway (University of York)
Lindsay Groves (Victoria University of Wellington)
Martin Henson (University of Essex)
Zhiming Liu (UNU-IIST, Macau)
David Naumann (Stevens Inst. of Technology, New Jersey)
Richard Paige (University of York)
Bill Stoddart (University of Teesside)

Additional Reviewers

Richard Banach (University of Manchester)
Phil Cook (University of Queensland)
Marcio Cornelio (University of Pernambuco)
Xiaoshan Li (University of Macau)
Vladimir Mencl (Charles University Prague)
Shengchao Qin (Durham University)

Sponsors

University of Teesside
HISE University of York
BCS-FACS
Microsoft Research

Table of Contents

Retrospective and Prospective for Unifying Theories of Programming

Eric Hehner

Department of Computer Science, University of Toronto
BA5224, 40 St. George St. Toronto ON Canada M5S 2E4
Tel.: 1 416 978 6026; Fax: 1 416 978 4765
hehner@cs.utoronto.ca
www.cs.utoronto.ca/~hehner

Abstract. This paper presents a personal account of developments leading to Unifying Theories of Programming, and some opinions about the direction the work should take in the future. It also speculates on consequences the work will have for all of computer science.

1 UTP and Me

My introduction to formal methods was the book *a Discipline of Programming* [3] by Edsger Dijkstra in 1976. I wrote a small contribution in a paper named **do** *considered* **od** [14] in that same year. In that paper I proposed recursive refinement as a way of composing programs, and a different way of generating the sequence of approximations for loop semantics that is more general than the one in Dijkstra's book, applying to all looping constructs, including general recursion.

It was standard in semantics work then (and for some people, it remains so today) to use a meaning function (sometimes written as double square brackets) that maps program text to its meaning. In Dijkstra's book, he used the *wp* function to map a program text and postcondition to a precondition. If S is some program text, and R is a postcondition, then $wp(S, R)$ is the exact precondition[1] for execution of S to terminate and establish postcondition R. In my 1976 paper, I made the proposal that we should stop thinking of programs as mere text, and start thinking of them as mathematical expressions in their own right. We should not need a function to map a program to its meaning. My proposal was that, like any mathematical expression, a program can stand for its meaning all by itself. So, in that paper, program S is a function that maps a postcondition R to a precondition, written $S(R)$. Sequential composition (semicolon) is just function composition. I proposed that the arrow in a guarded command is a lifted

[1] The English meaning of "precondition" is "something that is necessary beforehand". In Dijkstra's use, the "weakest precondition" *wp* was the weakest sufficient condition, *i.e.* the necesary and sufficient condition. To avoid misusing the word "precondition", I am saying "exact precondition" to mean the condition that is both necessary and sufficient.

S. Dunne and W. Stoddart (Eds.): UTP 2006, LNCS 4010, pp. 1–17, 2006.

implication, that the box connecting guarded commands is a lifted conjunction, and that the **if fi** brackets are a "totalizer". That proposal seems tame today, but in 1976 it was apparently bizarre, causing rejection of the paper in its first submission; and in its second submission the referees insisted that it be removed from the paper for publication. Since there were other contributions of the paper that I really wanted published, I obeyed the referees and removed it from the paper for publication in *Acta Informatica* in 1979. But it remains in the 1976 technical report version. Fortunately for all of us, Ralph Back in Finland read the technical report, adopted the proposal, and began the work called "Refinement Calculus", culminating in a wonderful book with that same name in 1998 [1].

Meanwhile, I made an amazing discovery: that Dijkstra's book was not the first work on formal methods; from the lack of references in the book, I had supposed it was. But it owed a lot to a paper by C.A.R.Hoare in 1969 [16]. That paper, and another in 1972 on data abstraction [17], and some lectures by Tony on CSP, convinced me to spend my sabbatical in 1981 in Oxford. It was an intellectually lively place, including Jean-Raymond Abrial, Steve Brookes, Peter Henderson, Cliff Jones, Lockwood Morris, David Park, Bill Roscoe, Dana Scott, Ib Sorensen, Joe Stoy, Bernard Sufrin, Jim Woodcock, and others. But it was not a good year for the Hoare family.

I had two projects while I was in Oxford. I had started writing a book in the year before going there, but then David Gries started writing the same book, and sending me the chapters for comment. David wrote much faster than I did, and quickly overtook me. So I decided to put my effort into comments on David's book, and abandon mine. But in Oxford, Tony persuaded me that there is room for another book, especially if I pitch my book at a different level than David's. So I resumed writing, aiming for a more advanced audience. The book [12] was published in Tony's series in 1984, and in it programs were predicate transformers.

My other project in Oxford in 1981 was to find a good model for CSP. I decided that in this project, programs were not predicate transformers, but predicates. Each day I would go into Tony's office before he arrived, and fill his board with my latest formulas, hoping that would catch his attention. I guess it worked. The paper [13] was a technical report in 1981, and published in *TCS* in 1983.

I liked the idea of using predicates for programs so much that I decided to apply it beyond CSP to a wide variety of programming constructs. My principles of "predicative programming" were:

- a specification is a predicate[2]
- refinement is implication
- a program is an implemented specification

[2] I am using the word "predicate" here as I used it back then, and as some people still use it today, to mean a boolean expression, particularly one that contains or may contain subexpression(s) of other type(s), and/or quantifiers. I now say "boolean expression" no matter what types its expressions have, and no matter what operators are used wihin. I now use "predicate" to mean a function whose result is boolean.

1982, IFIP Working Group 2.3 (Programming Methodology) allowed me an extraordinary 4 hours to present these ideas. For the most part, the presentation went very well, but there was one point that went badly. I wanted a "total correctness" formalism (who wouldn't?), and I achieved it by borrowing the weakest specification (given an initial state, any final state is satisfactory) to represent possibly nonterminating computations. I "justified" it by saying that if you don't care what the result is, then you don't care if there is a result (I am not defending that argument any more). I gained "total correctness" at the cost of making sequential composition (semicolon) almost but not quite associative. I had a theorem saying that if the state space is infinite (one integer variable makes it infinite) then semicolon is associative for all programs. I had another theorem saying that if there is at least one variable not appearing in any program (one unused boolean variable is enough), then again semicolon is associative for all programs. I remember Butler Lampson saying that I should just assume there's one extra variable, and get on with it. I also remember that Tony was unhappy; for him, associativity of semicolon had to be unqualified.

In 1982 March, Tony came to Toronto for a week, in part so that we could resolve the problem. I was opposed to adding an extra boolean variable that would not appear in any program, but would burden nearly every non-program specification. Tony was opposed to any qualification on associativity. In the end, Tony convinced me to add the alternative he preferred as an appendix to my paper. I tried to give the variable some physical motivation, so I called it s for "start/stop", saying that s with "initial" decoration means "the computation has started" and that s with "final" decoration means "the computation has stopped". That variable became the *ok* variable in UTP [15]. "Predicative Programming" was published [11] in *CACM* in 1984.

There was a growing number of theories of programming. I had predicative programming; Edsger Dijkstra had *wp* ; Cliff Jones had VDM; David Parnas had limited domain relations, and a second theory that he called "standard semantics"; and there was another theory of partial relations proposed by Bill Robison and independently by Bernard von Stengel, that later became the refinement semantics of Z. These were not just notationally different; they had substantive differences in expressive power and in their treatment of termination. So I set out to compare these different theories in a paper called "Termination Conventions and Comparative Semantics", published in *Acta Informatica* in 1988 [10]. The basis of the comparison was a translation from each of them to my own predicative semantics, and *vice versa*. I included a catalogue of semantics for all the aforementioned theories, expressed both with and without the extra boolean variable that indicates proper termination. So, in my mind at least, this paper was very much a forerunner of the UTP work.

One more idea that may have influenced UTP is parallel by merge. In 1990, Theo Norvell was my PhD student, and he suggested parallel by merge as a way of defining parallel composition that is both implementable and insensitive to frame. That is the form of parallelism in the 1993 edition of my book *a Practical Theory of Programming* [6], and in UTP in 1998. I have since abandoned it, and for the 2002 edition and onward I have returned to simple conjunction (to keep implementability, it must be sensitive to frame) that I had used from 1981 to 1989 [11, 13].

Since publication of UTP, both it and my work have been extended to include probabilistic computation [7], but I think neither work influenced the other; perhaps we were both influenced by the same source [18].

This history of work leading to UTP has been a personal one, and I am not sure it accords well with a history that Tony Hoare and He Jifeng might tell. My doubt comes from the fact that none of the work I have mentioned, except for the predicate model of CSP [13], was referenced in the UTP book.

2 UTP Without Me

I am pleased to think that I made some contribution to the UTP project. But there is an important point on which I have tried hard and so far failed to have any influence. I think the point is inevitable, so I will now make another attempt.

The tradition in programming theories is not to speak directly about execution time. To refer to theories that talk about whether a computation terminates, and the result upon termination, we commonly use the words "total correctness", suggesting that nothing else is of interest. I suspect the sentiment was (and maybe still is) that execution time is too dependent on factors (compiler, hardware) beyond the program. There are circumstances when time is important, called real-time or reactive programming. And theories have been invented [2], and new ones are still being invented [4], to reason about execution time. An entire logic, called temporal logic, was invented to specify and reason about timing. But none of that is necessary. All you need to do is add a time variable, placing increments ($t := t + \mathit{something}$) in the program wherever they are needed to account for the time required by the other operations in the program. Then you reason about the time variable exactly the same way you reason about the other variables, using exactly the same theory you were using before you added time. I presented this position in a paper [9] published in 1989 January.

Then in June of that year, in the opening address of the first MPC [8], I presented a more compelling reason for the inclusion of a time variable. To calculate the exact execution time, the time variable can be real-valued, and the increments should be exactly the execution time of the instructions compiled for the machine that will execute the instructions. A more abstract, machine-independent measure of time uses an integer-valued time variable, counting iterations of loops and recursive calls, ignoring all else. A still more abstract measure of time uses a boolean-valued time variable that just distinguishes finite execution time (termination) from infinite execution time (nontermination); that is the *ok* variable of UTP. But there's a big difference between numeric (real- or integer-valued) time and boolean time: the former can tick, and the latter cannot. We can do arithmetic on the time variable if it is a numeric type, but not if it is boolean. And that has a profound effect on the semantics and proof rules of the programming language, as I shall explain.

3 If and When

The acceptance of 0 as a number has taken a long time, and is still incomplete. In English, no-one quite knows whether to treat 0 as singular or plural, does he? On your keypad or telephone it is placed after 9, which is mathematically silly. In the 1991 Toronto phone book, there is a page that helpfully gives the time difference to various places in the world; to the U.K. it says "+5", and to Costa Rica it says "-1". But to Cuba it says "NA", and the legenda explains "time difference not applicable". By 1996 they tried to correct it; for Cuba it says "=", with the same explanation. In 1997 they discovered the number 0, but they felt the need then, and still do today, to explain that 0 means "no time difference".

When we say "There are a number of issues to discuss.", we don't mean there might be 0 of them. When 0 really is a possibility, people often add the phrase "if any", as in "Please put all the leftovers in the fridge, if there are any.". They create a case analysis, when none was needed. For example, the 1991 Canadian census asked the question "How many persons who have a usual home somewhere else in Canada stayed here overnight between 1991 June 3 and 4?", then offers a place to tick if there were none, and a box to fill with the number of persons if there were some. The people designing the form probably know perfectly well that the box is sufficient, but without the place to tick "if none" they would be overwhelmed by people complaining that they can't answer the question.

The Fortran language of 1955 had a loop construct, but its body had to be executed at least once; I suppose it seemed senseless to have a loop whose body might be executed 0 times. The error was corrected in Algol in 1958, and in PL/I, and in Pascal, in part: iteration might be 0 times, but the data structure over which one is iterating, the array, had to have at least one element. In Pascal that meant there was no null string. And that put the algebra of data structures back where the algebra of natural numbers was prior to 1930. We learn, but slowly; two steps forward, one step back.

The authors of UTP might have chosen to include a boolean variable to distinguish executions that take 0 time from those that take positive time. This variable would complicate the semantics to no advantage, and it would infect all specifications, causing the authors to invent "designs", which are specifications with this variable suppressed but still implicit. I commend the authors for not making this mistake. Perhaps someday, in English (or its successor), we won't feel the need to ask for "the number, if any"; we will simplify by just asking for "the number", accepting 0 as an answer.

In English, one sometimes hears the phrase "if ever", or "if and when", as in "I'll deal with that if and when it happens.". If we just say "I'll deal with that when it happens.", undoubtedly someone would immediately ask: "What if it never happens?". But it seems to me that case is already covered: if it never happens, I'll deal with it never. We simplify by eliminating the case analysis, and to do that we must learn to accept ∞ as an answer to the question "when?". We are not bothered by the different grammar in the two sentences "I don't have any bananas." and "I have 0 bananas."; one uses a negative verb and the other a positive verb, but we take them to mean the same thing. Likewise we should take "It never happens." and "It happens at time ∞." to mean the same thing. Perhaps someone in the future will show some census forms in which the case ∞ was separated off unnecessarily, and that speaker's audience can all have a good laugh at their ancestors' unwillingness to accept infinity as a number.

The authors of UTP have chosen to include a boolean variable *ok* to distinguish executions that take finite time from those that take infinite time. This variable complicates the semantics to no advantage, and it infects all specifications, causing the authors to invent "designs", which are specifications with this variable suppressed but still implicit. Worse than that, this variable causes duplication of work. Suppose I want to show that a computation involving loops delivers a certain result within a certain time bound. The next section shows that the work necessary to prove ok' is equivalent to finding an upper time bound, which I must repeat using a time variable in order to prove an upper time bound.

4 What Is the Meaning of Loops?

There are two usual ways to give meaning to loops (and recursions) in a total correctness semantics: the limit of a sequence of approximations, and a least fixpoint. To find the meaning of $b * S$ using the limit of approximations, define

$$\begin{aligned} W_0 &= \mathbf{true} \\ W_{n+1} &= (S;\ W_n) \lhd b \rhd II \end{aligned}$$

Then

$$b * S = (\forall n \,.\, W_n)$$

where the quantification may need to continue past the naturals and through the transfinite ordinals. As an example, we can find the semantics of

$$(x \neq 1) * (x := x \text{ div } 2)$$

in one integer variable x . We find

$$\begin{aligned} W_0 &= \mathbf{true} \\ W_1 &= (x := x \text{ div } 2\,;\, \mathbf{true}) \lhd x \neq 1 \rhd II \\ &\qquad = (x = 1 \Rightarrow x' = 1) \\ W_2 &= (x := x \text{ div } 2\,;\, x = 1 \Rightarrow x' = 1) \lhd x \neq 1 \rhd II \\ &= (1 \leq x < 4 \Rightarrow x' = 1) \end{aligned}$$

Jumping to the general case, which we could prove by induction,

$$W_n = (1 \leq x < 2^n \Rightarrow x' = 1)$$

And so

$$\begin{aligned} & (x \neq 1) * (x := x \text{ div } 2) \\ = \ & (\forall n \,.\, 1 \leq x < 2^n \Rightarrow x' = 1) \\ = \ & (1 \leq x \Rightarrow x' = 1) \end{aligned}$$

A sequence of approximations introduces an integer-valued time variable in disguise: it is the subscript n. W_n is the strongest specification of behavior that is observed before time n, in the measure that counts iterations. If we have an integer-valued time variable, it is unnecessary to introduce another one for the same purpose, and we can simplify the semantics of loops.

The other usual way to define loops is as a least fixpoint.

$$b * S \quad = \quad \mu X \,.\, (S \,;\, X) \lhd b \rhd \mathit{II}$$

This is closely analogous to defining the natural numbers $\mathbb{N}$ as a least fixpoint.

$$\mathbb{N} \quad = \quad \mu X \,.\, \{0\} \cup \{n+1 \mid n \in X\}$$

For more familiarity, we can remove μ by replacing the definition with two axioms called construction and induction. Loop construction

$$b{*}\mathrm{S} \quad = \quad (S \,;\, b * S) \lhd b \rhd \mathit{II}$$

says that a loop equals its first unrolling. Stated differently, $b * S$ is a solution (fixpoint) of the equation (in unknown X)

$$X \quad = \quad (S \,;\, X) \lhd b \rhd \mathit{II}$$

It is analogous to natural construction

$$\mathbb{N} \quad = \quad \{0\} \cup \{n+1 \mid n \in \mathbb{N}\}$$

which says that 0 is a natural number, and if n is a natural number, so is $n+1$ (II is analogous to 0, $\lhd b \rhd$ is analogous to $\cup$, and unrolling is analogous to adding 1). Stated differently, it says that $\mathbb{N}$ is a fixpoint of an equation. Loop induction

$$(\forall \sigma, \sigma' \,.\, X \quad = \quad (S \,;\, X) \lhd b \rhd \mathit{II}) \;\Rightarrow\; (\forall \sigma, \sigma' \,.\, X \Rightarrow b * S)$$

where σ is the state variables, says that $b * S$ is as weak as any fixpoint, so it is the weakest (least strong) fixpoint. It is analogous to natural induction, which can be written in a nontraditional form (to make the analogy clearer), replacing predicate satisfaction with set membership, as follows:

$$\forall X \,.\, X = \{0\} \cup \{n+1 \mid n \in X\} \;\Rightarrow\; \mathbb{N} \subseteq X$$

which says that $\mathbb{N}$ is a subset of any fixpoint, so it is the smallest fixpoint. Once again, if we lack an arithmetic time variable, then the loop semantics must compensate by introducing a kind of loop-arithmetic. If we have an arithmetic time variable, this is unnecessary, and we can simplify the semantics of loops.

Programming from specifications by means of refinement replaces the question "what does this program mean?" with the question "does this program refine that specification?" [5]. All a programmer needs to know about the meaning of program P is: for what specifications S is $S \Leftarrow P$ a theorem? What a programmer needs to know about II is

$$\sigma = \sigma' \;\Leftarrow\; \mathit{II}$$

In UTP (as in my work), II is defined by strengthening that refinement to equality, but for programming, all we need is the implication. The same comment applies to assignment, conditional, and sequential composition.

I am content to form loops by recursive refinement (as in my 1976 paper [14]). For example, if the specification (in one integer variable x) is $x \geq 1 \Rightarrow x' = 1$, I can refine it as follows:

$$(x \geq 1 \Rightarrow x' = 1) \;\Leftarrow\; II \lhd x = 1 \rhd (x := x \operatorname{div} 2 \,;\, x \geq 1 \Rightarrow x' = 1)$$

With this refinement, we can now execute the specification $x \geq 1 \;\Rightarrow\; x' = 1$ by executing what refines it, and when specification $x \geq 1 \;\Rightarrow\; x' = 1$ is encountered again, it is again executed by executing what refines it. That's a loop. Knowing what II, assignment, conditional, and sequential composition refine is sufficient for proof of this refinement; we do not need any further theory for loops.

If we are interested in execution time, we include a time variable. Let's make it integer-valued, and count iterations. We can prove

$$(x \geq 1 \Rightarrow t' \leq t + \mathit{log}\, x) \;\Leftarrow\; II \lhd x{=}1 \rhd (x := x \operatorname{div} 2 \,;\, t := t + 1 \,;\, t' \leq t + \mathit{log}\, x)$$

which says that for positive x, the execution time is bounded above by $\mathit{log}\, x$. We can also prove

$$(x < 1 \Rightarrow t' = \infty) \;\Leftarrow\; II \lhd x = 1 \rhd (x := x \operatorname{div} 2 \,;\, t := t + 1 \,;\, x < 1 \Rightarrow t' = \infty)$$

which says that for nonpositive x, the execution time is infinite. And for free we get the conjunction of all that we proved previously: execution satisfies

$$(x \geq 1 \Rightarrow x' = 1) \;\wedge\; (x \geq 1 \Rightarrow t' \leq t + \mathit{log}\, x) \;\wedge\; (x < 1 \Rightarrow t' = \infty)$$

It is extremely useful to be able to prove partial properties separately, and specifically to be able to prove results and timing separately, and then to combine them for free.

Although I am content to form loops without any loop syntax and without any theory that pertains to loops, apparently some people feel the need for loop syntax and theory. So UTP provides the syntax $b * P$. All we need to say about it is that

$$S \;\Leftarrow\; b * P$$

is syntactic sugar for

$$S \;\Leftarrow\; (P \,;\, S) \lhd b \rhd II$$

We do not attribute any meaning to $b * P$, but only to the refinement $S \Leftarrow b * P$. We do not need a limit of a sequence of approximations. We do not need least fixpoints. If we want to know about time (including termination), we add a time variable, but we don't have to complicate the semantics of loops.

My example recursive refinement has the form of a $*$ loop, but recursive refinement works for any loop structure, including loops with intermediate exits and deep exits, and for general recursion, not just tail recursion (see [6]).

5 What Can We Prove About Loops?

The two traditional ways of defining loop semantics (limit of a sequence of approximations, least fixpoint) for "total correctness" are too complicated to be used in proofs, and in practice they never are used. Instead, those who use formal methods split the problem into a "partial correctness" proof and a termination argument. "Partial correctness" of

$$(x \geq 1 \Rightarrow x' = 1) \;\Leftarrow\; (x \neq 1) * (x := x \,\mathsf{div}\, 2\, ;\, x \geq 1 \Rightarrow x' = 1)$$

is exactly

$$(x \geq 1 \Rightarrow x' = 1) \;\Leftarrow\; (x := x \,\mathsf{div}\, 2\, ;\, x \geq 1 \Rightarrow x' = 1) \lhd x \neq 1 \rhd II$$

For termination they use a "variant" or "bound function" or "well-founded set". In this example, they show that for $x > 1$, x is decreased but not below 0 by the body $x := x \,\mathsf{div}\, 2$ of the loop. The variant is again time in disguise; they are showing that the execution time is bounded by x in the measure that counts iterations. Then they throw away the bound, retaining only the one bit of information that there is a bound, and hence termination. In the example, this corresponds to a proof of

$$(x \geq 1 \Rightarrow t' \leq t + x) \Leftarrow (x := x \,\mathsf{div}\, 2\, ;\, t := t + 1\, ;\, x \geq 1 \Rightarrow t' \leq t + x) \lhd x \neq 1 \rhd II$$

This linear time bound is rather loose; for about the same effort we prove a logarithmic time bound. And in exactly the same way, we prove nontermination when $x < 1$. More generally, we can prove useful lower time bounds; we are not limited to the existence of an upper bound, which is what "total correctness" provides.

A "total correctness" semantics makes the proof of invariance properties difficult, or even impossible. For example, we cannot prove

$$x' \geq x \;\Leftarrow\; b * (x' \geq x)$$

which says, quite reasonably, that if the body of a loop doesn't decrease x, then the loop doesn't decrease x. The problem is that the semantics does not allow us to separate such invariance properties from the question of termination. If, in place of the above, we write

$$x' \geq x \;\Leftarrow\; (x' \geq x\, ;\, t := t + 1\, ;\, x' \geq x) \lhd x \neq 1 \rhd II$$

as I advocate, then the proof of the invariance property is easy.

6 What Can We Prove About Infinite Loops?

What can we prove about an infinite loop? According to the least fixpoint semantics, nothing. According to that semantics, $\mathbf{true} * P$ is equivalent to $\mathbf{true}$, which is completely arbitrary behavior. It does not imply $\neg\, ok'$; the behavior may be nonterminating, or terminating. If we add a time variable, we cannot prove $t' = t + \infty$. If the body of the loop includes communications (interactions), we cannot prove they happen. My way, to prove S, we must prove

$$S \Leftarrow (P\,;\,t := t+1\,;\,S) \lhd \mathbf{true} \rhd \mathit{II}$$

or more simply

$$S \Leftarrow (P\,;\,t := t+1\,;\,S)$$

(which is what I would write in the first place). Taking II as body for the moment, we cannot prove $t' \le t+n$ for finite n ; that would require proving

$$t' \le t+n \Leftarrow t' \le t+1+n$$

which is not so. But we can prove $t' > t+n$. We can also prove $t' = t+\infty$; that requires proving

$$t' = t+\infty \Leftarrow t' = t+1+\infty$$

and since, in my algebra, ∞ absorbs finite additions (∞ is a fixpoint of *tick*), that refinement is a theorem. If the body of the loop includes communications, we can prove that they do indeed happen.

A specification S is implementable (in UTP terminology, "healthy") if and only if for all initial states (including time) there is a final state (including time) that satisfies the specification with nondecreasing time (and non-undo-able communications, but I'll omit that for now):

$$\forall \sigma \,.\, \exists \sigma' \,.\, S \wedge t' \ge t$$

Refinement by a program is proof of implementability. For recursive refinement, we need to know separately that the specification is implementable. Although

$$\mathbf{false} \Leftarrow (P\,;\,t := t+1\,;\,\mathbf{false})$$

is a theorem, we reject **false** because it is unimplementable; we have not implemented a miracle.

Disturbingly, we can prove both of the implementable specifications $x' = 2$ and $x' = 3$. Both

$$x' = 2 \Leftarrow (t := t+1\,;\,x' = 2)$$
$$x' = 3 \Leftarrow (t := t+1\,;\,x' = 3)$$

are theorems. There is no inconsistency here. My theory of programming is sound in the following sense: if S is an implementable specification, and F is a program (possibly with call sites), and we can prove the refinement $S \Leftarrow F(S)$, then no observation of the corresponding computation will ever contradict S. The point is that observations are made at finite times, whereas the results $x' = 2$ and $x' = 3$ happen at time ∞ (never). For exactly the same reason, we can prove both

$$\neg\, ok' \Leftarrow (t := t+1\,;\,\neg\, ok')$$
$$ok' \Leftarrow (t := t+1\,;\,ok')$$

If this is at first disturbing, consider it the price to pay for the ability to prove results and timing separately, and combine them for free.

Perhaps more disturbingly, we can also prove

$$t < \infty \Rightarrow t' < \infty \Leftarrow (t := t+1\,;\,t < \infty \Rightarrow t' < \infty)$$

which seems to say that if the computation starts at a finite time, it will end at a finite time. But without a time bound, the specification offers no opportunity for complaint that the computation is taking too long. The theory should allow, and does allow, any computation whose observation does not contradict the specification.

The theory is incomplete in the following sense. Even if S is an implementable specification, and observations of the computation(s) corresponding to $S \Leftarrow F(S)$ never (in finite time) contradict S, the refinement might not be provable. But in that case, there is another implementable specification R such that the refinements $S \Leftarrow R$ and $R \Leftarrow F(R)$ are both provable. In that weaker sense, the theory is complete. There cannot be a theory of programming that is both sound and complete in the stronger sense.

7 The Problem with Halting

The halting function (predicate) is defined to tell whether a program's execution terminates. I will make two simplifications to the standard formulation, neither of which changes anything essential. We need to encode programs as data so we can apply the halting function to something that represents a program. In the standard formulation, programs are numbered, so we can apply the halting function to a number representing a program. Instead, I use a more transparent encoding: a program is represented by its text (character string). (That is how a program is presented to a compiler or interpreter.) The other simplification is to eliminate all mention of initial state (input). One way to do that is to define the halting function applied to program text p as saying whether "p halts from all initial states" or "p fails to halt on some initial state". Another way to do it is to pick some initial state as the one where execution of any program always starts; if you want some other initial state, just start the program with some initializing assignments to create the state you want. Define predicate $H : \mathbf{T} \longrightarrow \mathbf{B}$, where $\mathbf{T}$ is the text data type and $\mathbf{B}$ is the boolean data type, so that

$$\begin{aligned} H(\text{``} I\!I \text{''}) &= \mathbf{true} \\ H(\text{``}\mathbf{true} * I\!I \text{''}) &= \mathbf{false} \end{aligned}$$

and so on. Define text P as follows:

$$P = \text{``}(\mathbf{true} * I\!I) \lhd H(P) \rhd I\!I \text{''}$$

If we assume H is a functional program, then P represents a program. Now we ask: what is the result of $H(P)$? If the execution of P terminates, then $H(P)$ is **true**, and P represents a program that is equivalent to $\mathbf{true} * I\!I$, so execution of P does not terminate. And if the execution of P does not terminate, then $H(P)$ is **false**, and P represents a program that is equivalent to $I\!I$, and so execution of P does terminate. Conclusion: H cannot be a program; it's an incomputable function. That's the orthodox argument, and the orthodox conclusion, first made by Turing, and now found in many textbooks.

In UTP, programs are a special case of specification, so let me generalize H to apply to all specification texts, not just to program texts. In particular,

$$H(\text{“}ok'\text{”}) = \textbf{true}$$
$$H(\text{“}\neg\, ok'\text{”}) = \textbf{false}$$

And this time, we don't make any assumption that H is a functional program (computable function). Define specification text S as follows:

$$S = \text{“}\neg\, ok' \lhd H(S) \rhd ok'\text{”}$$

Now we ask: what is the result of $H(S)$? If S specifies terminating behavior, then $H(S)$ is **true**, and so S specifies nonterminating behavior. And if S specifies nonterminating behavior, then $H(S)$ is **false**, and so S specifies terminating behavior. What do you conclude from that?

This argument about specifications has exactly the same form as the orthodox argument about programs. Both arrive at a self-contradiction. We look for a way out by looking for an assumption that was wrong. In the argument about programs, the assumption was made that H is a program, so we withdrew that assumption. But from the argument about specifications, we see that the problem is still there, even without that assumption.

My conclusion is that we cannot consistently say the sentence "H tells us, for all specification texts S, whether S specifies terminating behavior.". The inconsistency is not immediately apparent, but the above argument shows us that it's there. This is similar to saying that the sentence "The barber, who is a man, shaves all and only the men in his town who do not shave themselves." is not obviously self-contradictory, but a short proof or argument shows it to be so. And from the first version of the story about H applied to program codes, I do not conclude that H is a perfectly well defined but incomputable function; I conclude there also that there is an inconsistency in the definition of H.

Let me try to make the inconsistency in the definition of H more apparent. Within S, $H(S)$ and ok' have the same role. So S represents

$$\neg\, ok' \lhd ok' \rhd ok'$$

which says, as directly as possible, that if execution terminates, then it doesn't terminate, and if it doesn't terminate then it does. There is nothing wrong with having a primed variable between the conditional triangles; for example, the specification

$$x' = 2 \lhd even(x') \rhd x' = 3$$

says quite reasonably that if the final value of x is even, then it should be 2, and if odd it should be 3; it is equivalent to $x' = 2 \vee x' = 3$. However, the specification $\neg\, ok' \lhd ok' \rhd ok'$ is equivalent to **false** (independent of the interpretation of ok'), so it is unimplementable (unhealthy). We are asking H to tell us the termination status of an unimplementable specification.

Returning to the "program" example

$$P = \text{“}(\textbf{true} * I\!I) \lhd H(P) \rhd I\!I\text{”}$$

is P an implementable specification? If we assume it is, then it might seem reasonable to ask H about its termination status (without any assumption that

H is computable), and we are led into the same contradiction as before. If we assume it isn't and don't ask H about its termination status, we lose the very specification we were using to demonstrate that H is incomputable.

The problem with H doesn't stop there. If we could define H consistently on just the implementable specifications, then we could consistently extend its definition to all specifications by, for example, saying $H(s) = \mathbf{false}$ for all unimplementable specifications s. If P is unimplementable, then P is equivalent to II, which is implementable. There is no way out.

The situation is exactly the same as for an interpreter of boolean expressions (also known as a prover). Suppose we try to define $I : \mathbf{T} \longrightarrow \mathbf{B}$ so that, when we apply I to a text representing a boolean expression, we get the result of evaluating the boolean expression. Now define

$$Q \quad = \quad \text{“}\,\mathbf{false} \lhd I(Q) \rhd \mathbf{true}\,\text{”}$$

or instead, to simplify, define

$$Q \quad = \quad \text{“}\,\neg\, I(Q)\,\text{”}$$

Applying I to Q yields inconsistency. This is exactly Gődel's incompleteness theorem: Q is saying that Q is not a theorem. Either we leave I incompletely defined (specifically, it does not interpret Q), or we suffer inconsistency. (I note with some irony that an interpreter is a meaning function, which I began this paper by eliminating!)

Wait a minute: there *is* a way out. Interpreter I is a program, and H is just a simplification of I: I tells us the result of evaluating, and H just tells us whether there is a result. So H really is a program. Applying H to P and to S results in an infinite loop (as does application of I to Q). We could say that H *does* deliver a result for P and for S, and I *does* deliver a result for Q, but only at time ∞. The “incomputable” function H is nothing but a program whose execution, for some input, is nonterminating. Such programs are common, and some of them are useful. This way out is a great mathematical simplification.

8 The Problem with Vacuum Cleaners

Here's a “proof” that a vacuum cleaner is unbuildable. If you could build one, then you could use it to clean out its own bag. But that's a self-contradiction (making the bag empty makes the bag full, and *vice versa*), so a vacuum cleaner is unbuildable. The “proof” that a vacuum cleaner is unbuildable is like the “proof” that the halting function is incomputable in the following ways. It accepts without question that a vacuum cleaner is at least a meaningful, consistent concept, just as the standard incomputability proof accepts without question that a halting function is at least a meaningful, consistent concept. Then the vacuum cleaner is applied to itself, just as the halting function is applied to itself. And, most importantly, time is not considered in the argument: in each case, there is no static solution, so we have inconsistency.

To restore consistency, we seem to have three options. The first option, à la Turing, is to remain steadfast in the belief that the vacuum cleaner and halting function are at least meaningful (consistent) concepts, but to label them as "unbuildable" and "incomputable" respectively. That withdraws an assumption made in the argument, but it was an irrelevant assumption. If you could just specify (never mind build) a vacuum cleaner, you arrive at the same contradiction. If you could just specify (never mind compute) the halting function, you arrive at the same contradiction. This option is not a way out. Neither "unbuildability" nor "incomputability" serve the purpose for which they were invented: to restore consistency.

The second option, à la Gődel, is to say that the definition of a vacuum cleaner, and the definition of the halting function, are inconsistent unless we leave them incomplete, and we do not apply them to the example that gives rise to the contradiction.

The third option is to add a time variable. Then we can ask what really does happen (over time) if we apply them to the troublesome examples. A vacuum cleaner really is buildable, and the halting function really is programmable. What really happens if someone uses a vacuum cleaner to clean out its own bag is that they create an infinite loop, blowing dirt forever around a circular hose. But that's not an inconsistency. Indeed, there are physical systems built intentionally as infinite loops; for example, pumping electrons around a circuit, doing useful work as they go. Likewise, applying the halting function to its troublesome example is an infinite computation, not a self contradiction.

A simpler, but maybe less visual, example, is the problem of the NOT gate. If we could build one, then we could use it in a closed circuit that includes just one NOT gate, and nothing else. If we ignore time, we find an inconsistency: assuming either final state of the circuit leads to a contradiction. The inconsistency is not eliminated by labeling NOT gates "unbuildable" or "incomputable". The problem is eliminated if we outlaw this particular use (and all similar uses) of the NOT gate. But the best solution is to admit that a NOT gate takes time; we look at the circuit's behavior over time, and we do not worry about what its final state might be. It is a useful circuit called an oscillator. (A practical oscillator is more complicated, but at its heart there is a NOT gate in a loop.)

9 What is a Time Bound?

I have argued that a claim of termination should be accompanied by a time bound. Now I ask: what is acceptable as a time bound?

Finding the execution time of any program can always be done by transforming the program into a function that expresses the execution time. To illustrate how, let us again look at the example

$$(n \neq 1) * (n := n \,\mathsf{div}\, 2)$$

in natural variable n. The first step in expressing the execution time is, not surprisingly, to get rid of the loop notation in favor of recursive refinement.

$$n' = 1 \ \Leftarrow\ I\!I \lhd n = 1 \rhd (n := n \,\mathsf{div}\, 2\,;\, n' = 1)$$

The next step is to add a time variable, and choose a timing policy. We express the execution time as $f(n)$, where function f must satisfy

$$t' = t + f(n) \Leftarrow I\!I \lhd n = 1 \rhd (n := n \operatorname{div} 2 \,;\, t := t + 1 \,;\, t' = t + f(n))$$

which can be simplified to

$$f(n) \quad = \quad 0 \lhd n = 1 \rhd (1 + f(n \operatorname{div} 2))$$

From this recursive definition of f, we see

$$\begin{array}{lllll} f(1) & = & 0 & & \\ f(2) & = & 1 + f(1) & = & 1 \\ f(3) & = & 1 + f(1) & = & 1 \\ f(4) & = & 1 + f(2) & = & 2 \end{array}$$

and so on. We also see

$$f(0) \quad = \quad 1 + f(0)$$

which has no finite solution, but according to my axioms for numbers [6], it has solution ∞ (because ∞ absorbs finite additions). This is exactly the right answer for how long the computation takes when n is 0. It would have been a duplication of effort to worry first about termination before calculating execution time.

Now consider this famous program whose execution time is considered to be unknown:

$$(n \neq 1) * ((n := n/2) \lhd even(n) \rhd (n := 3 \times n + 1))$$

where n is a natural variable. It is not even known whether the execution time is finite for all $n > 0$. Following the same steps as before, we find

$$f(n) \quad = \quad 0 \lhd n = 1 \rhd ((1 + f(n/2)) \lhd even(n) \rhd (1 + f(3 \times n + 1)))$$

or, more readably,

$$\begin{array}{lll} f(n) & = & \textbf{if } n = 1 \textbf{ then } 0 \\ & & \textbf{else if } even(n) \textbf{ then } 1 + f(n/2) \\ & & \textbf{else } 1 + f(3 \times n + 1) \end{array}$$

Thus we have an exact definition of the execution time. So why is the execution time considered to be unknown?

If the execution time of some program is n^2, we consider that the execution time of that program is known. Why is n^2 accepted as a time bound, and $f(n)$ as defined above not accepted? The reason is not that f is defined recursively; the square function is defined in terms of multiplication, and multiplication is defined recursively. The reason cannot be that n^2 is well behaved (finite, monotonic, and smooth), while f jumps around wildly and might sometimes be infinite-valued; every jump and change of value in f is there to fit the original program's execution time perfectly, and we shouldn't disqualify f for being perfect. One might propose the length of time it takes to compute the time bound as a reason to reject f. Since it takes exactly as long to compute the time bound $f(n)$ as to run the program, we might as well just run the original program and look at our watch and say that's the time bound. But *log log n* is accepted as a time bound even though it takes longer than *log log n* to compute *log log n*.

Could the reason be that function f is unfamiliar, that it has not been well studied and we don't know much about it? If it were as well studied and familiar as square, would we accept it as a time bound?

Consider the linear search program to find the first occurrence of a given item x in a given list L, and report its position as the final value of variable h. Suppose that L is infinitely long, and we are told that there is at least one occurrence of x in the list. We can prove that the execution time (counting iterations) is h'.

$$t' = t + h' \Leftarrow h := 0 \, ; t' = t + h' - h$$
$$t' = t + h' - h \Leftarrow \mathit{II} \lhd Lh = x \rhd (h := h + 1 \, ; t := t + 1 \, ; t' = t + h' - h)$$

Is this acceptable as a time bound? It gives us no indication of how long to wait for a result. On the other hand, there is nothing more to say about the execution time. The defect is in the given information: that x occurs somewhere, with no indication where.

10 Conclusion

When I began programming, I put my program, punched onto a deck of cards, in the "in" basket; hours later, the computer operator fed it into the computer, and put the output in the "out" basket, where I retrieved it. Computing involved an initial input and a final output, with no possibility of interaction. A "total correctness" theory is based on this out-of-date paradigm: without interaction, termination is essential. With the addition of interactive communication, nonterminating computations can be useful, so a semantics that does not insist on termination is useful. Furthermore, for some programs, for some inputs, we might well want to guarantee nontermination, which a "total correctness" formalism does not do. The operating system, even when I began programming, was an interacting, nonterminating computation. These days, every program I use terminates its execution when I click on "quit". Of course, each response to me must be a terminating computation; more than that, each response must come within the limit of my patience.

Throughout this paper, I have used annoying quotation marks around "total correctness" in order to provide some protection against the appeal of the phrase. It sounds like something very desirable, but it's a bad deal. It requires a complicated semantics of loops (either limit of a sequence of approximations, or least fixpoint) that is not easily used in proofs. To prove termination, you must do all the work of finding time bounds, but without the reward. And you must prove termination before you can conclude anything about results or time bounds. And when you have proven termination, you have proven something worthless, because no observation of a computation can falsify it (nontermination is unobservable). It is time to retire the concept of "total correctness", and to terminate our obsession with termination.

References

1. R.-J.R. Back and J.von Wright. *Refinement Calculus: a Systematic Introduction.* Springer, 1998.
2. P. Caspi, N. Halbwachs, D. Pilaud, and J.A. Plaice. LUSTRE: a declarative language for programming synchronous systems. In *14th ACM Symposium on Principles of Programming Languages*, pages 178–189, 1987.
3. E.W. Dijkstra. *A Discipline of Programming.* Prentice-Hall, 1976.
4. I.J. Hayes. Reasoning about real-time repetitions, terminating and nonterminating. *Science of Computer Programming*, 43(2-3):161–192, 2002.
5. E.C.R. Hehner and A.M. Gravell. Refinement semantics and loop rules. In J.M. Wing, J. Woodcock, and J. Davies, editors, *FM'99 - World Congress on Formal Methods, Toulouse*, number 1709 in Lecture Notes in Computer Science, pages 1497–1510. Springer-Verlag, 1999.
6. E.C.R Hehner. *a Practical Theory of Programming, first edition.* Springer, 1993. current edition www.cs.utoronto.ca/ hehner/aPToP.
7. E.C.R Hehner. Probabilistic predicative programming. In *Mathematics of Program Construction, Stirling, Scotland, July 12-14*, number 3125 in Lecture Notes in Computer Science, pages 169–185. Springer-Verlag, 2004.
8. E.C.R. Hehner. Termination is timing. In J. van de Snepscheut, editor, *Mathematics of Program Construction, Enschede, The Netherlands, June (opening address, invited)*, number 375 in Lecture Notes in Computer Science, pages 36–47. Springer-Verlag, 1989.
9. E.C.R. Hehner. Real-time programming. *Information Processing Letters*, 30:51–56, 1989 January 16.
10. E.C.R. Hehner and A.J. Malton. Termination conventions and comparative semantics. *Acta Informatica*, 25:1–14, 1988 January.
11. E.C.R. Hehner. Predicative programming. *Communications ACM*, 27(2):134–151, 1984 February.
12. E.C.R. Hehner. *the Logic of Programming.* International Series in Computer Science (ed. C.A.R. Hoare). Prentice-Hall, 1984.
13. E.C.R. Hehner and C.A.R. Hoare. a more complete model of communicating processes. *Theoretical Computer Science*, 26:105–120, 1983 September. Also as University of Toronto Technical Report CSRG-134, 1981 September.
14. E.C.R. Hehner. **do** considered **od**: a contribution to the programming calculus. *Acta Informatica*, 11:287–304, 1979. Also as University of Toronto Technical Report CSRG-75, 1976 November.
15. C.A.R. Hoare and He J. *Unifying Theories of Programming.* Prentice Hall, 1998.
16. C.A.R. Hoare. An axiomatic basis for computer programming. *Communications ACM*, 12(10):576–580, 583, 1969 October.
17. C.A.R. Hoare. A proof of correctness of data representations. *Acta Informatica*, 1(4):271–282, 1972.
18. C.C. Morgan, A.K. McIver, K. Seidel, and J.W. Sanders:. Probabilistic predicate transformers. *ACM Transactions on Programming Languages and Systems*, 18(3):325–353, 1996 May.

Object-Orientation in the UTP

Thiago Santos[1], Ana Cavalcanti[2], and Augusto Sampaio[1]

[1] Centre of Informatics, Federal University of Pernambuco
P.O. Box 7851, 50732-970 Recife-PE, Brazil
[2] Department of Computer Science, University of York,
Heslington York, YO10 5DD, United Kingdom

Abstract. In this paper, we study object-oriented programming concepts present in languages like Java and C++ in the framework of the Unifying Theories of Programming (UTP). This work shows how subtyping, data inheritance, (mutually) recursive methods, and dynamic binding can be described in the UTP by combining and extending the theories of designs and higher-order procedures. A distinguishing feature of our approach is modularity: following the style of the UTP, we deal with each concept in isolation; this makes our theory convenient to model integrated languages that include constructs from several paradigms.

1 Introduction

Since object-oriented languages have been widely used to develop software for different domains of application, there has been a strong need to understand and describe the meaning of object-oriented programs. Approaches like operational [1, 2], denotational [3], and algebraic semantics [4, 5] have been used to describe languages and how their concepts are related.

In the Unifying Theories of Programming (UTP) [6], Hoare and He establish a framework to allow reasoning about different programming paradigms using a relational calculus. In this paper, we describe in the UTP a subset of the object-oriented programming concepts found in languages like Java and C++. Our theory is an extension of the theories of designs and higher-order procedures.

In [7], we can find a description in the UTP of an object-oriented (OO) language that handles pointers and visibility mechanisms, among other OO features. The authors also present a set of rules related to refinement. However, (mutually) recursive methods are not described explicitly. Another example of an OO language described in UTP is presented in [8], where the semantics of TCOZ [9, 10], a language that combines processes, classes and time, is defined.

We target general object-oriented concepts, rather than any specific language. We introduce concepts of OO languages progressively and in isolation. We cover subtyping, single inheritance, dynamic binding, and (mutual) recursion, assuming a copy semantics. By introducing these features independently we provide a general theory of object-orientation that can be combined with other UTP theories in the usual way. In particular, our long-term goal is to define a combined theory for reactive, object-oriented designs, and use it to give a semantics to

S. Dunne and W. Stoddart (Eds.): UTP 2006, LNCS 4010, pp. 18–37, 2006.

OhCircus [11]. This is an object-oriented extension of *Circus* [12], a combination of Z [13] and CSP [14] whose semantics is based on the UTP.

In our theory, a class declaration is not a single block, as usual in object-oriented languages. We have separated constructs to declare a class and its immediate superclass, to declare an attribute, and to declare a method.

Example 1. Consider a simple banking system; we define a class *Account*, and its attributes and methods as follows:

$$\begin{array}{l}\mathbf{class}\ \mathit{Account};\\ \mathbf{att}\ \mathit{Account}\ \mathit{id} : \mathbb{Z}, \mathit{balance} : \mathbb{Z};\\ \mathbf{meth}\ \mathit{Account}\ \mathit{credit} = (\mathbf{val}\ x : \mathbb{Z} \bullet \mathbf{self}.\mathit{balance} := \mathbf{self}.\mathit{balance} + x)\end{array}$$

The declarations of the attributes and methods are independent, and combined in sequence. In particular, the declarations of the attributes and methods have to indicate their classes. We show that this approach simplifies the semantics, and makes the treatment of (mutual) recursion straightforward, as it should be.

It is well-known that, in the semantics of an object-oriented language, the types of the variables play a central role due to subtyping and dynamic binding [15]. In our theory, we have a collection of observational variables that are used to model declarations. They record important typing information and are used in the semantics of commands. We also drop the assumption that expressions are total; this is not realistic for object-oriented languages due to the possibility of attempts to access attributes and methods of a "**null** object" (that is, "**null** pointer exceptions"). As a consequence, we have to characterize well-defined expressions, and extend the semantics of assignments and conditionals.

Method names are also part of the alphabet of our theory. Their values are parametrised programs [16]. Their treatment follows the approach originally proposed in [17], and adopted in [15] to handle methods. It is also the approach followed in the UTP for higher-order procedures.

Dynamic binding is reflected in the value of a method variable. It is a conditional that checks the type of the target object and determines the right program that defines the behaviour of the method in each case. In this way, we capture dynamic binding in isolation. This follows the style adopted in an algebraic semantics for object-orientation [5].

This paper is organized as follows. In Section 2, we introduce the alphabet of our theory: observational variables related to the OO concepts of subtyping, inheritance and dynamic binding. In Section 3, we define class, attribute and method declaration. In Section 4, we review the concept of variables, to include type information explicitly. In Section 5, we describe well-definedness rules for expressions and the meaning of object creation, type test, type cast and attribute access. In Section 6, we review the semantics of commands emphasizing method call. Finally, in Section 7, we discuss related and future work.

2 Observational Variables

In addition to the programming variables and their dashed counterparts, and to *ok* and *ok*′ from the theory of designs, our theory includes two new observational variables: one to record the subclass relation; and another to record the types of attributes associated to a given class. For classes, we introduce:

$$\Gamma_{cls} : name \mapsto name$$

This is a mapping from class names to the corresponding name of their immediate superclasses. This observational variable allows us to introduce new types other than the primitive ones: booleans ($\mathbb{B}$) and integers ($\mathbb{Z}$).

Our second observational variable holds information about the attributes of each class and their types:

$$\Gamma_{att} : name \mapsto \{name \mapsto type\}$$

This is a mapping from a class name to a description of its attributes, which maps each attribute name to its type; *type* stands for any primitive type, or any name in dom Γ_{cls}.

The method names are also part of the alphabet of our theory. Their values are parametrised programs ($pds \bullet p$), where *pds* is a list of parameter declarations, and p is a program: the body of the parametrised program, which uses the parameters. Value (**val**), result (**res**), and value-result (**valres**) parameters are allowed. The notation *pds* stands for any parameter declaration list, possibly including the three parameter passing mechanisms. For example, **val** $x : X$; **res** $y : Y$; **valres** $z : Z$, is a valid instance of *pds*, where x, y, and z are variable names and X, Y, and Z are types. The function *types* applied to a list of parameter declarations returns the parameter types as a set. For example, *types* applied to the previous example yields $\{X, Y, Z\}$.

In bodies of the values of the observational variables named after methods nested conditionals with each branch representing the meaning of a method redefinition. For instance, considering that C is a subclass of B, which itself is a subclass of A, and that m is a parameterless method defined in A (with body *ma*), and redefined in both B and C (with bodies *mb* and *mc*), the m value is:

$$\begin{array}{l}\textbf{valres self} : \textbf{\textit{Object}} \bullet \\ \quad mc \lhd \textbf{self is } C \rhd (mb \lhd \textbf{self is } B \rhd (ma \lhd \textbf{self is } A \rhd \bot))\end{array}$$

Based on the type of the current object (**self**) the nested conditional allows selection of the more specialized version of m. When m is not defined for a given class, then the behaviour of a call to m with an object of this class as a target is unpredictable ($\bot$). The condition **self is** N, for a class name N, checks whether the value of **self** is an object of class N, or one of its subclasses. This is why the type of the object held by **self** is tested from the more specialized subclass to the less specialized one in the class hierarchy.

Finally, for each programming variable x, besides x itself, and x', we include in the alphabet two more observational variables (xt and xt') to record the declared type of x. This is potentially different from the actual (runtime) type of the value of x, which can be an object of a subclass of the type recorded in xt, when this is a class.

Object-oriented features such as attribute overriding, variable shading, and the use of **super** or related notations (to refer to elements of a superclass) are not considered here because they are only syntactic abbreviations that can be easily eliminated by preprocessing. We also consider that the names of classes, attributes, methods (except for method overriding), local variables and parameters are different. This allows us to write simpler predicates while not imposing any relevant practical limitation.

3 Declarations

In this section we provide the meaning, as designs, for class, attribute and method declarations.

3.1 Classes

As mentioned before, our aim is to add each feature of object-orientation in isolation. In this direction, a class declaration introduces just a new type, without any attribute or method. We use the notation of designs in the UTP to define each feature. The declaration **class** A, explained in the sequel, stands for the design:

$$\textbf{class } A =_{df} \begin{pmatrix} A \neq \textbf{\textit{Object}} \wedge \\ A \notin \operatorname{dom} \Gamma_{cls} \end{pmatrix} \vdash \begin{pmatrix} \Gamma'_{cls} = \Gamma_{cls} \cup \{A \mapsto \textbf{\textit{Object}}\} \wedge \\ w' = w \end{pmatrix}$$

where $w = in\alpha(\textbf{class } A) \setminus \{\Gamma_{cls}\}$.

By default, every class has as parent a special class named $\textbf{\textit{Object}}$, which has no attributes or methods. It cannot be redeclared, so the precondition of the design above requires A to be different from $\textbf{\textit{Object}}$. It also requires A to be a new class name: not in the domain of Γ_{cls}. The postcondition of the design specifies that the declaration includes A in Γ_{cls} with $\textbf{\textit{Object}}$ recorded as its immediate superclass. It also specifies that no other observational variable w is modified. In the UTP, $in\alpha(\textbf{class } A)$ is the input alphabet of the program **class** A, which includes all undashed observational variables of its alphabet. For the declaration **class** A **extends** B, we have:

$$\textbf{class } A \textbf{ extends } B =_{df} \begin{pmatrix} A \neq \textbf{\textit{Object}} \wedge \\ A \notin \operatorname{dom} \Gamma_{cls} \wedge \\ B \in \operatorname{dom} \Gamma_{cls} \end{pmatrix} \vdash \begin{pmatrix} \Gamma'_{cls} = \Gamma_{cls} \cup \{A \mapsto B\} \wedge \\ w' = w \end{pmatrix}$$

where $w = in\alpha(\textbf{class } A \textbf{ extends } B) \setminus \{\Gamma_{cls}\}$.

This introduces a record of class A with B as immediate superclass in Γ_{cls}. The class B needs to have been previously declared.

Using Γ_{cls}, we can define the subtyping relation $A \preceq B$, which holds if, and only if, both types are defined in Γ_{cls} and A is associated to B in the reflexive and transitive closure of Γ_{cls}, or if both types are equal and primitive. The inclusion of primitive types into the subtyping relation allows us to simplify definitions.

$$A \preceq B \equiv (A \in \operatorname{dom} \Gamma_{cls} \wedge (A, B) \in \Gamma^{*}_{cls}(\!|\ \{A\}\ |\!)) \vee (A \in \{\mathbb{B}, \mathbb{Z}\} \wedge A = B)$$

Example 2. Consider again a simple banking application, with classes *Account*, which depicts an account of a bank, *BAccount*, an extension of *Account* to hold bonus information, *Contact*, to hold traditional contact information, and *EContact*, an extension of *Contact* to hold electronic contact information. The meaning of the sequence of declarations of these classes is the design below.

class *Account*;
class *BAccount* **extends** *Account*;
class *Contact*;
class *EContact* **extends** *Contact*

$\equiv$

$$\begin{array}{l}
Account \neq \boldsymbol{Object} \wedge Account \notin \operatorname{dom} \Gamma_{cls} \vdash \\
\quad \Gamma'_{cls} = \Gamma_{cls} \cup \{Account \mapsto \boldsymbol{Object}\}; \\
BAccount \neq \boldsymbol{Object} \wedge BAccount \notin \operatorname{dom} \Gamma_{cls} \wedge Account \in \operatorname{dom} \Gamma_{cls} \vdash \\
\quad \Gamma'_{cls} = \Gamma_{cls} \cup \{BAccount \mapsto Account\}; \\
Contact \neq \boldsymbol{Object} \wedge Contact \notin \operatorname{dom} \Gamma_{cls} \vdash \\
\quad \Gamma'_{cls} = \Gamma_{cls} \cup \{Contact \mapsto \boldsymbol{Object}\}; \\
EContact \neq \boldsymbol{Object} \wedge EContact \notin \operatorname{dom} \Gamma_{cls} \wedge Contact \in \operatorname{dom} \Gamma_{cls} \vdash \\
\quad \Gamma'_{cls} = \Gamma_{cls} \cup \{EContact \mapsto Contact\}
\end{array}$$

The meaning of sequence in our theory is the same as that in the UTP.

3.2 Attributes

We can introduce attributes in Γ_{att} for those classes already in Γ_{cls}. All attributes are public. To introduce an attribute x of type T in class A we use the design:

$$\begin{array}{l}
\mathbf{att}\ A\ x : T =_{df} \\
\left(\begin{array}{l} A \in \operatorname{dom} \Gamma_{cls} \wedge \\ x \notin \operatorname{dom} \bigcup\{\Gamma_{att}(N) \mid N \in \operatorname{dom} \Gamma_{att}\} \wedge \\ T \in \{\mathbb{B}, \mathbb{Z}\} \cup \operatorname{dom} \Gamma_{cls} \end{array}\right) \vdash \\
\left(\begin{array}{l} \left(\begin{array}{l} A \notin \operatorname{dom} \Gamma_{att} \wedge \\ \Gamma'_{att} = \Gamma_{att} \cup \{A \mapsto \{x \mapsto T\}\} \end{array}\right) \vee \\ \left(\begin{array}{l} A \in \operatorname{dom} \Gamma_{att} \wedge \\ \Gamma'_{att} = \Gamma_{att} \oplus \{A \mapsto (\Gamma_{att}(A) \cup \{x \mapsto T\})\} \end{array}\right) \end{array}\right) \wedge\ w' = w
\end{array}$$

where $w = in\alpha(\mathbf{att}\ A\ x : T) \setminus \{\Gamma_{att}\}$.

If we try to declare an attribute of a class that has not been declared previously, with a name that was already used, or of a type that is not primitive or present in $\operatorname{dom} \Gamma_{cls}$, the declaration fails.

We can declare several attributes simultaneously, with the obvious meaning.

$$\begin{aligned} \mathbf{att}\ A\ x : T, y : U, \ldots &\equiv \mathbf{att}\ A\ x : T;\ \mathbf{att}\ A\ y : U;\ \ldots \\ \mathbf{att}\ A\ x : T, B\ y : U, \ldots &\equiv \mathbf{att}\ A\ x : T;\ \mathbf{att}\ B\ y : U;\ \ldots \end{aligned}$$

Our notation allows interleaving concerning the order of class, attribute and method declaration. For example, the sequence below is allowed.

$$\mathbf{class}\ A;\ \mathbf{att}\ A\ x : \mathbb{Z};\ \mathbf{class}\ B\ \mathbf{extends}\ A;\ \mathbf{att}\ A\ y : \mathbb{B};\ \mathbf{att}\ B\ z : A$$

In this case, the attribute y of the class A is declared after the declaration of the class B. In fact, if we have recursive classes, the required order of the declaration is different from that adopted in languages where classes are blocks. For example, if a class A has an attribute x whose type is a subclass B of A, then the following order of declaration is required.

$$\mathbf{class}\ A;\ \mathbf{class}\ B\ \mathbf{extends}\ A;\ \mathbf{att}\ A\ x : B$$

Transforming the class-based declarations of an object-oriented language into an appropriate sequence of class and attribute declarations is a simple task. For methods, similar considerations apply; mutual recursion, however, is further discussed in the Section 6.4.

Example 3. This example adds some attributes to the classes of Example 2.

$$\begin{aligned} &\mathbf{att}\ Account\ id : \mathbb{Z}, balance : \mathbb{Z}, contact : C; \\ &\mathbf{att}\ BAccount\ bonus : \mathbb{Z}; \\ &\mathbf{att}\ Contact\ phone : \mathbb{Z}; \\ &\mathbf{att}\ EContact\ icq : \mathbb{Z} \end{aligned}$$

$$\begin{aligned} \equiv\ & Account \in \operatorname{dom} \Gamma_{cls} \wedge id \notin \operatorname{dom} \bigcup \{\Gamma_{att}(N) \mid N \in \operatorname{dom} \Gamma_{att}\} \wedge \\ & \quad \mathbb{Z} \in \{\mathbb{B}, \mathbb{Z}\} \cup \operatorname{dom} \Gamma_{cls} \vdash \\ & \quad\quad \left(\begin{array}{l} \left(\begin{array}{l} Account \notin \operatorname{dom} \Gamma_{att} \wedge \\ \Gamma'_{att} = \Gamma_{att} \cup \{Account \mapsto \{id \mapsto \mathbb{Z}\}\} \end{array} \right) \vee \\ \left(\begin{array}{l} Account \in \operatorname{dom} \Gamma_{att} \wedge \\ \Gamma'_{att} = \Gamma_{att} \oplus \{Account \mapsto (\Gamma_{att}(Account) \cup \{id \mapsto \mathbb{Z}\})\} \end{array} \right) \end{array} \right) \\ & ;\ Account \in \operatorname{dom} \Gamma_{cls} \wedge balance \notin \operatorname{dom} \bigcup \{\Gamma_{att}(N) \mid N \in \operatorname{dom} \Gamma_{att}\} \wedge \ldots \end{aligned}$$

We apply the design definition of attribute declaration to each element of the sequence, starting with the attribute *id*, and ending with *icq*.

For a given class N we define $\mathcal{C}(N)$ to be a mapping that records all the attributes of N, including those declared in its superclasses. We define $\mathcal{C}(N)$ in terms of Γ_{cls}, and Γ_{att}.

$$\mathcal{C}(N) = \bigcup \Gamma_{att} (\!|\ \{\Gamma_{cls}^{+} (\!|\ \{N\}\ |\!) \cup \{N\}\} \setminus \{\boldsymbol{Object}\}\ |\!)$$

In words, $\mathcal{C}(N)$ contains all the attribute definitions of all classes related to N by the closure of the superclass relation, and N itself.

3.3 Methods

For a method declaration to succeed, the class to which it is associated must have been introduced before, and all formal parameters, passed as value (**val**), result (**res**) or value-result (**valres**), must have types introduced in Γ_{cls} or primitive ones. In any case, the meaning depends on whether the method is being declared for the first time or not. If it is ($m \notin \alpha(\textbf{meth } A\ m = (pds \bullet p))$), then the definition below applies. The new name m is introduced in the alphabet using a variable declaration. The design defines the value of m.

$$
\begin{array}{l}
\textbf{meth } A\ m = (pds \bullet p) =_{df} \\
\quad \textbf{var } m\ ; \\
\quad \left(\begin{array}{l} A \in \operatorname{dom} \Gamma_{cls} \wedge \\ \forall\, t \in types(pds) \bullet t \in \{\mathbb{B}, \mathbb{Z}\} \cup \operatorname{dom} \Gamma_{cls} \end{array}\right) \vdash \left(\begin{array}{l} m' = program \\ \wedge w' = w \end{array}\right)
\end{array}
$$

$$
\begin{array}{l}
\textbf{provided } m \notin \alpha(\textbf{meth } A\ m = (pds \bullet p)) \\
\textbf{where } program = \textbf{valres self} : \textbf{\textit{Object}};\ pds \bullet (p \lhd \textbf{self is } A \rhd \bot) \\
\textbf{and } w = in\alpha(\textbf{meth } A\ m = (pds \bullet p)) \setminus \{m\}.
\end{array}
$$

The value of m is a parametrised program. Methods are higher-order, predicate-valued variables as in the theory of higher-order procedures and parameters of the UTP. The parameters of m are those in *pds* and an extra parameter **self** to represent the target of a call; its type is ***Object***. Just as in **var** x, where we introduce in the alphabet new variables x and x', with **meth** $A\ m$, we introduce in the alphabet the variables m and m'. At the same time, we use a design to define the value of m'.

For the case of a redefinition of a method m ($m \in \alpha(\textbf{meth } A\ m = (pds \bullet p))$), we have the definition below.

$$
\begin{array}{l}
\textbf{meth } A\ m = (pds \bullet p) =_{df} \\
\quad \left(\begin{array}{l} A \in \operatorname{dom} \Gamma_{cls} \wedge \\ \forall\, t \in types(pds) \bullet t \in \{\mathbb{B}, \mathbb{Z}\} \cup \operatorname{dom} \Gamma_{cls} \wedge \\ \exists\, q \bullet m = \textbf{valres self} : \textbf{\textit{Object}};\ pds \bullet q \end{array}\right) \vdash \\
\qquad \left(\begin{array}{l} \exists\, q \bullet m = (\textbf{valres self} : \textbf{\textit{Object}};\ pds \bullet q) \\ \wedge m' = \textbf{valres self} : \textbf{\textit{Object}};\ pds \bullet join(A, p, q) \\ \wedge w' = w \end{array}\right)
\end{array}
$$

$$
\begin{array}{l}
\textbf{provided } m \in \alpha(\textbf{meth } A\ m = (pds \bullet p)) \\
\textbf{where } w = in\alpha(\textbf{meth } A\ m = (pds \bullet p)) \setminus \{m\}, \\
\textbf{and} \\
join(A, a, \bot) = a \lhd \textbf{self is } A \rhd \bot \\
join(A, a, b_l \lhd \textbf{self is } B \rhd b_r) = \\
\quad \begin{cases} a \lhd \textbf{self is } A \rhd (b_l \lhd \textbf{self is } B \rhd b_r), & \textit{if } A \preceq B \wedge A \neq B \\ b_l \lhd \textbf{self is } B \rhd join(A, a, b_r) & , \textit{otherwise} \end{cases}
\end{array}
$$

It is worth emphasizing that the definition of *join* deals with redefinition of m both in superclasses and in subclasses A of the class where the original definition is placed. The use of *join* allows us to introduce the method values, expressed as (parametrised) programs [16], in a form where dynamic binding is already resolved, as in algebraic methods [18, 5], and in the weakest precondition approach [15]. The special variable **self** denotes the instance of the target of the method call. All references to attributes on method bodies must be prefixed with **self**; variables without this prefix are formal parameters or local variables.

If the method is a redefinition, the method signatures must be exactly the same, and a new conditional is built to take into account the class hierarchy. Finally, if we try to make a call to m with an object of an inappropriate type as a target, the result is $\bot$ as well. Thus, a program with invalid method calls has unpredictable behavior.

We give the meaning of a parametrised program as a function from a value or a variable name to a program (or predicate). We consider each of the mechanisms of parameter passing individually; the definitions reflect the standard way of implementing them.

For a value parameter, the semantics is a higher-order function that takes the value of the argument and gives the program that declares the formal parameter as a local variable and initializes it with the argument.

$$(\mathbf{val}\ v : T \bullet p) = (\lambda\, w : T \bullet (\mathbf{var}\ v : T;\ v := w;\ p;\ \mathbf{end}\ v))$$

A function that models a parametrised program with a parameter passed by result takes as argument the name of a variable: an element of the syntactic category $\mathcal{N}$. This is the argument in a method call.

$$(\mathbf{res}\ v : T \bullet p) = (\lambda\, w : \mathcal{N} \bullet (\mathbf{var}\ v : T;\ p;\ w := v;\ \mathbf{end}\ v))$$

In this case, the local variable corresponding to the formal parameter is not initialized; its value is assigned to the argument.

For a value-result parameter, the definition is as expected: the local variable is initialized and then assigned to the argument in the end.

$$(\mathbf{valres}\ v : T \bullet p) = (\lambda\, w : \mathcal{N} \bullet (\mathbf{var}\ v : T;\ v := w;\ p;\ w := v;\ \mathbf{end}\ v))$$

The parameter of the function is again a program variable. This is an abstraction over three arguments: a variable, its dashed counterpart, and the type variable.

$$(\lambda\, x : \mathcal{N} \bullet p)(y) = p[y, y', yt/x, x', xt]$$

In this case, lambda-reduction is extended to cope with variable parameters: elements of the syntactic category $\mathcal{N}$. This semantics for methods was presented in [11].

Example 4. In this example we show the semantics of method declarations, considering that Γ_{cls} is the one defined in Example 2 and Γ_{att} that defined in Example 3. There is a method *credit* for *Account* and we redefine it for class *BAccount* to increase the value of a bonus variable before executing the *credit* behaviour.

$$\begin{array}{l}\textbf{meth}\ Account\ credit = (\textbf{val}\ x : \mathbb{Z} \bullet \\ \qquad \textbf{self}.balance := \textbf{self}.balance + x); \\ \textbf{meth}\ BAccount\ credit = (\textbf{val}\ x : \mathbb{Z} \bullet \\ \qquad \textbf{self}.bonus := \textbf{self}.bonus + 1;\ \textbf{self}.balance := \textbf{self}.balance + x)\end{array}$$

We observe that, in the body of the redefinition of *credit* for *BAccount* we have a repetition of the code in the body of *credit* as defined for *Account*. In a programming language, this is likely to be written as **super**.$credit(x)$ or using some other similar notation that avoids code repetition. As we explained in Section 2, however, semantically, these constructs can be removed using a copy rule. For this reason, do not consider such issue here. The meaning for the two method declarations is given by the sequence:

$$\begin{array}{l}\textbf{var}\ credit\ ; \\ \left(Account \in \operatorname{dom} \Gamma_{cls} \land \forall\, t \in types(\textbf{val}\ x : \mathbb{Z}) \bullet t \in \{\mathbb{B}, \mathbb{Z}\} \cup \operatorname{dom} \Gamma_{cls}\right) \\ \vdash \\ \left(credit' = \left(\begin{array}{l} \textbf{valres self} : \textbf{\textit{Object}};\ \textbf{val}\ x : \mathbb{Z} \bullet \\ \quad \textbf{self}.balance \ldots \lhd \textbf{self is}\ Account \rhd \bot \end{array} \right) \right) \\ ; \\ \left(\begin{array}{l} BAccount \in \operatorname{dom} \Gamma_{cls} \land \forall\, t \in types(\textbf{val}\ x : \mathbb{Z}) \bullet t \in \{\mathbb{B}, \mathbb{Z}\} \cup \operatorname{dom} \Gamma_{cls} \land \\ \exists\, q \bullet m = (\textbf{valres self} : \textbf{\textit{Object}};\ \textbf{val}\ x : \mathbb{Z} \bullet q) \end{array} \right) \\ \vdash \\ \left(\begin{array}{l} credit' = \textbf{valres self} : \textbf{\textit{Object}};\ \textbf{val}\ x : \mathbb{Z} \bullet \\ \qquad join \left(\begin{array}{l} BAccount, \\ (\textbf{self}.bonus := \textbf{self}.bonus + 1;\ \ldots), \\ \left(\textbf{self}.balance \ldots \lhd \textbf{self is}\ Account \rhd \bot\right) \end{array} \right) \end{array} \right)\end{array}$$

The value associated to *credit* after the second design is of the following form:

$$\begin{array}{l}\textbf{valres self} : \textbf{\textit{Object}};\ \textbf{val}\ x : \mathbb{Z} \bullet \\ \quad \textbf{self}.bonus \ldots \lhd \textbf{self is}\ BAccount \rhd \\ \qquad (\textbf{self}.balance \ldots \lhd \textbf{self is}\ Account \rhd \bot)\end{array}$$

The conditional type test created by *join* selects the appropriate command.

4 Variables

In [6], type information is not explicitly recorded for the variables. In an object-oriented language, where types play a central role, this is not appropriate. In our theory, the values of the variables are pairs, whose first element is the (runtime) type of the current value of the variable and the second is the value itself.

We give semantics to the construct **var** $x : T$, where T is the static (declared) type of the variable x. The new definition for a **var** that declares the types of the variables that it introduces is as follows:

$$\begin{array}{l}\textbf{var}\ x : T =_{df} \\ \quad \textbf{var}\ x, xt;\ T \in \{\mathbb{B}, \mathbb{Z}, \textbf{\textit{Object}}\} \cup \operatorname{dom} \Gamma_{cls} \vdash xt' = T \land x' \in T \land w' = w\end{array}$$

where $w = in\alpha(\textbf{var}\ x : T) \setminus \{x, xt\}$.

We use the existing **var** construct to introduce both x and xt in the alphabet. In the design, we check that T is a valid type. In this case, the type of x is defined to be T, and an arbitrary element of T is chosen as its initial value. All the other variables are not changed. In assignments to x, the pair (e_t, e_v) which denotes the value may change, but xt does not.

To complete this definition, we need to define the set of elements of a class type C. These are pairs in which the first element is C, and the second element is either the special value **null** or a mapping (record) that associates a value to the name of each of the attributes of C, and the values of the types determined by the subclasses of C. A formal definition is a function that takes Γ_{cls} and Γ_{att} as parameters; a similar function is specified in [15].

As within the UTP, **var** $x : T$ is a non-homogeneous relation: the alphabet of **var** $x : T$ does not include x or xt. The definition of **end** $x : T$ (the construct used to finalize the scope of x) is similar to that in the UTP. There are no concerns about type at the end of the scope of a variable, but we need to close the scope of both x and xt.

This discussion about the structure of values is extremely important to guide our concepts of what is an object value and how we can guarantee the correctness of assignments, and method requests, in an OO context. This interpretation of variables and values is not against the principles of the UTP; we have just made explicit representation of values in order to handle the concepts of OO.

5 Expressions

In this section we specify well-definedness rules for expressions, and the semantics of object creation, type test, type cast and attribute accesses.

5.1 Well-Definedness

Our theory includes new forms of expression e characterized by the following BNF-like definition.

$$e ::= v \mid le \mid \mathbf{new}\ N \mid e\ \mathbf{is}\ N \mid (N)e \mid f(e) \mid \mathbf{null}$$
$$le ::= x \mid \mathbf{self} \mid le.x$$

Here v is a primitive or object value. The expressions le, named left expressions, can be a variable, the special variable named **self**, or a sequence of dot-separated names. The expression **new** N stands for object creation, e **is** N for type test, and $(N)e$ for type cast. There is also a group of built-in operations over expressions, like, for instance, arithmetic and relational operators denoted by $f(e)$.

For an expression e, we write e_t to denote the first element of the value of e, and e_v to denote the second element. In other words, e_t is the type of the value of e, and e_v is the value itself forming a pair (e_t, e_v). The construct **null** actually stands for a family of values, one for each class. The type held by e_t in this case is inferred from the context. For instance, in an assignment $x :=$ **null**, $e_t = xt$. Which means that the runtime type of **null** is the declared type of x.

The well-definedness of expressions is specified by a function named $\mathcal{D}$. If an expression has a primitive value, it is well-defined if the value belong to the set of possible values of the type. For objects, we must check if the type belongs to $\mathrm{dom}\,\Gamma_{cls}$, and if the value belongs to the type.

Primitive Values

$$\mathcal{D}((\mathbb{B}, v)) \equiv v \in \mathbb{B}$$
$$\mathcal{D}((\mathbb{Z}, v)) \equiv v \in \mathbb{Z}$$

Objects

$$\mathcal{D}((T, \mathbf{null})) \equiv T \in \mathrm{dom}\,\Gamma_{cls}$$
$$\mathcal{D}((T, v)) \equiv T \in \mathrm{dom}\,\Gamma_{cls} \wedge v \in T$$

Variables are well-defined if their types are either primitive or present in the in $\mathrm{dom}\,\Gamma_{cls}$. If a variable has the special name **self**, it cannot be of a primitive type.

Variables

$$\mathcal{D}(x) \equiv xt \in \{\mathbb{B}, \mathbb{Z}, \textbf{\textit{Object}}\} \cup \mathrm{dom}\,\Gamma_{cls}$$
$$\mathcal{D}(\mathbf{self}) \equiv \mathbf{self}t \in \{\textbf{\textit{Object}}\} \cup \mathrm{dom}\,\Gamma_{cls}$$

An attribute access $le.x$ is valid only if le is well-defined, the value of le is different from **null** and x is in the domain of le.

Attribute Accesses

$$\mathcal{D}(le.x) \equiv \mathcal{D}(le) \wedge le_v \neq \mathbf{null} \wedge x \in \mathrm{dom}\, le_v$$

A **new** N declaration is valid only if the class N is recorded in $\mathrm{dom}\,\Gamma_{cls}$. The type test and casting can be done only if e is a well-defined expression and N belongs to $\mathrm{dom}\,\Gamma_{cls}$.

Typing

$$\mathcal{D}(\mathbf{new}\ N) \equiv N \in \mathrm{dom}\,\Gamma_{cls}$$
$$\mathcal{D}(e\ \mathbf{is}\ N) \equiv \mathcal{D}(e) \wedge N \in \mathrm{dom}\,\Gamma_{cls} \wedge e_t \preceq N$$
$$\mathcal{D}((N)e) \equiv \mathcal{D}(e) \wedge N \in \mathrm{dom}\,\Gamma_{cls} \wedge e_t \preceq N$$

The well-definedness restrictions for built-in operations for primitive types, $f(e)$, are defined individually and are very similar. We show the example of the remainder of a division operator, usually written '%' in programming languages:

Remainder

$$\mathcal{D}(x\%y) \equiv \mathcal{D}(x) \wedge \mathcal{D}(y) \wedge xt = \mathbb{Z} \wedge yt = \mathbb{Z} \wedge y \neq 0$$

In Section 6.1, we use the function $\mathcal{D}$ on expressions to define well-definedness rules for commands.

5.2 Object Creation

An object value is a pair $(type, value)$: the $type$ is a class name and the $value$ is a mapping from names to attribute values. Using Γ_{cls} and Γ_{att} to recover attributes and inheritance information, we provide a definition for **new** as:

$$\mathbf{new}\ N \equiv \left(N, \left\{ \begin{array}{l} x : \operatorname{dom} \Gamma_{cls}; \\ t : \{\mathbb{B}, \mathbb{Z}\} \cup \operatorname{dom} \Gamma_{cls}; \\ v : \mathbb{B} \cup \mathbb{Z} \cup \{\, T : \operatorname{dom} \Gamma_{cls};\ i : T \bullet i \,\} \\ | \\ (\mathcal{C}(N)(x) = \mathbb{B} \wedge t = \mathbb{B} \wedge v = \mathbf{false}) \vee \\ (\mathcal{C}(N)(x) = \mathbb{Z} \wedge t = \mathbb{Z} \wedge v = 0) \vee \\ (\exists\, T : \operatorname{dom} \Gamma_{cls} \bullet \mathcal{C}(N)(x) = T \wedge t = T \wedge v = \mathbf{null}) \\ \bullet\, x \mapsto (t, v) \end{array} \right\} \right)$$

This definition says that the value of a newly created object is a mapping from attribute names to values that associates all boolean attributes to **false**, all integer attributes to 0, and all class-typed attributes to **null**. For example, the value of **new** *BAccount* is:

$$(BAccount, \{id \mapsto (\mathbb{Z}, 0), balance \mapsto (\mathbb{Z}, 0), contact \mapsto (Contact, \mathbf{null})\})$$

5.3 Type Test

The expression e **is** N is a boolean that indicates whether the value of e belongs to the class N or one of its subclasses.

$$e\ \mathbf{is}\ N \equiv (\mathbb{B}, e_t \preceq N)$$

For example:

$$\begin{aligned} (\mathbf{new} BAccount)\ \mathbf{is}\ Account &\equiv (BAccount, \{\ldots\})\ \mathbf{is}\ Account \\ &\equiv (\mathbb{B}, BAccount \preceq Account) \\ &\equiv (\mathbb{B}, \mathbf{true}) \end{aligned}$$

This is justified by the definitions of **new**, type test, and $\preceq$, if we assume that Γ_{cls} is as defined in Example 2.

5.4 Type Cast

The result of a casting $(N)e$ is the expression e itself, if the casting is well defined. Since we are only defining the meaning of well-defined expressions, our specification is surprisingly trivial.

$$(N)e \ \equiv e$$

For example, provided that $BAccount \preceq Account$:

$$\begin{aligned} (Account)\ \mathbf{new}\ BAccount &\equiv (Account)(BAccount, \{\ldots\}) \\ &\equiv (BAccount, \{\ldots\}) \end{aligned}$$

In the semantics of assignments and conditionals, we guarantee that well-definedness is checked.

5.5 Attribute Access

An attribute access $le.x$ recovers from the object value mapping (le_v) the attribute named x.

$$le.x \equiv le_v(x)$$

Again, we have a very simple definition, because we are only considering well-defined attribute accesses.

6 Commands

In addition to the commands in the theory of designs, our theory includes assignments $le := e$ of a value e to a left expression le, and method calls $le.m(a)$ with target le and list of arguments a. Moreover, since expressions have changed, we need to consider well-definedness for some commands. We also consider mutual recursion. The other commands such as sequential composition $(P;\ Q)$ remain unchanged.

6.1 Well-Definedness

In this section, we specify well-definedness for assignments, conditionals and method calls. We consider two cases of assignments: assignments to variables, and assignments to object attributes. An assignment of an expression e to a variable x is considered well-defined if x is well-defined, e is well-defined and the type of e is a subtype of x.

Assignment to variables
$$\mathcal{D}(x := e) \equiv \mathcal{D}(x) \wedge \mathcal{D}(e) \wedge e_t \preceq xt$$

For an assignment of an expression e to an attribute x of le to be well-defined, the expression $le.x$ must be well-defined, e must be well-defined and the type of the expression e must be a subtype of the type of the attribute x in the class le_t $(\mathcal{C}(le_t)(x))$.

Assignment to attributes
$$\mathcal{D}(le.x := e) \equiv \mathcal{D}(le.x) \wedge \mathcal{D}(e) \wedge e_t \preceq \mathcal{C}(le_t)(x)$$

For a conditional to be well-defined, the conditional expression must be well-defined and yield a boolean value.

Conditional
$$\mathcal{D}(P \lhd e \rhd Q) \equiv \mathcal{D}(e) \wedge e_t = \mathbb{B} \wedge \mathcal{D}(P) \wedge \mathcal{D}(Q)$$

The well-definedness for method calls is the most extensive rule. A method call in the form $le.m(a)$ is valid if:

- le is well-defined;
- the method m is defined for the type of le;
- the value of le is different from **null**;

- to avoid aliasing, *le* is not passed as an argument and is not involved in any argument, or as part of a variable in these parameters. For further details about this restriction see [15];
- the types of the arguments in the list a must be compatible with the formal parameter list of m.

We present well-definedness rules according to the parameter mechanism. Starting with value parameters, we have:

$$\mathcal{D}(le.m(e)) \equiv \mathcal{D}(le) \wedge compatible(le, m) \wedge le_v \neq \mathbf{null} \wedge e_t \preceq T$$

$$\begin{array}{l} \mathbf{provided}\ \exists\, m, p \bullet m = (\mathbf{val}\ x : T \bullet p), \\ \mathbf{where}\ compatible(le, m)\ \text{is the predicate:} \\ \quad \exists\, pds, p \bullet m = (pds \bullet p) \wedge le_t \in scan(p) \\ \mathbf{and} \\ \quad scan(\bot) = \{\} \\ \quad scan(a_l \lhd \mathbf{self\ is}\ A \rhd a_r) = \{B : \operatorname{dom} \Gamma_{cls} \mid B \preceq A\} \cup scan(a_r) \end{array}$$

The *scan* function yields the set of class names for which the method m can have a definition different from abort. For result and value-result parameters we use the function *disjoint* described in [15], which verifies if *le* is involved in any of the arguments.

$$\begin{array}{l} \mathcal{D}(le.m(y)) \equiv \mathcal{D}(le) \wedge compatible(le, m) \wedge le_v \neq \mathbf{null} \wedge disjoint(le, y) \wedge T \preceq y_t \\ \mathbf{provided}\ \exists\, m, p \bullet m = (\mathbf{res}\ x : T \bullet p) \end{array}$$

$$\begin{array}{l} \mathcal{D}(le.m(z)) \equiv \mathcal{D}(le) \wedge compatible(le, m) \wedge le_v \neq \mathbf{null} \wedge disjoint(le, z) \wedge T = z_t \\ \mathbf{provided}\ \exists\, m, p \bullet m = (\mathbf{valres}\ x : T \bullet p) \end{array}$$

A method call with multiple arguments can be checked using combinations of these definitions.

6.2 Assignments

Now we give the semantics for assignments to variables, and assignments to attributes of object variables. In our theory, for assignments, we observe that modifying the value of method variables, the type variable xt, or Γ_{cls} and Γ_{att} is not allowed, in much the same way that assignments to *ok* are not allowed in the theory of designs.

If we establish the well-definedness of an assignment, we can update the value of the variable with that of the expression on the right side.

$$x := e =_{df} \mathcal{D}(x := e) \vdash x' = e \wedge w' = w$$

$$\mathbf{where}\ w = in\alpha(x := e) \setminus \{x\}.$$

For example, given a variable x of type *Account* ($xt = Account$), we can calculate the meaning of the assignment $x := \mathbf{new}BAccount$ as follows, provided that y

is the list of undashed variables in the alphabet, other than x, and that Γ_{cls} is as in Example 2.

$$
\begin{array}{l}
\mathcal{D}(x := (BAccount, \{\ldots\})) \vdash \\
\quad x' = (BAccount, \{\ldots\}) \land y' = y \\
\equiv \mathcal{D}(x) \land \mathcal{D}((BAccount, \{\ldots\})) \land BAccount \preceq xt \vdash \\
\quad x' = (BAccount, \{\ldots\}) \land y' = y \\
\equiv xt \in \{\mathbb{B}, \mathbb{Z}, \textbf{\textit{Object}}\} \cup \operatorname{dom} \Gamma_{cls} \land BAccount \in \operatorname{dom} \Gamma_{cls} \land \mathbf{true} \vdash \\
\quad x' = (BAccount, \{\ldots\}) \land y' = y \\
\equiv \mathbf{true} \vdash \\
\quad x' = (BAccount, \{\ldots\}) \land y' = y
\end{array}
$$

When we have to update an attribute of an object-valued expression, we must check the well-definedness of the assignment, and if it is valid, then we update the mapping that records the attribute value, maintaining the left expression type unchanged.

$$le.x := e =_{df} \mathcal{D}(le.x := e) \vdash le' = (le_t, le_v \oplus \{x \mapsto e\}) \land w' = w$$

$$\textbf{where } w = in\alpha(le.x := e) \setminus \alpha(le).$$

We use $\alpha(le)$ to denote a variable in the alphabet whose value is being inspected by the left-expression le. If le is a variable, then $\alpha(le)$ is the variable itself. For $x.y$ and $x.y.z$, the result is x. The equality $le' = (le_t, le_v \oplus \{\, x \mapsto e \,\})$ for the case in which le is itself an attribute access $y.z$ is an abbreviation of the equality $y' = (y_t, y_v \oplus \{\, z \mapsto y.z \oplus \{\, x \mapsto e \,\}\,\})$.

For example, given a variable x of type $Account$ ($xt = Account$), which has been initialized with **new** $BAccount$ ($x = (BAccount, \{id \mapsto (\mathbb{Z}, 0), \ldots\})$), we can calculate the attribute update $x.id := 1$ as follows, provided that y is the list of undashed variables in the alphabet, other than x, and that Γ_{cls} is as in Example 2.

$$
\begin{array}{l}
x.id := 1 \\
\equiv \mathcal{D}((BAccount, \{id \mapsto (\mathbb{Z}, 0), \ldots\}).id := (\mathbb{Z}, 1)) \vdash \\
\quad x' = (BAccount, \{id \mapsto (\mathbb{Z}, 0), \ldots\} \oplus \{id \mapsto (\mathbb{Z}, 1)\}) \land y' = y \\
\equiv \mathcal{D}((BAccount, \{id \mapsto (\mathbb{Z}, 0), \ldots\}).id) \land \mathcal{D}((\mathbb{Z}, 1)) \land \mathbb{Z} \preceq \mathcal{C}(xt)(id) \vdash \\
\quad x' = (BAccount, \{id \mapsto (\mathbb{Z}, 1), \ldots\}) \land y' = y \\
\equiv \mathcal{D}((BAccount, \{id \mapsto (\mathbb{Z}, 0), \ldots\})) \land \{id \mapsto (\mathbb{Z}, 0), \ldots\} \neq \mathbf{null} \land \\
id \in \operatorname{dom}\{id \mapsto (\mathbb{Z}, 0), \ldots\} \land \mathbf{true} \land \mathbb{Z} \preceq \mathbb{Z} \vdash \\
\quad x' = (BAccount, \{id \mapsto (\mathbb{Z}, 1), \ldots\}) \land y' = y \\
\equiv BAccount \in \{\mathbb{B}, \mathbb{Z}, \textbf{\textit{Object}}\} \cup \operatorname{dom} \Gamma_{cls} \land \mathbf{true} \land \mathbf{true} \land \mathbf{true} \land \mathbf{true} \vdash \\
\quad x' = (BAccount, \{id \mapsto (\mathbb{Z}, 1), \ldots\}) \land y' = y \\
\equiv \mathbf{true} \vdash \\
\quad x' = (BAccount, \{id \mapsto (\mathbb{Z}, 1), \ldots\}) \land y' = y
\end{array}
$$

Notice that if we had not initialized the variable x, the assignment would not be well-defined and would abort. The same behaviour would occur if we had tried to access the attribute $bonus$ of the $BAccount$ instance: since the variable has type $Account$, we cannot access variables from its subclass instance.

6.3 Conditional

We need to redefine the conditional to consider the well-definedness of the condition.

$$P \lhd e \rhd Q =_{df} \mathcal{D}(P \lhd e \rhd Q) \wedge ((e_v \wedge P) \vee (\neg e_v \wedge Q))$$

For example, suppose we have that **self** $= (BAccount, \{\ldots\})$, the type of **self** is a class, Γ_{cls} is that provided by Example 2, and both P and Q are well-defined ($\mathcal{D}(P) \wedge \mathcal{D}(Q) = \mathbf{true}$). The conditional $P \lhd \mathbf{self\ is}\ BAccount \rhd Q$ leads to the execution of P, as shown below.

$$\begin{aligned}
& P \lhd \mathbf{self\ is}\ BAccount \rhd Q \\
& \equiv \mathcal{D}(P \lhd \mathbf{self\ is}\ BAccount \rhd Q) \wedge \\
& \quad ((\mathbb{B}, \mathbf{self}_t \preceq BAccount)_v \wedge P) \vee (\neg(\mathbb{B}, \mathbf{self}_t \preceq BAccount)_v \wedge Q)) \\
& \equiv \mathcal{D}(\mathbf{self\ is}\ BAccount) \wedge (\mathbb{B}, \mathbf{self}_t \preceq BAccount)_t = \mathbb{B} \wedge \mathcal{D}(P) \wedge \mathcal{D}(Q) \wedge \\
& \quad ((\mathbf{true} \wedge P) \vee (\mathbf{false} \wedge Q)) \\
& \equiv \mathcal{D}(\mathbf{self}) \wedge BAccount \in \operatorname{dom} \Gamma_{cls} \wedge P \\
& \equiv \mathcal{D}(\mathbf{self}) \wedge P \\
& \equiv \mathbf{self}t \in \{\boldsymbol{Object}\} \cup \operatorname{dom} \Gamma_{cls} \wedge P \\
& \equiv P
\end{aligned}$$

If the type test were **false**, the branch selected would be Q. Moreover, according to the well-definedness rules for the variable **self**, it cannot be an instance of a primitive type. If this were the case, the meaning of the conditional would be abort.

6.4 Recursion

Basically, the meaning of recursion is as in the UTP: defined in terms of least fixed point. Our complete lattice is that of parametrised programs, with refinement as the partial order. The general form of a recursive method m of class A is the following.

$$\mathbf{meth}\ A\ m = \mu X \bullet \big(pds \bullet F(X)\big)$$

For example, the factorial function could be added to A as:

$$\mathbf{meth}\ A\ m = \mu X \bullet \begin{pmatrix} \mathbf{val}\ n : \mathbb{Z};\ \mathbf{res}\ r : \mathbb{Z} \bullet \\ \quad r := 1 \lhd n \leq 0 \rhd r := n * X(n-1, r) \end{pmatrix}$$

We observe that this is not in conflict with the expected form of a method declaration, **meth** $A\ m = (pds \bullet p)$, since, of course, the least fixed point operator results in a parametrised program. In particular, the parameters are the same as those in the body of the recursion. As a matter of fact, for each parameter declaration, we take the fixed point in the lattice of parametrised programs with those parameters.

Mutual recursion is easily addressed in our theory. It can be defined as:

$$\mathbf{meth}\ A\ m, B\ n = \mu\, X, Y \bullet \left(pds_m \bullet F(X, Y), pds_n \bullet G(X, Y) \right)$$

In this case, since m and n are mutually recursive, they are defined together, even though they are methods of different classes. This follows the standard approach to the definition of mutually recursive procedures. The vector of programs m, n is defined as the least fixed point of the function from vectors of programs to vectors of programs defined by the bodies of m and n: $pds_m \bullet F(X, Y)$ and $pds_n \bullet G(X, Y)$. As an example, calling the methods m or n defined below and a variable a as arguments results in the assignment of 0 to a.

$$\begin{array}{l}\mathbf{meth}\ A\ m, B\ n = \mu\, X, Y \bullet \\ \left(\begin{array}{l} \mathbf{val}\ x : \mathbb{Z};\ \mathbf{res}\ i : \mathbb{Z} \bullet i := x \lhd x = 0 \rhd Y(-x, i), \\ \mathbf{val}\ y : \mathbb{Z};\ \mathbf{res}\ j : \mathbb{Z} \bullet X(y - 1, j) \lhd x > 0 \rhd X(y + 1, j) \end{array} \right)\end{array}$$

In many theories of object-orientation, mutual recursion is a difficulty. The complication is really attached to the fact that the mutually recursive methods may be declared in an independent way in separate classes. By splitting the block structure of a class into its basic semantic blocks, we trivially overcome this difficulty.

6.5 Method Call

The most interesting feature of this work is the resolution of a method call. Since we have already solved dynamic binding when dealing with the semantics of method declaration (Section 3.3), the semantics of method call is just a call to the value of the method. In other words, we have isolated the several aspects involved in a method call, so that dynamic binding is captured in the definition of the value of the method variable, which holds a parametrised program, and a method call is just a simple call to a higher-order procedure. Thus, we can defined the method call as:

$$le.m(args) =_{df} \mathcal{D}(le.m(args)) \land \neg(m(le, args)[\mathbf{false}/okay']) \vdash m(le, args)$$

The condition $\neg(m(args)[\mathbf{false}/okay'])$ is the precondition of the design that characterises the method call.

Suppose we start with $\Gamma_{cls} = \{\}$ and $\Gamma_{att} = \{\}$, and execute the declaration of classes, attributes and methods in the Examples 2 and 3. Then consider the program fragment below.

$$\begin{array}{l}\mathbf{var}\ a : Account; \\ a := \mathbf{new}\ BAccount; \\ a.credit(10)\end{array}$$

Due to dynamic binding, $a.credit(10)$ must execute the body of the method *credit* defined for the subclass *BAccount*. As described in Section 3, we have solved this problem using a conditional test over the special variable named **self**. Below, we show how the method call is expanded and how the program associated to variable *credit* resolves the dynamic binding. Due to lack of space, we omit the precondition of $a.credit(10)$, and calculate only $credit(a, 10)$.

$$
\begin{array}{l}
credit(a, 10) \\
\equiv\{ \text{ method expansion } \} \\
\left(\begin{array}{l}\textbf{valres self}: \textbf{\textit{Object}};\ \textbf{val}\ x : \mathbb{Z} \bullet \\ \quad \textbf{self}.bonus \ldots \lhd \textbf{self is}\ BAccount \rhd (\ldots \lhd \textbf{self is}\ Account \rhd \bot)\end{array}\right)(a, 10) \\
\\
\equiv\{ \text{ semantics of } \textbf{valres} \ \} \\
\textbf{var self}: \textbf{\textit{Object}}; \\
\quad \textbf{self} := a; \\
\quad \left(\begin{array}{l}\textbf{val}\ x : \mathbb{Z} \bullet \\ \quad \textbf{self}.bonus \ldots \lhd \textbf{self is}\ BAccount \rhd (\ldots \lhd \textbf{self is}\ Account \rhd \bot)\end{array}\right)(10); \\
\quad a := \textbf{self}; \\
\textbf{end self} \\
\\
\equiv\{ \text{ semantics of } \textbf{val} \ \} \\
\textbf{var self}: \textbf{\textit{Object}}; \\
\quad \textbf{self} := a; \\
\quad\quad \textbf{var}\ x : \mathbb{Z}; \\
\quad\quad\quad x := 10; \\
\quad\quad\quad \textbf{self}.bonus \ldots \lhd \textbf{self is}\ BAccount \rhd (\ldots \lhd \textbf{self is}\ Account \rhd \bot); \\
\quad\quad \textbf{end}\ x; \\
\quad a := \textbf{self}; \\
\textbf{end self} \\
\\
\equiv\{ \text{ the conditional reduces to its left branch } \} \\
\textbf{var self}: \textbf{\textit{Object}}; \\
\quad \textbf{self} := a; \\
\quad\quad \textbf{var}\ x : \mathbb{Z}; \\
\quad\quad\quad x := 10; \\
\quad\quad\quad \textbf{self}.bonus := \textbf{self}.bonus + 1; \\
\quad\quad\quad \textbf{self}.balance := \textbf{self}.balance + x; \\
\quad\quad \textbf{end}\ x; \\
\quad a := \textbf{self}; \\
\textbf{end self}
\end{array}
$$

This can be expanded to a predicate that establishes the final value of a to be its initial value with attributes updated by assignments. The expansion of this sequential composition is exactly the expected meaning of the method call.

7 Conclusions

We have demonstrated that object-orientation with subtyping, data inheritance and dynamic binding can be defined in the UTP, using a theory that combines designs and higher-order procedures. In particular, we have introduced two observational variables to capture information about class declarations, extra variables xt and xt', for each programming variable x, to capture the type of the variables, and, finally, variables m and m' to capture the meaning (parameters and body) of each method named m. In our theory, recursion and mutual recursion are handled in a very simple way.

The concept of variable in the object-orientation context requires explicit typing information to allow the specification of well-definedness rules for expressions and commands, and to provide the correct semantics of object-oriented expressions and commands such as assignments, conditional and method calls. We have a strong type system where all operations, and commands, over variables, values and expressions must be checked to be considered correct. We have seen that invalid declarations and commands associated to OO elements lead to $\perp$; in other words, the meaning of a badly-typed program is $\perp$, which has the unpredictable behavior that we would expect.

In contrast to [7], we do not use a runtime environment; we adopt a copy semantics, as in [15]. In the future, we intend to introduce the concept of object sharing; we plan to include extra information about variables, and review well-definedness, expressions and commands. With object sharing, the view of the target of a method call as a value-result parameter, whose value is updated to reflect changes carried out by the method, becomes unnecessary since changes are reflected directly in the objects, not in a copy. Other features that we will explore in the future are visibility mechanisms and exception handling.

The work reported in [19] presents a method for defining object specifications and refinement in a predicative style [20]. The idea is to decouple the concepts associated with general OO features, like, for instance, inheritance and class specification. This results in very general specification constructs, of which those usually found in object-oriented languages are a special case. Here, we also pursue modularity and decoupling, but we only consider object-oriented constructs.

This work was our first step towards the definition of a semantics for *OhCircus*, our object-oriented combination of Z and CSP. Our next concern is with the proposal and proof of refinement laws. Afterwards, we plan to combine our theory with that of CSP processes.

Acknowledgements. The work of Thiago Santos and Augusto Sampaio are funded by the Brazilian Research Council (CNPq grants 141301/2004-0 and 521039/95-9). The work of Ana Cavalcanti is partially funded by the Royal Society and QinetiQ. A preliminary approach to the semantics of methods was previously studied in conjunction with Jim Woodcock; we benefitted from several discussions with him. We also thank to the reviewers for their very detailed and relevant comments and the symposium participants for their challenger questions.

References

1. Plotkin, G.: A structural approach to operational semantics. Technical Report DAIMI FN-19, Aarhus University (1981)
2. Drossopoulou, S., Eisenbach, S. In: Towards an Operational Semantics and Proof of Type Soundness for Java. Springer-Verlag (1998)

3. Schmdit, D.A.: Denotational Semantics. A Methodology for Language Development. Allyn and Bacon,Inc (1986)
4. Hoare, C.A.R., Hayes, I.J., Jifeng, H., Morgan, C.C., Roscoe, A.W., Sanders, J.W., Sorensen, I.H., Spivey, J.M., Sufrin, B.A.: Laws of programming. Commun. ACM **30** (1987) 672–686
5. Borba, P.H.M., Sampaio, A.C.A., Cavalcanti, A.L.C., Cornélio, M.L.: Algebraic Reasoning for Object-Oriented Programming. Science of Computer Programming **52** (2004) 53–100
6. Hoare, C.A.R., He, J.: Unifying Theories of Programming. Prentice-Hall (1998)
7. Jifeng, H., Li, X., Liu, Z.: A Refinement Calculus for Object Systems. Technical report 322, UNU-IIST, P.O.Box 3058, Macau (2005)
8. Qin, S.C., Dong, J.S., Chin, W.N.: A Semantic Foundation of TCOZ in Unifying Theory of Programming. In: FM'03. Lecture Notes in Computer Science, Pisa, Italy, Springer-Verlag (2003) 321–340
9. Mahony, B., Dong, J.: Blending Object-Z and Timed CSP: An introduction to TCOZ. In: Proceedings of the 20th International Conference on Software Engineering (ICSE'98), Kyoto, Japan, IEEE Computer Society Press (1998) 95–104
10. Mahony, B.P., Dong, J.S.: Timed Communicating Object Z. IEEE Transactions on Software Engineering **26** (2000) 150–177
11. Cavalcanti, A.L.C., Sampaio, A.C.A., Woodcock, J.C.P.: Unifying Classes and Processes. Software and System Modelling **4** (2005) 277–296
12. Woodcock, J.C.P., Cavalcanti, A.L.C.: The Semantics of *Circus*. In Bert, D., Bowen, J.P., Henson, M.C., Robinson, K., eds.: ZB 2002: Formal Specification and Development in Z and B. Volume 2272 of Lecture Notes in Computer Science., Springer-Verlag (2002) 184–203
13. Woodcock, J.C.P., Davies, J.: Using Z-Specification, Refinement, and Proof. Prentice-Hall (1996)
14. Roscoe, A.W.: The Theory and Practice of Concurrency. Prentice-Hall Series in Computer Science. Prentice-Hall (1998)
15. Cavalcanti, A.L.C., Naumann, D.A.: A Weakest Precondition Semantics for Refinement of Object-oriented Programs. IEEE Transactions on Software Engineering **26** (2000) 713–728
16. Back, R.J.R.: Procedural Abstraction in the Refinement Calculus. Technical report, Department of Computer Science, Åbo, Finland (1987) Ser. A No. 55.
17. Naumann, D.A.: Predicate transformers and higher-order programs. Theor. Comput. Sci. **150** (1995) 111–159
18. Borba, P.H.M., Sampaio, A.C.A.: Basic Laws of ROOL: an object-oriented language. In: 3rd Workshop on Formal Methods, Brazil (2000) 33–44
19. Kassios, I.T.: Decoupling in Object Orientation. In Fitzgerald, J., Tarlecki, A., Hayes, I., eds.: FME 2005: Formal Methods. Volume 3582 of Lecture Notes in Computer Science., Springer-Verlag (2005) 43–58
20. Hehner, E.: A Practical Theory of Programming, the second edition. Springer-Verlag, New York (2004)

CSP Is a Retract of CCS

He Jifeng[1] and Tony Hoare[2]

[1] Software Engineering Institute, East China Normal University
[2] Microsoft Research Cambridge

Summary. Theories of concurrency can be distinguished by the set of processes that they model, and by their choice of pre-ordering relation used to compare processes and to prove their correctness. For example, theories based on CCS are often pre-ordered by simulation (or more commonly bisimulation), of which the main varieties are strong or weak or barbed. Theories based on CSP choose as their pre-order a refinement relation, defined as inclusion over sets of observations. The main varieties of observation are just traces, or failures and/or divergences. The processes of the CSP model are restricted to those that satisfy certain naturally arising 'healthiness conditions'. This paper gives a unifying treatment of simulation and refinement, and illustrates it by the familiar varieties of CCS and CSP that are mentioned above.

We consider the variations two at a time. A link between two theories is a function L, which maps the processes of its source theory onto those of its target theory. The image of L defines exactly the set of processes of the target theory. The ordering relation of the target theory is obtained by applying the link L to one or both operands before applying the source theory ordering. We will use the normal transition rules of a structured operational semantics to define a series of linking functions: W for weak simulation, T for trace refinement, R for refusals, D for divergences. We then show that each function is a retraction, in the sense that it is idempotent and decreasing and (in most cases) monotonic in its source ordering. Finally, we show that certain compositions of these functions are also retractions.

The definition of a retraction ensures that (1) the processes of the target theory are a subset of those of the source theory; (2) all ordering theorems of the source theory are preserved in the target theory; (3) the healthiness conditions of the target theory are expressed as fixed-point equivalences of the form $p \equiv Lp$; (4) model-checking the target theory can be optimised, by applying L to only one of the two operands of the ordering. Finally, we show how the separately defined retractions can be composed in a way that preserves these important properties. In other words, the transition systems of several alternative versions of CCS, as well as the main standard versions of CSP, are retracts of the universal transition system that underlies CCS.

The research reported here is a step towards completion of the unfinished business of the original ESPRIT Basic Research Action CONCUR [BRA 3009, 1989-92], which aimed to assimilate the theories and notations of CSP, ACP and CCS. A retraction is a good tool for this purpose, because it precisely codifies the similarities between the theories, and enables them to be used in combination, while preserving their essential and beneficial differences. Such unified families of theories may in due course serve as a rigorous foundation for

S. Dunne and W. Stoddart (Eds.): UTP 2006, LNCS 4010, pp. 38 – 62, 2006.

a comprehensive programming toolset, one that provides reliable assistance at all stages of program design, development, testing and evolution. In this working draft, some of the later sections are incomplete.

1 Introduction

The immediate aim of this paper is to improve our understanding of the relationship between some of the many varieties of process algebra which have been developed by researchers in the last quarter century. The primary definition of a process algebra may be presented in a number of different styles – for example, operational, algebraic, or denotational. For a mature calculus, there will usually be several consistent or even equivalent presentations, which can include sections classified under the following headings:

1. an edge-labelled **graph**, known as a transition system; its nodes are the states of a process, and the arcs are labelled with the kind of observation made as a process passes from its source to its target;
2. a **pre-order** (*i.e.*, a reflexive transitive relation) over the nodes of the graph; It expresses some useful notion of conformity, refinement, approximation or equivalence of processes;
3. a **signature** of constants and operators used to describe process behaviour; all processes of the theory are denoted by a term that is constructed by repeated application of the operators to the constants;
4. an operational **semantics**, presented in the form of a set of transition rules relating the terms of the language to the nodes in the graph by consideration of the labels on their outgoing edges; the transition rules describe in an abstract machine-independent way how the language can be implemented;
5. a set of algebraic **equations** over terms of the language; they define a structural equivalence relation, by which the term model for the language may be quotiented;
6. a **specification language** for describing properties of processes, including their criterion of correctness;
7. a **deductive system** for proving the conformity of processes to their specifications.

Nearly all process algebras are based on the first two headings, a transition system and a pre-order. Various classes of algebra give differing emphases to the other headings. CCS [14] and its successors express their definitive semantics by a signature and an operational semantics. The underlying transition system is assumed to be universal, in the sense that it contains a sub-graph isomorphic to the whole of every other transition system. The commonly adopted pre-order is bisimulation, which is in fact an equivalence relation. The modal μ-calculus [8] provides a specification language, and the deductive system is provided by the satisfaction rules for this modal logic. The various versions of ACP [4] start by a statement of a signature for process terms, accompanied by a set of algebraic postulates; an operational semantics is then proved consistent with these postulates. The other calculi have to prove their algebraic laws as theorems. The π-calculus [15] is presented by a combination of algebraic postulates together with an operational semantics; a number of sitable pre-orders have been proposed. The original CSP [3] and its derivatives start with the simple standard mathematics of sets and sequences. This serves as a specification language, and permits a denotational definition of the concept of a process as a set which satisfies certain healthiness conditions. The constants and operators of the calculus are given direct mathematical definitions. Conformity of a process to an arbitrary specification is identified with inclusion of sets of sequences of observations (known as traces): no special deductive system is needed, because normal mathematics is the basis of all proofs.

Since our goal is to find links between theories of all these classes, we concentrate on what they have in common, namely the first two headings, a transition system and a pre-ordering relation. For the same reason, our development starts with the universal transition system of CCS. It is universal in the sense that every other transition system can be mapped (isomorphically up to bisimulation) onto a subset of its objects and transitions. Finally, we select as our initial pre-order the CCS concept of strong simulation (denoted $\leq$). Equivalence of processes (denoted by $\equiv$) is defined in this paper as mutual simulation (known also as observational equivalence). The familiar deficiencies of simulation as a notion of correctness is resolved by introduction of a well-chosen notion of tests or barbs.

In section 3 we will show how a particular theory of concurrency can be defined as a subset of another by means of a function L (for link). It maps the nodes of the source theory surjectively onto the nodes of the target theory. Furthermore, the pre-order of the target theory is defined, as in [6], by applying L to the two processes of the source theory, and using the pre-order of the source theory to compare them. More formally, Lp and Lq are ordered in the target theory if and only if p and q are ordered in the source theory. Since the source theory uses simulation as its pre-order, the pre-orders of all the linked theories can be efficiently model-checked by the same standard algorithm; such a facility is now part of the Concurrency Workbench [5].

In section 4, we explore some of the desirable properties of the link L. The first and most desirable property is that it should be idempotent, in the sense that applying it twice is equivalent to applying it just once. Secondly it should be monotonic, in the sense that it preserves the source ordering. Thirdly, it should be decreasing, in the sense that its result is always lower in the source ordering than its argument. A function that has all these three properties is called a retraction. It turns out that an ordering defined by a retraction permits a more efficient mechanical test; this fact has been industrially exploited in the model-checking algorithm of FDR [20].

The claim of our title that CSP is a retract of CCS applies only to representative samples of the two process calculi:

1. the trace model of CSP (with τ recorded) is a retract of CCS modulo strong simulation, by a retraction T (section 5.1);
2. CCS modulo weak simulation is a retract of CCS modulo strong simulation, by a retraction W (Section 5.2);
3. the trace model of CSP (with τ omitted) is a retract of CCS modulo weak simulation, by a retraction $(W\,;\,T)$ (Section 5.3);

4. CCS modulo refusal-barbed simulation is a retract of CCS modulo two-thirds simulation, by a retraction R (Section 6.1);
5. CCS modulo divergence-barbed simulation is a retract of CCS modulo strong simulation, by a retraction D (Section 6.2).

The long-term goal of the research reported in this paper is to contribute to unifying theories of concurrent programming [10]. The effort will be successful only if it helps in revealing the distinctive merits of each theory, permitting them to be exploited in combination, ideally with the aid of a coherent suite of mechanical tools. There is no intention or desire that any one of the theories should dominate or supersede any of the others.

2 Background

We start with the usual definition of a labelled transition system as

a set P of processes:	$nil, p, q, Lp, \ldots$
a set A of observations:	$a, b, \ldots$
including communications:	$x, y, \ldots$
and hidden symbols:	$\tau, \sigma, \ldots$
and barbs, which have special meanings:	$ref(X), \delta, \ldots$
a transition relation $T \subseteq P \times A \times P$	

The fact that $(p,a,q) \in T$ means that a process in state p can make a transition to state q, and simultaneously admit or emit the observation a. As usual, we will implicitly work in the single fixed labeled transition system of CCS. Other transition systems for other theories will be defined as subsets of the processes of this universal system.

We will exploit infix relational notation, and define

$$\xrightarrow{<a>} \quad \cong \quad \{(p,q) \mid (p,a,q) \in T\}$$

We use the identity relation (Id), forward relational composition (;), the universal relation ($U = P{\times}P$), relational union ($\cup$), relational converse (superscript $^{\cup}$) and inclusion ($\subseteq$); we appeal without mention to the familiar algebraic properties of the relational calculus: unit laws, associativity, monotonicity, distribution through union.

The concept of an observation extends to sequences of none or more observations, denoted by $s, t, \ldots \in A^*$. The following definitions are standard:

$$p \xrightarrow{\varepsilon} q \quad \cong \quad p = q$$

$$p \xrightarrow{<a>s} r \quad \cong \quad p\,(\xrightarrow{<a>}\;;\;\xrightarrow{s})\,r$$

$$p \xrightarrow{s} \_ \quad \cong \quad \exists q \,.\, p \xrightarrow{s} q$$

$$traces(p) \quad \cong \quad \{\, s \mid p \xrightarrow{s} \_ \,\}$$

Simulation is defined co-inductively as the weakest solution of a set of equations. (For bisimulation, R must be symmetric – but we shall not be using bisimulation in this paper):

$$\leq \text{ is the weakest relation } R \subseteq P{\times}P \text{ such that}$$
$$\forall a : A \;.\; R \,;\, \xrightarrow{<a>} \;\subseteq\; \xrightarrow{<a>} \,;\, R$$

An important practical advantage in the choice of simulation as the standard pre-order for a theory of concurrency is that its definition describes abstractly but exactly the algorithm for an efficient model checker; model checking can be used automatically to disprove false conjectures in the theory, and often also to prove true ones.

Theorem 2.1. $\leq$ is a pre-order.

Proof: (for reflexivity): Id (the identity relation on processes) satisfies the equations that define simulation. It is therefore included in the weakest such relation, or more formally, Id $\subseteq \leq$. That is just the relational definition of reflexivity.

(for transitivity): similarly, ($\leq ; \leq$) is included in $\leq$.

Lemma 2.1. $\forall s : A^* \;.\; \leq \,;\, \xrightarrow{s} \;\subseteq\; \xrightarrow{s} \,;\leq$

Proof: By induction on the length of s.

CSP refinement can be defined in the same style as simulation:

$$\sqsubseteq \text{ is the weakest relation } R \subseteq P{\times}P \text{ such that}$$
$$\forall s : A^* \;.\; R \,;\, \xrightarrow{s} \,;\, U \;\subseteq\; \xrightarrow{s} \,;\, U$$

Theorem 2.2. $\sqsubseteq$ is a pre-order.

Proof: Similar to the above.

Theorem 2.3. $\leq \;\subseteq\; \sqsubseteq$

Proof: By the preceding Lemma, a trivial proof in the relational calculus shows that $\leq$ satisfies the defining equation for $\sqsubseteq$.

We would like to confirm that $\sqsubseteq$ satisfies its own defining property:

Lemma 2.2. $\sqsubseteq \,;\, \xrightarrow{s} \,;\, U \;\subseteq\; \xrightarrow{s} \,;\, U$

Proof: $\sqsubseteq$ is the union of all solutions. Composition distributes through union.

Even more important is a proof that $\sqsubseteq$ coincides with the usual trace refinement:

Theorem 2.4. $p \sqsubseteq q \quad \Leftrightarrow \quad traces(q) \subseteq traces(p)$

Proof: RHS

$$\begin{array}{clcllr}
 & \mathit{traces}(q) & \subseteq & \mathit{traces}(p) & & \\
\Leftrightarrow & q \xrightarrow{s} _ & \Rightarrow & p \xrightarrow{s} _\,, & \forall s \in A^* & \{\text{by defn } \mathit{traces}\} \\
\Leftrightarrow & \{(p,q)\} ; \xrightarrow{s} ; U & \subseteq & \xrightarrow{s} ; U & & \{\text{rewriting}\} \\
\Rightarrow & \{(p,q)\} & \subseteq & \sqsubseteq & & \{\text{by defn } \sqsubseteq\} \\
\Leftrightarrow & p & \sqsubseteq & q & & \{\text{rewriting}\} \\
\Rightarrow & q \xrightarrow{s} _ & \subseteq & p \xrightarrow{s} _\,, & \forall s \in A^* & \{\text{by prev. lemma}\} \\
\Leftrightarrow & \mathit{traces}(q) & \subseteq & \mathit{traces}(p) & & \{\text{by defn } \mathit{traces}\}
\end{array}$$

3 Functions Defined by Transition Rules

A new function symbol L can be introduced into a process algebra by transition rules of the form

$$\frac{p\ (fa)\ q}{Lp \xrightarrow{\langle a\rangle} Lq}$$

where fa is a relation defined in terms of the observation a. By suitable definition of the relation fa, a multiplicity of transition rules defining the same symbol L can often be reduced to a single rule of the form shown above.

L is intended to be a syntactic operator on expressions denoting processes. It is therefore an injection, *i.e.*, a total invertible function. The image of L is a region of the source transition system which constitutes the transition system of the target theory of concurrency. This region will contain an edge labelled a if and only if the existence of that edge can be deduced from this single transition rule displayed above.

Relational notation can be used to express and prove the properties of functions, by defining pLq and $qL^{\cup}p$ both to mean $q = Lp$. The fact that L is an injection can be expressed relationally:

because L is single-valued:	$L^{\cup} ; L \subseteq \mathrm{Id}$	
because L is a total many-one function:	$L ; L^{\cup} = \mathrm{Id}$	......{L inj.}

At the start of this section we defined the function L by means of a single transition rule. Recall that the rule defines exactly the set of all transitions involving L that can be deduced from it. As a result, the single transition rule can be read as an equivalence:

$$p\ (fa)\ q \quad \Leftrightarrow \quad Lp \xrightarrow{\langle a\rangle} Lq$$

Because all transitions deducible by the single rule lead from the image of L to the range of L, two further equivalences may be derived from the same rule:

$$\begin{array}{lcl}
Lp \xrightarrow{\langle a\rangle} r & \Leftrightarrow & \exists q.\ r = Lq \wedge p\ (fa)\ q \\
r \xrightarrow{\langle a\rangle} Lq & \Leftrightarrow & \exists p.\ r = Lp \wedge p\ (fa)\ q
\end{array}$$

All three equivalences can be neatly coded in the relational calculus:

$$fa = L ; \xrightarrow{a} ; L^{\cup}$$
$$L ; \xrightarrow{<a>} = fa ; L$$
$$\xrightarrow{<a>} ; L^{\cup} = L^{\cup} ; fa \qquad \ldots \quad \ldots.\{\text{L commut.}\}$$

An immediate consequence is a useful commuting law for $(L ; \leq)$:

Lemma 3.1. $(L ; \leq) ; \xrightarrow{a} \quad \subseteq \quad fa ; (L ; \leq) \qquad \ldots\ldots..\{L ; \leq \text{ commut.}\}$

This property can be strengthened to a co-inductive characterisation of $L ; \leq$, as follows:

Theorem 3.1. $L ; \leq$ is the weakest relation $R \subseteq P \times P$ such that

$$\forall a : A \,.\quad R ; \xrightarrow{<a>} \quad \subseteq \quad fa ; R$$

Proof: Let R satisfy the commuting property quoted in the theorem.

$$L^{\cup} ; R ; \xrightarrow{<a>} \subseteq L^{\cup} ; fa ; R = \xrightarrow{<a>} ; L^{\cup} ; R \qquad \{L \text{ commut.}\}$$

$\Rightarrow \quad L^{\cup} ; R \subseteq \leq \qquad \{\text{defn } \leq\}$
$\Rightarrow \quad L ; L^{\cup} ; R \subseteq L ; \leq \qquad \{L \text{ inj.}\}$
$\Rightarrow \quad L ; \leq$ is weaker than R.
$\Rightarrow \quad L ; \leq$ has the relevant commuting property $\qquad$ {Lemma 3.1}

Being weaker than an arbitrary R, $(L ; \leq)$ is the weakest such commuting relation.

Let L be a function from processes to processes. A new ordering on processes can be defined by applying L to both operands of the source ordering:

$$p \leq_L q \quad \cong \quad Lp \leq Lq \,, \qquad \text{all } p \,, q$$

An algebraic presentation of the same definition is

$$\leq_L \quad \cong L ; \leq ; L^{\cup}$$

Lemma 3.2. $\leq_L$ is a pre-order.

Proof: $(\leq_L \text{ reflexive}) \quad \text{Id} \subseteq L ; L^{\cup} \subseteq L ; \leq ; L^{\cup} \qquad \{\leq_L \text{ transitive}\}$

$$(L ; \leq ; L^{\cup}) ; (L ; \leq ; L^{\cup}) \subseteq L ; \leq ; \leq ; L^{\cup} \qquad \{L \text{ inj.}\}$$
$$\subseteq L ; \leq ; L^{\cup}$$

The following theorem gives a co-inductive characterisation of this pre-order.

Theorem 3.2. $\leq_L$ is the weakest relation $R \subseteq P \times P$ such that

$$\forall a : A \,.\quad R ; fa \subseteq fa ; R$$

Proof: Similar to Theorem 3.1.

The same definition and lemma apply to refinement ordering.

$$\sqsubseteq_L \quad \cong \quad L \,;\, \sqsubseteq \,;\, L^{\cup}$$

4 Retractions

In this section we discuss the desirable properties of the ordering $\leq_L$ of the target theory, and relate them to desirable properties of the function L.

Monotonicity. First, we would like $\leq_L$ to be uniformly weaker than standard simulation, so that all the simulations provable in CCS will still be valid for the new theory as well, and the new calculus will be a member of the CCS family. This is just the condition that L should be monotonic in the source ordering, which can be expressed relationally in two ways:

$$\leq \quad \subseteq \quad \leq_L$$
$$\leq ;L \quad \subseteq \quad L;\leq \qquad \{L \text{ mon.}\}$$

Monotonicity can be proved easily by from the definition of L , using the defining relation *fa,* as described in section 3. The theorem follows the spirit of the congruence rules given in [9].

Theorem 4.1. L is monotonic if $\leq ;fa \;\subseteq\; fa;\leq$, all a

Proof: $L^{\cup};\leq ;L \,;\, \xrightarrow{<a>} \;=\; L^{\cup};\leq ;fa\,;L$ $\{L$ commut.$\}$

$\subseteq\; L^{\cup};fa\,;\leq ;L$ $\{\text{proviso}\}$

$=\; \xrightarrow{<a>} ;L^{\cup};\leq;L$ $\{L$ commut.$\}$

Hence $L^{\cup};\leq ;L \;\subseteq\; \leq$,

from which $\leq ;L \;\subseteq\; L;\leq$ $\{\text{by } L \text{ inj.}\}$

Decrease. The simulation ordering $p \leq q$ can reasonably be interpreted as a statement that p is a more general or more abstract description of the behaviour of q. For example, p may be a specification, expressing abstractly the desirable general properties of a system, and q may be a more detailed description of the behaviour of the system implementation The relationship $p \leq q$ then states that the implementation meets its specification.

If we are going to use the target theory for specifications, it is desirable that it should be in principle more abstract than the source theory. In particular, we would like every target process Lp to be a more abstract description of the source process p:

$$Lp \quad \leq \quad p$$

This has two equivalent more algebraic formulations

$$L^{\cup} \quad \subseteq \quad \leq$$
$$\leq \quad \subseteq \quad L;\leq \qquad \text{......}\{L \text{ dec.}\}$$

Theorem 4.2. L is decreasing if $\xrightarrow{<a>} ; L \subseteq L ; \xrightarrow{<a>}$, all a

(or equivalently, if $L^{\cup} ; \xrightarrow{<a>} \subseteq \xrightarrow{<a>} ; L^{\cup}$)

Proof:

$$L^{\cup} ; \xrightarrow{<a>} ; L ; L^{\cup} \subseteq L^{\cup} ; L ; \xrightarrow{<a>} ; L^{\cup} \qquad \{\text{proviso}\}$$

$$L^{\cup} ; \xrightarrow{<a>} \subseteq \xrightarrow{<a>} ; L^{\cup} \qquad \{L \text{ inj.}\}$$

$$L^{\cup} \subseteq \leq \qquad \{\text{defn of simulation}\}$$

Idempotence. The processes of our new calculus will be defined as just the image of the function L. We would like to ensure that over the image of L, $\leq_L$ has the same meaning as $\leq$. This is obviously desirable, simply as a unification of the theories in question. But it also has practical value. One or both of the operands of $\leq$ are often expressed in the notations of the target calculus, and these can be proved in advance to remain in the image of L. For such operands there is no need to apply the function L before model-checking. This desirable property is defined formally:

$$p\,(L ; \leq ; L^{\cup})\, q \quad \text{iff} \quad p \leq q, \qquad \text{for all } p, q \text{ in the image of } L$$

i.e., $$L ; L ; \leq ; L^{\cup} ; L^{\cup} = L ; \leq ; L^{\cup}$$

It is simpler to state a slightly stronger requirement, that L is an idempotent function, in that applying it twice is observationally equivalent to applying it just once. (Note that this is not true idempotence, but only idempotence up to equivalence):

$$L(Lp) \equiv Lp$$

i.e., $$L ; L ; \leq \; = \; L ; \leq \qquad \ldots .\{L \text{ idem.}\}$$

If L is already known to be decreasing, idempotence can be proved simply by

$$Lp \leq L(Lp)$$

A desirable consequence of idempotence is that the image of L is just the same as its fixed points; as a result, the processes of the new theory are just those processes of the source theory that satisfy the healthiness condition that

$$Lp \equiv p$$

Another desirable consequence of idempotence of a decreasing function L is that it maps each p of the source theory to the strongest process in the target theory that approximates p.

Theorem 4.3. Decreasing L is idempotent if $L ; fa \subseteq fa ; L$, all a

(or equivalently, if $\xrightarrow{<a>} ; L^{\cup} \subseteq L^{\cup} ; \xrightarrow{<a>}$)

Proof:

$$L^{\cup} ; L ; L ; \xrightarrow{<a>} \subseteq L^{\cup} ; L ; fa ; L \qquad \{L \text{ commut.}\}$$

$$\subseteq L^{\cup} ; fa ; L ; L \qquad \{\text{proviso}\}$$

$$\subseteq \xrightarrow{<a>} ; L^{\cup} ; L ; L \qquad \{L \text{ commut.}\}$$

Retraction. A retraction is defined as a function that is monotonic, decreasing and idempotent. In summary, a retraction L satisfies the three inequations

$$\begin{array}{rcll} \leq & \subseteq & L\,;\leq & \text{..... \{dec.\}} \\ \leq\,;L & \subseteq & L\,;\leq & \text{..... \{mon.\}} \\ L\,;L\,;\leq & \subseteq & L\,;\leq & \text{..... \{idem.\}} \end{array}$$

Efficiency. To test the relation $\leq_L$ by model checking it is generally necessary to pre-process both operands in advance, by application of the function L. It would obviously be more efficient to apply L to only one of the operands, and still be sure of getting the same result of the test. Preferably, it is the specification that should be processed, because specifications are in general simpler than their implementations.

In order to validate this optimisation, it is obviously essential that the meaning of the optimised ordering should be the same as the original:

$$L\,;\leq \quad = \quad \leq_L$$

Surprisingly, a function is efficient if and only if it is a retraction, as shown by the following theorems.

Theorem 4.4. L is a retraction iff $L\,;\leq$ is a pre-order.

Proof: Assume that $L\,;\leq$ is a pre-order.

$$\begin{array}{llcll} \{L \text{ dec}\} & \leq & \subseteq & L\,;\leq\,;\leq & \{L\,;\leq \text{ reflexive}\} \\ & & \subseteq & L\,;\leq & \{\leq \text{ is transitive}\} \\ \{L \text{ mon}\} & \leq\,;\,L & \subseteq & L\,;\leq\,;L & \{\text{just proved}\} \\ & & \subseteq & L\,;\leq\,;L\,;\leq & \{\leq \text{ reflexive}\} \\ & & \subseteq & L\,;\leq & \{L\,;\leq \text{ transitive}\} \\ \{L \text{ idem}\} & L\,;L\,;\leq & \subseteq & L\,;\leq\,;L\,;\leq & \{\leq \text{ reflexive}\} \\ & & \subseteq & L\,;\leq & \{L\,;\leq \text{ transitive}\} \end{array}$$

Now assume that L is a retraction.

$$\begin{array}{llcll} \{L\,;\leq \text{ refl}\} & \text{Id} & \subseteq & \leq & \{\leq \text{ reflexive}\} \\ & & \subseteq & L\,;\leq & \{L \text{ dec.}\} \\ \{L\,;\leq \text{ trans}\} & L\,;\leq\,;L\,;\leq & \subseteq & L\,;L\,;\leq\,;\leq & \{L \text{ mon.}\} \\ & & \subseteq & L\,;\leq\,;\leq & \{L \text{ idem.}\} \\ & & \subseteq & L\,;\leq & \{\leq \text{ trans.}\} \end{array}$$

Theorem 4.5. L is a retraction iff $L\,;\leq \;=\; L\,;\leq\,;L^{\cup}$

Proof: ($\Leftarrow$): trivially by the preceding theorem, because $L\,;\leq\,;L^{\cup}$ is a pre-order.

$$\begin{array}{llcll} (\Rightarrow): & L\,;\leq\,;L^{\cup} & \subseteq & L\,;\leq\,;\leq & \{L \text{ dec.}\} \\ & & = & L\,;\leq & \\ & L\,;\leq & \subseteq & L\,;\leq\,;L\,;L^{\cup} & \{L \text{ inj.}\} \\ & & \subseteq & L\,;L\,;\leq\,;L^{\cup} & \{L \text{ mon.}\} \\ & & \subseteq & L\,;\leq\,;L^{\cup} & \{L \text{ idem.}\} \end{array}$$

5 Simulation and Refinement

In this section, we will prove the basic retraction property of the traces model of CSP. In the first subsection we will deal with strong simulation, by assuming that the hidden symbol τ is either absent, or treated in the same way as all other symbols. In the second subsection we will define weak simulation, and show how its retract gives the standard trace model of CSP, in which τ is effectively removed from all the traces. The effect of removal is actually achieved by saturating the transition system with τ-transitions.

5.1 Trace Refinement and Strong Simulation

Let s be a trace of the process p. Suppose p has already engaged in all the actions recorded in s. Then the possible future behaviour of p is denoted by $\text{Д}_s\, p$, the s-derivative of p; it is pronounced 'p after s'. The process $\text{Д}_s\, p$ can perform an action a just if the process p can perform the sequence of actions $s\langle a\rangle$. After this action a has happened, subsequent behaviour is of course described by $\text{Д}_{s\langle a\rangle}\, p$.

$$p \xrightarrow{s\langle a\rangle} \_ \quad \Leftrightarrow \quad \text{Д}_s\, p \xrightarrow{\langle a\rangle} \text{Д}_{s\langle a\rangle}\, p$$

This equivalence is a consequence of a family of transition rules, parameterised by s

$$\frac{p \xrightarrow{s\langle a\rangle} \_}{\text{Д}_s\, p \xrightarrow{\langle a\rangle} \text{Д}_{s\langle a\rangle}\, p} \qquad \{\text{defn } \text{Д}_s\}$$

As usual, $\text{Д}_s\, p$ is taken to be the solution of these equivalences that has the minimal number of transitions. It has no transitions at all in the case that s is not a trace of p. This case is of no interest to us, and we shall take care to avoid it.

Because the rule given above is the only way of deriving an $\xrightarrow{\langle a\rangle}$ transition for $\text{Д}_s\, p$

$$\text{Д}_s\, p \xrightarrow{\langle a\rangle} r \quad \Leftrightarrow \quad p \xrightarrow{s\langle a\rangle} \_ \;\wedge\; r = \text{Д}_{s\langle a\rangle}\, p \qquad \{\text{Д}_s \text{ det.}\}$$

By existentially quantifying r on both sides, we get

$$\text{Д}_s\, p \xrightarrow{\langle a\rangle} \_ \quad \Leftrightarrow \quad p \xrightarrow{s\langle a\rangle} \_$$

We would like to generalise this property to longer traces than just $\langle a\rangle$.

Theorem 5.1.1. $p \xrightarrow{st} \_ \quad \Leftrightarrow \quad p \xrightarrow{s} \_ \;\wedge\; \text{Д}_s p \xrightarrow{t} \_$

Proof: By induction on t:

$$\begin{aligned} p \xrightarrow{s\varepsilon} \_ \quad &\Leftrightarrow \quad p \xrightarrow{s} \_ \\ &\Leftrightarrow \quad p \xrightarrow{s} \_ \;\wedge\; \text{Д}_s\, p \xrightarrow{\varepsilon} \_ \qquad \{\text{added clause is true}\} \end{aligned}$$

The induction hypothesis can be specialised by substituting $s<a>$ for s :

$$
\begin{array}{lll}
& p \xrightarrow{s<a>t} \_ & \\
\Leftrightarrow & p \xrightarrow{s<a>} \_ \;\wedge\; \text{Д}_{s<a>}\, p \xrightarrow{t} \_ & \{\text{ind. hyp.}\} \\
\Leftrightarrow & p \xrightarrow{s<a>} \_ \;\wedge\; \text{Д}_s\, p \xrightarrow{<a>} \text{Д}_{s<a>}\, p \;\wedge\; \text{Д}_{s<a>}\, p \xrightarrow{t} \_ & \{\text{defn } \text{Д}_s\} \\
\Rightarrow & p \xrightarrow{s} \_ \;\wedge\; \text{Д}_s\, p \xrightarrow{<a>t} \_ & \{\text{defn } ;\} \\
\Rightarrow & \text{Д}_s\, p \xrightarrow{<a>} \text{Д}_{s<a>}\, p \;\wedge\; \text{Д}_{s<a>}\, p \xrightarrow{t} \_ & \{\text{Д}_s \text{ det.}\} \\
\Rightarrow & p \xrightarrow{s<a>} \_ \;\wedge\; \text{Д}_{s<a>}\, p \xrightarrow{t} \_ & \{\text{defn } \text{Д}_s\} \\
\Leftrightarrow & p \xrightarrow{s<a>t} \_ & \{\text{ind. hyp.}\}
\end{array}
$$

To simplify the statement and use of this theorem, we define a partial functional relation H_s that excludes the uninteresting case:

$$p\, H_s\, q \quad \cong \quad p \xrightarrow{s} \_ \;\wedge\; q = \text{Д}_s\, p$$

The theorem proved above can now be given an algebraic formulation:

Theorem 5.1.2. $\xrightarrow{st}\, ;\, U \quad = \quad H_s\, ;\, \xrightarrow{t}\, ;\, U$ .....$\{H_s\text{intro.}\}$

Corollary. $p \xrightarrow{s} \_ \quad \Rightarrow \quad traces(\text{Д}_s\, p) \;=\; \{t \mid st \in traces(p)\}$

The corollary expresses the intuitive trace definition of the derivative that is given by CSP.

Theorem 5.1.3. $\sqsubseteq\, ;\, \xrightarrow{s} \quad \subseteq \quad H_s\, ;\, \sqsubseteq$ .....$\{H_s\text{comm.}\}$

Proof: p LHS q

$$
\begin{array}{llll}
\Leftrightarrow & p \sqsubseteq v \;\wedge\; v \xrightarrow{s} q, & & \textit{for some } v \\
\Rightarrow & traces(v) \subseteq traces(p) \;\wedge & \multicolumn{2}{l}{traces(q) \subseteq \{\, t \mid st \in traces(v)\} \;\wedge\; p \xrightarrow{s} \_} \\
\Rightarrow & traces(\text{Д}_s\, p) & = & \{\, t \mid st \in traces(p)\} \\
& & \supseteq & \{\, t \mid st \in traces(v)\} \\
& & \supseteq & traces(q) \\
\Rightarrow & p\, H_s (\text{Д}_s\, p) \;\wedge\; \text{Д}_s\, p \sqsubseteq q & & \\
\Rightarrow & p \text{ RHS } q & &
\end{array}
$$

Although $\text{Д}_a(p)$ describes the behaviour of p after it has done a , there is no guarantee that p itself can actually make an a-transition to $\text{Д}_a(p)$. In the general transition system of CCS, each a-transition of p may simultaneously make an internal commitment preventing it from behaving henceforth with the full generality of $\text{Д}_a(p)$, as shown in the left diagram of Figure 1.However, in all models of CSP, a guarantee of the existence of such an a-transition is given. This is displayed in the right diagram of Figure 1, which shows the corresponding CSP process in the trace model. To map CCS to CSP, we define a retraction T, which supplies the missing a-transitions when necessary. Henceforth we will use H_a in place of $H_{<a>}$.

$$\frac{p\ H_a\ q}{Tp \xrightarrow{<a>} Tq}$$

From these we get the standard commuting laws

$$T;\xrightarrow{<a>} \;=\; H_a\ ;\ T$$
$$\xrightarrow{<a>}\ ;T^{\cup} \;=\; T^{\cup};H_a \qquad \{T\text{ commut.}\}$$

Theorem 5.1.4. $T;\xrightarrow{s}\ ;U \quad = \quad \xrightarrow{s};U$

Proof: By induction on s :

$$T;\xrightarrow{\varepsilon};U = U = \xrightarrow{\varepsilon};U \qquad T\text{ and }\xrightarrow{\varepsilon}\text{ are total relations}\}$$
$$T;\xrightarrow{<a>s}\ ;U \;=\; H_a\ ;\ T;\xrightarrow{s}\ ;U \qquad \{T\text{ commut.}\}$$
$$=\; H_a\ ;\ \xrightarrow{s};U \qquad \{\text{ind. hyp.}\}$$
$$=\; \xrightarrow{<a>s}\ ;U \qquad \{H_s\ \text{intro.}\}$$

Corollaries.
$$T \subseteq \sqsubseteq \qquad \{\text{defn } \sqsubseteq\}$$
$$T;\sqsubseteq \;\subseteq\; \sqsubseteq$$
$$T;\leq \;\subseteq\; \sqsubseteq \qquad \{\text{because } \leq\ \subseteq\ \sqsubseteq\}$$

Theorem 5.1.5. $T^{\cup} \subseteq \sqsubseteq$

Proof:
$$T^{\cup};\xrightarrow{s}\ ;U \;=\; T^{\cup};\ T;\xrightarrow{s}\ ;U \qquad \{\text{Theorem 5.1.4}\}$$
$$\subseteq\; \xrightarrow{s}\ ;U \qquad \{T\ \text{inj.}\}$$

Corollaries.
$$\sqsubseteq;T^{\cup} \;\subseteq\; \sqsubseteq \qquad \{\sqsubseteq\ \text{trans.}\}$$
$$traces(p) \;=\; traces(Tp) \qquad \{\text{Theorem 2.3}\}$$

Theorem 5.1.6. $T^{\cup};\sqsubseteq \;\subseteq\; \leq$

Proof:
$$T^{\cup};\sqsubseteq;\xrightarrow{<a>} \;\subseteq\; T^{\cup};H_a;\sqsubseteq \qquad \{H_a\text{comm.}\}$$
$$=\; \xrightarrow{<a>}\ ;T^{\cup};\sqsubseteq \qquad \{T\text{ commut.}\}$$

Corollary. $\sqsubseteq \;\subseteq\; T;\leq$

Theorem 5.1.7. $T;\leq \;=\; \sqsubseteq$ {from previous corollaries}

Corollary. T is a retraction {Theorem 4.4, since $\sqsubseteq$ is an order}

Note that this proof has not used Theorems 4.1 to 4.3, which are not applicable to the transition rule that defines T.

It follows that the trace model of CSP is a retract of CCS modulo strong simulation. It remains to explore the other models of CSP in relationship with other orderings over CCS; these orderings give special roles to hidden symbols and to barbs.

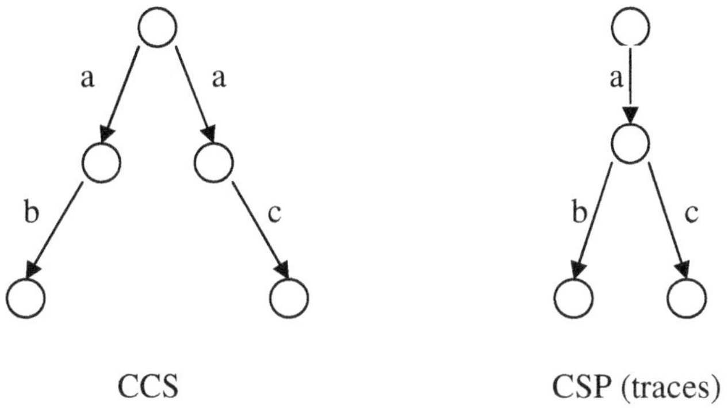

Fig. 1

5.2 Weak Simulation

The special symbol τ is intended to stand for an event that is internal to a process; its occurrence or non-occurrence is not observable from outside. So any number of occurrences of τ are indistinguishable from any other number – even none. Furthermore, any observable event may be preceded or followed by any number of occurrences of τ. These intentions are encoded in the following definition of a weak transition in CCS (for convenience, slightly different from the familiar definition):

$$= \tau => \quad \cong \quad (\xrightarrow{<\tau>})^*$$

$$= a => \quad \cong \quad (\xrightarrow{<\tau>})^* \; ; \xrightarrow{<a>} ; (\xrightarrow{<\tau>})^* , \qquad \text{if } a \neq \tau$$

We define a retraction W which turns weak transitions of the source theory into ordinary strong transitions of the target theory. It thereby allows an implementation to optimise responsiveness by proceeding more directly to the next visible action, omitting any or all of the hidden actions which precede it or follow it.

$$\frac{p \;= a =>\; q}{Wp \xrightarrow{<a>} Wq}$$

In Figure 2, the right diagram shows a fragment of the target theory on the right; it is derived from the fragment of the source theory on the left. The right diagram also contains a τ-loop on every node.

Theorem 5.2.1. W is a retraction.

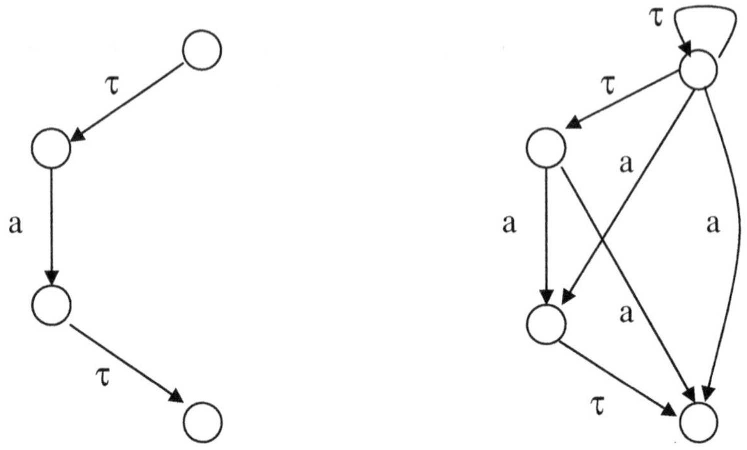

before W after W

Fig. 2

Proof: By Theorems 4.1 to 4.3, it suffices to prove the following lemmas:

$$\text{(mon)} \quad \leq\, ;\, = a \Rightarrow \;\subseteq\; = a \Rightarrow ;\, \leq \qquad \{\text{induction on def simulation}\}$$

$$\text{(dec)} \quad \xrightarrow{\langle a \rangle} ;\, L \;\subseteq\; = a \Rightarrow ;\, L \qquad \{\text{because } \xrightarrow{\langle a \rangle} \;\subseteq\; = a \Rightarrow\}$$

$$= \quad L ;\, \xrightarrow{\langle a \rangle} \qquad \{L \text{ commut.}\}$$

$$\text{(idem)} \quad L ;\, = a \Rightarrow \;\subseteq\; (\xrightarrow{\langle \tau \rangle})^* ;\, = a \Rightarrow ;\, (\xrightarrow{\langle \tau \rangle})^* ;\, L \qquad \{\text{induction on } L \text{ commut.}\}$$

$$= \quad = a \Rightarrow ;\, L$$

$$\{\, = a \Rightarrow \;=\; (\xrightarrow{\langle \tau \rangle})^* ;\, = a \Rightarrow ;\, (\xrightarrow{\langle \tau \rangle})^* \,\}$$

By Theorem 3.1, $(W ; \leq)$ is the weakest relation satisfying the inequation

$$(W ; \leq) ;\, \xrightarrow{\langle a \rangle} \;\subseteq\; = a \Rightarrow ;\, (W ; \leq) \qquad \{W ; \leq \text{ commut.}\}$$

This is essentially the standard co-inductive definition of weak simulation (expressed in a single clause, rather than separating the case that $a = \tau$). We therefore claim that weak simulation is the same as $\leq_W$, which is of course the same as $(W ; \leq)$. We conclude that CCS modulo weak simulation is a retract (by W) of CCS modulo strong simulation.

Our next claim will be that $\sqsubseteq_w$ expresses exactly the CSP notion of trace inclusion, where all occurrences of the hidden symbol τ are removed from the traces on both sides. We define by induction a minus operator which effects this removal, and lift the definition to sets in two ways:

$$
\begin{array}{lcl}
(<>)- & = & <> \\
(<\tau>\, t)- & = & t- \\
(<a>\, t)- & = & <a>\,(\,t\,) \\
S- & \cong & \{\, s \mid s- \in S\} \\
S+ & \cong & \{\, s \mid s- \in S-\,\}
\end{array}
$$

Note that + and – are monotonic with respect to set inclusion, + is increasing, and

$$
\begin{array}{lclcl}
S{+}{+} & = & (S-)+ & = & S+ \\
S- & = & (S+)- & = & S-
\end{array}
$$

The function *traces*(p)– gives the normal CSP traces of a process p, with all occurrences of τ removed. The function *traces*(p)+ inserts τ arbitrarily often into these reduced traces. It does not matter which of these functions is used to model CSP refinement, because of the simple property that

Lemma 5.2.1. $S- \subseteq T-$ iff $S+ \subseteq T+$

Proof: Properties of + and –, operating on sets.

The following lemma shows that the traces of Wp are closed with respect addition or removal of τ :

Lemma 5.2.2. $W ; \xrightarrow{t-} ; U \quad = \quad W ; \xrightarrow{t} ; U$

Proof:

$$
\begin{array}{lcll}
W ; \xrightarrow{<\tau>t} ; U & = & W ; \xrightarrow{t} ; U & \{\text{induction on } t\} \\
W ; \xrightarrow{s<\tau>t} ; U & = & W ; \xrightarrow{s\,t} ; U & \{\text{induction on } s\}
\end{array}
$$

The result follows by induction on the number of τ in t.

Lemma 5.2.3. $s \in traces(q)+$ iff $q = s- =>\_$

Proof:

$$
\begin{array}{lcll}
s \in traces(q)+ & \Leftrightarrow & s- \in traces(q)- & \{\text{defn } +\} \\
 & \Rightarrow & q \xrightarrow{t} \_ & \text{for some } t \text{ satisfying } t- = s \\
 & \Rightarrow & q = s- =>\_ & \\
 & & & \text{since } t \text{ is just } (s-) \text{ interleaved with } \tau\text{s} \\
 & \Rightarrow & s \in traces(q)+ & \\
 & & & \text{since } s \text{ is just } (s-) \text{ interleaved with } \tau\text{s}
\end{array}
$$

Theorem 5.2.2. $traces(Wq) \quad = \quad traces(q)+$

Proof:

$$
\begin{array}{lcll}
s \in \text{RHS} & \Leftrightarrow & q = s- =>\_ & \{\text{Lemma 5.2.3}\} \\
 & \Leftrightarrow & Wq \xrightarrow{s-} \_ & \{\text{defn } W\} \\
 & \Leftrightarrow & Wq \xrightarrow{s} \_ & \{\text{Lemma 5.2.2}\} \\
 & \Leftrightarrow & s \in traces(Wq) &
\end{array}
$$

Theorem 5.2.3. $p \sqsubseteq_w q$ iff $traces(q) - \subseteq traces(p) -$

Proof: Lemma 5.2.1 and Theorem 5.2.2 .

This confirms that $\sqsubseteq_w$ corresponds to the familiar CSP concept of τ-hidden trace inclusion. We now proceed to relate it to weak simulation.

Lemma 5.2.4. $T ; \sqsubseteq_w \;=\; \sqsubseteq_w$

Proof:

$$\begin{array}{llll} traces(W(Tq)) & = & traces(Tq)+ & \{\text{Theorem 5.2.2}\} \\ & = & traces(q)+ & \{\text{Theorem 5.1.5 corollary}\} \\ & = & traces(Wq) & \{\text{Theorem 5.2.2}\} \end{array}$$

Lemma 5.2.5. $W ; \sqsubseteq_w \;=\; \sqsubseteq_w$

Proof:

$$\begin{array}{llll} \text{LHS} & = & W ; W ; T ; \leq ; W^{\smile} & \{\text{defn } \sqsubseteq_w\} \\ & \subseteq & W ; W ; \leq ; T ; \leq ; W^{\smile} & \{\leq \text{ reflexive}\} \\ & = & W ; \leq ; T ; \leq ; W^{\smile} & \{W \text{ idempotent}\} \\ & \subseteq & W ; T ; \leq ; \leq ; W^{\smile} & \{T \text{ monotonic}\} \\ & = & \text{RHS} & \\ & \subseteq & W ; \leq ; T ; \leq ; W^{\smile} & \\ & \subseteq & W ; W ; \leq ; T ; \leq ; W^{\smile} & \{W \text{ idempotent}\} \\ & \subseteq & W ; W ; T ; \leq ; \leq ; W^{\smile} & \{T \text{ monotonic}\} \\ & = & \text{LHS} & \end{array}$$

The following theorem shows that τ-hidden trace refinement is a retract of weak simulation.

Theorem 5.2.4. $\sqsubseteq_w \;=\; W ; T ; \leq_w$

Proof:

$$\begin{array}{llll} \sqsubseteq_w & = & W ; \sqsubseteq ; W^{\smile} & \{\text{definition}\} \\ & = & W ; (T ; \leq) ; W^{\smile} & \{\text{Theorem 5.1.7}\} \\ & \subseteq & W ; T ; (W ; \leq) ; W^{\smile} & \{\leq \;\subseteq\; W ; \leq\} \\ & = & \text{RHS} & \{\text{definition } \leq_w\} \\ & \subseteq & W ; T ; \sqsubseteq_w & \{\leq \;\subseteq\; \sqsubseteq\} \\ & = & \sqsubseteq_w & \{\text{Lemmas 5.2.4 and 5.2.5}\} \end{array}$$

Corollary. $W ; T$ is a retraction wrto $\leq_w$. $\{\sqsubseteq_w$ is a pre-order$\}$

The next and final theorem of this section shows the efficient way of computing trace refinement in CSP by model-checking.

Theorem 5.2.5. $\sqsubseteq_w \;=\; W ; T ; \leq$

Proof:

$$\begin{array}{llll} \text{LHS} & = & W ; T ; \leq ; T^{\smile} ; W^{\smile} & \{\text{definition}\} \\ & \subseteq & \text{RHS} & \{T \text{ and } W \text{ dec.}\} \end{array}$$

$$
\begin{array}{llll}
p \text{ RHS } q & \Leftrightarrow & traces(q) \subseteq traces(Wp) & \{\text{Theorem 5.1.7}\} \\
& \Leftrightarrow & traces(q) \subseteq traces(p)+ & \{\text{Lemma 5.2.3}\} \\
& \Rightarrow & traces(q)+ \subseteq traces(p)++ & \{+ \text{ mon.}\} \\
& \Leftrightarrow & traces(Wq) \subseteq traces(Wp) & \{\text{Lemma 5.2.3}\} \\
& \Leftrightarrow & p \text{ LHS } q &
\end{array}
$$

Corollary. $W ; T$ is a retraction wrto $\leq$. {Theorem 4.4}

We conclude that CSP modulo τ-hidden trace refinement is a retract (by $W ; T$) of CCS modulo either weak simulation or strong simulation.

6 Barbs

A barb is an event which represents an observation of the current state of a process. It is effectively inserted into a transition system by a function B at all places where the state has the property that is intended to be observed. It records the result of the kind of test defined in [1] and [6]. Barbed simulation and barbed refinement are then defined in the usual way as $B ; \leq ; B^{\cup}$ and $B ; \sqsubseteq ; B^{\cup}$ respectively. In general, B is not a retraction. The purpose of the barb is usually to define a form of simulation which is stronger than strong simulation, so B cannot be monotonic.

In a theory used for program proofs, the most important properties (to prove the absence of) are those that indicate that the program has gone wrong. And two of the most prevalent risks of concurrent programming are deadlock and livelock. Deadlock occurs when two processes are waiting for each other, but refuse to participate in communications offered by the other. Livelock occurs when a process can engage in an infinite series of hidden events, and never has to wait for a communication to be offered by its environment. These two barbs have proved to widely useful in practice. A recently discovered barb is the *revival* of [22].

Simulation cannot deal properly with deadlock. Indeed, a process that never engages in any event whatsoever displays immediate deadlock; but simulation actually proves that it meets every specification whatsoever. Weak simulation cannot deal properly with livelock, because all hidden events are effectively concealed, including infinite sequences of them. The FDR model of CSP deals with both these problems, by making their observation explicit in the form of refusal barbs and divergence barbs, which are effectively added at the end of each trace. These will be the topic of this section.

6.1 Refusals

Many of the events modelled in a process algebra are communication events. Their successful completion depends on participation not only by the process itself, but also by some other process in its environment. If either participant refuses to engage in the events offered by the other, nothing further can happen. This is the notorious phenomenon of deadlock. This is the primary cause of unexpected deadlock.

Let X be a set of communication events. Then '*ref*(X)' is an observation (barb) meaning that the process is deadlocked, even though its environment is prepared to synchronise with any the communications in X, and even allows the selection to be made by the process itself. This concept of a refusal is introduced by a function R, defined by the transition rules

$$\frac{p \; ref_X \; q}{Rp \xrightarrow{ref(X)} Rq} \qquad\qquad \frac{p \xrightarrow{a} q}{Rp \xrightarrow{a} Rq}$$

where $p \; ref_X \; q \;\; \widehat{=} \;\; \forall x : X \cup \{\tau\} . \;\; \neg p \xrightarrow{x} \_ \;\; \wedge \;\; q = p$

One of the standard healthiness conditions of CSP is that every event that cannot happen can be added to the refusal set. This follows from the definition of ref_X, because

$$ref_X \quad \subseteq \quad \xrightarrow{x} \; ; U \cup ref_{X \cup \{x\}}$$

Furthermore, every subset of a refusal set can also be refused. These two healthiness conditions can be coded algebraically

$$\begin{array}{rcl} R \; ; \xrightarrow{ref(X \cup Y)} & \subseteq & R \; ; \xrightarrow{ref(X)} \\ R \; ; \xrightarrow{ref(X)} & \subseteq & R \; ; (\xrightarrow{x} \; ; U \cup \xrightarrow{ref(X \cup \{x\})}) \end{array}$$

Of course, the validity of these conditions depends on the assumption that they are satisfied by any *a priori* refusals in the transition system, namely ones that possibly existed before application of R. To avoid such non-standard refusals, a process algebra usually forbids the explicit occurrence of *ref(X)* (and other barbs) in its process descriptions.

We define refusal-barbed simulation in the usual way:

$$\leq_r \quad \widehat{=} \quad (R \; ; \leq \; ; R^{\cup})$$

By Theorem 3.2, $\leq_r$ is the weakest relation S satisfying

$$\begin{array}{rcll} S \; ; \xrightarrow{a} & \subseteq & \xrightarrow{a} \; ; S & \text{if } a \text{ is not a refusal} \\ S \; ; ref_X & \subseteq & ref_X & \end{array}$$

The second clause can be expanded

$$p \, S \, q \Rightarrow \forall X . \, [\, (\forall x : X \cup \{\tau\} \, . \neg q \xrightarrow{x}) \Rightarrow (\forall x : X \cup \{\tau\} \, . \neg p \xrightarrow{a})]$$

By simple contraposition of implication and set-theoretic simplification, this is equivalent to

$$p \, S \, q \Rightarrow (\forall x . \;\; p \xrightarrow{x} \;\; \Rightarrow \;\; q \xrightarrow{x} \vee \; q \xrightarrow{\tau})$$

As a result, $\leq_r$ comes quite close to satisfying the defining property of two-thirds simulation [13]. We will therefore give it that name.

Refusal-barbed refinement is also defined in the standard way:

$$\sqsubseteq_r \quad \widehat{=} \quad R \; ; \sqsubseteq \; ; R^{\cup}$$

This relation can be fairly efficiently computed using model checking, using the formula $R \,;\, T \,;\, \leq \,;\, R^{\cup}$. Unfortunately, the final $R^{\cup}$ cannot be omitted, because R is not monotonic and cannot be a retraction.

Having defined $\sqsubseteq_r$ in a standard way, we are obliged to show that it is essentially the same as the standard CSP notion of failures refinement. In CSP, refusal barbs are restricted to appear only at the very end of a trace, whereas in a trace of Rp they can occur anywhere, any number of times. Let E be the set of all sequences that contain at most one refusal, and the refusal is at the end. We use E to select the failures of p from the traces of Rp:

$$failures(p) \quad \cong \quad traces(Rp) \cap E$$

Note that this definition of failures differs from the original one, in that it includes also traces which do not end in a refusal.

Lemma 6.1.1. $traces(Rq) \subseteq traces(Rp) \quad \Rightarrow \quad failures(q) \subseteq failures(p)$

For the reverse implication, we define a function *close* which adds into any subset of E all those additional traces which could have been introduced by R.

$$close(S) \quad \cong \quad S \cup \{s\langle r\rangle t \mid s\langle r\rangle \in S \wedge st \in close(S)\,,\ \ r \text{ a refusal}\}$$

This is clearly a monotonic function. Furthermore

Lemma 6.1.2. $traces(Rq) \quad = \quad close(traces(Rq) \cap E\,)$

Theorem 6.1.1. $p \sqsubseteq_r q \quad \Leftrightarrow \quad failures(q) \subseteq failures(p)$

Proof: From the preceding two lemmas.

We have now shown how two-thirds simulation and failures refinement can both be defined in terms of R. As a result, failures refinement can be fairly efficiently computed by model-checking, just exploiting Theorem 5.1.7 to get

$$\sqsubseteq_r \quad = \quad R \,;\, T \,;\, \leq \,;\, R^{\cup}$$

But we still have to make good the claim that the simple failures of CSP is a retract of CCS modulo two-thirds simulation. The relevant retraction will be $(R \,;\, T\,)$. That will take the rest of this subsection.

Lemma 6.1.3.

$$R \,;\, \xrightarrow{a} \quad = \quad \xrightarrow{a} ;\, R \qquad \text{if } a \text{ is not a refusal}$$

$$R \,;\, \xrightarrow{ref(X)} \quad = \quad (\,\xrightarrow{ref(X)} \cup\ ref_X\,) \,;\, R$$

$$R \,;\, ref_X \quad = \quad ref_X \,;\, R$$

Although R is not a retraction it is an idempotent function, and a decreasing one.

Theorem 6.1.2.

$$\leq \ \subseteq \ R \,;\, \leq$$

$$R \,;\, R \,;\, \leq \quad = \quad R \,;\, \leq$$

Proof: From the preceding lemma by Theorems 4.2 and 4.3.

Corollary. R is a retraction with respect to $\leq_r$. {because $R ; \leq_r = \leq_r$}

This section is incomplete.

6.2 Failures with Hiding

In CSP, the standard model combines refusals barbs with the concealment of hidden events. The relevant refinement ordering is defined by composing W with R:

$$\sqsubseteq_{rw} \quad = \quad R ; W ; \sqsubseteq ; W^{\cup} ; R^{\cup}$$

Two-thirds simulation also has a weak form, which can be similarly defined:

$$\leq_{rw} \quad = \quad R ; W ; \leq ; W^{\cup} ; R^{\cup} \quad = \quad R ; W ; \leq ; R^{\cup}$$

One of the effects of W is to insert a τ transition from every process to itself. Any subsequent application of R will discover that all states are unstable; so it will never insert a refusal. As a result,

Lemma 6.2.1. $W ; ref_X \quad = \quad \{\}$

Lemma 6.2.2. $W ; R ; \leq \quad = \quad W ; \leq$

Proof: If a is not a refusal

$$\begin{array}{lll} W^{\cup} ; W ; R ; \xrightarrow{a} & = W^{\cup} ; W ; \xrightarrow{a} ; R & \{\text{Lemma 6.1.3}\} \\ & = W^{\cup} ; = a => ; W ; R & \{W \text{ commut.}\} \\ & = \xrightarrow{a} ; W^{\cup} ; W ; R & \{R ; \xrightarrow{\tau} = \xrightarrow{\tau} ; R\} \end{array}$$

$$\begin{array}{lll} W^{\cup} ; W ; R ; \xrightarrow{ref(X)} & = W^{\cup} ; W ; (\xrightarrow{ref(X)} \cup ref_X) ; R & \{R \text{ commut.}\} \\ & = W^{\cup} ; = ref(X) => ; W ; R & \{W ; ref_X = \{\}\} \\ & = \xrightarrow{ref(X)} ; W^{\cup} ; W ; R & \{W \text{ commut.}\} \end{array}$$

Theorem 6.2.1. $R ; W$ is idempotent.

Proof:

$$\begin{array}{lll} R ; W ; R ; W ; \leq & \subseteq R ; W ; R ; \leq ; W ; \leq & \\ & = R ; W ; \leq ; W ; \leq & \{\text{Lemma 6.2.2}\} \\ & = R ; W ; W ; \leq & \{W \text{ mon.}\} \\ & = R ; W ; \leq & \{W \text{ idem.}\} \\ & \subseteq R ; W ; R ; W ; \leq & \{R, W \text{ dec.}\} \end{array}$$

Corollary. $R ; W$ is a retraction with respect to $\leq_{rw}$.

This section is incomplete.

6.3 Divergence

Live-lock, also known as divergence, is a phenomenon that occurs when a process is engaged in an unbounded series of internal events, each of which consumes some resource. It typically arises from an unguarded recursion in a program, for example an iteration with a permanently false exit condition. Because live-lock cannot be observed from any finite trace, it is called a 'liveness' property, rather than a safety property of a process.

One of the applications of a theory of programming is to prove the validity of optimising transformations. To prove the justifying equations, it is necessary that the theory should ignore consumption of resources. That is why each finite subsequence of hidden events is legitimately regarded as hidden, but hiding an infinite sequence is usually inadvisable, since there is no limit on the computational resources that may be consumed. Even if there are other concurrent processes behaving properly, live-lock is often regarded as undesirable. We therefore introduce a special symbol σ to denote a hidden event that consumes resources.

CSP provides a method of proving the absence of divergence by making it observable as a barb, for which we choose the symbol δ. This turns absence of divergence from a liveness property into a safety property, which can be proved by the normal method of refinement. The barb is introduced into a transition system by a function D, which also turns any bounded sequence of σ into the harmless ignorable τ. D is defined by the transition rules

$$\frac{p\ \tau^{\infty}\ q}{Dp \xrightarrow{<\delta>} Dq} \qquad\qquad \frac{p \xrightarrow{<a>} q}{Dp \xrightarrow{<a>} Dq}$$

where τ^{∞} is the greatest binary relation r satisfying the equation

$$r \quad = \quad \xrightarrow{\tau}\ ;\ r$$

Theorem 6.3.1. D is a retraction.

Note that the definition of $p\ \tau^{\infty}\ q$ does not depend on q, so the behaviour of Dp after divergence is arbitrary. This is in accordance with the basic philosophy of CSP, which was primarily intended to support a top-down procedure for designing correct implementations from their specifications. It took the view that divergence was never a desirable behaviour for an implementation, and that any process that contains a potential divergence cannot satisfy any reasonable specification. A divergent process must therefore be placed at the bottom of the refinement ordering. This is enforced by a healthiness condition stating that any process that can diverge at any point can also do anything else whatsoever from that point on. Of course, this condition makes CSP entirely unsuitable to help in debugging a program that suffers from a divergence error. For debugging, a purely operational language definition is more suitable. That is why it is so important to establish a link between an operationally defined theory and one which takes a more abstract and idealistic point of view that supports proofs that a well-designed system will never diverge.

In fact CSP took a stronger view, that even the possibility of divergence is equivalent to arbitrary behaviour, and the divergence barb does not even have to be selected. A slight change in the definition of D would model different choices of divergent behaviour. These topics will not be pursued further at this point.

We define divergence-barbed simulation and the trace-divergence model of CSP in the usual way

$$\leq_d \quad \cong \quad D\,;\, \leq\,;\, D^{\cup}$$

$$\sqsubseteq_d \quad \cong \quad D\,;\, \sqsubseteq\,;\, D^{\cup}$$

A development similar to that of section 5.2 leads to the conclusion that CCS modulo divergence-barbed simulation is a retract of CCS modulo strong simulation, and that the trace-divergence model of CSP is a retract (by $D\,;\,T$) of CCS modulo divergence-barbed simulation.

This section is incomplete.

7 Conclusion

The ideas of this paper have been derived from many sources. The concept of a retraction was introduced from topology to Computer Science by [23]. Relationships between families of process algebras and their orderings have been comprehensively explored in [25]. The algebraic expressive power of CCS and CSP have been analysed and compared in [2, 24] and elsewhere. The use of transition rules to define functions is due to [18]. Barbed simulation was introduced in [16], and refusal barbs have been comprehensively treated in [17]. A series of testing equivalences (including traces and refusals) have been defined in [1]; they culminate in a testing equivalence identical to observation equivalence. Saturation of a transition system has been used in [6] as a means to relate testing pre-orders with simulation. Refinement has been related to a higher-order version of simulation by [7]. The efficiency of retractions has been exploited in the model-checking tool FDR [20].

This paper has put these original ideas together, and applied them specifically to illuminate the relationship between various versions of CCS and of CSP. Only the simplest standard definitions of simulation and trace refinement have been used. All the interesting variation is provided by the definition of the links between the theories. In many cases, a link translates each process of the source theory onto a process of the target theory that is its closest approximation. A link simultaneously specifies the healthiness conditions and the ordering of the target theory. The links are surprisingly simply defined by transition rules. They can be applied separately or (for suitable cases) in combination. The proofs are mostly trivial, and have been presented in an unusually algebraic style. There are no complex constructions or ingenious algorithms. Perhaps similar techniques may be found useful in the study of more modern process algebras like the π-calculus [15] and bigraphical systems [12].

The inspiration for the research reported in this paper arose at a Workshop held in Microsoft Research Ltd., in Cambridge on 22-23 July 2002. Those who contributed were Ernie Cohen, Cedric Fournet, Paul Gardiner, Andy Gordon, Tony Hoare, Robin Milner, Sriram Rajamani, Jacob Rehof and Bill Roscoe. Some of the ideas from the Workshop have been incorporated in the model checking tool Zing [19].

An unexpected result of this research is that a specification-oriented denotational semantics like that of CSP can be systematically derived from a purely operational semantics like that of CCS, by means of operationally defined links. Our first attempt at a derivation in the reverse direction could only prove partial correctness of an operational implementation of CSP [10]. A unifying theory that reconciles these two styles of semantic presentation may be influential when model-checking tools based on simulation are used in combination with theorem-proving tools based on specification. Perhaps one day such tools will be regularly applied together for reliable system design and validation [11].

References

1. Samson Abramsky, *Observation equivalence as a testing equivalence,* TCS 53 (1987) 225-241
2. S.D. Brookes, *On the relationship of CCS and CSP*, LNCS 154 (1983)
3. S.D. Brookes, C.A.R. Hoare and A.W. Roscoe, *A theory of communicating sequential processes,* JACM (1984) 31
4. J.A. Bergstra and J.W. Klop, *Algebra of communicating processes with abstraction,* TCS 37(1) 77-121 (1985)
5. R. Cleaveland, J. Parrow and B. Steffen, *The Concurrency Workbench,* LNCS 407 (1989) 24-37
6. Rance Cleaveland and Matthew Hennessy, *Testing Equivalence as a Bisimulation Equivalence,* FACS (1992) 3
7. P. Gardiner, *Power simulation and its relation to traces and failures refinement,* TCS 309(1) 157-176 (2003)
8. Matthew Hennessy and Robin Milner, *Algebraic laws for non-determinism and concurrency*, JACM 31(1) 137-161 (1985)
9. J.F. Groote and F. Vaandrager. *Structured operational semantics and bisimulation as a congruence,* Information and Computation 100(2) 202-260 (1992)
10. C.A.R. Hoare and He Jifeng, *Unifying theories of programming,* Prentice Hall (1998)
11. C.A.R. Hoare and J. Misra, *Verified Software: theories, tools, experiments,* VSTTE conference (2005)
12. O.H. Jensen and R. Milner, *Bigraphs and mobile processes (revised),* UCAM-CL-TR-580 (2004)
13. K. Larsen and A. Skou, *Bisimulation through probabilistic testing,* POPL proceedings (1989)
14. R. Milner, *Communication and concurrency,* Prentice Hall (1985).
15. R. Milner, *Communicating and mobile systems: the π-calculus*, Cambridge University Press (1999)
16. R. Milner and D. Sangiorgi, *Barbed Bisimulation*, ICALP 1992
17. I. Phillips, *Refusal testing,* Springer LNCS 226 (1986) 304-313
18. G.D. Plotkin, *A structural approach to operational semantics,* DAIMI-FN-19, Aarhus University, Denmark (1981)
19. Sriram K. Rajamani, Jakob Rehof, Shaz Qadeer, Yichen Xie and Tony Andrews, *Zing: a model checker for concurrent software*, CAV 2004, Springer. 484-487
20. A.W. Roscoe, *The theory and practice of concurrency,* Prentice Hall (1998)
21. A.W. Roscoe, *Revivals, stuckness and responsiveness,* unpublished draft.

22. A.W. Roscoe, *Model checking in CSP*, in A classical mind: essays in honour of C.A.R. Hoare, Prentice-Hall (1994)
23. Dana Scott, *Data types as lattices,* SIAM Journal on Computing 5 (1976) 522-587
24. R.J. van Glabbeek, *Notes on the methodology of CCS and CSP*, CWI report CS-R8624 (1986)
25. R.J. van Glabbeek, *The Linear Time – Branching time Spectrum*, Handbook of Process Algebra, Elsevier (2001) 3-39

A Design-Based Model of Reversible Computation

Bill Stoddart, Frank Zeyda, and Robert Lynas

University of Teesside, UK

Abstract. We investigate, within the UTP framework of Hoare He Designs, the effect of seeing computation as an essentially *reversible* process. We describe the theoretical link between reversibility and the minimum power requirements of a computation, and we review Zuliani's work on Reversible Probabilistic Guarded Command Language. We propose an alternative formalisation of reversible computing which accommodates backtracking. To obtain a basic backtracking language able to search for a single result we exploit the already recognised properties of non-deterministic choice, using it as provisional choice rather than implementor's choice. We add a "prospective values" formalism which can describe programs that return all the possible results of a search, and we show how to formally describe the premature termination of such a search, a mechanism analogous to the "cut" of Prolog. An appendix describes some aspects of the **wp** calculus in terms of Designs, as needed for our proofs.

Support for the programming structures described has been incorporated in a reversible virtual machine for i386 platforms with Posix compatibility.

Keywords: reversible computing, backtracking, Hoare He Designs, wp calculus, prospective values.

1 Introduction

We investigate the effect on formal software development of regarding computation as an essentially *reversible* process. Programs written in sequential programming languages normally erase information as they run: for example the assignment `x:=7` erases the former value of `x`. Our target execution platform will be a reversible virtual machine which preserves such information. This incurs an efficiency penalty on current architectures, but, looking at the efficiency of computation in absolute terms, we will see that it is precisely the erasure of information during irreversible computing steps which *inescapably* requires the expenditure of energy during a computation, and imposes a lower bound on its energy requirements.

The thermodynamics of computation was first formulated by R Landauer of IBM Research in 1961 [10]. It was developed to give a theory of reversible computation by C Bennett [2]. A tutorial exposition can be found in the Feynman

S. Dunne and W. Stoddart (Eds.): UTP 2006, LNCS 4010, pp. 63–83, 2006.

Computing Lectures [4]. The MIT Pendulum project was a recent attempt to produce an efficient reversible processor using current technologies [6]. P Zuliani has expounded the essential theory using a guarded command language with predicate transformer semantics, thus bringing it within the realm of practical software development [21].

In this paper we look at reversible computing within the framework of "Designs", the formalism proposed by Hoare and He in their work on Unifying Theories of Programming [9]. We exploit the reversible nature of our computing model to handle garbage collection and to introduce backtracking constructs. The latter will require some modification of the standard UTP approach, in that we will repeal the "Law of the Excluded Miracle" We include in our language the naked guarded command $g \Longrightarrow P$, with the operational interpretation that an attempt to execute an infeasible command will cause computation to reverse back to the most recent point at which an unexplored choice is available for execution.

The paper is organised as follows. In Section 2 we review the concept of logical reversibility and establish the relationship between irreversible operations and necessary power consumption. In Section 3 we consider "reversible pGCL", Zuliani's adaptation of Morgan and McIver's probabilistic guarded command language [13], and we begin to tackle an issue not fully covered in Zuliani's work, that of "stepwise reversibility". In Section 4 we consider the use of non-deterministic choice as a tool for describing a backtracking search. In Section 5 we begin to consider the problem of formally expressing collections of results, and we outline our adaptation of "bunches". In Section 6 we propose a "prospective value" formalism to describe all the results of a search. In Section 7 we show how to formally describe the premature termination of a search by a mechanism analogous to the "cut" of Prolog. In Section 8 we draw our conclusions and outline future work. Some proofs linking designs and weakest preconditions are given in an appendix.

One aspect of this work that we would like to stress, although the details are not discussed, is the existence of an associated execution platform. We have written a reversible virtual machine which runs on i386 platforms under Linux, BSD Unix or Windows with a Posix compatibility layer. It provides an interactive intermediate level postfix language and development environment and closely supports the programming structures described here. Various articles, manuals and the current source files are available from *http://www.tees.ac.uk/formalmethods.*

2 Logical Reversibility

As computer scientists we are accustomed to abstracting away from particular computing mechanisms. Our aim in this section, however, is to consider a computation as a physical process with particular regard to its necessary energy requirements. One way to anticipate our arguments is to to consider a collection of balls moving on an idealised billiard table, with no pockets and on which balls roll and rebound from the cushions with no energy loss. The laws of motion in such a "conservative system" are deterministic and reversible, and at any time its previous history could be recovered if we could exactly reverse the direction of movement of each of the balls. On a system where damping occurs, however, the balls will eventually come to rest, and the system no longer contains the information required to recover its past history. This example provides an association between damping (energy consumption) and loss of information (irreversibility) which we will now attempt to develop, along with the minimum energy requirements involved.

In a talk given in 1949 and later published in [18], John von Neumann remarked that there must be a dissipation of $k * T * ln(2)$ units of energy per "elementary act of information, that is per elementary decision of a two way alternative and per elementary transmission of one unit of information". His analysis is based on the assumption that each "elementary act" removes one bit of uncertainty from the result of a computation, thus reducing the entropy within the computer by the classical thermodynamic quantity $k * T * ln(2)$, and requiring an equivalent energy dissipation to the environment.

This roughly sketched theory remained unchallenged until 1961 when Rolf Landauer provided an analysis based on determining the essential function of energy consumption during computation.[10], and found that it was only necessary for "standardizing signals and making them independent of their exact logical history", i.e. that energy consumption was only required for the irreversible steps of a computing process.

To explore these concepts we need a physical model that allows information to be registered in a material way. Because the laws of thermodynamics apply in a very general way, we will not analyse a practical model of memory storage, but rather one which allows us to perform our demonstrations in the simplest way. Figure 1 shows a cylinder containing a single molecule of ideal gas and having a piston at each end. Initially the molecule is free to move anywhere within the piston. A zero is registered by moving in the piston on the left and restricting the molecule to the right half of the cylinder.

A value of one is similarly registered by moving in the piston on the right. This model has been used by Feynman [4], Bennett [3] and others, and in a slightly more elaborate form dates back to a paper from 1929 by Szilard [17].

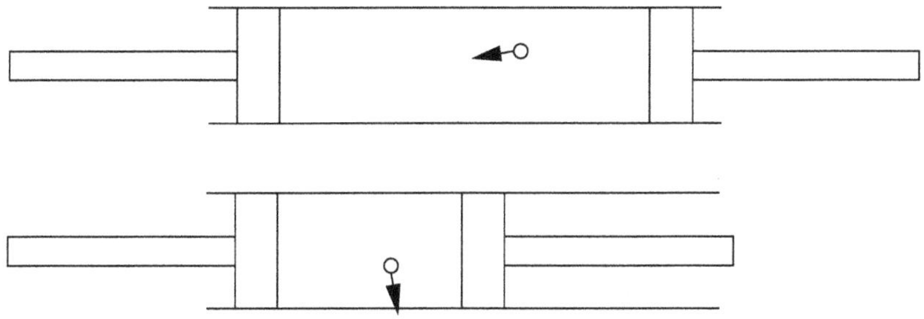

Fig. 1. Cylinder containing one molecule of gas

In the lower diagram of Figure 1 the piston on the right has been moved in against the pressure of the gas (whose molecular movement we interpret in a time-averaged sense) so that the gas is compressed to half its previous volume. As the piston starts to move the initial effect is to increase the energy in the molecule, which is now rebounding from a moving surface and thus gains speed. However, we will assume an isothermal compression, that is one in which the additional energy of the molecule is rapidly absorbed by the environment, so that we can assume the compression of the gas takes place at a constant temperature. The Ideal Gas Law tells us that the pressure and volume of a gas at temperature T are related by $P * V = N * k * T$ where k is Boltzmann's constant, N is the number of molecules in the gas and T is the absolute temperature. If the distance between the pistons in our cylinder is L and the area presented to the gas by each piston is A, the volume of the gas is $V = A * L$ For a single molecule we thus have $P * A * L = k * T$. The force exerted by the gas on one piston is thus $P * A = k * T/L$. To find the minimum work needed to compress the gas to half its volume we need to integrate this force between an initial distance separating the pistons, L_0 say, and $L_0/2$.

$$W = \int_{L_0}^{\frac{L_0}{2}} \frac{k*T}{L}\, dL = k * T * ln(\tfrac{L_0}{2}) - k * T * ln(L_0) = -k * T * ln(2)$$

A very interesting property of this result is that it depends neither on the mass of the molecule or on the size of the cylinder, and is, in fact, the general result for the change of entropy associated with constraining a particle to half its phase space along one of its degrees of freedom in any thermal system.

We can similarly recover from this compressed gas $k * T * ln(2)$ of free energy when allowing it to re-expand. We note too that this energy is not obtained from the gas, but from the environment: its availability is due to the *configuration* of the system.

Representation of a bit of data is more realistically characterised as some form of bistable well. Figure 2 represents orientations of a pair of magnets, linked so that they are always at the same angle. The ensemble has two positions of stable equilibrium, representing 1 and 0 states.

In the figure we see the magnets being moved from a 1 to a 0 state. The graph below represents the potential energy of the ensemble as the two linked needles pass through different angles of rotation. The reversible operation of switching from 1 to zero can essentially be performed without consumption of energy, since the energy required to move "up" to the state of unstable equilibrium can, in principle, be recovered whilst moving "down" to the 0 state. The same analysis applies to switching from 0 to 1, but what about the operation of just toggling the bit (without knowing its current state)? This can be done in an energy free manner by rotating the whole ensemble about its centre point as shown in Figure 3.

Now let us consider the irreversible operation "set to 1" illustrated in figure 4. Recall that a conservative system obeying the laws of motion is both reversible and deterministic. An energy free "set to 1", therefore, would have a deterministic reverse trajectory. However, the reverse trajectory of "set to 1" is

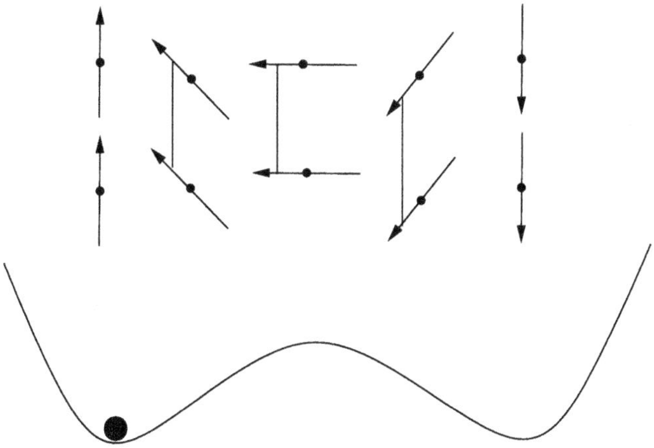

Fig. 2. Pair of compass needles forming a bistable well

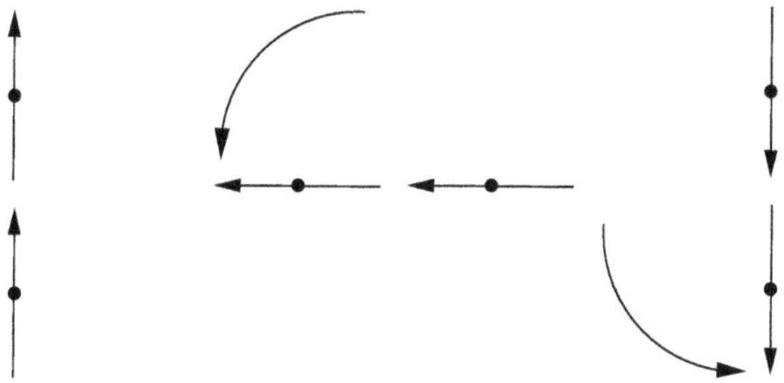

Fig. 3. Energy free toggling of a bit

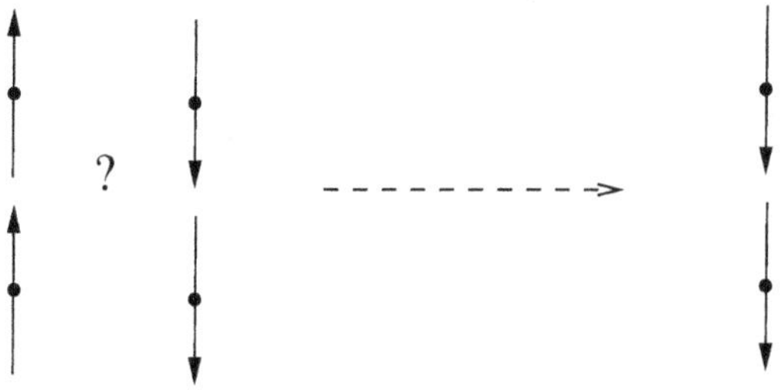

Fig. 4. The irreversible "set to 1" operation

non-deterministic, since it has to include the possibilities of returning to a previous state of either 0 or 1. This contradiction tells us that our assumption that "set to 1" can be performed in a conservative system is incorrect, and therefore some damping is required in this case. Before we definitively accept this conclusion however we must dispose of the following counter argument. "The reverse trajectory need only be non-deterministic if all previous history has been lost

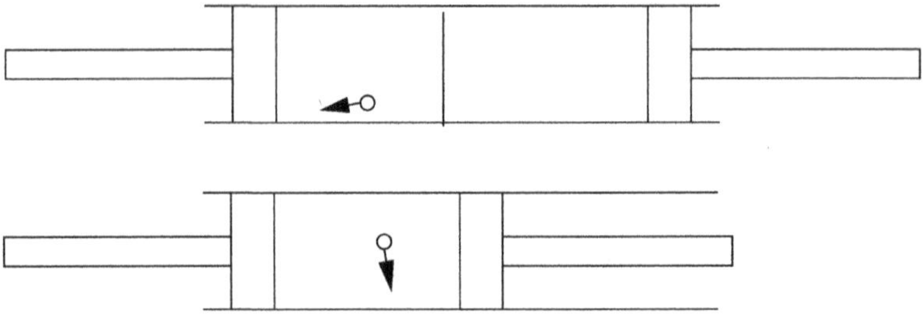

Fig. 5. Szilard's Cylinder

by the "set to 1" operation. So long as we allow some residual difference in the configuration of a 1 bit that was previously a 1 and a 1 bit that was previously a zero, the argument breaks down. Also, such differences are seen on real devices, as, for example, in the ability to perform forensic analysis of a blanked area of a hard disc and retrieve its previous contents." Although this argument has some force as far as one single operation is concerned, it is not possible to employ it in any physically realistic way over a continued sequence of operations without the necessary residuals building up and disabling the devices capacity to store information. As Landauer says "the physical many to one mapping, which is the source of the entropy change, need not happen in full detail during the machine cycle which performed the logical function, but it must eventually take place, and this is all that is relevant for the heat generation argument".

So far we have considered two separate arguments based respectively on the energy needed to constrain a particle along an information bearing degree of freedom and on the reversibility of the laws of motion in a conservative system. To draw these together consider again our cylinder of gas. What if, instead of compressing the molecule into one half of the cylinder by exerting force on one of the pistons, we had instead trapped the molecule on one side of the cylinder by inserting a partition, as shown in the upper cylinder of figure 5. This is an operation that, in principle, requires no work.

We could then push in the piston from the side that does not contain the gas. Since we are not moving the piston against any resisitng force this action again, in principle, requires no work. We could then remove the partition and be in a position to extract work from the piston without having put any work in.

This apparent paradox was proposed by L Szilard[17] in 1929 as an aid to analysing the closely related "paradox" of Maxwell's Demon. Szilard looked for a compensating energy input in the measurement that would need to be made before it could be decided which piston to move. His analysis was universally accepted until Landauer's colleague at IBM Research, Charles Bennet, showed that measurement is not intrinsically an energy consuming process, and, applying Landauer's analysis, pointed out that the mechanism that registered which side the molecule was on would itself have to perform an irreversible operation analogous to the "set to 1" operation described above, and that this was where a necessary energy input must occur.

Landauer's analysis led him to the conclusion that a computation which is reversible *at each step* would, in principle, have a zero minimum energy requirement. However, he also reasoned that computing inevitably uses irreversible steps, for example the assignment $x := 0$ cannot be reversed because it destroys the value of x. Such steps are inevitably associated with the consumption of a certain minimum amount of energy. If a computing process could be contrived which used only reversible steps, then the laws of thermodynamics would not impose any minimum energy requirement for the computation. He notes that individual steps in a computing process can be made reversible by providing additional memory storage to preserve data that would otherwise be lost, but rejects this as a general technique as the result would be an unpredictable requirement for additional memory which would need to be irreversibly initialised to a known value: "Our unwieldy machine has therefore avoided the irreversible operations during the running of the program, only at the expense of added comparable irreversibility during the loading of the program."[10]

This conclusion was incorrect, because we can organise the required additional memory efficiently as a stack, and regard its initialisation as a one-off cost which, once paid, will allow us to run all subsequent programs in a reversible manner. Despite this one erroneous conclusion Landauer's 1961 paper made the seminal contribution in setting the terms for a debate on reversibility and was republished in volume 44 of the IBM Journal of Research and Development in 2000.

In 1963 Y Lecerf [11] formulated a reversible Turing Machine which potentially indicated how reversible computations could be managed, but this work did not feed into the reversible computing debate. However in 1973, C Bennett described[2] how an arbitrary (one tape) Turing Machine could be translated into a reversible 3 tape machine. The latter performs the calculation of the original machine, storing any overwritten data on the (originally blank) second tape. It then copies the result to the third tape. Finally it reverses its calculations so as to terminate with the first tape back in its original condition, the second tape once again blank and the result left on the third tape. Fundamental to Bennett's analysis is that writing to a blank tape is a reversible operation. The blank second tape plays the role of the pre-initialised memory mentioned above. Bennett linked his machines to the energy requirements of computing with the comment that Turing "machines may be made logically reversible at every step.. This .. makes plausible the existence of thermodynamically reversible computers which could perform useful computations at useful speed while dissipating considerably less than kT of energy per logical step."

3 Reversible pGCL

An interesting contribution to reversible computing is given in the paper "Logical Reversibility" by P Zuliani [21]. The author provides a similar formulation of non-reversible computation in terms of reversible computation. However, rather than using Turing Machines, he formulates his translation in terms of pGCL[13].

His work extends reversibility to computations involving non-deterministic and probabilistic choice, and presents it in a form suitable for incorporation into a software development method.

His technique for making an irreversible language reversible is to add some extra state, in the form of a single boolean variable b and a history stack, and to transform each operation S in the language into a reversible operation S_r which has the same effect as S on the original state space and which uses the history stack to preserve any information that would otherwise be lost when S is executed. For each S_r he provides an inverse operation (actually a right inverse) S_i such that $S_r\,;\;S_i \;=\; II$. The technique is illustrated in the following table where we give these constructs for the assignment and choice statements.

S	Reversible Operation S_r	Inverse Operation S_i
$v := e$	$push\ v;\ \ v := e$	$pop\ v$
$R \sqcap S$	$push\ b;\ \ (R_r;\ push\ true) \sqcap (S_r;\ push\ false)$	$pop\ b;\ \ R_i \lhd b \rhd S_i;\ \ pop\ b$

We would like to take this analysis a stage further because it does not, as it stands, provide the *stepwise reversibility* we require. For example the inverse of the assignment to v is $pop\ v$, a non-reversible operation, and the transformed assignment statement, $push\ v;\ \ v := e$, contains the irreversible step $v := e$.

We will show an alternative approach to the construction of a reversible assignment which gives a transformation consisting of the sequential composition of *reversible steps.* We initially limit our discussion to a language with integer variables and we consider only the assignment of a single variable rather than a variable list. We first note that we have some reversible assignment statements to call upon, namely those of the form $x := x + e$, where $x \setminus e$, i.e. x does not occur free in e. Such a statement has an inverse $x := x - e$. We set ourselves the problem of implementing general assignment purely in terms of reversible assignment statements.

We note that assignment to a zero valued variable is reversible, since:

$$(x = 0 \vdash x := e) \;=\; (x = 0 \vdash x := x + e[0/x])$$

Here the precondition $x = 0$ allows us the freedom to implement $x := e$ by the reversible command $x := x + e$.

The role of the history stack will be taken by an integer array, h, having a large enough size *hsize*, and with an array index i which will, loosely speaking, be used as a stack pointer. h and i are fresh variables with respect to the original program. We assume the elements of h are initialised to zero and i is initialised to one (requiring an initial investment of energy).

We can give a reversible transformation of $x := e$ as a sequence of reversible commands, as shown in the following trace:

assignment	$h(i-1)$	$h(i)$	$h(i+1)$	x
	?	0	0	x_0
$h(i) := h(i) + x$	?	x_0	0	x_0
$h(i+1) := h(i+1) + e$	?	x_0	e	x_0
$x := x - h(i)$	?	x_0	e	0
$x := x + h(i+1)$	?	x_0	e	e
$h(i+1) = h(i+1) - x$	?	x_0	0	e
$i := i + 1$	x_0	0	0	e

The reverse operation may be formed from the inverse operations of each of the above steps:

assignment	$h(i-1)$	$h(i)$	$h(i+1)$	x
	x_0	0	0	e
$i := i - 1$	?	x_0	0	e
$h(i+1) := h(i+1) + x$	?	x_0	e	e
$x := x - h(i+1)$	?	x_0	e	0
$x := x + h(i)$	?	x_0	e	x_0
$h(i+1) := h(i+1) - e$	?	x_0	0	x_0
$h(i) := h(i) - x$	?	0	0	x_0

The transformation of $x := e$ and the inverse operation given above are only correct under the assumption $h(i) = 0 \land h(i+1) = 0$, which is implied by the stronger condition:

$$i \in 1..hsize - 1 \land \forall j \bullet j \in i..hsize \Rightarrow h(j) = 0$$

which is *invariant* in the sense that it is established by the initialisation of the history stack and preserved by each forward and reverse assignment (under the assumption that hsize is sufficiently large). It must similarly be preserved by all other operations, but we do not have space to detail that here.

A second remark we need to make concerning the above analysis is that we consider the expression value e to have been computed and stored in some suitable register before the assignment is made. Subsequent to the reverse execution of the assignment would therefore be the "uncomputation" of the value e.

We can describe the stepwise construction of non-integer assignments using an extra level of refinement in which we introduce some details that, for normal purposes, can be left to the compiler of our implementation-level code. This extra level will interpret the execution of our assignment statements in terms of a reference semantics. Let the values of some type D that arise during a calculation be denoted by $d_1, d_2...$ With each value d_i we associate a unique reference rd_i of type $\mathbb{N}$. Let Ref_D be the partial injection $\{rd_1 \mapsto d_1, rd_2 \mapsto d_2...\}$. We now consider $v := d_i$, which would normally be an assignment at the implementation level, to be an *abstract assignment* implemented, in our further level of refinement, by $v_r := dr_i$. The refinement requires an abstraction predicate which tells us that $Ref_D(v_r) = v$. Since all assignment is now implemented as integer assignment, our previous analysis will suffice.

4 Reversible Computing and Backtracking

Our aim is to exploit reversible computation to introduce automatic backtracking and more abstract (mathematical) data types into an implementation level language. Rather than adding additional state to provide reversibility, as described in the previous section, the formal technique we employ is to use non-deterministic choice as *provisional choice* instead of (or as well as) implementor's choice. Though not often discussed, this idea has a long history. As far back as 1967, in his paper "Non-deterministic Algorithms" [5], Floyd talked of "programs governed in part .. by final causes for the sake of which their effects are carried out". In "The Specification Statement"[12] Carroll Morgan mentions the possibility as follows: "Ordinarily we limit the syntax of our programming language so that miracles cannot be written in it. If we relax this restriction, allowing naked guarded commands, then operational reasoning suggests a backtracking implementation". He gives as an example this refinement of the program $i : [a[i] = v]$ which finds one position of an element in an array.

if
$\quad i := 0 \sqcap .... \sqcap i := N - 1;$
$\quad a[i] = v \longrightarrow \mathit{skip}$
fi

He comments: "We are using the generalised *if* .. *fi* which allows abortion if its body is miraculous, and the body is miraculous *only* when no branch of the alternative can avoid the miraculous behaviour to follow. In this context *if* .. *fi* resembles the "cut" of Prolog, allowing failure (preventing backtracking) if no solution is found.."

A similar possibility is noted by Eric Hehner in [8], although, as he remarks, his timing calculus does not work in conjunction with a backtracking interpretation.

To begin with, we will introduce a limited form of backtracking simply by allowing naked guarded commands of the form $g \Longrightarrow S$.[1] This requires the repeal of Dijkstra's "Law of the Excluded Miracle" *at the implementation level.* In UTP this means suspending healthiness condition **H4**, which insists that Designs should be feasible. In the following discussion S will denote a program with alphabet s and with design $P \vdash Q$, i.e. a program with assumption P and commitment Q. We remind the reader that such a design $P \vdash Q$ satisfies **H4** if $\exists\, ok', s' \bullet (P \vdash Q)$.

We define $g \Longrightarrow (P \vdash Q) \mathrel{\widehat=} (g \Rightarrow P \vdash g \wedge Q)$. Note that this is a design, but not one that will obey **H4**, other than in the trivial case where $g = \mathit{true}$.

With this definition we separate the concepts of guard and choice. One effect is that the conditional $S \lhd b \rhd T$ no longer needs to be a primitive construct, as it can be defined as $S \lhd b \rhd T \mathrel{\widehat=} b \Longrightarrow S \sqcap \neg\, b \Longrightarrow T$.

As a simple example of the backtracking effect obtained with guards and choice consider $S \mathrel{\widehat=} x := 1 \sqcap x := 2;\ x = 2 \Longrightarrow II$. An operational interpretation of this program is that it first makes a choice of assigning 1 or 2 to x. If it

[1] The use of '$\Longrightarrow$' for guards is borrowed from B and preferred over the normal '$\longrightarrow$' because we will presently be using the latter to represent a different form of guard.

assigns 1 the following statement is infeasible, which provokes reverse execution. The second alternative is then tried, making $x = 2$. The following command is now feasible and the program terminates with $x = 2$. Alternatively, if the first command initially assigns $x := 2$, the second command is immediately feasible and again the program terminates with $x = 2$. The formal calculation is:

$x := 1 \sqcap x := 2;\ x = 2 \Longrightarrow II \quad = \quad$ "writing each operation as a design"

$true \vdash x' = 1 \vee x' = 2;\ true \vdash x = 2 \wedge x' = x \quad = \quad$ "defn of $P \vdash Q$"

$ok \Rightarrow (x' = 1 \vee x' = 2) \wedge ok';\ ok \Rightarrow x = 2 \wedge x' = x \wedge ok' \quad = \quad$ "seq comp"

$\exists\, x'', ok'' \bullet (ok \Rightarrow (x'' = 1 \vee x'' = 2) \wedge ok'') \wedge (ok'' \Rightarrow x'' = 2 \wedge x' = x'' \wedge ok')$

$\quad = \quad$ "disjunction of the cases $ok'' = false$ and $ok'' = true$"

$\exists\, x'' \bullet \neg\, ok \vee (ok \Rightarrow (x'' = 1 \vee x'' = 2)) \wedge x'' = 2 \wedge x' = x'' \wedge ok'$

$\quad = \quad$ "$x'' \setminus \neg\, ok$"

$\neg\, ok \vee \exists\, x'' \bullet (ok \Rightarrow (x'' = 1 \vee x'' = 2)) \wedge x'' = 2 \wedge x' = x'' \wedge ok'$

$\quad = \quad$ "one point rule"

$\neg\, ok \vee (ok \Rightarrow x' = 2 \wedge ok') \quad = \quad$ "logic $\neg\, a \vee (a \Rightarrow b) \quad = \quad a \Rightarrow b$"

$ok \Rightarrow x' = 2 \wedge ok' \quad = \quad$ "definition of $P \vdash Q$"

$true \vdash x' = 2$

Note that the symbols $=$ and $\quad = \quad$ both denote equality, but with different binding power. The latter binds more weakly than the logical connectives, and is often used between the steps of a proof or derivation. We write equality between predicates A and B to indicate that they are equivalent at the top level, i.e. $\vdash A \Leftrightarrow B$.

For a more extensive example of the use of this form of backtracking see [19] where we present a specification and refinement proof of the Knight's Tour problem in a version of B modified to accept naked guarded commands. In this treatment the specification of the problem obtains the solution in a single choice which details a sequence of moves which satisfies the requirements of the problem. The implementation uses a loop which finds the solution step by step, and our refinement proof ensure the result meets the specification. Search heuristics may be introduced, such as making the most constrained choice first. These make use of our knowledge of the order in which non-deterministic choices are taken in our implementation. This knowledge is not recorded in our semantics of choice, so any performance gains are outside the scope of our formal analysis.

An advantage of reversibility is that it provides a simple basis for the management of garbage collection, and we have found it possible to provide a complete and efficient reversible implementation of finite sets which potentially reduces the semantic distance between specifications and implementations and, along with the availability of automatic backtracking, gives a very expressive implementation level language. A disadvantage of this language is that we cannot always rely on its syntax to protect us against over-refinement. We have to perform a syntactic analysis on an implementation to see if the commands used could introduce infeasibility, and, in such cases, protect against this by generating appropriate proof obligations. Without this precaution *magic* would qualify as an implementation of any design. How these advantages and disadvantages will impact on proof effort over a range of example programs remains to be investigated.

5 Bunches

A shortcoming of the backtracking technique introduced in the previous section is that it is limited to finding a single solution and that backtracking completely erases any information found. We may wish to find and record all solutions to a problem, or a set of solutions that collectively satisfy some criteria. This will be the focus of our investigation for the rest of the paper. For the purposes of our theory presentation it will be convenient to use "bunches" [7, 8]. A bunch is the "contents of a set" (Hehner) without the packaging that allows set representation to build up nested structures. A bunch of bunches is self-flattening, and that property will simplify our presentation.

Any value is an elementary bunch or element. For example 2 is a bunch. In set theory we must distinguish between 2 and $\{2\}$, i.e. between an element and a set containing just that element. In bunch theory there is no distinction.

The empty bunch is written as *null*. If A and B are bunches then their union and intersection, written A, B and $A'B$ respectively, are also bunches. We write $A : B$ to say A is a sub-bunch of B. As with sets, the repetition and order of elements has no significance. Some examples:

$$
\begin{array}{l}
2, 3 : 1, 2, 3, 4 \\
2 : 2 \\
A : A, B \\
null : 1, 2
\end{array}
$$

Operators applied to bunches are lifted in an obvious way: they distribute through bunch union and are strict with respect to *null*. For example, $1, 2 + 3, 4 = 1 + 3, 1 + 4, 2 + 3, 2 + 4 = 4, 5, 6$ and $1, 2 + null = null$.

We adopt bunch theory to our particular ends, which are to use it in a typed (or multi-sorted) theory which uses partial functions together with classical logic and takes a total correctness view of program description, i.e. the approach of B and Z. All identifiers in our theory denote elements. Bunches only arise as expressions. Bunches have no effect on our treatment of types, which are maximal sets. The type of any non-empty bunch is the same as the type of its elements. We also have an empty bunch of each type. To model non-termination we introduce an improper bunch $\perp$, or more strictly an improper bunch for each type. Given a type (maximal set) T the associated improper bunch is $\perp_T$. Where context can determine its type we write the bottom bunch as $\perp$. The bunches of any type form a complete lattice under bunch inclusion with the improper bunch as its bottom element. For any proper bunch E we have $E : \perp$ and $\neg \perp : E$. The improper bunch is strict with respect to bunch union, i.e. $E, \perp = \perp$. It is strict with respect to any operation applying to bunches of its type, e.g. $E + \perp = \perp$.

The "guarded bunch" $g \longrightarrow E$ is defined by the property:

$(g \Rightarrow (g \longrightarrow E = E)) \wedge (\neg\, g \Rightarrow (g \longrightarrow E = \mathit{null}))$

The "preconditioned bunch" $p \mid E$ is defined as $p \longrightarrow E, \neg\, p \longrightarrow \bot$

The bunch comprehension $\S\, x \bullet E$, where E must include information that determines the type of x, is the bunch of all values that can be taken by E as x ranges over the values of its type. For example $\S\, n \bullet 2 * n$ is the bunch of even numbers, and $\S\, x \bullet 0 < x \wedge x < 3 \longrightarrow 10 * x$ is the bunch $10, 20$.

Where we need to distinguish bunches from other comma-separated lists we enclose them in bunch brackets $({}_b ..){}_b$.

We write $E[F/w]$, where E and F are expressions and w a variable to denote the substitution of F for w in E. If F and w are lists they must be of the same arity and the substitution is made term-wise. Substitution distributes over bunch union. For example $E_1, E_2[F/w] = E_1[F/w], E_2[F/w]$ and $E[({}_b F_1, F_2){}_b/w] = E[F_1/w], E[F_2/w]$. So long as $F \neq \bot$ the value of the expression $E[F/w]$ is given as a bunch comprehension by $E[F/w] = \S\, w' \bullet w' : F \longrightarrow E[w'/w]$.

To remain within two-valued logic we avoid bunches of predicates by interpreting inner predicates (membership and equality) in a way that always makes them either true or false. Given expressions X and S of types T and $\mathbb{P}\; T$, the membership predicate $X \in S$ is true if it is point-wise true for each $x : X$ and $s : S$. Predicates such as $a < b$ are interpreted as set membership, i.e. $a \mapsto b \in \_ < \_$. Thus $1, 2 < 3$ is true, and both $1, 3 < 3$ and $4, 5 < 3$ are false. Expressions A and B are equal if $A : B$ and $B : A$.

Bunches allow us to define function application in a generalised way. Given $r \in A \leftrightarrow B$ and $a \in A$ we define the application of r to a by:

$r\, a \mathrel{\widehat=} \S\, b \bullet a \mapsto b \in r \longrightarrow b$

This generalisation of function application renders the separate notion of relational image superfluous, but more importantly it allows us to write $r\, x = y$ to express that r is functional at x and the unique value associated with x in r is y, a luxury not usually permitted in systems which use two-valued logic together with a relational model of function application. For example given a partial function f and $f\, x = 3$ we are not entitled, under the classical dispensation, to deduce $x \in \operatorname{dom} f$ [16, 1]. With the definition of application given here we can make this deduction, because were it false we would have $f\, x = \mathit{null}$.

Some further details of our use of bunches can be found in [20]. For a more extensive description of the use of bunches in the context of predicative program description see Paige and Hehner[15]. Morris and Bunkenburg have developed a theory which accommodates boolean bunches and an associated four-valued logic.[14]

6 Prospective Values

The following program finds one of the positions of an element with value e in an array a of size asize, and leaves this position in i:

$P \mathrel{\widehat=} i :\in 1..\mathit{asize};\; a[i] = e \longrightarrow \mathit{II}$

If more than one element in the array has value e, there is more than one possible result that can be left in i. We would like to be able to use the program P to find and record all of them. With this aim in view let $S \diamond E$ represent the bunch of possible values (the *prospective values*) expression E could take after running program S. The symbol '$\diamond$' has a binding power just below the program connective symbol '; '. Relating this to our example program, the set of all positions at which the value e occurs is now given by $\{P \diamond i\}$. Aside: we write this result as a set rather than a bunch because we use sets rather than bunches to represent collectivities on our implementation platform. One property of bunches that makes them attractive for theory description is that they do not make a distinction between the integer n and a bunch of integer that just contains n. However, this also makes their implementation less convenient than that of sets, where the distinction between n and $\{n\}$ allows us to represent the first as a simple integer and the second using reference semantics. End of aside.

For a design $S = P \vdash Q$ with an alphabet s we define:

$$S \diamond E = P \mid \S\, s'.Q \longrightarrow E[s'/s]$$

In this definition, within the assumption P of S, the commitment Q of S is used as a guard which selects those values of s' which S may allow to occur. For each such value we obtain a possible value that E could take after the execution of S by substituting s' for s in E.

The following proposition is useful for proving further properties of $S \diamond E$.

Proposition 1. *Let $P \vdash Q$ be a design, E be an expression and z be a fresh variable, i.e. $z \setminus P \vdash Q$ and $z \setminus E$. Then:*
$z : (P \vdash Q) \diamond E \Leftrightarrow \neg\, ((P \vdash Q)\ \mathbf{wp} \neg\, (z : E))$

This proposition was suggested to us by Louis Mussat. The proof uses the following lemma, which is proved in an appendix.

Lemma 1. *Let $\alpha(P \vdash Q) = s$, then:*
$(P \vdash Q)\ \mathbf{wp}\ r = \neg\, (P \Rightarrow \exists\, s'' \bullet (Q[s''/s'] \wedge \neg\ r[s''/s]))$

We now prove the proposition.

Proof. *We distinguish the cases $\neg\, P$ and P.*

Assuming $\neg\, P$

$z : (P \vdash Q) \diamond E \quad = \quad$ *"definition of $(P \vdash Q) \diamond E$"*

$z : P \mid \S\, s' \bullet Q \longrightarrow E[s'/s] \ \Leftrightarrow\ $ *"assumption $\neg\, P$"*

$z : \mathit{false} \mid \S\, s' \bullet Q \longrightarrow E[s'/s] \quad = \quad$ *"defn of preconditioned bunch"*

$z : \bot \quad = \quad$ *"property of the improper bunch"*

true

also

$\neg\, ((P \vdash Q)\ \mathbf{wp} \neg\, z : E) \ \Leftrightarrow\ $ *"assumption $\neg\, P$"*

$\neg\,((\mathit{false} \vdash Q)\ \mathbf{wp} \neg\, z : E) \quad = \quad$ *"false precondition"*

$\neg\, \mathit{false} \quad = \quad \mathit{true}$

this completes the proof for the case $\neg\, P$

Assuming P

$z : (P \vdash Q) \diamond E \quad = \quad$ *"definition of* $(P \vdash Q) \diamond E$*"*

$z : P \mid \S\, s' \bullet Q \longrightarrow E[s'/s] \;\Leftrightarrow\;$ *"assumption* P*"*

$z : \mathit{true} \mid \S\, s' \bullet Q \longrightarrow E[s'/s] \;\Leftrightarrow\;$ *"bunch precondition"*

$z : \S\, s' \bullet Q \longrightarrow E[s'/s] \;\Leftrightarrow\;$ *"existential property of bunch comprehension"*

$\exists\, s' \bullet (Q \wedge z : E[s'/s]) \;\Leftrightarrow\;$ *"assumption* P *and logic* $(\mathit{true} \Rightarrow a) \;=\; a$*"*

$P \Rightarrow \exists\, s' \bullet (Q \wedge z : E[s'/s])$

$\quad = \quad$ *"change in bound variable name, noting* $s'' \setminus Q \wedge z : E[s'/s]$*"*

$P \Rightarrow \exists\, s'' \bullet (Q[s''/s'] \wedge z : E[s'/s][s''/s'])$

$\quad = \quad$ *"property of substitution"*

$P \Rightarrow \exists\, s'' \bullet (Q[s''/s'] \wedge z : E[s''/s])$

$= \quad$ *"by logic* $a \;=\; \neg\neg\, a$ *and lemma 1"*

$\neg\,((P \vdash Q)\ \mathbf{wp} \neg\, z : E)$

this completes the proof for the case P*.* □

Using this result, or directly from its definition, we can now readily prove each of the following rules for $S \diamond E$ which cover the syntactic forms that can be used for an operation S at the specification level.

Name	Rule	Side Cond
Assumption	$(P \vdash Q) \diamond E = P \mid (\mathit{true} \vdash Q) \diamond E$	
Skip	$I\!I \diamond E = E$	
Assignment	$x := F \diamond E = E[F/x]$	
Guard	$g \Longrightarrow S \diamond E = g \longrightarrow S \diamond E$	
Choice	$S \sqcap T \diamond E = (S \diamond E), (T \diamond E)$	
Choice from set	$(x :\in A) \diamond E = \S\, a \bullet a \in A \longrightarrow E[a/x]$	$a \setminus E$
Seq Comp	$S;\ T \diamond E = S \diamond T \diamond E$	
Local Variable	$(\mathit{var}\ z.S.\mathit{end}\ z) \diamond E = \S\, z \bullet S \diamond E$	$z \setminus E$

We limit ourselves to two examples of such proofs. The first is for assumption, and in this case we work directly from the definition:

$(P \vdash Q) \diamond E = P \mid \mathit{true} \vdash Q \diamond E$

Proof. $(P \vdash Q) \diamond E \quad = \quad$ "by definition of $(P \vdash Q) \diamond E$"

$P \mid \S\, s' \bullet Q \longrightarrow E[s'/s] \quad = \quad$ "since for any bunch E, $E = \mathit{true} \mid E$"

$P \mid (\mathit{true} \mid \S\, s' \bullet Q \longrightarrow E[s'/s]) \quad = \quad$ "by definition of $(P \vdash Q) \diamond E$"

$P \mid (\mathit{true} \vdash Q) \diamond E$ □

The second result we prove is for sequential composition, Here we make use of Mussat's proposition:

$S;\ T \diamond E = S \diamond T \diamond E$

Proof. Let z be a fresh variable, then:

$z : S;\ T \diamond E \quad = \quad$ "proposition 1"

$\neg\,(S;\ T\ \mathbf{wp} \neg\, z : E) \quad = \quad$ "by **wp** property of sequential composition"

$\neg\,(S\ \mathbf{wp}\ (T\ \mathbf{wp} \neg\, z : E)) \quad = \quad$ " logic, $\neg\neg\, a \;=\; a$ "

$\neg\,(S\ \mathbf{wp} \neg\,(\neg\ T\ \mathbf{wp} \neg\, z : E)) \quad = \quad$ "proposition 1"

$\neg\,(S\ \mathbf{wp} \neg\,(z : T \diamond E) \quad = \quad$ "proposition 1"

$z : S \diamond T \diamond E$

Hence by extensionality the required result holds. □

7 Non-backtracking Choice and Cutting Short a Search

We can call upon mathematical constants to help us describe our programs. We call these "abstract constants" if they appear only at the specification level, and "concrete constants" if they appear at the implementation level, and therefore need some representations in executable code.

For each type T we loosely define a concrete constant $ichoice_T$ which is a partial function whose domain is the finite non-empty subsets of T. The only additional information we provide concerning this function is that for any set W in its domain, $ichoice_T(W) \in W$. We write $ichoice$ for $ichoice_T$ in applications of these functions since the particular function intended can be determined from the type of its argument.

Now consider the following two ways of making a choice from $W \in \mathbb{P}\ T$ and assigning this to a variable x: first $x :\in W$ and second $x := ichoice(W)$. Both these assignments involve making a choice from a set, and in neither case does our description detail exactly what the choice will be. Otherwise, however, these choices are quite different. The first will generate alternative choices under backtracking, the second is an irrevocable choice. We can compare them by considering what happened if each of the choices is sequentially composed with $x = w \Longrightarrow II$. First the backtracking choice:

$x :\in W;\ x = w \Longrightarrow II \diamond x \quad = \quad$ "sequential composition"

$x :\in W \diamond x = w \Longrightarrow II \diamond x \quad = \quad$ "guard"

$x :\in W \diamond x = w \longrightarrow II \diamond x \quad = \quad$ "skip"

$x :\in W \diamond x = w \longrightarrow x \quad = \quad$ "choice from a set"

$\S\, x' \bullet x' \in W \longrightarrow (x = w \longrightarrow x)[x'/x] \quad = \quad$ "substitution"

$\S\, x' \bullet x' \in W \longrightarrow (x' = w \longrightarrow x') \quad = \quad$ "property of guarded bunch"

$\S\, x' \bullet x' \in W \wedge x' = w \longrightarrow x') \quad = \quad$ "$x' = w$"

w

Here the operational interpretation is that if a choice of $x :\in W$ is made such that $x \neq w$, the false guard will provoke reverse execution and another choice will be made. Eventually the choice $x = w$ has to be made since $w \in W$, so the final result is w. Now consider the irrevocable choice:

$$x := ichoice(W);\ x = w \Longrightarrow II \diamond x \quad = \quad \text{"sequential composition"}$$
$$x := ichoice(W) \diamond x = w \Longrightarrow II \diamond x \quad = \quad \text{"guard"}$$
$$x := ichoice(W) \diamond x = w \longrightarrow II \diamond x \quad = \quad \text{"skip"}$$
$$x := ichoice(W) \diamond x = w \longrightarrow x \quad = \quad \text{"assignment"}$$
$$x = w \longrightarrow x[ichoice(W)/x] \quad = \quad \text{"substitution"}$$
$$ichoice(W) = w \longrightarrow ichoice(W)$$

Here the result is null unless $ichoice(W) = w$, in which case it is w.

The use of irrevocable choice is sometimes desirable during a search. Consider a Sodoku game solver for example. At each step we decide which square to work with, and which number to put in that square. The square is best chosen irrevocably, because *we cannot fail to obtain a solution because of the choice of square.* The choice of number to place in the square however, could result in a position from which no solution exists, so this choice must be provisional.

An important use of irrevocable choice is in giving a semantics to a backtracking search which will be curtailed on discovery of a certain condition P on the set z of results obtained so far. The condition is checked after each result is generated. If it is true, a "cut" is applied, which stops any further backtracking. The results found so far are then returned. For this we use the notation $S \diamond_{z:P} E$. Under the assumption of $trm(S) \wedge \exists\, z.(z \in \mathbb{P}\{S \diamond E\} \wedge P)$ this has the value:

$$\{S \diamond_{z:P} E\} = ichoice\,\{z \mid z \in \mathbb{P}\{S \diamond E\} \wedge P\}$$

Thus, unlike Prolog, we are able to hide the use of cut and provide a description of its effect which does not compromise the rest of our semantics.

8 Conclusions and Future Work

In this paper we bring together the physics and the formal description of reversible computations. We are motivated by the desire to relate computation both to the physical constraints imposed by the second law of thermodynamics and the need to find tractable and expressive programming languages that are amenable to incorporation within a formal development framework. Within this framework there are many interesting issues we have been unable to develop here, and we mention a few now.

The usual approach to refinement of sequential programs relies on the syntax of the implementation level language to protect the user against over-refinement. Due to this protection, the refinement lattice of programs can have *magic* as its bottom (most refined) element, without any fear that any development will propose a miraculous implementation. In our approach we do not always have this luxury, since naked guarded commands may introduce infeasibility. They do not always risk doing so however. When such a command occurs in the program S in an expression $\{S \diamond E\}$, it does not introduce infeasibility, since if S is infeasible $\{S \diamond E\}$ (which is just an expression) is simply the empty set. Operations that encapsulate provisional choice have their own special requirements; their refinement must not entail any loss of choice. We cannot, for example, reduce the choices available for a Knight's move, and still expect to find a solution to the Knight's tour. As a result of such considerations it becomes necessary to show how the program development process can be handled in a way that minimises the need for extra proof obligations.

At a more theoretical level, the prospective value descriptions which we have introduced appear general enough to provide a semantic foundation for computing in their own right. There are obvious relationships between potential values and the predicative and **wp** formalisms. We propose to investigate these and see whether PV descriptions are sometimes more tractable than the other forms. In the spirit of UTP we will also investigate the healthiness conditions of the PV formalism. Just as not all predicates over program states plus auxiliary variables represent computations, and we apply healthiness conditions to limit our interest to those that do, not all transformations of value expressions represent computations either. Once these healthiness conditions have been formulated it will be interesting to see if they are a complete characterisation of PV semantics, i.e. whether we can recover from them the definition of $S \diamond E$.

Acknowledgements. We acknowledge the suggestions made in a number of interesting conversations and electronic discussions with J-R.Abrial, S Dunne, R Floyd and L Mussat, and also the useful comments of the anonymous referees.

References

1. J-R Abrial and W J Mussat. On Using Conditional Definitions in Formal Theories. In Bert D, Bowen J, Henson M, and Robinson K, editors, *ZB2002*, number 2272 in Lecture Notes in Computer Science, 2002.
2. C Bennett. The Logical Reversibility of Computation. *IBM Journal of Research and Development*, 6, 1973.
3. C Bennett. The Thermodynamics of Computation. *International Journal of Theoretical Physics*, 21 pp 905-940, 1982.
4. R P Feynman. *Lectures on Computation.* Westview Press, 1996.
5. R W Floyd. Non-deterministic Algorithms. *Journal of the ACM*, 14(4), 1967.
6. M P Frank. *Reversibility for Efficiant Computing.* PhD thesis, MIT, 1999.
7. E C R Hehner. Bunch theory: A simple set theory for computer science. *Information Processing Letters*, 12.1 pp26-31, 1981.
8. E C R Hehner. *A Practical Theory of Programming.* Springer Verlag, 1993.
9. C A R Hoare and He Jifeng. *Unifying Theories of Programming.* Prentice Hall, 1998.
10. R Landauer. Irreversibility and Heat Generated in the Computing Process. *IBM J R&D*, 5, 1961.
11. Yves Lecerf. Machines de Turing Reversibles. *Comptes rendus de l'Académie Française des Sciences*, 257(1963), 1963.

12. C Morgan. The specification statement. *ACM Transactions on Programming Systems*, 10(3), 1988.
13. Carroll Morgan and Annabel McIver. pGCL: Formal Reasoning for Random Algorithms. *South African Computer J.*, 22:14–27, 1999.
14. J Morris and A Bunkenburg. A theory of bunches. *Acta Informatica*, 37(8), 2001.
15. R F Paige and E C R Hehner. Bunches for Object Oriented, Current and Real Time Specification. In J M Wing, Woodcock J, and Davies J, editors, *FM99 vol 1*, number 1708 in Lecture Notes in Computer Science. Springer Verlag, 1999.
16. W J Stoddart, S E Dunne, and Galloway A J. Undefined Expressions and Logic in Z and B. *Formal Methods in System Design*, 15(3), 1999.
17. L Szilard. On the Decrease of Entropy in a Thermodynamic System by the intervention of Intelligent Beings. *Z Phys*, 53, 1929.
18. J von Neumann. *Theory of Self Reproducing Automata.* University of Illinois Press, Year of book publication 1966. The remark was originally made in a talk given in 1949. Edited and completed by Arthur Burks.
19. F Zeyda, W J Stoddart, and S E Dunne. The Refinement of Reversible Computations. In T Muntean and K Sere, editors, *2nd International Workshop on Refinement of Critical Systems*, 2003. Available from www.esil.univ-mrs.fr/ spc/rcs03/rcs03.
20. Frank Zeyda, Bill Stoddart, and Steve Dunne. A Prospective-value Semantics for the GSL. In M Henson, S King, S Schneider, and H Treharne, editors, *ZB2005*, number 3455 in Lecture Notes in Computer Science, 2005.
21. P Zuliani. Logical reversibility. *IBM J R&D*, 45(6), 2001.

Appendix. Designs and Weakest Preconditions

In this appendix we relate Hoare/He designs to the **wp** calculus. We prove an important lemma used in the paper and some other results which reinforce our confidence in the definition of **wp** that we use.

The weakest precondition that a program S will establish a post-condition r us given in by Hoare and He in [9] for a predicative program S as $S \; \mathbf{wp} \; r = \neg \, (S; \neg \; r)$. The definition is given before designs are introduced, and needs some modification to cope with non-termination, as can be seen from the following successful attempt to prove the termination of $abort \mathrel{\widehat{=}} false \vdash Q$.

We first simplify the definition of *abort*.

$abort = false \vdash Q \quad = \quad$ "defn of $P \vdash Q$"

$false \wedge ok \Rightarrow Q \wedge ok' \quad = \quad$ "logic, $false \wedge a \; = \; false$ and $false \Rightarrow a \; = \; true$"

$true$

Now working from the given definition of **wp** :

$trm \; abort \quad = \quad$ "defn of trm S"

$abort \; \mathbf{wp} \; true \quad = \quad$ "from defn of abort"

$true \; \mathbf{wp} \; true \quad = \quad$ "defn of **wp** "

$\neg \, (true; \neg \; true) \quad = \quad$ "sequential composition"

$\neg \; (\exists \, s'', ok'' \bullet true \wedge false) \quad = \quad$ "logic"

$\neg \; (\exists \, s'', ok'' \bullet false) \quad = \quad$ "$s'', ok'' \setminus false$"

$\neg\, \mathit{false} \;=\;$ "logic"

true

We have proved is that *abort* always terminates, and our intention, of course, is that it should never terminate. The problem is with the definition of S **wp** r. We will therefore work with the following definition which was communicated to us by S Dunne and which arose in his informal discussions with A Galloway.

Definition. $(P \vdash Q)\ \mathbf{wp}\ r \mathrel{\widehat=} \neg\,((P \vdash Q);\ \neg\,(r \wedge ok))[\mathit{true}/ok]$

The following lemma is a re-expression of this definition:

Lemma 1. *Let* $\alpha(P \vdash Q) = s$*, then:*
$(P \vdash Q)\ \mathbf{wp}\ r = \neg\,(P \Rightarrow \exists\, s'' \bullet (Q[s''/s'] \wedge \neg\, r[s''/s]))$

Proof. $(P \vdash Q)\ \mathbf{wp}\ r \;=\;$ "definition of **wp**"

$\neg\,(P \vdash Q;\ \neg\,(r \wedge ok))[\mathit{true}/ok] \;=\;$ "definition of $P \vdash Q$"

$\neg\,(P \wedge ok \Rightarrow Q \wedge ok';\ \neg\,(r \wedge ok))[\mathit{true}/ok] \;=\;$ "sequential composition"

$\neg\,\exists\, s'', ok'' \bullet ((P \wedge ok \Rightarrow Q[s''/s'] \wedge ok'') \wedge \neg\,(r[s''/s] \wedge ok''))[\mathit{true}/ok]$

$=$ "substituting true/ok"

$\neg\,\exists\, s'', ok'' \bullet ((P \Rightarrow Q[s''/s'] \wedge ok'') \wedge \neg\,(r[s''/s] \wedge ok''))$

$=$ " disjoining cases $\neg\, ok''$ and ok'' "

$\neg\,\exists\, s'' \bullet (\neg\, P \vee ((P \Rightarrow Q[s''/s']) \wedge \neg\, r[s''/s]))$

$=$ "logic, $\neg\, a \vee b \;=\; a \Rightarrow b$"

$\neg\,\exists\, s'' \bullet (P \Rightarrow ((P \Rightarrow Q[s''/s']) \wedge \neg\, r[s''/s]))$

$=$ "logic, $a \Rightarrow (a \Rightarrow b) \wedge c \;=\; a \Rightarrow b \wedge c$"

$\neg\,\exists\, s'' \bullet (P \Rightarrow Q[s''/s'] \wedge \neg\, r[s''/s])$

$=$ "since $s'' \setminus P$"

$\neg\,(P \Rightarrow \exists\, s'' \bullet (Q[s''/s'] \wedge \neg\, r[s''/s]))$ □

Proposition 1. *For any design* $P \vdash Q$ *define* $\mathit{wpterm}(P \vdash Q) \mathrel{\widehat=} (P \vdash Q)\ \mathbf{wp}\ \mathit{true}$*. Then:* $\mathit{wpterm}(P \vdash Q) = P$

This confirms that the view of termination provided by our definition of **wp** *accords with the idea of termination given by the assumption of a design.*

Proof. $\mathit{wpterm}(P \vdash Q) \;=\;$ "Definition of *wpterm*"

$(P \vdash Q)\ \mathbf{wp}\ \mathit{true} \;=\;$ "lemma 1"

$\neg\,(P \Rightarrow \exists\, s'' \bullet (Q[s''/s'] \wedge \neg\, \mathit{true}[s''/s]))$

$=$ "properties of substitution and logic"

$\neg\,(P \Rightarrow \exists\, s'' \bullet (Q[s''/s'] \wedge \mathit{false})$

$=$ "logic, $a \wedge \mathit{false} \;=\; \mathit{false}$"

$\neg\,(P \Rightarrow \exists\, s'' \bullet \mathit{false})$

$=$ "since no existential quantification can satisfy false"

$\neg\,(P \Rightarrow \mathit{false}) \quad = \quad$ " logic $a \Rightarrow \mathit{false} \;=\; \neg\, a$"

$\neg\,\neg\, P \quad = \quad$ "logic $\neg\,\neg\, a \;=\; a$"

P □

Proposition 2. $\neg\,(P \vdash Q)$ **wp** $\neg\,(s' = s) = (P \Rightarrow Q)$

This confirms that the **wp** *derivation of the commitment of a program (under its assumption) agrees with the commitment given in the design. The qualification "under its assumption" leads, in the total correctness framework of* **wp** *analysis, to the commitment being extracted as $P \Rightarrow Q$ rather than Q, reflecting the fact that, outside of the assumption P, any result might be obtained.*

Proof. $\neg\,(P \vdash Q)$ **wp** $\neg\,(s' = s) \quad = \quad$ "Lemma 1"

$\neg\,\neg\,(P \Rightarrow \exists\, s'' \bullet (Q[s''/s'] \wedge \neg\,\neg\,(s' = s)[s''/s]))$

$=$ "substitution and logic"

$(P \Rightarrow \exists\, s'' \bullet (Q[s''/s'] \wedge s' = s''$

$=$ "one point rule"

$P \Rightarrow Q[s''/s'][s'/s'']) \quad = \quad$ "substitution" $\; P \Rightarrow Q$ □

Proposition 3. *Assuming $s' \setminus r$, then:*

$((P \vdash Q)$ **wp** $r) = (P \wedge \forall\, s' \bullet (Q \Rightarrow r[s'/s]))$

This is a development of lemma 1 for the case when $s' \setminus r$. The result is an intuitively appealing representation of **wp** *which, along with the previous propositions, confirms our confidence in our definition of* **wp** .

Proof. $(P \vdash Q)$ **wp** $r \quad = \quad$ "lemma 1"

$\neg\,(P \Rightarrow \exists\, s'' \bullet (Q[s''/s'] \wedge \neg\; r[s''/s]))$

$=$ "change of bound variable name, $s' \setminus (Q[s''/s'] \wedge \neg\; r[s''/s])$"

$\neg\,(P \Rightarrow \exists\, s' \bullet (Q[s''/s'][s'/s''] \wedge \neg\; r[s''/s][s'/s'']))$

$=$ "substitution"

$\neg\,(P \Rightarrow \exists\, s' \bullet (Q \wedge \neg\; r[s'/s]))$

$=$ " logic, $a \Rightarrow b \;=\; \neg\, a \vee b$ "

$\neg\,(\neg\, P \vee \exists\, s' \bullet (Q \wedge \neg\; r[s'/s]))$

$=$ "logic, de Morgan"

$P \wedge \neg\; \exists\, s' \bullet (Q \wedge \neg\; r[s'/s]))$

$=$ " logic, $\neg\; \exists\, x \bullet P \;=\; \forall\, x \bullet \neg\; P$"

$P \wedge \forall\, s' \bullet \neg\,(Q \wedge \neg\, r[s'/s]))$

$=$ "logic, de Morgan"

$P \wedge \forall\, s' \bullet \neg\; Q \vee r[s'/s]))$

$=$ "logic, de Morgan"

$P \wedge \forall\, s' \bullet Q \Rightarrow r[s'/s]))$ □

An Operational Semantics in UTP for a Language of Reactive Designs (Abstract)

Jim Woodcock

Computer Science Dept., University of York,
York, UK

Abstract. Following the approach in UTP, we describe a language of state-rich processes with communication, concurrency, and imperative commands on program variables. We give this language an operational semantics, with states and transitions represented symbolically. The semantics is described in Z, allowing us to execute the semantics using an animator, and to start work on a mechanical proof of correctness using the deep embedding in ProofPowerZ of the existing denotational semantics for the language. An extension of the operational semantics has been used in an algorithm to construct automata as part of the Circus model checker. This is joint work with Ana Cavalcanti and Leonardo Freitas.

S. Dunne and W. Stoddart (Eds.): UTP 2006, LNCS 4010, p. 84, 2006.

Constructing Property-Oriented Models for Verification

Jifeng He[1,⋆], Shengchao Qin[2,⋆⋆], and Adnan Sherif[3]

[1] Software Engineering Institute, East China Normal University
jifeng@sei.ecnu.edu.cn
[2] Department of Computer Science, Durham University
shengchao.qin@durham.ac.uk
[3] Centro de Informatica, Federal University of Pernambuco

Abstract. This paper advocates a general approach to formal verification by constructing property-oriented models. We instantiate the approach using timing properties, and construct a heterogeneous untimed model in which time is abstracted away, so that we can verify timing properties in an untimed framework. The correctness of property-oriented model construction is ensured by the conformance of semantic and syntactic mappings.

1 Introduction

It has been noticed that a single software development method is not sufficient to solve all types of problems found in complex software systems. The integration of software development methods has been proposed and investigated in the recent years, for example, the integration of state-modeling and process languages has become an active area of research ([19, 6, 1, 11]). Such blending of different notations can provide us more powerful languages for specifying very complex software systems. Unified observation-oriented models behind the integrated languages (like [14], [23]) can ensure the soundness of the integration of different notations, and can be used as a reference document for developing tool supports. However, such complete models are usually very complicated and thus hard to use for the verification purpose.

Properties to be verified or analysed can be divided into different categories, each kind of properties only refer to part of the whole observation model, such as safety properties that are not time dependent, timing properties, deadlock-free properties. Recent work [4] suggests a projection approach to the verification of timing properties. The projection can be conducted in a syntax-directed manner, where the soundness proof replies on a deep projection from the whole model to the sub-model, thus the whole model should be built first, which is usually very time-consuming. Therefore, we propose to construct (small) property-oriented models for the verification of any particular kind of properties. We shall guarantee that different property-oriented sub-models can be integrated into the whole model in a later stage, where necessary. In this paper, we elaborate this general idea using timing properties. We construct an untimed heterogeneous model, where time information is abstracted away, and handled by a special

⋆ Supported in part by China 973 Project 2002CB312001.
⋆⋆ Author for Correspondence. Supported in part by China NNSFC Project 60573081.

S. Dunne and W. Stoddart (Eds.): UTP 2006, LNCS 4010, pp. 85–100, 2006.

Timer process. With such a property-oriented model we can verify certain kind of timing properties using the simpler untimed model, either by model checking or theorem proving. This greatly simplifies the verification process.

We demonstrate our approach using a small language CZ, which is a subset of the combination of CSP [7] and Z [20]. It can be regarded as a subset of the *Circus* [21] language, or a subset of another powerful specification language TCOZ [11]. We shall focus on timing properties that can be described in programming languages, rather than specification languages, like:

- the delay between two consecutive events should at least be t units of time;
- a program awaits an event at most t units of time before it does something else.

More general timing properties that can be described in specification languages but difficult in programming languages, like deadline and waituntil in TCOZ, will not be covered here.

This paper makes the following contributions:

- We propose a general approach to verification by constructing *property-oriented* models for integrated formal languages.
- We demonstrate our approach in terms of timing properties. We build an untimed model for the verification of real-time properties.
- We build a deep link between timed traces and untimed heterogeneous traces (with timer events). From that, we can generate the provably-correct untimed model.
- We illustrate our approach through an alarm controller example.
- As a byproduct, we explore some healthiness conditions and interesting algebraic laws for heterogeneous communicating processes.

The rest of the paper is organized as follows. Section 2 introduces the illustrative example. Section 3 describes the language model. The approach is presented in detail in Section 4, followed by related work and conclusion.

2 An Illustrative Example

In this section, we use a small example to illustrate a novel approach to the verification of timing properties for reactive systems.

2.1 The Alarm Controller

The alarm system was first used in [9]. The system is a common alarm controller that can be found in buildings and cars. The controller is connected to a sensor which detects movements or changes in the environment monitored by the alarm. The controller operates in two modes: when disabled, it will ignore any disturbance detected by the sensor; when enabled, the controller will sound an alarm when the sensor signals a disturbance.

There are two timing requirements on the alarm controller: the first states that after the controller is enabled, there is a period of t_1 units of time before a disturbance can cause the alarm to ring. The period t_1 permits a person to enable the alarm and then leave without causing it to sound. The second requirement states that when a detected disturbance is received, the controller will wait for another period of t_2 units of time before activating the alarm. The period t_2 leaves some time to the legal user to disable it before it sounds.

Let us analyse the first timing requirement, that is, when the controller is enabled, there is a delay of t_1 units of time before it can receive any disturbance from its sensor. As a first attempt, we can specify this requirement in terms of the following action:

$$R_1 \mathrel{\widehat=} enable \rightarrow Wait\ t_1; disturb \rightarrow R$$

Notice the event *enable* indicates the alarm system is enabled, while the event *disturb* denotes a disturbance detected by the sensor. At this moment, we ignore the subsequent behaviour after a disturbance is received and simply use R to denote it.

The key idea of our approach is to separate timing properties from logical properties by introducing a specific component, called *Timer*, to take care of the timing features. Thus we can use existing untimed verification tools like model checkers to verify that certain time properties are met, rather than construct a new tool for verification from scratch.

For R_1, we can transform it to the following untimed action:

$$R_1' \mathrel{\widehat=} enable \rightarrow set! \rightarrow reset? \rightarrow disturb \rightarrow R$$

The two new events *set* and *reset* are used to interact with the following *Timer* action:

$$Timer \mathrel{\widehat=} set? \rightarrow Wait\ t_1; reset! \rightarrow Skip$$

Note that the *Timer* component is in charge of time control. It is activated by *set* signal, and after t_1 time elapses, it notifies the process R_1' via signal *reset*.

To verify R_1 meets the property that a disturbance can only be received after the controller is enabled for t_1 units of time (we refer to it as t_1-*delay property* in what follows), we only need to check the following untimed property for R_1':

$$\begin{array}{l}\forall utr_0, utr_1, utr_2 \cdot ((utr = utr_0 ^\frown \langle enable \rangle ^\frown utr_1 ^\frown \langle disturb \rangle ^\frown utr_2 \ \wedge \\ \quad utr_1 \upharpoonright \{enable, disturb\} = \langle\rangle) \Rightarrow utr_1 = \langle set, reset \rangle)\end{array}$$

It states that there are only two timer events *set* and *reset* between an *enable* event and its consecutive *disturb* event. The event *set* activates the timer, while *reset* deactivates the timer, which indicates t_1 time is passed. Together with the timer action, it ensures the t_1-delay property. Note that *utr* denotes the (untimed) trace, i.e. a sequence of events, while utr_i's are segments of the trace. Formal definitions will be given in a later section.

The soundness for the separation of timing features from logical features can be specified in terms of the following equation:

$$R_1 = (R_1' |[\{set, reset\}]| Timer) \setminus \{set, reset\}$$

This can be easily proved using the expansion laws for parallel composition. The right hand side is a parallel composition of an untimed action (R_1') and a timer action (*Timer*) which communicate with each other via two internal events *set* and *reset* (hidden from outside). Such a parallel composition is the normal form we shall adopt for verification.

2.2 The Normal Form

In this subsection, we shall deal with the complete specification for the alarm controller.

The complete timed specification for the alarm controller is given as follows.

$$\begin{aligned} Disable &\mathrel{\widehat{=}} disable \rightarrow Skip \\ Running &\mathrel{\widehat{=}} Disable \mathbin{\Box} (disturb \rightarrow Active) \\ Active &\mathrel{\widehat{=}} Disable \overset{t_2}{\rhd} (alarm \rightarrow Disable) \\ Alarm &\mathrel{\widehat{=}} \mu X \bullet enable \rightarrow (Disable \overset{t_1}{\rhd} Running); X \end{aligned}$$

Note that event *disable* is used to disable the controller, event *alarm* signals the firing of the alarm. For more flexibility, we allow the controller to be disabled at any point during running. We use timeout constructs (defined later in Section 3.2) to capture this requirement. Take *Alarm* as an example, once the controller is enabled, it is either disabled (and then waits for *enable* again), or is ready to receive any disturbance after t_1 (*Running*).

As explained in last subsection, we shall transform the timed specification *Alarm* to a normal form composed of an untimed specification in parallel with a *Timer* action.

We shall use function Φ to abstract away timing features from a timed action. The complete definition for Φ will be given when we present the syntax of the language. The following is the result after applying it to the above specification.

$$\begin{aligned} \Phi(Disable) &\mathrel{\widehat{=}} disable \rightarrow Skip \\ \Phi(Running) &\mathrel{\widehat{=}} \Phi(Disable) \mathbin{\Box} (disturb \rightarrow \Phi(Active)) \\ \Phi(Active) &\mathrel{\widehat{=}} set!t_2 \rightarrow \\ &\quad ((disable \rightarrow halt! \rightarrow Skip) \mathbin{\Box} (reset? \rightarrow alarm \rightarrow \Phi(Disable))) \\ \Phi(Alarm) &\mathrel{\widehat{=}} \mu X \bullet enable \rightarrow set!t_1 \rightarrow \\ &\quad ((disable \rightarrow halt! \rightarrow Skip) \mathbin{\Box} (reset? \rightarrow \Phi(Running))); X \end{aligned}$$

Note that a new timer event *halt* is used to stop the timer when event *disable* arrives during the ticking of the clock. There are two timing requirements in the specification, thus we design the general timer action as follows:

$$Timer \mathrel{\widehat{=}} \mu X \bullet set?x \rightarrow ((halt? \rightarrow Skip) \mathbin{\Box} (Wait\ x; reset! \rightarrow Skip)); X$$

Note that when the timer is *set* to work, a value is passed to it (stored in x) to indicate the time duration that it should count before it generates a *reset* signal.

Now the timed specification *Alarm* is transformed to the following normal form:

$$(\Phi(Alarm)|[\{set, reset, halt\}]|Timer)\backslash(\{set, reset, halt\}$$

The following theorem ensures the soundness of the abstraction.

Theorem 1. *We have*

$$Alarm \; = \; (\Phi(Alarm)|[\{set, reset, halt\}]|Timer)\backslash\{set, reset, halt\}$$

It is proved using algebraic laws for parallel expansion and hiding.

2.3 Verification of Timing Properties in the Untimed Model

In this subsection we shall demonstrate that timing requirements can be verified in the untimed framework.

There are two timing requirements for the alarm controller, namely,

- once enabled, the controller should wait at least t_1 units of time before it can receive any disturbance from the sensor.
- once a disturbance is received, the controller should wait at least t_2 units of time before it fires the alarm.

As timing is controlled by the timer actions in our normal form, we can abstract away timing from the above requirements by adding in timer events that are in charge of activating/deactivating the timers. The timing requirements are thus specified in terms of timer events as follows:

$$\begin{aligned} R_1(utr) \mathrel{\widehat{=}} \forall utr_0, utr_1, utr_2 \cdot (&utr = utr_0 \frown \langle enable \rangle \frown utr_1 \frown \langle disturb \rangle \frown utr_2 \ \wedge \\ &utr_1 \upharpoonright \{enable, disturb\} = \langle\rangle) \Rightarrow (utr_1 = \langle set.t_1, reset \rangle) \\ R_2(utr) \mathrel{\widehat{=}} \forall utr_0, utr_1, utr_2 \cdot (&utr = utr_0 \frown \langle disturb \rangle \frown utr_1 \frown \langle alarm \rangle \frown utr_2 \ \wedge \\ &utr_1 \upharpoonright \{disturb, alarm\} = \langle\rangle) \Rightarrow (utr_1 = \langle set.t_2, reset \rangle) \end{aligned}$$

The overall timing requirement for the alarm controller is thus as below:

$$Req(utr) \mathrel{\widehat{=}} R_1(utr) \wedge R_2(utr)$$

To verify the timed specification ($Alarm$) meets the timing requirements, we only need to demonstrate that the untimed specification ($\Phi(Alarm)$) meets the above requirement, that is, $\Phi(Alarm) \Rightarrow Req(utr)$.

Theorem 2. *Suppose $\Phi(Alarm)$ and $Req(utr)$ are given as above, we have*

$$[\![\Phi(Alarm)]\!] \Rightarrow Req(utr)$$

where $[\![P]\!]$ denotes the observation-oriented semantics for program P.

Proof. From the definition of $\Phi(Alarm)$,

$$\Phi(Alarm) = P; \Phi(Alarm)$$

where $P \mathrel{\widehat{=}} enable \rightarrow set!t_1 \rightarrow ((disable \rightarrow halt! \rightarrow Skip) \,\Box\, (reset? \rightarrow \Phi(Running)))$.

Thus the semantic predicate $[\![\Phi(Alarm)]\!]$ is subject to

$$[\![\Phi(Alarm)]\!] = [\![P]\!]; [\![\Phi(Alarm)]\!]$$

That is, it is the fixed point of the equation $X = \mu X \cdot ([\![P]\!]; X)$.

Note that we also use the operator (;) to represent the concatenation of two observational predicates. The formal definition is given in [8].

Due to the following fixed point theorem ([8]):

$$F(S) \sqsupseteq S \text{ implies } \nu X \cdot F(S) \sqsupseteq S$$

and the fact that there is only one fixed point in this case, we only need to prove

$$[\![P]\!]; Req(utr) \Rightarrow Req(utr)$$

It is thus straightforward as all possible traces of P lie in the following set:

$$\begin{aligned}trace(P) = \{&\langle enable, set.t_1, disable\rangle,\ \langle enable, set.t_1, disable, halt\rangle,\\ &\langle enable, set.t_1, reset, disable\rangle,\ \langle enable, set.t_1, reset, disturb, set.t_2, disable\rangle,\\ &\langle enable, set.t_1, reset, disturb, set.t_2, disable, halt\rangle\}\\ &\cup \{utr \mid utr \preceq \langle enable, set.t_1, reset, disturb, set.t_2, reset, alarm, disable\rangle\}\end{aligned}$$

□

Note that the proof is much simpler and more straightforward in comparison with the existing proof given in [9] due to the property-oriented model we use.

3 The Language

This section introduces our language CZ that we use to instantiate our method. We shall give both the untimed and timed models.

3.1 The Untimed Model

The syntax for CZ is given in Fig. 1.

$$\begin{array}{lll} Action & ::= & Skip \mid Stop \mid Chaos \\ & & \mid Communication \rightarrow Action \mid b\&Action \\ & & \mid Action; Action \mid Action \Box Action \mid Action \sqcap Action \\ & & \mid Action |[E]| Action \mid Action \backslash E \mid \mu X \bullet Action \\ & & \mid Command \\ Command & ::= & x := e \mid Action \lhd b \rhd Action \\ Communication & ::= & c?[x] \mid c![e] \mid c[.e] \end{array}$$

Fig. 1. CZ : the untimed model

Note that e represents an expression, while b a boolean expression. The set E denotes channel names. The notation $[u]$ indicates that term u is optional.

Skip is a basic action that terminates immediately. *Stop* represents an abnormal termination which simply puts a program in an ever waiting state. *Chaos* is the worst action, nothing can be said about its behaviour. In a *guarded action* (*b&Action*), the action is preceded by a predicate which has to be true for the action to take place, otherwise the guarded action behaves as *Stop*. An *internal choice* between two actions ($Action \sqcap Action$) selects one of the two actions in a non-deterministic manner, whereas the *external choice* ($Action \Box Action$) waits for any of the two actions to interact with the environment. The first action that interacts with the environment (either by synchronising on an event or terminating) is the resulting action.

The *sequential composition* of two actions (*Action*; *Action*) behaves as the first action, followed immediately by the second action upon termination of the first. An action can be prefixed with a communication event (input or output) which will take place before the action starts. The action waits for the other actions that need to synchronise on the channel before the communication can take place. The *parallel composition* of two actions

$(Action|[cs]|Action)$ involves a set (cs) containing the events they need to synchronise on. A *hiding* operation also takes a set of events (cs). The set is to be excluded from the resulting observation of the action, hidden events can no longer be seen by other actions.

An observation-oriented model for the *Circus* language based on Hoare and He's Unifying Theories of Programming [8] is explored in detail in [23, 21], while the unified model for TCOZ is reported in [14]. As our language CZ is a subset of the above two languages, we can borrow the following observation variables from them.

- ok, ok' : Boolean. When ok is $true$, it states that the program has started and $ok' = true$ indicates that the program has terminated or is in an intermediate stable state.
- $wait, wait'$: Boolean. When $wait$ is $true$, the program starts in an intermediate state. When $wait'$ is $true$ the program has not terminated; when it is $false$, it indicates a final observation.
- $state, state'$ are mappings from program variable names to values. The undashed variable represents the initial valuation of the program variables, while the dashed one denotes the valuation at the final observation.
- utr, utr' : $\mathsf{seq}\, Event$ are the sequence of observations on the program's interactions with its environment. utr denotes the observations that occur before the program starts, and utr' the final observation. Each element of the sequence is an event.
- ref, ref' : $\mathbb{P}\, Event$ stands for the set of events the program can refuse.

A single observation is given by the combination of the above variables. A program is given as predicates over the observation variables. We give the semantics for basic actions and communication events in what follows to show the use of the above semantic variables. Readers can refer to [23, 14] for the complete set of semantic definitions.

Basic Action. The semantics of the action *Skip* is given as a program that can only terminate normally and has no interaction with the environment.

$$[\![Skip]\!] \mathrel{\widehat=} ok' \wedge \neg wait' \wedge utr' = utr \wedge state' = state$$

The action *Stop* is given as a predicate that waits for ever; it does not change the state.

$$[\![Stop]\!] \mathrel{\widehat=} ok' \wedge wait' \wedge utr' = utr$$

The assignment attributes a value to a variable in the current state. If the variable does not exist it will be added, otherwise its value will be over written. The assignment operation is instantaneous and does not consume time.

$$[\![x := e]\!] \mathrel{\widehat=} ok' \wedge \neg wait' \wedge utr' = utr \wedge state' = state \oplus \{x \mapsto e\}$$

Note that we abuse the same e in the right hand side to denote the value of e in *state*.

Communication. An action can engage in a communication if all the other actions involved in the same communication are ready to do so. We model this with the help of two predicates. $wait\_com(c)$ models the waiting state of an action to communicate on channel c. The only possible observation is that the communication channel cannot appear in the refusal set during the observation period. *term_com*$(c.e)$ represents the act of communicating a value e over a channel c.

$$\begin{aligned} wait\_com(c) &\mathrel{\widehat{=}} ok' \wedge wait' \wedge c \notin ref' \wedge utr' = utr \\ term\_com(c.e) &\mathrel{\widehat{=}} ok' \wedge \neg wait' \wedge utr' = utr ^\frown \langle c \rangle \end{aligned}$$

The semantics of the output command is given below.

$$[\![c!e]\!] \mathrel{\widehat{=}} wait\_com(c) \;\vee\; term\_com(c.e) \wedge state' = state$$

The input command can be defined in a similar manner.

$$[\![c?x]\!] \mathrel{\widehat{=}} wait\_com(c) \;\vee\; term\_com(c.e) \wedge state' = state \oplus \{x \mapsto e\}$$

The semantics of the communication prefix can be given in terms of communication and of the sequential composition. The action *comm* is either an input or an output event, or an abstract event name.

$$[\![comm \rightarrow Action]\!] \mathrel{\widehat{=}} [\![comm; Action]\!]$$

3.2 The Timed Model

The timed language TCZ extends the untimed language CZ with two new time operators given in Fig. 2.

$$\begin{aligned} Action ::= &\cdots \\ &\mid Wait\ t \text{ (time delay)} \\ &\mid Action \overset{t}{\rhd} Action \text{ (timeout)} \end{aligned}$$

Fig. 2. TCZ: the timed model

The action ($Wait\ t$) will delay the system for an amount of time determined by the positive integer expression t before terminating normally. The timeout construct ($Action \overset{t}{\rhd} Action$) takes a positive integer value as the length of the timeout. The timeout operator acts as a time guarded choice. It behaves as either the first or the second action. If the first action performs an observable event or terminates before the specified time elapses, it is chosen. Otherwise, the first action will be suspended and the only possible observations are those produced by the second action.

The semantics for the timed language is given with the same observation variables $ok, ok', wait, wait', state$ and $state'$, while the variables utr, utr' and ref' are replaced by a new pair of variables ttr, ttr' denoting communication traces in the timed model.

The variable *ttr* records the observations of communication events that occur before the program starts, and ttr' records the final observation. Each element of the sequence represents an observation in one time unit. Each observation element is composed of a tuple, where the first element of the tuple is the sequence of events that occur in the time unit, and the second is the associated set of refusals at the end of the same time unit.

$$ttr, ttr' : \mathsf{seq}(\mathsf{seq}\, Event \times \mathbb{P}\, Event)$$

We maintain an auxiliary variable *utr* that represents a sequence of events that have occurred since the last observation. In this observation we are interested in recording only the events without time.

$$utr : \mathsf{seq}\, Event$$
$$utr = flat(ttr') - flat(ttr)$$

$$\text{where } flat : \mathsf{seq}(\mathsf{seq}\, Event \times \mathbb{P}\, Event) \rightarrow \mathsf{seq}\, Event$$
$$flat(\langle\rangle) = \langle\rangle$$
$$flat(\langle el, ref\rangle ^\frown S) = el ^\frown flat(S)$$

We show the use of these new variables in the definition of the $(Wait\ d)$ action. The only possible behaviour for this action is to wait for the specified number of units of time to pass before terminating immediately.

$$[\![Wait\ d]\!]_{time} \mathrel{\widehat{=}} ((ok' \land wait' \land (\#ttr' - \#ttr) < d) \\ \lor(ok' \land \neg wait' \land (\#ttr' - \#ttr) = d)) \land utr = \langle\rangle$$

The timeout action can be defined in terms of external choice as in [17]. The following is a direct definition.

$$[\![P \overset{t}{\rhd} Q]\!]_{time} \mathrel{\widehat{=}} (P \land utr = \langle\rangle \land \#ttr' - \#ttr \le t)\lor \\ (\exists k : \#ttr < k \le \#ttr{+}t, \exists \tilde{ttr} \bullet \pi_1(ttr'(k)) \neq \langle\rangle \land ttr \preceq \tilde{ttr} \land \#\tilde{ttr} - \#ttr = k\land \\ (\forall i : \#ttr < i < \#ttr{+}k \bullet \pi_1(ttr'(i)) = \langle\rangle \land \tilde{ttr}(i) = ttr'(i)) \land P[\tilde{ttr}/ttr]) \lor \\ (\exists \tilde{ttr} \bullet ttr \preceq \tilde{ttr} \land \#\tilde{ttr} - \#ttr = t\land \\ (\forall i : \#ttr < i < \#ttr{+}t \bullet \pi_1(ttr'(i)) = \langle\rangle \land \tilde{ttr}(i) = ttr'(i)) \land Q[\tilde{ttr}/ttr])$$

Note that if P is ready to react to the environment exactly when it has waited for time t, the timeout process chooses P or Q non-deterministically.

Given the semantic model for a TCZ program, we can use the linking function given in [17] to abstract away time information, and thus obtain the corresponding untimed model. This abstraction is useful when we are interested in the verification of time-independent safety properties. In this paper, we shall not elaborate on this aspect but focus more on timing properties.

4 The Approach

This section is devoted to the general approach that we propose to the verification of real-time systems. The verification framework is given in Fig. 3.

Fig. 3 shows us two different approaches. The first one is a top down approach where we start with a timed program and we are interested in checking if the timed program satisfies the time requirements. The second approach is a bottom up method where we start with an untimed program and add time information where requested. The need for the second one is due to the fact that system development is usually done in stages, in the early stages of development the system designer concentrates on the behaviourial/logical properties of the system, while leaving timing requirement to a

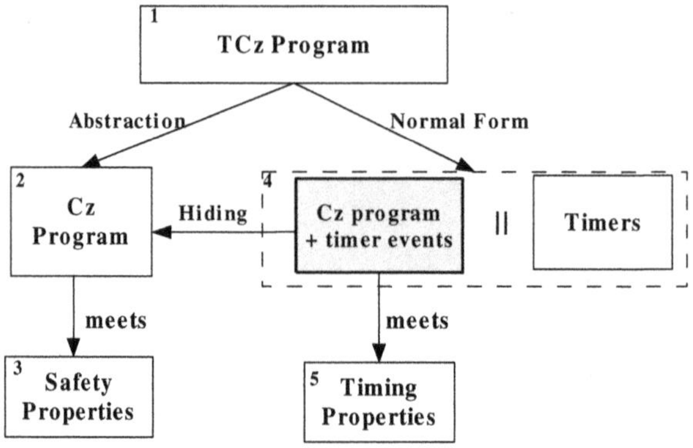

Fig. 3. The Property-Oriented Models for Verification

later stage. Another aspect is that in some cases it is necessary to identify the hardware used in the implementation to have a clear understanding of the time delays and time-outs that can occur in the system and the points in which they may occur. In the rest of this section we present our approach in detail.

4.1 The Validation Approach

This approach is concerned with the validation of the time requirements of the system using the untimed model. Fig. 3 illustrates the steps for using the framework. The steps to carry out the validation of the time requirements are summarised as follows.

- We start with a specification of our system in the timed model using the timed version of the language. The system designer gives a complete description of the system. All the operators of the language can be used at this stage including parallel composition The timed semantic model of the language is used in this step.
- If we need to verify untimed safety properties, we can use an abstraction function (e.g. the one given in [17]) to obtain an untimed version of the original specification. Such an untimed program can be used to validate the behaviour requirements and safety requirements that are not time dependent. We do not elaborate this aspect in this paper.
- With the help of the normal form function Φ, we obtain a version of the program that has the same semantics as the original program but contains internal timer events. In this step the expansion laws should be used as well to remove all the parallel compositions.
- Time requirements can be expressed in the untimed model with timer events. We can use this untimed model to prove the design meets the time requirements. This can be done using theorem provers or existing (untimed) model checkers.

4.2 The Normal Form

Usually timed programs are implemented with timers, this can be either the system clock or a dedicated timer. Following the same criteria we give a normal form for the time operators. The implementation of the time operators is given as a timer and an untimed program that is synchronised with the timer on dedicated events.

As mentioned above, the events *set*, *halt*, and *reset* are timer events, used by the program to synchronise with and control a timer. The following is the timer program:

$$\mathit{Timer} \mathrel{\widehat{=}} \mu X \bullet \mathit{set}?x \rightarrow ((\mathit{halt}? \rightarrow \mathit{Skip})\Box(\mathit{Wait}\ x; (\mathit{reset}! \rightarrow \mathit{Skip}))); X$$

The timer is initiated with the event *set* which serves as a trigger. The behaviour of the timer is as follows: after set by its environment, it waits for the *set* signal to set the timer again if an interrupt event *halt* arrives before the timeout, or it emits a signal *reset* and starts to wait for another *set* after it has counted for the designated period of time (stored in x) set by the environment. The event *reset* is similar to other events used in the language, whereas the events *set* and *halt* have special properties. We shall explore these differences further in the next subsection.

Given the definition for a timer action, we aim to generate a function Φ that takes as input a timed program and returns the corresponding untimed program with timer events. That is, for any sequential program *P*, the function Φ should satisfy the following equation:

$$(\dagger) \qquad P = \Phi(P) \ \textbf{par}\ \mathit{Timer}$$

Given actions *X* and *Y*, such that $\alpha X \cap \alpha Y = \{\mathit{set}, \mathit{reset}, \mathit{halt}\}$,

$$X \ \textbf{par}\ Y \mathrel{\widehat{=}} (X \,|[\{\mathit{set}, \mathit{reset}, \mathit{halt}\}]|\, Y) \backslash \{\mathit{set}, \mathit{reset}, \mathit{halt}\}$$

Note that in the action (*X* **par** *Y*), *X* behaves as a master action, while *Y* acts as a slave action. The overall action terminates if and only if the master action *X* terminates.

As timers are not allowed to be shared by parallel actions, several timer actions are needed in the equation ($\dagger$) in case that *P* is a parallel action.

We shall first give a mapping ψ to abstract away time information from timed traces, while adding timer events properly. This can be regarded as a deep semantic link between a timed process and a heterogeneous communicating process. We only need to define the mapping ψ on *maximal traces*.

Definition 1. *A timed trace ttr_0 from a prefix-closed trace set is* maximal, *if for any trace ttr_1 that satisfies $\#ttr_0 = \#ttr_1$, and $\forall i : 1..\#ttr_0 \cdot \pi_1(ttr_0(i)) = \pi_1(ttr_1(i))$, we have $\forall i : 1..\#ttr_0 \cdot \pi_2(ttr_0(i)) \supseteq \pi_2(ttr_1(i))$.*

Definition 2. *Given a set of timed traces TTR, and a single prefix s, we define a set of timed traces "after" s as follows:*

$$\mathit{TTR}/s \mathrel{\widehat{=}} \{\mathit{ttr} \mid (s ^\frown \mathit{ttr}) \in \mathit{TTR}\}$$

Given a trace ttr, we use pref(ttr) to denote the prefix-closed set of traces made out of all prefixes of ttr. We extend it to a set of traces TTR as

$$\mathit{pref}(\mathit{TTR}) \mathrel{\widehat{=}} \bigcup\{\mathit{pref}(\mathit{ttr}) \mid \mathit{ttr} \in \mathit{TTR}\}$$

Given two set of traces TTR_1, and TTR_2, the concatenation of them is given as

$$\mathit{TTR}_1 ^\frown \mathit{TTR}_2 \mathrel{\widehat{=}} \{\mathit{ttr}_1 ^\frown \mathit{ttr}_2 \mid \mathit{ttr}_i \in \mathit{TTR}_i,\ \mathit{for}\ i = 1, 2\}$$

Definition 3 (Semantic Mapping). *Let $\mathcal{A}$ denote the maximal set of events of interest, and $\mathcal{A}^*$ denote the sequence closure over $\mathcal{A}$. Given a set of maximal traces TTR, the corresponding set of heterogeneous traces $\psi(TTR)$ is defined as follows:*

- $TTR = \{\langle(\langle\surd\rangle, X)\rangle\}$.
  $\psi(TTR) \mathrel{\widehat{=}} \{\langle\surd\rangle\}$.
- $\exists ttr \in TTR \cdot \forall i : 1{\le}i{\le}\#ttr \cdot \pi_1(ttr(i)) = \mathcal{A}^* \wedge \pi_2(ttr(i)) = \mathcal{A}$.
  $\psi(TTR) \mathrel{\widehat{=}} \mathcal{A}^*$.
- $\forall ttr \in TTR \cdot \forall i : 1{\le}i{\le}\#ttr \cdot \pi_1(ttr(i)) = \langle\rangle \wedge \pi_2(ttr(i)) = \mathcal{A}$.
  $\psi(TTR) \mathrel{\widehat{=}} \{\langle\rangle\}$.
- $TTR = pref(ttr)$, *where* $ttr = \langle(\langle\rangle, \mathcal{A}), .., (\langle\rangle, \mathcal{A})\rangle$, *and* $\#ttr = n$.
  $\psi(TTR) \mathrel{\widehat{=}} pref(\langle set.n, reset\rangle)$.
- $pref(ttr) \subseteq TTR$, *where* $ttr{=}\langle(\langle\rangle, \mathcal{A}{-}C), .., (\langle\rangle, \mathcal{A}{-}C), (\langle\rangle, \mathcal{A}{-}C{-}B), (\langle\rangle, \mathcal{A}{-}B)\rangle$, $\#ttr = n{+}1$, *and B and C are finite sets of events,* $C = \{c_1, .., c_k\}$.
  Let $ttr_i = \langle(\langle\rangle, \mathcal{A}{-}C), .., (\langle\rangle, \mathcal{A}{-}C)\rangle ^\frown \langle(s_i, X_i)\rangle$, *where* $head(s_i) = c_i \in C$, *for* $i = 1, .., k$.
  $$\psi(TTR) \mathrel{\widehat{=}} pref(\langle set.n, reset\rangle) \cup \{\langle set.n, reset\rangle ^\frown s \mid s \in \psi(TTR/ttr)\} \cup \bigcup_{i=1}^{k}(pref(\langle set.n, c_i, halt\rangle) \cup\{\langle set.n, c_i, halt\rangle ^\frown tail(s_i) ^\frown s \mid s \in \psi(TTR/ttr_i)\})$$
- *For other cases,* $\psi(TTR) \mathrel{\widehat{=}} \cup \{flat(ttr) \mid ttr \in TTR\}$.

We assume that any sequential action can be written in the guarded normal form $\Box_{i=1}^{n}(c_i \rightarrow P_i)$. We construct Φ as follows.

Definition 4 (Syntactic Mapping).

$$\begin{aligned}
\Phi(Skip) &\mathrel{\widehat{=}} Skip\\
\Phi(Chaos) &\mathrel{\widehat{=}} Chaos\\
\Phi(Stop) &\mathrel{\widehat{=}} Stop\\
\Phi(x := e) &\mathrel{\widehat{=}} x := e\\
\Phi(b\&P) &\mathrel{\widehat{=}} b\&\Phi(P)\\
\Phi(P \lhd b \rhd Q) &\mathrel{\widehat{=}} \Phi(P) \lhd b \rhd \Phi(Q)\\
\Phi(Wait\ t) &\mathrel{\widehat{=}} set!t \rightarrow reset? \rightarrow Skip\\
\Phi(\Box_{i=1}^{k}(c_i \rightarrow P_i)) &\mathrel{\widehat{=}} \Box_{1\le i\le k}(c_i \rightarrow \Phi(P_i))\\
\Phi(P\Box Q) &\mathrel{\widehat{=}} \Phi(P)\Box\Phi(Q)\\
\Phi(P \sqcap Q) &\mathrel{\widehat{=}} \Phi(P) \sqcap \Phi(Q)\\
\Phi(P; Q) &\mathrel{\widehat{=}} \Phi(P); \Phi(Q)\\
\Phi(P\backslash E) &\mathrel{\widehat{=}} \Phi(P)\backslash E\\
\Phi((\Box_{i=1}^{n}(c_i{\rightarrow}P_i)) \overset{t}{\rhd} Q) &\mathrel{\widehat{=}} set!t{\rightarrow}((\Box_{i=1}^{n}(c_i{\rightarrow}halt!{\rightarrow}\Phi(P_i)))\Box\ (reset?{\rightarrow}\Phi(Q)))\\
\Phi(\mu X \bullet \Box_{i=1}^{n}(c_i \rightarrow P_i(X))) &\mathrel{\widehat{=}} \mu X \bullet \Box_{i=1}^{n}(c_i \rightarrow \Phi(P_i(X)))
\end{aligned}$$

Theorem 3. *The syntactic mapping Φ conforms with the semantic mapping ψ. That is, given any program P from* TCZ, *we have*

$$\psi([\![P]\!]_{time}) = [\![\Phi(P)]\!]$$

The proof is straightforward by a structural induction on *P*.

Theorem 4. *The syntactic mapping Φ is a homomorphic solution to the equation (†).*

4.3 Algebraic Laws

The set of processes generated by function Φ are called as *heterogeneous communicating processes* (HCP). It can be regarded as an extension of Communicating Sequential Processes (CSP) (if we ignore state features). It enriched CSP with timer events, thus is also subject to the healthiness conditions for CSP (Chapter 8 of [8]). However, as timer events have the same behaviour in both synchronous and asynchronous models, it satisfies some additional healthiness conditions. These additional properties will yield a subset of CSP processes. Therefore, although heterogeneous communicating processes are an extension of CSP, they can be simulated by a subset of CSP.

We shall present the additional properties in what follows.

HC1 $[\![P]\!] \ \wedge \ utr^\frown \langle set_1, set_2\rangle \preceq utr' \ = \ [\![P]\!] \ \wedge \ utr^\frown \langle set_2, set_1\rangle \preceq utr'$

It states that, if a heterogeneous communicating process sets two timers consecutively, then it can set them in any order.

Similarly, we have the following healthiness conditions.

HC2 $[\![P]\!] \ \wedge \ utr^\frown \langle set_1, halt_2\rangle \preceq utr' \ = \ [\![P]\!] \ \wedge \ utr^\frown \langle halt_2, set_1\rangle \preceq utr'$

HC3 $[\![P]\!] \ \wedge \ utr^\frown \langle halt_1, halt_2\rangle \preceq utr' \ = \ [\![P]\!] \ \wedge \ utr^\frown \langle halt_2, halt_1\rangle \preceq utr'$

The following condition indicates that no heterogeneous communicating process can refuse both events *halt* and *reset* simultaneously when the timer is activated.

HC4 $[\![P]\!] \wedge utr' = utr_0{}^\frown \langle set\rangle^\frown utr_1 \ \wedge \ utr_1 \lceil \{halt, reset\} = \langle\rangle \ \Rightarrow \ \{halt, reset\} \not\subseteq ref'$

In what follows, we give some expansion laws to transform a parallel action into a sequential one. Take note that timer events play different roles from normal events.

In the following laws, we assume P and Q are already in guarded normal forms: $P \ = \ \Box_{i=1}^{n}(c_i \rightarrow P_i)$, $Q \ = \ \Box_{k=1}^{m}(d_k \rightarrow Q_k)$, where for all i, k, $c_i \neq d_k$, and c_i, d_k are not timer events. Let $cs \ = \ (\alpha P \cap \alpha Q)\backslash\{set, halt, reset\}$.

The following one is the standard expansion law where no timer events are involved.

Law 1 $$P|[cs]|Q \ = \ \begin{cases} \Box_{i,k:c_i=d_k\in cs}(c_i \rightarrow (P_i|[cs]|Q_k)) \\ \Box\Box_{i:c_i\notin cs}(c_i \rightarrow (P_i|[cs]|Q)) \\ \Box\Box_{k:d_k\notin cs}(d_k \rightarrow (P|[cs]|Q_k)) \end{cases}$$

If timer events are involved, we should use the following expansion laws.

Law 2 $$(set_1 \rightarrow P)|[cs]|(set_2 \rightarrow Q) \ = \\ (set_1 \rightarrow set_2 \rightarrow (P|[cs]|Q)) \sqcap (set_2 \rightarrow set_1 \rightarrow (P|[cs]|Q))$$

Note that the two output events set_1 and set_2 can occur in any order, which is reflected by the internal choice. So do the two *halt* events or a mix of them, as illustrated by the following two laws.

Law 3 $$(set_1 \rightarrow P)|[cs]|(halt_2 \rightarrow Q) \ = \\ (set_1 \rightarrow halt_2 \rightarrow (P|[cs]|Q)) \sqcap (halt_2 \rightarrow set_1 \rightarrow (P|[cs]|Q))$$

Law 4 $(halt_1 \rightarrow P)|[cs]|(halt_2 \rightarrow Q) =$
$(halt_1 \rightarrow halt_2 \rightarrow (P|[cs]|Q)) \sqcap (halt_2 \rightarrow halt_1 \rightarrow (P|[cs]|Q))$

The events *set* and *halt* from the master process have higher priority than the *reset* event emitted by the slave process. This is reflected in the following two laws:

Law 5 $(set_1 \rightarrow P)|[cs]|(reset_2 \rightarrow Q) = set_1 \rightarrow (P|[cs]|(reset_2 \rightarrow Q))$

Law 6 $(halt_1 \rightarrow P)|[cs]|(reset_2 \rightarrow Q) = halt_1 \rightarrow (P|[cs]|(reset_2 \rightarrow Q))$

Law 7 $(reset_1 \rightarrow P)|[cs]|(reset_2 \rightarrow Q) =$
$(reset_1 \rightarrow (P|[cs]|(reset_2 \rightarrow Q))) \Box (reset_2 \rightarrow ((reset_1 \rightarrow P)|[cs]|Q))$

Take note that different from **Law 2**, external choice is used here as the two input events $reset_1$ and $reset_2$ have to wait for the corresponding output events from the environment (Timer processes).

5 Related Work and Conclusion

The two mostly related integrated formal specification languages are TCOZ [11] and *Circus* [21]. *Circus* is a combination of CSP and Z. It also includes specification statements found in Morgan's refinement calculus [13] and Dijkstra's language of guarded commands [3]. *Circus* has a well-defined syntax and a formal semantics [23, 21] based on Hoare and He's unifying theories of programming [8]. Case studies using the language are explored in [22] to show its power of expressiveness. A development method for *Circus* using refinement is described in [15]. A timed model for *Circus* was provided in [17]. Our untimed model Cz is a subset of *Circus*.

TCOZ is a blending of Object-Z [5, 18] and Timed CSP [16, 2], aiming at specification for complex real-time systems. The semantic link between the two formalisms Timed CSP and Object-Z is reported in [12]. TCOZ was enriched with sensors/actuators in [10]. A unified observation model for TCOZ is presented in [14]. Recent work [4] proposed a projection from TCOZ specifications to Timed Automata Patterns for model-checking timing properties using UPPAAL. Their syntactical mapping is proved sound under bisimulation. In our paper, we propose to verify timing properties in untimed framework by constructing a property-oriented untimed model, which, we believe, should be much simpler than doing it within the timed model.

Instead of using the same complex model as both semantic and reasoning models, we advocate the construction of small property-oriented models, that are separated from the whole semantic model, for verification of particular kinds of properties. In our instantiation in terms of timing properties, the approach does make analysis and reasoning about certain timing properties simpler and easier. A deep semantic link has been built between the timed model and the untimed model in the observation level, which ensures that it is safe to use a smaller property-oriented model for verification.

References

1. M. Butler. csp2B: A Practical Approach to Combining CSP and B. *Formal Aspects of computing*, 12:182–196, 2000.
2. J. Davies and S. Schneider. A brief history of Timed CSP. *Theoretical Computer Science*, 138:243–271, 1995.
3. E. W. Dijkstra. Guarded Commands, Nondeterminacy and Formal Derivation of Programs. *Communications of the ACM*, 18(8):453 – 457, 1975.
4. J. S. Dong, P. Hao, S.C. Qin, J. Sun, and Y. Wang. Timed Patterns: TCOZ to Timed Automata. In *6th International Conference on Formal Engineering Methods, ICFEM 2004*, Seattle, WA, USA, November 2004.
5. R. Duke and G. Rose. *Formal Object Oriented Specification Using Object-Z.* Cornerstones of Computing Series. Macmillan, March 2000.
6. C. Fischer. CSP-OZ: A combination of Object-Z and CSP. In H. Bowmann and J.Derrick, editors, *Formal Methods for Open Object-Based Distributed Systems (FMOODS '97)*, volume 2, pages 423–438. Chapman & Hall, 1997.
7. C. A. R. Hoare. *Communicating Sequential Processes.* Prentice Hall, 1985.
8. C.A.R. Hoare and J. He. *Unifying Theories of Programming.* Prentice-Hall, 1998.
9. L. Li and J. He. Towards a Denotational Semantics of Timed RSL using Duration Calculus. Technical Report 161, UNU/IIST, April 1999.
10. B. Mahony and J. S. Dong. Sensors and Actuators in TCOZ. In *FM'99: World Congress on Formal Methods*, volume 1709 of *Lect. Notes in Comput. Sci.*, Toulouse, France, September 1999. Springer-Verlag.
11. B. Mahony and J. S. Dong. Timed Communicating Object Z. *IEEE Transactions on Software Engineering*, 26(2):150–177, February 2000.
12. B. Mahony and J. S. Dong. Deep Semantic Links of TCSP and Object-Z: TCOZ Approach. *Formal Aspects of Computing*, 13(2):142–160, 2002.
13. C. C. Morgan. *Programming from Specifications.* Prentice Hall, 1994.
14. S.C. Qin, J.S. Dong, and W.N. Chin. A Semantics Foundation for TCOZ in Unifying Theories of Programming. In K. Araki, S. Gnesi, and D. Mandrioli, editors, *Formal Methods: International Symposium of Formal Methods Europe*, volume 2805 of *Lect. Notes in Comput. Sci.*, pages 321–340. Springer, 2003.
15. A. Sampaio, J. Woodcock, and A. Cavalcanti. Refinement in Circus. In *FME2002: International Symposium of Formal Methods Europe*, volume 2391 of *Lect. Notes in Comput. Sci.*, pages 451–470. Springer-Verlag, 2002.
16. S. Schneider, J. Davies, D. M. Jackson, G. M. Reed, J. N. Reed, and A. W. Roscoe. Timed CSP: Theory and practice. In J. W. de Bakker, C. Huizing, W. P. de Roever, and G. Rozenberg, editors, *Real-Time: Theory in Practice*, volume 600 of *Lect. Notes in Comput. Sci.*, pages 640–675. Springer-Verlag, 1992.
17. A. Sherif and J. He. Towards a Timed Model for Circus. In C. George and H. Miao, editors, *ICFEM'02 Formal Methods and Software Engineering*, volume 2495 of *Lect. Notes in Comput. Sci.*, pages 613–624. Springer-Verlag, 2002.
18. G. Smith. *The Object-Z Specification Language.* Advances in Formal Methods. Kluwer Academic Publishers, 2000.
19. G. Smith and J. Derrick. Refinement and verification of concurrent systems specified in Object-Z and CSP. In *International Conference on Formal Engineering Methods*, pages 293–302. IEEE Computer Society, 1997.
20. J. M. Spivey. *The Z Notation: A Reference Manual.* Prentice Hall International Series in Computer Science, Prentice-Hall, 1992.

21. J. Woodcock and A. Cavalcanti. Circus: a concurrent refinement language. Technical report, Oxford University Computing Laboratory, Wofson Building, Parks Road, Oxford OX1 3QD, UK, July 2001.
22. J. Woodcock and A. Cavalcanti. The steam boiler in a unified theory of Z and CSP. In J. He, Y. Li, and G. Lowe, editors, *The 8th Asia-Pacific Software Engineering Conference (APSEC'01)*, pages 291–298. IEEE Press, 2001.
23. J. Woodcock and A. Cavalcanti. The Semantics of Circus. In *2nd International Conference on Z and B*, volume 2272 of *Lect. Notes in Comput. Sci.*, pages 184–203. Springer-Verlag, 2002.

A Relational Investigation of UTP Designs and Prescriptions

Moshe Deutsch and Martin C. Henson

Department of Computer Science, University of Essex, UK
{mdeuts, hensm}@essex.ac.uk

Abstract. This paper presents a mathematical investigation of the relationships among a number of approaches for specification and refinement in two well-known paradigms based on the idea of *Unifying Theories of Programming*: Hoare and He's *designs* and Dunne's *prescriptions*. We present the technical analysis in a proof-theoretic relational framework based on two-predicate schema specifications. This enables us to demonstrate the relationships among (what *prima facie* seem to be) different models of refinement associated with each of these paradigms.

1 Introduction

In this paper, we review a number of formalisms for specification and refinement; in particular, we seek to explore the mathematical relationships among them. For this, we use a logical framework which captures the properties of specifications, described in some language of schema expressions, whose underlying model is relational. We consider schema-based specifications in four different frameworks: a logic for *Z-like* specifications, a logic for *non-lifted-totalised* specifications reminiscent of the one introduced in [11], the logic given in [23] for specifications called *designs* and the logic given in [15, 16] for specifications called *prescriptions* (both of which are interpreted as predicates). We will deal here only with *atomic schemas*, namely unstructured schemas involving no schema combinators.

We begin by introducing the semantics of schema specifications in a logical framework similar to that of Z and the semantics of non-lifted-totalised specifications (section 2). In addition to that, we provide two purely proof-theoretic characterisations of refinement[1] for schema-based specifications. We then introduce the concepts of both specification and refinement in two schema-based paradigms based on the idea of UTP: Hoare and He's designs (section 3) and Dunne's prescriptions (section 4). This enables us to examine the nature of refinement in each of these two paradigms (section 5): for each one, we develop a theory of refinement expressed in a purely homogeneous relational form and prove that it is *equivalent* to both the appropriate theory of refinement in the paradigm in question and the appropriate purely proof-theoretic characterisation introduced in section 2. We conclude the paper with some final comments and indications of several directions for future investigation (section 6); these are mainly to do with the interpretations of *compound* schema expressions and their impact on "stepwise" and "piecewise" development by refinement in these paradigms.

[1] Since we only deal here with *operation-refinement*, we will drop this qualification: unless we specify otherwise, refinement is short for *operation*-refinement.

S. Dunne and W. Stoddart (Eds.): UTP 2006, LNCS 4010, pp. 101–122, 2006.

Our investigation takes place in $\mathcal{Z}_C$, the logic for Z reported in [21]. For technical convenience, we summarise few relevant features of this, and additional notational conventions, in appendix A.

2 Specification and Refinement in a Z-Like Framework

2.1 The "Z" Interpretation

This paper is concerned with capturing a variety of specification and refinement paradigms in a schema-based logical framework.[2] In the following, we write U_i (*etc.*) for $[\,T \mid P_i \mid Q_i]$. This is an atomic operation schema whose type is $\mathbb{P}\,T$. T stands for $T^{in} \curlyvee T^{out'}$, where T^{in} is the type of the *before* sub-bindings and $T^{out'}$ is the type of the *after* sub-bindings. Since types can be recovered from the alphabets of P and Q for atomic schemas, we can and will write $[P \mid Q]$ for $[\,T \mid P \mid Q]$ in the sequel (and suppress types) where possible.[3]

The Z interpretation of atomic schemas is the following:

Definition 1.

$$[\![[P \mid Q]]\!]_Z =_{df} \{z_0 \star z_1' \mid z_0.z_1'.(P \wedge Q)\}$$

Membership in the Z interpretation is defined as follows:

Definition 2. $[\![z \in_Z U]\!]_Z =_{df} z \in [\![U]\!]_Z$

The following introduction and elimination rules are derivable for specifications in the Z interpretation:

Proposition 1.

$$\frac{t_0.t_1'.P \quad t_0.t_1'.Q}{t_0 \star t_1' \in_Z U}\,(Z^+) \qquad \frac{t_0 \star t_1' \in_Z U}{t_0.t_1'.P}\,(Z_0^-) \qquad \frac{t_0 \star t_1' \in_Z U}{t_0.t_1'.Q}\,(Z_1^-) \qquad \square$$

Note that this is, obviously, not quite the Z interpretation as introduced in its standard [27] or in other accounts in the literature (*e.g.* [14], [28] and [4]): Z is based on an underlying partial relation semantics that employs the "postcondition only" approach, in which preconditions are logically induced as *feasibility conditions*. Conversely, the above interpretation is based on (two-predicate) specifications whose preconditions and postconditions are *syntactically separated*; this concept coincides with, and casts the technical material in a similar style to, specifications in the UTP designs and prescriptions paradigms.

2.2 Non-lifted-Totalised Specifications

Another important concept is the *totalisation* of specifications. The standard model for Z is a partial relation semantics; the (*de facto*) standard notion of refinement in Z is based on *total correctness*: it involves the process of relational completion often referred

[2] Recall that we will deal only with atomic schemas.

[3] We provide further notational conventions in appendix A.

to as the *lifted-totalisation* semantics. This is a *model-theoretic* characterisation (that mediates between the underlying Z semantics and the interpretation of refinement), in which specifications (partial relations) are both *completed* (made total) and *extended* by means of an additional semantic element, often known as "bottom" and written $\perp$. This approach was first introduced in [28] (chapter 16 *et seq.*) and further elaborated in [4, ch.2-3]. In previous work (*e.g.* [10, 11, 8, 7, 6]), we examined carefully the essence of the lifted-totalisation semantics, in general, and the mathematical (as well as the conceptual) role of the $\perp$ values, in particular, in model-theoretic refinement. In the process, we demonstrated why a straightforward *non-lifted-totalisation* interpretation cannot underlie any reasonable model-based theory of refinement in Z. We did show, however, that a novel notion of what it means for a value to be in the precondition of a specification leads to a non-lifted-totalisation interpretation which underlies a valid theory of *operation-refinement*. Unfortunately, this cannot be generalised to any valid theory of simulation-based *data-refinement*.[4]

The investigation of data-refinement is beyond the scope of this paper and it will need to be examined carefully in the context of the technical material we explore here. In any case, we shall demonstrate in the sequel that the (straightforward) interpretation of non-lifted-totalised schema specifications, in the two-predicate model, lays a foundation for a relational framework in which both UTP designs and UTP prescriptions can be refined. This framework is free of auxiliary semantic elements [28] and propositional auxiliary variables [23].

Definition 3. *The interpretation of atomic non-lifted-totalised schemas:*

$$[\![[P \mid Q]]\!]_{NLT} =_{df} \{z_0 \star z_1' \mid z_0.z_1'.(P \Rightarrow Q)\}$$

Membership in the non-lifted-totalisation interpretation is simply:

Definition 4. $[\![z \in_{NLT} U]\!]_{NLT} =_{df} z \in [\![U]\!]_{NLT}$

The following rules are derivable for non-lifted-totalised specifications:

Proposition 2.

$$\frac{t_0.t_1'.P \vdash t_0.t_1'.Q}{t_0 \star t_1' \in_{NLT} U}\ (NLT^+) \qquad \frac{t_0 \star t_1' \in_{NLT} U \quad t_0.t_1'.P}{t_0.t_1'.Q}\ (NLT^-)$$

□

The following additional rules are derivable for non-lifted-totalised specifications:

Lemma 1.

$$\frac{\neg t_0.t_1'.P}{t_0 \star t_1' \in_{NLT} U}\ (i) \qquad \frac{t_0.t_1'.Q}{t_0 \star t_1' \in_{NLT} U}\ (ii)$$

□

This interpretation is reminiscent of the semantics underlying Henson and Reeves's method for program development and specification refinement within a single *Z-like* semantic framework [22]; though in *ibid.*, the semantics of an atomic operation schema is given in terms of a *set of total functions*, each of which takes any state satisfying the precondition of the operation to a state satisfying its postcondition.

[4] For further detail see [8],[7] and [6, ch.7].

2.3 Proof-Theoretic Refinement

In this section we introduce two purely proof-theoretic characterisations of refinement for (two-predicate) schema specifications. These are closely connected to refinement as introduced by Spivey in, for example, [26] and as discussed in [24], [25] and [4]. In those contexts we do not so much have an alternative notion of refinement as two sufficient conditions (essentially the premises of the introduction rules in propositions 3 and 4 below). By adding the two elimination rules we add necessary conditions, and thus formalise an independent theory in each case.

These notions are based on two basic observations regarding the properties one expects in a refinement: firstly, that a refinement may involve the reduction of non-determinism; secondly, that a refinement may involve the expansion of the domain of definition. Put another way, we have a refinement providing that *postconditions do not weaken* (we do not permit an increase in non-determinism in a refinement) and that *preconditions do not strengthen* (we do not permit requirements in the domain of definition to disappear in a refinement).

We name these notions S-refinement and SP-refinement; each of them can be captured by forcing the refinement relation to hold *exactly* when these conditions apply. S-refinement is written $U_0 \sqsupseteq_s U_1$ and is given by the definition that leads directly to the following introduction and elimination rules:

Proposition 3. *Let z, z_0, z_1 be fresh variables.*

$$\frac{z.P_1 \vdash z.P_0 \quad z_0.P_1, z_0.z_1'.Q_0 \vdash z_0.z_1'.Q_1}{U_0 \sqsupseteq_s U_1} \; (\sqsupseteq_s^+)$$

$$\frac{U_0 \sqsupseteq_s U_1 \quad t.P_1}{t.P_0} \; (\sqsupseteq_{s_0}^-) \qquad \frac{U_0 \sqsupseteq_s U_1 \quad t_0.P_1 \quad t_0.t_1'.Q_0}{t_0.t_1'.Q_1} \; (\sqsupseteq_{s_1}^-)$$

□

SP-refinement is written $U_0 \sqsupseteq_{sp} U_1$ and is given by the definition that leads directly to the following rules:

Proposition 4. *Let z, z_0, z_1 be fresh variables.*

$$\frac{z.P_1 \vdash z.P_0 \quad z_0.z_1'.Q_0 \vdash z_0.z_1'.Q_1}{U_0 \sqsupseteq_{sp} U_1} \; (\sqsupseteq_{sp}^+)$$

$$\frac{U_0 \sqsupseteq_{sp} U_1 \quad t.P_1}{t.P_0} \; (\sqsupseteq_{sp_0}^-) \qquad \frac{U_0 \sqsupseteq_{sp} U_1 \quad t_0.t_1'.Q_0}{t_0.t_1'.Q_1} \; (\sqsupseteq_{sp_1}^-)$$

□

In the context of single-predicate schema specifications, S-refinement and SP-refinement respectively represent refinement in the *contractual* and *behavioural* approaches [4]: the former represents a more sequential view in which preconditions may be weakened in a refinement process, whereas the latter represents a more concurrent view in which preconditions remain fixed.[5]

[5] In our previous work, we respectively referred to these as the *chaotic* (*e.g.* [11, 8]) and the *abortive* (*e.g.* [9] and [6, ch.5,9]) approaches.

This is not the case when we consider specifications whose pre and postconditions are syntactically separated. The behaviour imposed on preconditions is identical in S-refinement and SP-refinement: weakening of preconditions is viable in both. The difference between them lies in the behaviour each of them imposes on postconditions: both of them sanction strengthening of postconditions, yet SP-refinement is more strict - it forbids weakening of postconditions; S-refinement, on the other hand, does not restrict the behaviour of postconditions in the region where the (initial) precondition does not hold. We will demonstrate in section 5 that S-refinement is equivalent to refinement in the UTP designs paradigm and SP-refinement is equivalent to refinement in the UTP prescriptions paradigm.

3 UTP Designs

3.1 Background

In [23], Hoare and He develop a common framework for unifying theories of programming. This framework is based on a *total correctness* setting in which a *predicative model* is employed for modelling programs. In other words, what they are seeking to do in *ibid.* is to model all programs as single *homogeneous* relations called *designs*, where a relation here is simply a *predicate* over a given alphabet of variables. Furthermore, in order to address behaviours that specifically concern with *initiation* and *termination* of programs, the authors adopt an idea that originated from Eric Hehner [18]: they add two auxiliary *boolean* variables, ok and ok', to the alphabet of every relation; these respectively record whether or not the program has *started* and *terminated*. In this way, they retain the *homogeneity* of the relations.

In this section we rehearse the basic material concerning designs as described in [23], recasting this in proof-theoretic and relational form in so doing. This reformulation eases the comparisons we go on to make in the sequel and brings out some of the structure implicit in [23].

3.2 Logic and Semantics

First we have designs themselves. These are written, by Hoare and He, as precondition/postcondition pairs: $P \vdash Q$. In this paper, however, we need not overburden the notation and simply give the Hoare-He design semantics for atomic schemas.

Definition 5. *The interpretation of atomic schemas:*

$$[\![[P \mid Q]]\!]_H =_{df} \{z_0 \star z_1' \mid \mathsf{ok} \wedge z_0.P \Rightarrow \mathsf{ok}' \wedge z_0.z_1'.Q\}$$

Note that this interesting definition establishes the meaning of schema (design) as a *parameterised* relation: it depends on two propositional variables ok and ok'. We will need to write $U(u, v')$ in the language of specifications, to refer to certain substitutions for the parameters in the interpretation. Thus $[\![U(u, v')]\!]_H$ is the relation $[\![U]\!]_H\,[\mathsf{ok}/u, \mathsf{ok}'/v']$. With this notation in place we can define H-membership, noting that U and $U(\mathsf{ok}, \mathsf{ok}')$ are equivalent:

Definition 6. $[\![z \in_H U(u, v')]\!]_H =_{df} z \in [\![U(u, v')]\!]_H$

The rules for this, then, are also parameterised:

Proposition 5.

$$\frac{\mathsf{ok}, t_0.P \vdash \mathsf{ok}' \quad \mathsf{ok}, t_0.P \vdash t_0.t_1'.Q}{t_0 \star t_1' \in_H U}\ (H^+)$$

$$\frac{t_0 \star t_1' \in_H U \quad \mathsf{ok} \quad t_0.P}{\mathsf{ok}'}\ (H_0^-) \qquad \frac{t_0 \star t_1' \in_H U \quad \mathsf{ok} \quad t_0.P}{t_0.t_1'.Q}\ (H_1^-)$$

□

These rules simplify in the various cases in which the two parameters take on values.

Proposition 6. *The following rules are all derivable:*

$$\frac{t_0.P \vdash t_0.t_1'.Q}{t_0 \star t_1' \in_H U(t,t)}\ (H(tt)^+) \qquad \frac{t_0 \star t_1' \in_H U(t,t) \quad t_0.P}{t_0.t_1'.Q}\ (H(tt)^-)$$

$$\frac{\neg t_0.P}{t_0 \star t_1' \in_H U(t,f)}\ (H(tf)^+) \qquad \frac{t_0 \star t_1' \in_H U(t,f)}{\neg t_0.P}\ (H(tf)^-)$$

$$\frac{}{t_0 \star t_1' \in_H U(f,t)}\ (H(ft)) \qquad \frac{}{t_0 \star t_1' \in_H U(f,f)}\ (H(ff))$$

□

H-refinement (refinement of designs) closes these relational expressions by quantification over the propositional variables:

Definition 7. $[\![U_0 \sqsupseteq_H U_1]\!]_H =_{df} \forall\, \mathsf{ok}, \mathsf{ok}' \bullet [\![U_0]\!]_H \subseteq [\![U_1]\!]_H$

Though, H-refinement can be simplified as follows:

Proposition 7. $U_0 \sqsupseteq_H U_1 \Leftrightarrow [\![U_0(t,t)]\!]_H \subseteq [\![U_1(t,t)]\!]_H \wedge [\![U_0(t,f)]\!]_H \subseteq [\![U_1(t,f)]\!]_H$

Proof. This follows from the observation that, when v is a propositional variable, $\forall\, v \bullet P(v)$ is equivalent to $P[v/t] \wedge P[v/f]$ and from the two degenerate axioms (*H(ft)*) and (*H(ff)*). □

Thus, we have the following rules for H-refinement:

Proposition 8. *Let z be fresh.*

$$\frac{z \in_H U_0(t,t) \vdash z \in_H U_1(t,t) \quad z \in_H U_0(t,f) \vdash z \in_H U_1(t,f)}{U_0 \sqsupseteq_H U_1}\ (\sqsupseteq_H^+)$$

$$\frac{U_0 \sqsupseteq_H U_1 \quad t \in_H U_0(t,t)}{t \in_H U_1(t,t)}\ (\sqsupseteq_{H_0}^-) \qquad \frac{U_0 \sqsupseteq_H U_1 \quad t \in_H U_0(t,f)}{t \in_H U_1(t,f)}\ (\sqsupseteq_{H_1}^-)$$

□

4 UTP Prescriptions

Another concept concerning UTP was developed by Steve Dunne of the University of Teesside (UK) in seminal work reported in [15, 16]. In *ibid.*, Dunne develops a predicative model that generalises Hoare and He's designs to a framework based on a *general correctness* setting; specifications in this framework are called *prescriptions*.

In this section we introduce the technical material underlying prescriptions, recasting it in our relational framework based on two-predicate schema specifications. We then review some interesting properties of specification and refinement in this paradigm and in comparison to UTP designs.

4.1 Logic and Semantics

We begin with the definition of prescriptions. Akin to Hoare and He's designs, these are written in [15, 16] as precondition/postcondition pairs: $P \Vdash Q$. In the same manner as in definition 5, we give Dunne's prescription semantics for atomic schemas:

Definition 8.

$$[\![[P \mid Q]]\!]_D =_{df} \{z_0 \star z_1' \mid (\mathsf{ok} \wedge z_0.P \Rightarrow \mathsf{ok}') \wedge (\mathsf{ok}' \Rightarrow z_0.z_1'.Q \wedge \mathsf{ok})\}$$

Similarly to the interpretation of designs, we write $[\![U(u, v')]\!]_D$ for the relation $[\![U]\!]_D\,[\mathsf{ok}/u, \mathsf{ok}'/v']$; thus membership in the prescriptions interpretation is merely:

Definition 9. $[\![z \in_D U(u, v')]\!]_D =_{df} z \in [\![U(u, v')]\!]_D$

Then the following rules are immediately derivable for prescriptions:[6]

Proposition 9.

$$\frac{\mathsf{ok}, t_0.P \vdash \mathsf{ok}' \quad \mathsf{ok}' \vdash t_0.t_1'.Q \quad \mathsf{ok}' \vdash \mathsf{ok}}{t_0 \star t_1' \in_D U}\ (D^+)$$

$$\frac{t_0 \star t_1' \in_D U \quad \mathsf{ok} \quad t_0.P}{\mathsf{ok}'}\ (D_0^-) \qquad \frac{t_0 \star t_1' \in_D U \quad \mathsf{ok}'}{t_0.t_1'.Q}\ (D_1^-) \qquad \frac{t_0 \star t_1' \in_D U \quad \mathsf{ok}'}{\mathsf{ok}}\ (D_2^-)$$

□

Likewise, we simplify these rules in the various instantiations of ok and ok'.

Proposition 10. *The following rules are derivable:*

$$\frac{t_0.t_1'.Q}{t_0 \star t_1' \in_D U(t, t)}\ (D(tt)^+) \qquad \frac{t_0 \star t_1' \in_D U(t, t)}{t_0.t_1'.Q}\ (D(tt)^-)$$

$$\frac{\neg t_0.P}{t_0 \star t_1' \in_D U(t, f)}\ (D(tf)^+) \qquad \frac{t_0 \star t_1' \in_D U(t, f)}{\neg t_0.P}\ (D(tf)^-)$$

$$\frac{t_0 \star t_1' \in_D U(f, t)}{\mathit{false}}\ (D(ft)) \qquad \frac{}{t_0 \star t_1' \in_D U(f, f)}\ (D(ff))$$

□

We are now in position to define the concept of prescriptions refinement. We name this D-refinement, whose definition closes the relational expressions above by quantification over the auxiliary variables:

Definition 10. $[\![U_0 \sqsupseteq_D U_1]\!]_D =_{df} \forall\, \mathsf{ok}, \mathsf{ok}' \bullet [\![U_0]\!]_D \subseteq [\![U_1]\!]_D$

Again, this notion can be simplified by the following proposition:

Proposition 11. $U_0 \sqsupseteq_D U_1 \Leftrightarrow [\![U_0(t, t)]\!]_D \subseteq [\![U_1(t, t)]\!]_D \wedge [\![U_0(t, f)]\!]_D \subseteq [\![U_1(t, f)]\!]_D$

Proof. Similar to the proof of proposition 7. □

Therefore, the following introduction and elimination rules are derivable for D-refinement:

[6] Again, note that U and $U(\mathsf{ok}, \mathsf{ok}')$ are equivalent.

Proposition 12. *Let z be fresh.*

$$\frac{z \in_D U_0(t,t) \vdash z \in_D U_1(t,t) \quad z \in_D U_0(t,f) \vdash z \in_D U_1(t,f)}{U_0 \sqsupseteq_D U_1} \; (\sqsupseteq_D^+)$$

$$\frac{U_0 \sqsupseteq_D U_1 \quad t \in_D U_0(t,t)}{t \in_D U_1(t,t)} \; (\sqsupseteq_{D_0}^-) \qquad \frac{U_0 \sqsupseteq_D U_1 \quad t \in_D U_0(t,f)}{t \in_D U_1(t,f)} \; (\sqsupseteq_{D_1}^-)$$

□

4.2 Some Interesting Properties

There are two very interesting properties that specifically characterise prescriptions.[7] First, the prescription form $[\![[P \mid Q]]\!]_D$ is *canonical* in a sense that:

$$[\![[P_0 \mid Q_0]]\!]_D = [\![[P_1 \mid Q_1]\!]_D \;\; \textit{iff} \;\; P_0 = P_1 \text{ and } Q_0 = Q_1$$

This contrasts with Hoare and He's design form $[\![[P \mid Q]]\!]_H$ which is *not canonical* since, for example:

$$[\![[P \mid Q]]\!]_H , \;\; [\![[P \mid P \Rightarrow Q]]\!]_H \text{ and } [\![[P \mid P \wedge Q]]\!]_H$$

all represent the same design.

Secondly, the assortment of *extreme specifications* in Dunne's framework induces a very neat characterisation for prescriptions. Consider the definition of the four possible extreme specifications in a two-predicate model:

Definition 11.

$$\begin{array}{llll} abort =_{df} [false \mid false] & chaos =_{df} [false \mid true] \\ magic =_{df} [true \mid false] & chance =_{df} [true \mid true] \end{array}$$

And then the meaning of these in each of the two paradigms of designs and prescriptions:[8]

Proposition 13.

$$\begin{array}{llll} [\![abort]\!]_H & \equiv true & [\![abort]\!]_D & \equiv \neg \mathsf{ok}' \\ [\![chaos]\!]_H & \equiv true & [\![chaos]\!]_D & \equiv \mathsf{ok}' \Rightarrow \mathsf{ok} \\ [\![magic]\!]_H & \equiv \neg \mathsf{ok} & [\![magic]\!]_D & \equiv \neg \mathsf{ok} \wedge \neg \mathsf{ok}' \\ [\![chance]\!]_H & \equiv \mathsf{ok} \Rightarrow \mathsf{ok}' & [\![chance]\!]_D & \equiv \mathsf{ok}' \Leftrightarrow \mathsf{ok} \end{array}$$

□

Hence, we can observe that the following characterisation holds for prescriptions: D is a *prescription iff*

$$magic \sqsupseteq D \sqsupseteq chaos$$

Namely, a prescription is any relation which fits within the sub-lattice between *chaos* and *magic*; this is delineated in Fig. 1. This, of course, does not hold for the designs paradigm because its assortment of extreme specifications is more confined: the specifications *chaos* and *abort* are both equivalent to *true*.

[7] The material in this section is based on the summary introduced in [15] and [16].

[8] Note that *chaos* is named "*anarchy*" in [15, 16].

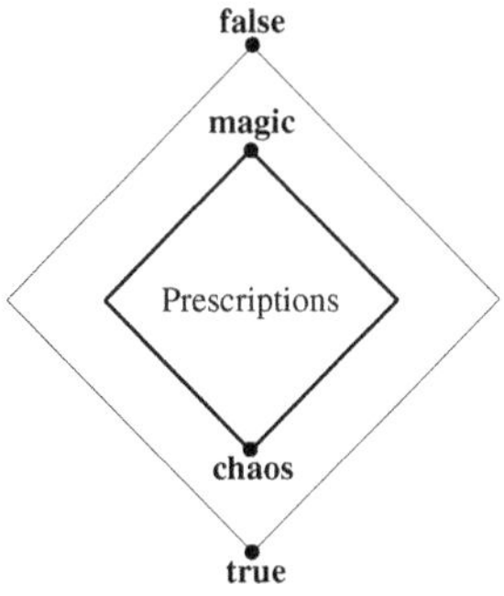

Fig. 1. The lattice of prescriptions

5 A Basis for Unification: Equivalence of Refinement Theories

This section constitutes the core of our technical investigation. For each of the two paradigms of designs and prescriptions, we will establish a theory of refinement which involves simple relational operations on specifications in the Z and the non-lifted-totalisation semantics (sections 2.1 and 2.2). Subsequently, we will demonstrate that this theory is equivalent to both the appropriate theory of refinement in the paradigm in question and the proof-theoretic characterisation of refinement for two-predicate schema specifications (section 2.3). In doing this, we will bring together a number of models for specification and refinement, which *prima facie* look radically different, and demonstrate that they are in fact intimately related mathematically.

Methodologically, we shall be showing that all judgements of refinement in one theory are contained among the refinements sanctioned by another. Such results can always be established proof-theoretically because we have expressed all our approaches as theories (sets of introduction and elimination rules). Specifically, we will show that the refinement relation of a theory $\mathcal{T}_0$ satisfies the elimination rule (or rules) for refinement of another theory $\mathcal{T}_1$. Since the elimination rules and introduction rules of a theory enjoy the usual symmetry properties, this is sufficient to show that all $\mathcal{T}_0$-refinements are also $\mathcal{T}_1$-refinements. Equivalence can then be shown by interchanging the roles of $\mathcal{T}_0$ and $\mathcal{T}_1$ in the above.

5.1 Designs Refinement

HH-Refinement. This notion is written $U_0 \sqsupseteq_{HH} U_1$ and given by the following definition:

Definition 12.

$$\begin{aligned} U_0 \sqsupseteq_{HH} U_1 =_{df} & \llbracket U_0 \rrbracket_{NLT} \subseteq \llbracket U_1 \rrbracket_{NLT} \wedge \\ & (\llbracket U_0 \rrbracket_{NLT} - \llbracket U_0 \rrbracket_Z) \subseteq (\llbracket U_1 \rrbracket_{NLT} - \llbracket U_1 \rrbracket_Z) \end{aligned}$$

The following rules are derivable for HH-refinement:

Proposition 14. *Let z be fresh.*

$$\frac{z \in_{NLT} U_0 \vdash z \in_{NLT} U_1 \quad z \in_{NLT} U_0, z \notin_Z U_0 \vdash z \notin_Z U_1}{U_0 \sqsupseteq_{HH} U_1} \; (\sqsupseteq^+_{HH})$$

$$\frac{U_0 \sqsupseteq_{HH} U_1 \quad t \in_{NLT} U_0}{t \in_{NLT} U_1}\ (\sqsupseteq^-_{HH_0}) \qquad \frac{U_0 \sqsupseteq_{HH} U_1 \quad t \in_{NLT} U_0 \quad t \notin_Z U_0}{t \notin_Z U_1}\ (\sqsupseteq^-_{HH_1})$$

□

H-Refinement and S-Refinement Are Equivalent. This result recasts Hoare and He's theorem 3.1.2 [23, p.77] in our mathematical framework. We begin by showing that H-refinement satisfies the two S-refinement elimination rules.

Proposition 15. *The following rule is derivable:*

$$\frac{U_0 \sqsupseteq_H U_1 \quad t_0.P_1}{t_0.P_0}$$

Proof.

$$\frac{\dfrac{\dfrac{\dfrac{\overline{\neg t_0.P_0}\ (1)}{t_0 \star t_1' \in_H U_0(t,f)} \quad U_0 \sqsupseteq_H U_1}{t_0 \star t_1' \in_H U_1(t,f)}}{\neg t_0.P_1} \qquad t_0.P_1}{\dfrac{false}{t_0.P_0}\ (1)}$$

□

Turning to the second elimination rule.

Proposition 16. *The following rule is derivable:*

$$\frac{U_0 \sqsupseteq_H U_1 \quad t_0.P_1 \quad t_0.t_1'.Q_0}{t_0.t_1'.Q_1}$$

Proof.

$$\frac{t_0.P_1 \qquad \dfrac{U_0 \sqsupseteq_H U_1 \quad \dfrac{t_0.t_1'.Q_0}{t_0 \star t_1' \in_H U_0(t,t)}\ (1)}{t_0 \star t_1' \in_H U_1(t,t)}}{t_0.t_1'.Q_1}$$

□

Then it is an immediate consequence that H-refinement is *sound* with respect to S-refinement:

Theorem 1.

$$\frac{U_0 \sqsupseteq_H U_1}{U_0 \sqsupseteq_s U_1}$$

Proof. Follows directly from propositions 15 and 16, in addition to the rule $(\sqsupseteq_s^+)$.[9] □

Now we show that S-refinement satisfies the H-refinement elimination rules.

Proposition 17. *The following rule is derivable:*

$$\frac{U_0 \sqsupseteq_s U_1 \quad t_0 \star t_1' \in_H U_0(t,t)}{t_0 \star t_1' \in_H U_1(t,t)}$$

[9] The proofs of such theorems are always automatic by the structural symmetry between introduction and elimination rules. We shall, therefore, not provide them explicitly.

Proof.

$$\dfrac{\dfrac{U_0 \sqsupseteq_s U_1 \quad \overline{t_0.P_1}^{\,(1)} \quad \dfrac{t_0 \star t_1' \in_H U_0(t,t) \quad \dfrac{U_0 \sqsupseteq_s U_1 \quad \overline{t_0.P_1}^{\,(1)}}{t_0.P_0}}{t_0.t_1'.Q_0}}{t_0.t_1'.Q_1}}{t_0 \star t_1' \in_H U_1(t,t)}\ (1)$$

□

And now the second elimination rule.

Proposition 18. *The following rule is derivable:*

$$\frac{U_0 \sqsupseteq_s U_1 \quad t \in_H U_0(t,f)}{t \in_H U_1(t,f)}$$

Proof.

$$\dfrac{\dfrac{\dfrac{\dfrac{U_0 \sqsupseteq_s U_1 \quad \overline{t_0.P_1}^{\,(1)}}{t_0.P_0} \quad \dfrac{t_0 \star t_1' \in_H U_0(t,f)}{\neg t_0.P_0}}{false}}{\neg t_0.P_1}\ (1)}{t_0 \star t_1' \in_H U_1(t,f)}$$

□

Then the following theorem immediately follows, by $(\sqsupseteq_H^+)$, from propositions 17 and 18; namely, H-refinement is *complete* with respect to S-refinement:

Theorem 2.

$$\frac{U_0 \sqsupseteq_s U_1}{U_0 \sqsupseteq_H U_1}$$

□

Together, theorems 1 and 2 establish that the theories of H-refinement and S-refinement are equivalent.

H-Refinement and HH-Refinement Are Equivalent. We begin by showing that HH-refinement satisfies the two H-refinement elimination rules. For this, we will require an auxiliary lemma demonstrating that HH-refinement guarantees that preconditions do not strengthen (*i.e.* it satisfies the rule $(\sqsupseteq_{s_0}^-)$).

Lemma 2. *The following rule is derivable:*

$$\frac{U_0 \sqsupseteq_{HH} U_1 \quad t_0.P_1}{t_0.P_0}$$

Proof.

$$\dfrac{\dfrac{\dfrac{\dfrac{U_0 \sqsupseteq_{HH} U_1 \quad \dfrac{\overline{\neg t_0.P_0}^{\,(1)}}{t_0 \star t_1' \in_{NLT} U_0}\ (L.\ 1(i)) \quad \dfrac{\overline{\neg t_0.P_0}^{\,(1)}}{t_0 \star t_1' \notin_Z U_0}}{t_0 \star t_1' \notin_Z U_1}}{\neg t_0.P_1 \vee \neg t_0.t_1'.Q_1} \quad \dfrac{\overline{\neg t_0.P_1}^{\,(2)} \quad t_0.P_1}{false} \quad \begin{matrix}\delta\\ \vdots\\ false\end{matrix}}{false}\ (2)}{t_0.P_0}\ (1)$$

Where δ stands for the following branch:

$$\dfrac{\dfrac{\dfrac{U_0 \sqsupseteq_{HH} U_1 \quad \dfrac{\overline{\neg t_0.P_0}\ (1)}{t_0 \star t_1' \in_{NLT} U_0}\ (L.\ 1(i))}{t_0 \star t_1' \in_{NLT} U_1} \quad t_0.P_1}{t_0.t_1'.Q_1} \quad \overline{\neg t_0.t_1'.Q_1}\ (2)}{false}$$

□

Now considering the first H-refinement elimination rule.

Proposition 19. *The following rule is derivable:*

$$\frac{U_0 \sqsupseteq_{HH} U_1 \quad t \in_H U_0(t,t)}{t \in_H U_1(t,t)}$$

Proof.

$$\dfrac{\dfrac{\dfrac{U_0 \sqsupseteq_{HH} U_1 \quad \dfrac{\dfrac{t_0 \star t_1' \in_H U_0(t,t) \quad \dfrac{U_0 \sqsupseteq_{HH} U_1 \quad \overline{t_0.P_1}\ (1)}{t_0.P_0}\ (L.\ 2)}{t_0.t_1'.Q_0}}{t_0 \star t_1' \in_{NLT} U_0}\ (L.\ 1(ii))}{t_0 \star t_1' \in_{NLT} U_1} \quad \overline{t_0.P_1}\ (1)}{t_0.t_1'.Q_1}}{t_0 \star t_1' \in_H U_1(t,t)}\ (1)$$

□

Turning now to the second elimination rule in H-refinement.

Proposition 20. *The following rule is derivable:*

$$\frac{U_0 \sqsupseteq_{HH} U_1 \quad t \in_H U_0(t,f)}{t \in_H U_1(t,f)}$$

Proof.

$$\dfrac{\dfrac{U_0 \sqsupseteq_{HH} U_1 \quad \dfrac{t_0 \star t_1' \in_H U_0(t,f)}{\neg t_0.P_0}}{\neg t_0.P_1}\ (L.\ 2)}{t_0 \star t_1' \in_H U_1(t,f)}$$

□

Then by propositions 19 and 20, in addition to the rule $(\sqsupseteq_H^+)$, we get the following theorem immediately:

Theorem 3.

$$\frac{U_0 \sqsupseteq_{HH} U_1}{U_0 \sqsupseteq_H U_1}$$

□

We now show that H-refinement satisfies the two HH-elimination rules.

Proposition 21. *The following rule is derivable:*

$$\frac{U_0 \sqsupseteq_H U_1 \quad t \in_{NLT} U_0}{t \in_{NLT} U_1}$$

Proof.

$$\cfrac{U_0 \sqsupseteq_H U_1 \quad
\cfrac{t_0 \star t_1' \in_{NLT} U_0 \quad \cfrac{U_0 \sqsupseteq_H U_1 \quad \overline{t_0.P_1}^{\ (1)}}{t_0.P_0}\ {}^{(P.\,15)}}
{\cfrac{t_0.t_1'.Q_0}{t_0 \star t_1' \in_H U_0(t,t)}\ {}^{(2)}}}
{\cfrac{t_0 \star t_1' \in_H U_1(t,t) \qquad\qquad \overline{t_0.P_1}^{\ (1)}}
{\cfrac{t_0.t_1'.Q_1}{t_0 \star t_1' \in_{NLT} U_1}\ {}^{(1)}}}$$

$\square$

Now the second elimination rule in HH-refinement.

Proposition 22. *The following rule is derivable:*

$$\frac{U_0 \sqsupseteq_H U_1 \quad t \in_{NLT} U_0 \quad t \notin_Z U_0}{t \notin_Z U_1}$$

Proof. Consider the following derivation which requires the the *law of excluded middle* (*tertium non datur*):

$$\cfrac{\cfrac{t_0 \star t_1' \notin_Z U_0}{\neg t_0.P_0 \vee \neg t_0.t_1'.Q_0} \quad
\cfrac{U_0 \sqsupseteq_H U_1 \quad \overline{\neg t_0.P_0}^{\ (1)}}{\cfrac{\neg t_0.P_1}{t_0 \star t_1' \notin_Z U_1}}\ {}^{(P.\,15)} \quad
\cfrac{\delta}{\ \vdots\ }{t_0 \star t_1' \notin_Z U_1}}
{t_0 \star t_1' \notin_Z U_1}\ {}^{(1)}$$

Where δ stands for the following branch:

$$\cfrac{\overline{t_0.P_1 \vee \neg t_0.P_1}\ {}^{(LEM)} \quad
\cfrac{\beta}{\ \vdots\ }{t_0 \star t_1' \notin_Z U_1} \quad
\cfrac{\overline{\neg t_0.P_1}^{\ (2)}}{t_0 \star t_1' \notin_Z U_1}\ {}^{(2)}}
{t_0 \star t_1' \notin_Z U_1}$$

Where β is:

$$\cfrac{\cfrac{t_0 \star t_1' \in_{NLT} U_0 \quad \cfrac{U_0 \sqsupseteq_H U_1 \quad \overline{t_0.P_1}^{\ (2)}}{t_0.P_0}\ {}^{(P.\,15)}}{t_0.t_1'.Q_0} \qquad \overline{\neg t_0.t_1'.Q_0}^{\ (1)}}
{\cfrac{false}{t_0 \star t_1' \notin_Z U_1}}$$

$\square$

Then by propositions 21 and 22, as well as the rule ($\sqsupseteq_{HH}^+$), the following theorem is immediately derivable:

Theorem 4.

$$\frac{U_0 \sqsupseteq_H U_1}{U_0 \sqsupseteq_{HH} U_1}$$

$\square$

Theorems 3 and 4 together establish that the theories of H-refinement and HH-refinement are equivalent. Despite their superficial dissimilarity, H-refinement, HH-refinement and S-refinement are all equivalent to one another. Not only these results reinforce theorem 3.1.2 in [23], they also demonstrate that the ideas of specification and development (by stepwise, and piecewise, refinement), in the UTP designs paradigm, can be unified within a homogeneous relational framework which involves neither the introduction of auxiliary semantic elements, nor the deployment of auxiliary propositional variables.

5.2 Prescriptions Refinement

DD-Refinement. In the following, we write $U_i^\dagger$ (*etc.*) for the schema $[Q_i \mid P_i]$; thus, DD-refinement is written $U_0 \sqsupseteq_{DD} U_1$ and given by the following definition:

Definition 13.

$$U_0 \sqsupseteq_{DD} U_1 =_{df} (\llbracket U_1^\dagger \rrbracket_{NLT} - \llbracket U_1^\dagger \rrbracket_Z) \subseteq (\llbracket U_0^\dagger \rrbracket_{NLT} - \llbracket U_0^\dagger \rrbracket_Z) \land$$
$$(\llbracket U_0 \rrbracket_{NLT} - \llbracket U_0 \rrbracket_Z) \subseteq (\llbracket U_1 \rrbracket_{NLT} - \llbracket U_1 \rrbracket_Z)$$

The following rules are derivable for DD-refinement:

Proposition 23. *Let z be fresh.*

$$\frac{\begin{array}{cc} z \in_{NLT} U_1^\dagger, z \notin_Z U_1^\dagger \vdash z \in_{NLT} U_0^\dagger & z \in_{NLT} U_0, z \notin_Z U_0 \vdash z \in_{NLT} U_1 \\ z \in_{NLT} U_1^\dagger, z \notin_Z U_1^\dagger \vdash z \notin_Z U_0^\dagger & z \in_{NLT} U_0, z \notin_Z U_0 \vdash z \notin_Z U_1 \end{array}}{U_0 \sqsupseteq_{DD} U_1} (\sqsupseteq_{DD}^+)$$

$$\frac{U_0 \sqsupseteq_{DD} U_1 \quad t \in_{NLT} U_1^\dagger \quad t \notin_Z U_1^\dagger}{t \in_{NLT} U_0^\dagger} (\sqsupseteq_{DD_0}^-) \qquad \frac{U_0 \sqsupseteq_{DD} U_1 \quad t \in_{NLT} U_1^\dagger \quad t \notin_Z U_1^\dagger}{t \notin_Z U_0^\dagger} (\sqsupseteq_{DD_1}^-)$$

$$\frac{U_0 \sqsupseteq_{DD} U_1 \quad t \in_{NLT} U_0 \quad t \notin_Z U_0}{t \in_{NLT} U_1} (\sqsupseteq_{DD_2}^-) \qquad \frac{U_0 \sqsupseteq_{DD} U_1 \quad t \in_{NLT} U_0 \quad t \notin_Z U_0}{t \notin_Z U_1} (\sqsupseteq_{DD_3}^-)$$

□

D-Refinement and SP-Refinement Are Equivalent. This result formalises, in our mathematical framework, Dunne's informal summary given in [16]. Using our usual strategy involving elimination rules, we begin by showing that D-refinement is *sound* with respect to SP-refinement. Firstly, the rule for preconditions.

Proposition 24. *The following rule is derivable:*

$$\frac{U_0 \sqsupseteq_D U_1 \quad t_0.P_1}{t_0.P_0}$$

Proof. The proof is identical to the proof of proposition 15, modulo the following substitutions: $\in_D$ replaces $\in_H$ and $\sqsupseteq_D$ replaces $\sqsupseteq_H$.

□

Now the rule for postconditions.

Proposition 25. *The following rule is derivable:*

$$\frac{U_0 \sqsupseteq_D U_1 \quad t_0.t_1'.Q_0}{t_0.t_1'.Q_1}$$

Proof.

$$\frac{\dfrac{U_0 \sqsupseteq_D U_1 \quad \dfrac{t_0.t_1'.Q_0}{t_0 \star t_1' \in_D U_0(t,t)}}{t_0 \star t_1' \in_D U_1(t,t)}}{t_0.t_1'.Q_1}$$

□

Then by propositions 24 and 25, in addition to the rule ($\sqsupseteq_{sp}^{+}$), the following theorem is immediate:

Theorem 5.

$$\frac{U_0 \sqsupseteq_D U_1}{U_0 \sqsupseteq_{sp} U_1}$$

□

Turning now to showing the D-refinement is *complete* with respect to SP-refinement.

Proposition 26. *The following rule is derivable:*

$$\frac{U_0 \sqsupseteq_{sp} U_1 \quad t \in_D U_0(t,t)}{t \in_D U_1(t,t)}$$

Proof.

$$\frac{\dfrac{U_0 \sqsupseteq_{sp} U_1 \quad \dfrac{t_0 \star t_1' \in_D U_0(t,t)}{t_0.t_1'.Q_0}}{t_0.t_1'.Q_1}}{t_0 \star t_1' \in_D U_1(t,t)}$$

□

Now the second elimination rule in D-refinement.

Proposition 27. *The following rule is derivable:*

$$\frac{U_0 \sqsupseteq_{sp} U_1 \quad t \in_D U_0(t,f)}{t \in_D U_1(t,f)}$$

Proof. The proof is identical to the proof of proposition 18, modulo the following substitutions: $\in_D$ replaces $\in_H$, $\sqsupseteq_{sp}$ replaces $\sqsupseteq_s$ and the application of ($\sqsupseteq_{sp_0}^{-}$) replaces the application of ($\sqsupseteq_{s_0}^{-}$).

□

This leads directly to the following theorem:

Theorem 6.

$$\frac{U_0 \sqsupseteq_{sp} U_1}{U_0 \sqsupseteq_D U_1}$$

□

Theorems 5 and 6 together establish that D-refinement and SP-refinement are equivalent.

D-Refinement and DD-Refinement Are Equivalent. We begin by showing that DD-refinement satisfies the two D-refinement elimination rules. Similarly to the counterpart investigation in the designs framework (section 5.1), one of these results relies on an auxiliary lemma demonstrating that DD-refinement guarantees that preconditions do not strengthen (*i.e.* satisfies the rule $(\sqsupseteq^{-}_{spo})$).

Lemma 3. *The following rule is derivable:*

$$\frac{U_0 \sqsupseteq_{DD} U_1 \quad t_0.P_1}{t_0.P_0}$$

Proof. The bulk of the proof is identical to the proof of lemma 2. That is, the basic derivation is, *mutatis mutandis*, identical to its counterpart: $\sqsupseteq_{DD}$ replaces $\sqsupseteq_{HH}$. Where δ proof branch is:

$$\cfrac{\cfrac{}{\neg t_0.t_1'.Q_1}\,(2) \quad \cfrac{\cfrac{U_0 \sqsupseteq_{DD} U_1 \quad \cfrac{\cfrac{}{\neg t_0.P_0}\,(1)}{t_0 \star t_1' \in_{NLT} U_0}\,(L.\ 1(i)) \quad \cfrac{\cfrac{}{\neg t_0.P_0}\,(1)}{t_0 \star t_1' \notin_Z U_0}}{t_0 \star t_1' \in_{NLT} U_1} \quad t_0.P_1}{t_0.t_1'.Q_1}}{false}$$

□

Now considering the first elimination rule in D-refinement.

Proposition 28. *The following rule is derivable:*

$$\frac{U_0 \sqsupseteq_{DD} U_1 \quad t \in_D U_0(t,t)}{t \in_D U_1(t,t)}$$

Proof. Consider the following derivation which requires the *law of excluded middle*:

$$\cfrac{\cfrac{\cfrac{}{\neg t_0.t_1'.Q_1 \lor t_0.t_1'.Q_1}\,(LEM) \quad \begin{array}{c}\delta_0\\ \vdots \\ t_0.t_1'.Q_1\end{array} \quad \cfrac{}{t_0.t_1'.Q_1}\,(1)}{t_0.t_1'.Q_1}\,(1)}{t_0 \star t_1' \in_D U_1(t,t)}$$

Where δ_0 stands for the following branch:

$$\cfrac{\begin{array}{c}\beta_0\\ \vdots\\ \neg t_0.t_1'.Q_0 \lor \neg t_0.P_0\end{array} \quad \cfrac{\cfrac{\cfrac{}{\neg t_0.t_1'.Q_0}\,(2) \quad \cfrac{t_0 \star t_1' \in_D U_0(t,t)}{t_0.t_1'.Q_0}}{false}}{t_0.t_1'.Q_1} \quad \begin{array}{c}\beta_1\\ \vdots\\ t_0.t_1'.Q_1\end{array}}{t_0.t_1'.Q_1}\,(2)$$

Where β_0 is:

$$\cfrac{\cfrac{U_0 \sqsupseteq_{DD} U_1 \quad \cfrac{\cfrac{}{\neg t_0.t_1'.Q_1}\,(1)}{t_1' \star t_0 \in_{NLT} U_1^\dagger}\,(L.\ 1(i)) \quad \cfrac{\cfrac{}{\neg t_0.t_1'.Q_1}\,(1)}{t_1' \star t_0 \notin_Z U_1^\dagger}}{t_1' \star t_0 \notin_Z U_0^\dagger}}{\neg t_0.t_1'.Q_0 \lor \neg t_0.P_0}$$

and β_1 is:

$$\dfrac{\dfrac{\dfrac{}{\neg t_0.P_0}\,(2) \quad \dfrac{\dfrac{U_0 \sqsupseteq_{DD} U_1 \quad \dfrac{\dfrac{}{\neg t_0.t_1'.Q_1}\,(1)}{t_1' \star t_0 \in_{NLT} U_1^{\dagger}}\,(L.\ 1(i)) \quad \dfrac{\dfrac{}{\neg t_0.t_1'.Q_1}\,(1)}{t_1' \star t_0 \notin_{Z} U_1^{\dagger}}}{t_1' \star t_0 \in_{NLT} U_0^{\dagger}} \quad \dfrac{t_0 \star t_1' \in_D U_0(t,t)}{t_0.t_1'.Q_0}}{t_0.P_0}}{\mathit{false}}}{t_0.t_1'.Q_1}$$

□

Turning to the second elimination rule in D-refinement.

Proposition 29. *The following rule is derivable:*

$$\frac{U_0 \sqsupseteq_{DD} U_1 \quad t \in_D U_0(t,f)}{t \in_D U_1(t,f)}$$

Proof.

$$\dfrac{\dfrac{U_0 \sqsupseteq_{DD} U_1 \quad \dfrac{t_0 \star t_1' \in_D U_0(t,f)}{\neg t_0.P_0}}{\neg t_0.P_1}\,(L.\ 3)}{t_0 \star t_1' \in_D U_1(t,f)}$$

□

Then by propositions 28 and 29, in addition to the rule $(\sqsupseteq_D^{+})$, we get the following theorem immediately:

Theorem 7.

$$\frac{U_0 \sqsupseteq_{DD} U_1}{U_0 \sqsupseteq_D U_1}$$

□

We now demonstrate that D-refinement satisfies the four DD-refinement elimination rules.

Proposition 30. *The following rule is derivable:*

$$\frac{U_0 \sqsupseteq_D U_1 \quad t \in_{NLT} U_1^{\dagger} \quad t \notin_Z U_1^{\dagger}}{t \in_{NLT} U_0^{\dagger}}$$

Proof.

$$\dfrac{\dfrac{\dfrac{t_1' \star t_0 \notin_Z U_1^{\dagger}}{\neg t_0.P_1 \vee \neg t_0.t_1'.Q_1} \quad \dfrac{\dfrac{\dfrac{}{\neg t_0.P_1}\,(2) \quad \dfrac{t_1' \star t_0 \in_{NLT} U_1^{\dagger} \quad \overset{\delta}{\vdots}\; t_0.t_1'.Q_1}{t_0.P_1}}{\mathit{false}}}{t_0.P_0} \quad \dfrac{\dfrac{\dfrac{}{\neg t_0.t_1'.Q_1}\,(2) \quad \overset{\delta}{\vdots}\; t_0.t_1'.Q_1}{\mathit{false}}}{t_0.P_0}}{t_0.P_0}\,(2)}{t_1' \star t_0 \in_{NLT} U_0^{\dagger}}\,(1)$$

Where δ stands for the following branch:

$$\dfrac{U_0 \sqsupseteq_D U_1 \qquad \dfrac{\overline{t_0.t_1'.Q_0}\ (1)}{t_0 \star t_1' \in_D U_0(t,t)}}{\dfrac{t_0 \star t_1' \in_D U_1(t,t)}{t_0.t_1'.Q_1}}$$

□

Now the second elimination rule in DD-refinement.

Proposition 31. *The following rule is derivable:*

$$\frac{U_0 \sqsupseteq_D U_1 \quad t \in_{NLT} U_1^\dagger \quad t \notin_Z U_1^\dagger}{t \notin_Z U_0^\dagger}$$

Proof. Consider the following derivation which requires the *law of excluded middle*:

$$\dfrac{\dfrac{}{t_0.t_1'.Q_0 \vee \neg t_0.t_1'.Q_0}\ (LEM) \qquad \begin{matrix}\beta\\ \vdots\\ t_1' \star t_0 \notin_Z U_0^\dagger\end{matrix} \qquad \dfrac{\dfrac{}{\neg t_0.t_1'.Q_0}\ (1)}{t_1' \star t_0 \notin_Z U_0^\dagger}}{t_1' \star t_0 \notin_Z U_0^\dagger}\ (1)$$

Where β is:

$$\dfrac{\dfrac{\dfrac{t_1' \star t_0 \notin_Z U_1^\dagger}{\neg t_0.P_1 \vee \neg t_0.t_1'.Q_1} \qquad \dfrac{\dfrac{\dfrac{}{\neg t_0.P_1}\ (2) \quad \dfrac{t_1' \star t_0 \in_{NLT} U_1^\dagger \quad \begin{matrix}\delta\\ \vdots\\ t_0.t_1'.Q_1\end{matrix}}{t_0.P_1}}{false}}{\neg t_0.t_1'.Q_0} \qquad \dfrac{\dfrac{\dfrac{}{\neg t_0.t_1'.Q_1}\ (2) \quad \begin{matrix}\delta\\ \vdots\\ t_0.t_1'.Q_1\end{matrix}}{false}}{\neg t_0.t_1'.Q_0}}{\neg t_0.t_1'.Q_0}\ (2)}{t_1' \star t_0 \notin_Z U_0^\dagger}$$

and δ is identical to δ branch in the proof of proposition 30.

□

Turning to the third elimination rule in DD-refinement.

Proposition 32. *The following rule is derivable:*

$$\frac{U_0 \sqsupseteq_D U_1 \quad t \in_{NLT} U_0 \quad t \notin_Z U_0}{t \in_{NLT} U_1}$$

Proof.

$$\dfrac{\dfrac{\dfrac{t_0 \star t_1' \notin_Z U_0}{\neg t_0.P_0 \vee \neg t_0.t_1'.Q_0} \qquad \dfrac{\dfrac{\dfrac{}{\neg t_0.P_0}\ (2) \quad \dfrac{U_0 \sqsupseteq_D U_1 \quad \dfrac{}{t_0.P_1}\ (1)}{t_0.P_0}\ (P.\,24)}{false}}{t_0.t_1'.Q_1} \qquad \begin{matrix}\delta\\ \vdots\\ t_0.t_1'.Q_1\end{matrix}}{t_0.t_1'.Q_1}\ (2)}{t_0 \star t_1' \in_{NLT} U_1}\ (1)$$

Where δ stands for the following branch:

$$\cfrac{\cfrac{}{\neg t_0.t_1'.Q_0}\,(2) \quad \cfrac{t_0 \star t_1' \in_{NLT} U_0 \quad \cfrac{U_0 \sqsupseteq_D U_1 \quad \cfrac{}{t_0.P_1}\,(1)}{t_0.P_0}\,(P.24)}{t_0.t_1'.Q_0}}{\cfrac{false}{t_0.t_1'.Q_1}}$$

□

And, finally, the fourth elimination rule in DD-refinement.

Proposition 33. *The following rule is derivable:*

$$\frac{U_0 \sqsupseteq_D U_1 \quad t \in_{NLT} U_0 \quad t \notin_Z U_0}{t \notin_Z U_1}$$

Proof. The proof is, *mutatis mutandis*, identical to the proof of proposition 22: $\sqsupseteq_D$ replaces $\sqsupseteq_H$ and the applications of proposition 24 replace proposition 15.

□

Then by propositions 30, 31, 32 and 33, in addition to the rule ($\sqsupseteq^+_{DD}$), the following theorem is immediately derivable:

Theorem 8.

$$\frac{U_0 \sqsupseteq_D U_1}{U_0 \sqsupseteq_{DD} U_1}$$

□

Together, theorems 7 and 8 establish that the theories of D-refinement and DD-refinement are equivalent. Therefore, D-refinement, DD-refinement and SP-refinement are all equivalent. Once again, we have demonstrated that the concepts of specification and refinement in the UTP prescriptions paradigm can be unified within a homogeneous relational framework without any artificial auxiliary mechanisms.

6 Conclusions and Further Work

In this paper, we have analysed the mathematical relationships amongst a number of formalisms using a proof-theoretic relational framework based on two-predicate schema specifications. In particular, we have conducted an examination of the concepts of specification and refinement in two paradigms based on the idea of UTP: Hoare and He's *designs* [23] and Dunne's *prescriptions* [15, 16]. We have shown that the theory of refinement in each of the two paradigms is related to both an appropriate proof-theoretic characterisation of refinement for two-predicate schema specifications and a certain theory of refinement expressed in a purely homogeneous relational form.

What we have not examined here is the way *compound* schema expressions are interpreted in these formalisms and the manner in which refinement *interacts* with such expressions. Z provides a very rich calculus of schema operations for structuring specifications in a modular manner, but none of these operators is *monotonic* with respect to its standard notion of refinement; this has a major effect on their usefulness in the context of program development. The reasons for this deficiency are explored in great detail in [13], [12] and [6, ch.6]. However, there is a very interesting way which enables us to rehabilitate monotonicity in schema-based formalisms: we could take the interpretation of designs (definition 5) or the interpretation of prescriptions (definition 8) as the semantics for atomic schemas and then introduce interpretations for compound operation schema expressions by recursion over their structure using (almost) the standard relational operations. In this way, refinement could then be the subset relation on the semantics and the calculus of schema operations would be (trivially) *fully-monotonic*.

There are various examples of formalisms which employ a similar strategy: the model described in [22] is an example of this where the interpretation of atomic operation schemas is taken to be *sets of permissible implementations*, [17] is closely related to an example in which the underlying semantics is given by a *weakest precondition* semantics and νZ [19, 20] is an example of this where the underlying interpretation is taken to be Woodcock's *lifted-totalisation* semantics [28].

There are two major ramifications to this approach. Firstly, the fundamental relation here is *refinement* (as opposed to *equality* in Z); equality would then appear as inter-refinability. Secondly, partiality in this model denotes over-constrained specifications (*i.e. magic*), whereas all partiality in Z (arising from either under-constrained or over-constrained specifications) is interpreted as chaotic divergence (including $\perp$). Therefore, the *nature* of the schema operations in this approach is different: the operations no longer express exactly their usual informal semantics. These changes are explored, to a certain extent, in νZ. Nonetheless, much work remains to be done both at the level of infrastructure and at the pragmatic level. Furthermore, it would be very interesting to explore the relationship between νZ and a similar approach based on designs/prescriptions as the underlying interpretation.

Acknowledgements

This work has been influenced in its development by too many people to name explicitly. However, special thanks for particularly important discussions and comments go to Steve Dunne, Steve Reeves, Ray Turner, John Derrick, Steve Schneider, Bill Stoddart and Frank Zeyda. We would like to thank one of the referees for spotting an presentational inconsistency in the original submission.

References

1. D. Azada and P. Muenchaisri, editors. *APSEC 2003: 10th Asia-Pacific Software Engineering Conference, Chiangmai, Thailand, December 10-12, 2003, Proceedings*. IEEE Computer Society Press, December 2003.
2. D. Bjørner, C. A. R. Hoare, and H. Langmaack, editors. *VDM '90, VDM and Z – Formal Methods in Software Development, Third International Symposium of VDM Europe, Kiel, FRG, April 17-21, 1990, Proceedings*, volume 428 of *Lecture Notes in Computer Science*. Springer, 1990.
3. D.Bert, J. P. Bowen, S. King, and M. Waldén, editors. *ZB 2003: Formal Specification and Development in Z and B, Third International Conference of B and Z Users, Turku, Finland, June 4-6, 2003, Proceedings*, volume 2651 of *Lecture Notes in Computer Science*. Springer, 2003.
4. J. Derrick and E. A. Boiten. *Refinement in Z and Object-Z: Foundations and Advanced Applications*. Formal Approaches to Computing and Information Technology – FACIT. Springer, May 2001.
5. J. Derrick and E. A. Boiten, editors. *REFINE 2005 International Workshop*, Electronic Notes in Theoretical Computer Science. BCS-FACS, April 2005.

6. M. Deutsch. *An Analysis of Total Correctness Refinement Models for Partial Relation Semantics*. PhD thesis, University of Essex, 2005.
7. M. Deutsch and M. C. Henson. An Analysis of Backward Simulation Data-Refinement for Partial Relation Semantics. In *APSEC 2003 [1]*, pages 38–48, 2003.
8. M. Deutsch and M. C. Henson. An Analysis of Forward Simulation Data Refinement. In *ZB 2003 [3]*, pages 148–167, 2003.
9. M. Deutsch and M. C. Henson. An Analysis of Operation-Refinement in an Abortive Paradigm. In *REFINE 2005 [5]*, 2005.
10. M. Deutsch, M. C. Henson, and S. Reeves. Results on Formal Stepwise Design in Z. In P. Strooper and P. Muenchaisri, editors, *APSEC 2002: 9th Asia-Pacific Software Engineering Conference, Gold Coast, Queensland, Australia, December 4-6, 2002, Proceedings*, pages 33–42. IEEE Computer Society Press, December 2002.
11. M. Deutsch, M. C. Henson, and S. Reeves. An analysis of total correctness refinement models for partial relation semantics I. *Logic Journal of the IGPL*, 11(3):287–317, 2003.
12. M. Deutsch, M. C. Henson, and S. Reeves. Modular reasoning in Z: scrutinising monotonicity and refinement. *University of Essex, technical report CSM-407 (under consideration of FACJ)*, December 2003.
13. M. Deutsch, M. C. Henson, and S. Reeves. Operation Refinement and Monotonicity in the Schema Calculus. In *ZB 2003 [3]*, pages 103–126, 2003.
14. A. Diller. *Z: An Introduction to Formal Methods*. J. Wiley and Sons, 2nd edition, 1994.
15. S. E. Dunne. Recasting Hoare and He's Unifying Theory of Programs in the Context of General Correctness. In A. Butterfield, G. Strong, and C. Pahl, editors, *IWFM 2001: 5th Irish Workshop on Formal Methods, Dublin, Ireland, 16-17 July 2001*, Workshops in Computing. BCS, 2001.
16. S. E. Dunne. A Predicative Model for General Correctness. *Departmental Seminar, Department of Computer Science, University of Essex*, March 2004.
17. L. J. Groves. *Evolutionary Software Development in the Refinement Calculus*. PhD thesis, Victoria University, 2000.
18. E. C. R. Hehner. *The Logic of Programming*. Prentice Hall International, 1984.
19. M. C. Henson, M. Deutsch, and B. Kajtazi. The Specification Logic νZ. *University of Essex, technical report CSM-421*, 2004.
20. M. C. Henson and B. Kajtazi. The Specification Logic νZ. In *REFINE 2005 [5]*, 2005.
21. M. C. Henson and S. Reeves. Investigating Z. *Logic and Computation*, 10(1):43–73, 2000.
22. M. C. Henson and S. Reeves. A logic for schema-based program development. *Formal Aspects of Computing*, 15(1):84–99, 2003.
23. C.A.R Hoare and J. He. *Unifying Theories of Programming*. Prentice Hall International, 1998.
24. S. King. Z and the Refinement Calculus. In *VDM '90 [2]*, pages 164–188, 1990.
25. B. Potter, J. Sinclair, and D. Till. *An Introduction to Formal Specification and Z*. Prentice Hall, 2nd edition, 1996.
26. J. M. Spivey. *The Z Notation: A Reference Manual*. Prentice Hall, 2nd edition, 1992.
27. I. Toyn, editor. *Z Notation: Final Committee Draft, CD 13568.2*. Z Standards Panel, 1999.
28. J. C. P. Woodcock and J. Davies. *Using Z: Specification, Refinement and Proof*. Prentice Hall, 1996.

A Specification Logic - A Synopsis

In this appendix, we will summarise only few relevant features of the Z-logic, settling some notational conventions in the process. This is included for convenience only and the reader may wish to consult [21] and [11] for a more leisurely treatment of our notational and meta-notational conventions.

Our analysis takes place in the "Church-style" version of the Z-logic due to Henson and Reeves, namely $\mathcal{Z}_C$ [21]. This provides a convenient basis, in particular a satisfactory logical account, upon which the present work can be formalised.

$\mathcal{Z}_C$ is a typed theory in which the types of higher-order logic are extended with *schema types* whose values are unordered, label-indexed tuples called *bindings*. For example, if the T_i are types and the z_i are labels (constants) then: $[\cdots \mathsf{z}_i : T_i \cdots]$ is a (schema) type. Values of this type are bindings, of the form: $\langle\!| \cdots \mathsf{z}_i \Rrightarrow t_i \cdots |\!\rangle$, where the term t_i has type T_i.

The symbols $\preceq$, $\curlywedge$, $\curlyvee$ and $-$ denote the *schema subtype* relation, and the operations of *schema type intersection* and (compatible) *schema type union* and *schema type subtraction*. *Binding selection*, written $t.\mathbf{x}$, is axiomatised so that, for example: $\langle\!| \mathsf{x} \Rrightarrow 2, \mathsf{y} \Rrightarrow 3 |\!\rangle.\mathsf{x} = 2$. Selection generalises so that $t.P$ denotes the predicate P in which each observation $\mathbf{x}$ is replaced by $t.\mathbf{x}$. We let U (with diacriticals when necessary) range over atomic operation schemas of the form $[T \mid P \mid Q]$. These are sets of bindings linking, as usual, before observations with after observations. We also permit *binding concatenation*, written $t_0 \star t_1$, when the alphabets of t_0 and t_1 are disjoint:

Definition 14. *Suppose that* $l_i \neq k_j \quad (0 \leq i \leq n, 0 \leq j \leq m)$.

$$\langle\!| l_0 \Rrightarrow t_0 \cdots l_n \Rrightarrow t_n |\!\rangle \star \langle\!| k_0 \Rrightarrow s_0 \cdots k_m \Rrightarrow s_m |\!\rangle =_{df} \langle\!| l_0 \Rrightarrow t_0 \cdots l_n \Rrightarrow t_n, k_0 \Rrightarrow s_0 \cdots k_m \Rrightarrow s_m |\!\rangle$$

This is, in fact, exclusively used for partitioning bindings in operation schemas into before and after components, so the terms involved are necessarily disjoint.

Unifying Theories in ProofPower-Z

Marcel Oliveira, Ana Cavalcanti, and Jim Woodcock

Department of Computer Science, The University of York
Heslington, York, YO10 5DD, United Kingdom

Abstract. The increasing interest in the combination of different computational paradigms is very well represented by Hoare & He in the *Unifying Theories of Programming*. In this paper, we present a mechanisation of part of that work in a theorem prover, ProofPower-Z; the theories of alphabetised relations, designs, reactive and CSP processes are in the scope of this paper. An account of how this mechanisation is done, and more interestingly, of what issues were raised and of our decisions, is presented here. We aim at providing tool support for further explorations of Hoare & He's unification, and for the mechanisation of languages based on this unification. More specifically, *Circus*, a specification language that combines Z, CSP, specification statements, and Dijkstra's guarded command language is our final target.

Keywords: Unifying Theories of Programming, theorem prover.

1 Introduction

Researchers have concentrated their interest in the combination of programming paradigms, which consider different aspects and stages of software development. Hoare & He did one of the most significant works towards unification [9]. In the *Unifying Theories of Programming* (UTP), they use Tarski's relational calculus to give a denotational semantics to constructs from several programming paradigms. Relations between an initial and a subsequent observation of computer devices are used to give meaning to specifications, designs, and programs. Observational variables and associated healthiness conditions characterise theories for imperative, communicating, or sequential processes and their designs.

Following this trend of research, *Circus* [21, 2] combines a model-based language, Z [22], a process algebra, CSP [8], Dijkstra's language of commands, and specification statements [10]. It differs from other combinations [19, 16, 5, 20] in that it has an associated refinement theory [2, 14, 13]. The mechanical proof of more than one hundred refinement laws requires the mechanisation of the *Circus* semantics, and will be the basis for its theorem prover. In previous work [21], we define a Z semantics for *Circus*. Although usable for reasoning about systems specified in *Circus*, it is not appropriate to prove properties of the language itself.

In early work [18], Sherif and He present a time model for *Circus*. Qin *et.al.* [15] used the UTP to formalise the semantics of TCOZ and capture some of its new features for the first time. This semantics is being used as a reference document

S. Dunne and W. Stoddart (Eds.): UTP 2006, LNCS 4010, pp. 123–140, 2006.

in the development of tools for TCOZ and as a semantics foundation for proving soundness of these tools. Woodcock and Hughes use the UTP model [23] in order to give a formal semantics to a programming language that contains shared variables. Our work provides mechanical support not only to *Circus*, but also to any language that has the UTP as its theoretical basis.

In recent work [3], we summarise the alphabetised relational calculus, and the theory of precondition-postcondition specifications, called designs. A detailed theory for reactive processes is presented, and then combined with the theory of designs, to provide the model for CSP. By mechanising the theories of reactive processes and CSP, we enable a further exploration on these results.

We present here the first step towards mechanising the *Circus* semantics and the proof of its refinement laws: the mechanisation of the UTP in the theorem prover ProofPower-Z [1]. The definitions of the theories of relations, designs, reactive processes, and CSP, and more than three-hundred and seventy theorems, is the result of our work. Many issues arose from the existence of an alphabet and from our intention of proving refinement laws; we discuss them here.

Section 2 presents the UTP and ProofPower-Z. In Section 3, we discuss design issues and describe the theory hierarchy we created. Section 4 describes the mechanisation of the UTP relations, designs, reactive processes, and CSP. The proof of one theorem illustrates our approach. Finally, in Section 5, we draw our conclusions and describe future work.

2 Preliminaries: UTP and ProofPower-Z

The UTP is a framework based on an alphabetised extension of Tarski's relational calculus. Every program, design, and specification is interpreted in the UTP as a relation between an initial observation and a single subsequent observation, which may be either an intermediate or a final observation of the behaviour of a program execution. The relations are defined as predicates over observational variables. The initial observations of each variable are undecorated, and subsequent observations are decorated with a dash.

Several theories share common ideas; sequential composition, conditional, nondeterminism, and parallelism are some of them. Refinement is interpreted as inclusion of relations: reverse implication. Every relation is a pair $(\alpha P, P)$, where αP is the alphabet: set of observational variables that can be free in the predicate P. Healthiness conditions are used to test a specification or design for feasibility, and reject it, if it makes implementation impossible in the target language. They are often expressed in terms of an idempotent function ϕ that makes a program healthy. Every healthy program P must be a fixed point $P = \phi\, P$).

Figure 1 presents how some UTP theories [9] are related. Relations are predicates with an input and an output (dashed) alphabet. Designs are specifications written in terms of pre and postconditions. Reactive processes are programs whose behaviour may depend on interactions with an environment. Finally, CSP processes is a failures-divergences model for CSP, enriched with

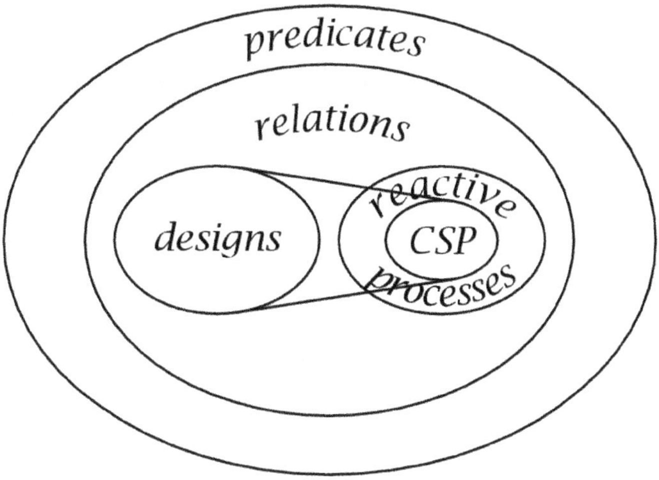

Fig. 1. Theories in the UTP

state; they can be characterised as relations that result from applying R to designs.

ProofPower-Z is a higher-order tactic based theorem prover implemented using New Jersey SML, that supports specifications and proofs in Z. It extends ProofPower-HOL, which builds on ideas arising from research at the Universities of Cambridge [7] and Edinburgh [6]. Some of the extensions provided by the New Jersey SML were used in ProofPower-Z, in order to achieve features such as a theory hierarchy, extension of the character set accepted by the metalanguage ML, and facilities for quotation of object language (Z or HOL) expressions, and for automatic pretty-printing of the representation of such expressions.

As it is an extension of ProofPower-HOL, definitions can be made using Z, HOL, and even SML, which is the input command language. ProofPower-Z also offers the possibility of defining proof tactics, which can be used to reduce, and modularise proofs. Among other analysis support, ProofPower-Z provides syntax and type checking, schema expansion, precondition calculation, domain checking, and general theorem proving. Using the subgoal package, goals can be split in simpler subgoals. The Z notation used in ProofPower-Z is almost the same as that of the Z standard. We explain the differences as needed.

ProofPower-Z comes with a large number of verified theories. However, as it supports a powerful logic, the level of automation is lower than in theorem provers that support, for example, first-order logic. On the other hand, it has been successfully used in industry, and was a natural choice as a basis for a *Circus* theorem prover, as it is routinely used by our industrial partner: QinetiQ.

3 Design Issues

This section describes the issues raised during the automation of the UTP. The first difficulty that we faced was that the name of a variable is used to refer both to the name itself and to its value. For instance, in the relation $(\{x\}, x = 0)$, the left-most x indicates the name x, while the right-most x stands for the value of x. We make explicit the difference between a variable name and a variable value.

We discarded the option of giving an axiomatic semantics to relations, since we would not be able to use most of the theorems that are built-in in ProofPower-Z to reason about sets and other models. Our relations are pairs of sets.

Since we want to prove refinement laws, our mechanisation gives the possibility of expressing and proving meta-theorems. A shallow-embedding, in which the mapping from language constructs to their semantic representation is part of the meta-language, would not allow us to express such theorems. We use a deep-embedding, where the syntax and the semantics of the alphabetised relations is formalised inside the host language. The deep-embedding has the additional advantage of providing the possibility of introducing new predicate combinators.

The syntax of relations and designs could be expressed as a data type (Z free types), say *PRED*, for the relations. In this case, the semantics would be given as a partial ($\nrightarrow$) function $f : PRED \nrightarrow PRED$. If we took this approach, most of the proofs would be by induction over *PRED*. Any extension to the language would require proving most of the laws again. Instead, we express the language constructors as functions; this is a standard approach in functional languages. Extensions require only the definition of the new constructors, and that they preserve any healthiness conditions; no proofs need to be redone.

Using SML as a meta-language would not give us a deep-embedding. We were left with the choice of Z or HOL. If we used HOL as meta-language, reusing the definitions of Z constructs would not be possible, because they are written in SML. Because of our knowledge of Z, and the expressiveness of its toolkit, we have used Z as our meta and target language.

In Figure 2, we present our hierarchy of theories. In order to handle sequences, we extend the ProofPower-Z's theory *z-library*; the result is *utp-z-library*. The theory *utp-rel* is that of general UTP relations. It includes basic alphabetised operators like conjunction and existential quantification; relational operators like alphabet extension, sequential composition, and skip; and refinement. Like all our theories, it includes the operator definitions and their laws.

Two theories inherit from *utp-rel*: *utp-okay* is concerned with an observational variable *okay*, and *utp-wtr* with *wait*, *trace*, and *ref*. These are the main variables of the theory of reactive processes. The theory *utp-okay* is the parent of *utp-des*, the theory for designs. Along with *utp-wtr*, *utp-okay* is also the parent of the reactive processes theory (*utp-rea*), which redefines part of *utp-rel*. The theory for CSP processes, *utp-csp*, inherits from both *utp-rea* and *utp-des*. The theory for *Circus* (*utp-circus*) inherits from *utp-csp*; it is under development. Our proofs of the laws of a theory does not expand definitions of its parent theory; it uses the parent's laws. This provides modularisation and encapsulation.

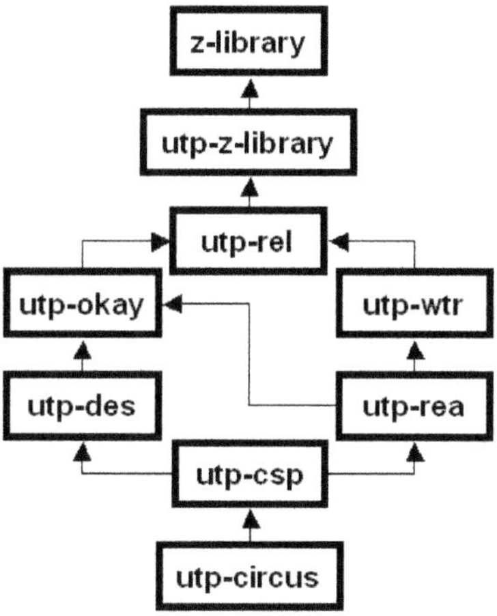

Fig. 2. Theories in the UTP

4 Mechanisation

In this section we describe in detail our ProofPower-Z theories. For the sake of presentation, we do not present the Z generated by the ProofPower-Z document preparation tool, which has an awkward indentation for expressions. Instead, we present a better indented copy of the pretty-printed ProofPower-Z expressions.

4.1 Relations

A name is an element of the given set $[NAME]$. Each relation has an alphabet of type $ALPHABET \mathrel{\widehat{=}} \mathbb{P}\, NAME$ (the Z abbreviation $N == A$ is provided as $N \mathrel{\widehat{=}} A$ in ProofPower-Z; it gives a name N to the mathematical object A). Every alphabet a contains an input alphabet of undashed names, and an output alphabet of dashed names. Instead of using free types, which would lead to more complicated proofs in ProofPower-Z, we use the injective ($\rightarrowtail$) function $dash : NAME \rightarrowtail NAME$ to model name decoration. The set of *dashed* names is defined as the range of *dash*. The complement of this set is the set of *undashed* names; hence, names are either *dashed* or *undashed*, but multiple dashes is allowed. For the sake of conciseness, we omit the definitions of the functions in_a and out_a, which return the input and the output alphabets of a given alphabet. All the definitions and proof scripts can be found elsewhere [12].

An alphabet a in which $n \in a \Leftrightarrow n' \in a$, for every undashed name n, is called *homogeneous*. For us, n' is mechanised as $dash\ n$. Similarly, a pair of alphabets $(a1, a2)$ is *composable* if $n \in a2 \Leftrightarrow n' \in a1$, for every undashed name n.

A value is an element of the free-type $VALUE$, which can be an integer, a boolean, a set of values, a sequence of values, a pair of values, a channel, or a special synchronisation value.

$$\begin{array}{rl} VAL ::= & Int(\mathbb{Z}) \mid Bool(BOOL) \mid Set(\mathbb{P}\ VAL) \mid Seq(\mathrm{seq}\ VAL) \\ \mid & Pair(VAL \times VAL) \mid Channel(NAME) \mid Sync \end{array}$$

In ProofPower-Z, $Bool(BOOL)$ stands for the Z constructor $Bool\langle\!\langle BOOL\rangle\!\rangle$, which introduces a collection of constants, one for each element of the set $BOOL$. The ProofPower-Z type $BOOL$ is the booleans. The type VAL can be extended without any impact on the proofs.

Although we are defining an untyped theory, the observational variables have types; for instance, *okay* is a boolean. For this reason, we specify some types; for instance, booleans are in the set $BOOL\_VAL \mathrel{\widehat=} \{Bool(true), Bool(false)\}$, channels are in the set $CHANNEL\_VAL \mathrel{\widehat=} \{n : NAME \bullet Channel(n)\}$, and events are in the set $EVENT\_VAL \mathrel{\widehat=} \{c : CHANNEL\_VAL;\ v : VAL \bullet Pair(c, v)\}$.

Three definitions allow us to abstract from the syntax of expressions. The set of relations ($\leftrightarrow$) between values is $RELATION \mathrel{\widehat=} VAL \leftrightarrow VAL$. The set of unary functions is $UNARY\_F \mathrel{\widehat=} VAL \nrightarrow VAL$; similarly, for binary functions we have the set $BINARY\_F \mathrel{\widehat=} (VAL \times VAL) \nrightarrow VAL$, which defines the set of partial functions from pairs of values to values. For instance, the sum function is $\{(Int(0), Int(0)) \mapsto Int(0), (Int(0), Int(1)) \mapsto Int(1), \ldots\}$. An expression can be a value, a name, a relation, or a unary or binary function application.

$$\begin{array}{rl} EXP ::= & Val(VAL) \mid Var(NAME) \mid Rel(RELATION \times EXP \times EXP) \\ \mid & Fun_1(UNARY\_F \times EXP) \mid Fun_2(BINARY\_F \times EXP \times EXP) \end{array}$$

The definitions for unary functions, binary functions, and relations only deal with values; $Fun_1(f, e)$ can only be evaluated once e is evaluated to some VAL.

A binding is defined as $BINDING \mathrel{\widehat=} NAME \nrightarrow VAL$, and $BINDINGS$ is the set of bindings. Given a binding b and an expression e with free-variables in the domain (dom) of b, $Eval(b, e)$ gives the value of e in b (beta-reduction). A relation is modelled in our work by the type REL_PRED defined below. Basically, a relation is a pair: the first element is its alphabet, and the second is a set of bindings, which gives us all bindings that satisfy the UTP predicate modelled by the relation. The domain of the bindings must be equal to the alphabet. Optional models in which this restriction could be relaxed are possible; however, they would lead us to more complex definitions as we discuss in Section 5. The set-comprehension $\{x : s \mid p \bullet e\}$ denotes the set of all expressions e such that x is taken from s and satisfies the condition p. Usually, e contains one or more free occurrences of x. The *true* condition and the constructor x may be omitted.

$$\begin{array}{l} REL\_PRED \mathrel{\widehat=} \\ \quad \{a : ALPHABET;\ bs : BINDINGS \mid (\forall\, b : bs \bullet \mathrm{dom}\, b = a) \bullet (a, bs)\} \end{array}$$

This follows directly from the definition of alphabetised predicates of the UTP.

In our work, we use Z axiomatic definitions, which introduce constrained objects, to define our constructs. For instance, let us consider the following axiomatic definition.

$$\begin{array}{|l} x : s \\ \hline p \end{array}$$

It introduces a new symbol x, an element of s, satisfying the predicate p.

Our first construct represents the truth. For a given alphabet a, $True_R\ a$ is defined as the pair with alphabet a, and with all the bindings with domain a.

$$\begin{array}{|l} True_R : ALPHABET \rightarrow REL\_PRED \\ \hline \forall\, a : ALPHABET \bullet True_R\ a = (a, \{b : BINDING \mid \operatorname{dom} b = a\}) \end{array}$$

In our work, we subscript the constructs in order to make it easier to identify to which theory they belong to; we use R for the theory of relations.

Nothing satisfies *false*: the second element of $False_R\ a$ is the empty set.

$$\begin{array}{|l} False_R : ALPHABET \rightarrow REL\_PRED \\ \hline \forall\, a : ALPHABET \bullet False_R\ a = (a, \varnothing) \end{array}$$

This operator is the main motivation for representing relations as pairs. If we had defined relations just as a set of bindings with the same domain a, which would be considered as the alphabet, we would not be able to tell the difference between $False_R\ a_1$ and $False_R\ a_2$, since both sets would be empty. Besides, it is important to notice the difference between $True_R\ \varnothing$ and $False_R\ \varnothing$: the former has a set that contains one empty set of bindings as its second element, and the latter has the empty set as its second element.

As we are working directly with the semantics of predicates, we are not able to give a syntactic characterisation of free variables. Instead, we have the concept of an unrestricted variable.

$$\begin{array}{|l} UnrestVar : REL\_PRED \rightarrow \mathbb{P}\, NAME \\ \hline \forall\, u : REL\_PRED \bullet \\ \quad UnrestVar\ u = \{n : u.1 \mid \forall\, b : u.2;\ v : VAL \bullet b \oplus \{n \mapsto v\} \in u.2\} \end{array}$$

For a relation u, a name n from its alphabet is unrestricted if, for every binding b of u, all the bindings obtained by changing the value of n in b are in u. In Z, $f \oplus g$ stands for the relational overriding of f with g; furthermore, $t.n$ refers to the *n-th* element of a tuple t.

All usual predicate combinators are defined. Conjunctions and disjunctions extend the alphabet of each relation to the alphabet of the other. The function $\oplus_R$ is alphabet extension; the values of the new variables are left unconstrained. In the following definition we make use of the Z domain restriction $A \lhd R$: it restricts a relation $R : X \leftrightarrow Y$ to a set A, which must be a subset of X, ignoring any member of R whose first element is not a member of A.

$$\begin{array}{|l} \_ \oplus_R \_ : REL\_PRED \times ALPHABET \rightarrow REL\_PRED \\ \hline \forall\, u : REL\_PRED;\ a : ALPHABET \\ \bullet\ u \oplus_R a = (u.1 \cup a, \{b : BINDING \mid (u.1 \lhd b) \in u.2 \wedge \operatorname{dom} b = u.1 \cup a\}) \end{array}$$

The conjunction is defined as the union of the alphabets and the intersection of the extended set of bindings of each relation.

$$\_ \wedge_R \_ : REL\_PRED \times REL\_PRED \rightarrow REL\_PRED$$

$$\forall u1, u2 : REL\_PRED \bullet$$
$$u1 \wedge_R u2 = (u1.1 \cup u2.1, (u1 \oplus_R u2.1).2 \cap (u2 \oplus_R u1.1).2)$$

The definition of disjunction is similar, but the union of the extend set of bindings is the result. We have proven that these definitions are idempotent, commutative, and associative, and that they distribute over each other. We have also proven that $True_R$ is the zero for disjunction and the unit for conjunction; similar laws were also proved for $False_R$. However, restrictions on the alphabets must be taken into account. For example, we have the unit law for conjunction. The ProofPower-Z output notation $n \vdash t$ gives name n to a theorem t. Besides, in Z, the quantification $\forall x : a \mid p \bullet q$ corresponds to the predicate $\forall x : a \bullet p \Rightarrow q$.

$$REL\_True\_\wedge_R\_id\_thm1$$
$$\vdash \forall a : ALPHABET;\ u : REL\_PRED \mid a \subseteq u.1 \bullet u \wedge_R True_R\ a = u$$

As expected, the conjunction of a relation u with $True_R$ is u, but the alphabet of $True_R$ must be a subset of the alphabet of u. Otherwise, the conjunction may have an alphabet other than that of u and the theorem does not hold.

The negation of a relation r does not change its alphabet. Only those bindings b that do not satisfy r ($b \notin r.2$) are included in the resulting bindings. For the sake of conciseness, we omit the trivial definitions of implication ($\_ \Rightarrow_R \_$), equivalence ($\_ \Leftrightarrow_R \_$), conditional ($\_ \lhd_R \_ \rhd_R \_$), that can be trivially be defined in terms of the previously defined operators.

The function $-_R$ removes variables from the alphabet of a relation using domain anti-restriction (domain removal) to remove names from the set of bindings. It is defined as $u -_R a = (u.1 \setminus a, \{b : u.2 \bullet a \Leftarrow b\})$. Complementary to domain restriction, the domain anti-restriction $A \Leftarrow R$, ignores any member of R, whose first element is a member of A. Existential quantification $\exists_{-R}$ simply removes the quantified variables from the alphabet and changes the bindings accordingly.

$$\exists_{-R} : (ALPHABET \times REL\_PRED) \rightarrow REL\_PRED$$

$$\forall a : ALPHABET;\ u : REL\_PRED \bullet \exists_{-R}(a, u) = u -_R a$$

Universal quantification $\forall_{-R}(a, u)$ is defined as $\neg_R \exists_{-R}(a, \neg_R u)$.

In the definition of the CSP *SKIP*, Hoare and He seem to use another existential quantification, in which the quantified variables are not removed from the alphabet. We define this new quantifier $\exists_R(a, u)$ as $(\exists_{-R}(a, u)) \oplus a$. Basically, we remove the quantified variables from the alphabet and include them again, leaving their values unrestricted.

Our sequential composition $u1;\ u2$ is not defined as in the UTP [9], an existential quantification on the intermediary state; the motivation is simplifying our proofs. In the UTP definition [9], the existential quantification is described using new 0-subscripted names to represent the intermediate state. Its mechanisation requires two functions: one for creating new names, and another one for expressing substitution of names. Any proof on sequential composition would require induction on both functions.

Relations can only be combined in sequence if their alphabets are *composable*. If we defined sequential composition as a partial function, domain checks would be required during proofs. Instead, we define a total function on well-formed pairs of relations, WF_Semi_R, which have composable alphabets.

$$
\begin{array}{|l}
\_;_R\_ : WF\_Semi_R \rightarrow REL\_PRED \\
\hline
\forall u1\_u2 : WF\_Semi_R \bullet \\
\quad u1\_u2.1 \;;_R\; u1\_u2.2 = \\
\quad\quad (in\_a\; u1\_u2.1.1 \cup out\_a\; u1\_u2.2.1, \\
\quad\quad \{b1 : u1\_u2.1.2;\; b2 : u1\_u2.2.2 \\
\quad\quad \mid (\forall n : \mathrm{dom}\, b2 \mid n \in undashed \bullet b2(n) = b1(dash\; n)) \\
\quad\quad \bullet (undashed \lhd b1) \cup (dashed \lhd b2)\})
\end{array}
$$

The alphabet of a sequential composition is composed of the input alphabet of the first relation and the output of the second relation. For each pair of bindings (b_1,b_2) from u_1 and u_2, respectively, we make a combination of all input values in b_1 (undashed names) with output values in b_2(dashed names). However, only those pairs of bindings in which the final values of all names in b_1 correspond to their initial values in b_2 are taken into consideration in this combination.

The UTP defines an alphabet extension that enables sequential composition to be applied to operands with non-composable alphabets. The function $+_R$ differs from $\oplus_R$ in that it restricts the value of the new name to be left unchanged. For a given predicate P and name n, it returns the predicate $P \wedge_R (n' =_{\{n',n\}} n)$.

Although useless for practical purposes, the Π (skip) is very useful for reasoning about programs. In our work it is defined as the function defined below. Given a well-formed alphabet a, it does not change the alphabet and returns all the bindings b with domain a, in which for every undashed name n in a, $b\,n = b\,n'$. The type WF_Skip_R is the set of all *homogeneous* alphabets.

$$
\begin{array}{|l}
\Pi_R : WF\_Skip_R \rightarrow REL\_PRED \\
\hline
\forall a : WF\_Skip_R \bullet \\
\quad \Pi_R\; a = (a, \{b : BINDING \\
\quad\quad\quad \mid \mathrm{dom}\, b = a \\
\quad\quad\quad \wedge (\forall n : a \mid n \in undashed \bullet b(n) = b(dash\; n))\})
\end{array}
$$

Other programming constructs like variable blocks and assignments are also included in this theory; their definitions can also be found in [12].

We now turn to the definition of refinement as the universal implication of relations. The universal closure used in UTP [9] is defined $\langle_R\, u \,\rangle_R = \forall\_{_R}(u.1, u)$. For a pair of relations (u_1,u_2), such that $(u_1, u_2) \in WF\_REL\_PRED\_PAIR$ (both have the same alphabet), we have that u_1 is refined by u_2, if, and only if, for all names in their alphabets, $u_2 \Rightarrow u_1$. This is expressed by the definition below.

$$
\begin{array}{|l}
\_\sqsubseteq_R\_ : WF\_REL\_PRED\_PAIR \rightarrow REL\_PRED \\
\hline
\forall u1\_u2 : WF\_REL\_PRED\_PAIR \bullet \\
\quad u1\_u2.1 \sqsubseteq_R u1\_u2.2 = \langle_R\, (u1\_u2.2 \Rightarrow_R u1\_u2.1) \,\rangle_R
\end{array}
$$

We have proved that our interpretation of refinement is, as expected, a partial order [12]. Moreover, the set of relations with alphabet a is a complete lattice.

Only functions $f : REL\_PRED \nrightarrow REL\_PRED$ whose domain is a set of relations with the same alphabet are considered in the theory of fixed points. We call the set of such functions $REL\_FUNCTION$. The definition of the weakest fixed point of a function $f : REL\_FUNCTION$ is standard. The greatest fixed point is defined as the least upper bound of the set $\{X \mid X \sqsubseteq f(x)\}$. This is different from Hoare and He's definition [9], which is not convenient for proofs. However, it is trivial to prove that we have an equivalent definition.

4.2 Proving Theorems

We have built a theory with more than two-hundred and seventy laws on alphabets, bindings, relational predicates, and laws from the predicate calculus. In what follows, we illustrate our approach in their proofs.

The proof of one of our laws is shown in Figure 3: the weakest fixed point law ($\forall F, Y \bullet F(Y) \sqsubseteq Y \Rightarrow \mu F \sqsubseteq Y$). We set our goal to be the law we want to prove using the SML command *set_goal*. It receives a list of assumptions and the proof goal. In our case, since we are not dealing with standard predicates, we must explicitly say that relations are $True_R$.

We start our proof by rewriting the Z empty set definition (*rewrite_tac*) and stripping the left-hand side of the implication into the assumptions (*z_strip_tac*). The SML command *a* applies a tactic to the current goal; the tactical *REPEAT* applies the given tactic as many times as possible. The next step is to rewrite the definition of least fixed point in the conclusion: we use forward chaining in the assumptions (*all_asm_fc_tac*), giving our Z definition of least fixed point as argument, and use the new assumption to rewrite the conclusion(*asm_rewrite_tac*).

The application of a previously proved theorem, *REL_lower_bound_thm*, concludes our proof. However, it requires some assumptions, before being applied. We introduce them in the assumption list using the tactic *lemma_tac*. The first condition is that Y is an element of the set of relations u, with an alphabet a, such that $F(u) \sqsubseteq_R u$. We use the tactical PC_T1 to stop ProofPower-Z from rewriting our expression by using the proof context *initial*, which is the most basic proof context. Furthermore, to avoid a new subgoal, we use the tactical $THEN1$ that applies the tactic in the right-hand side to the first subgoal generated by the tactic in the left-hand side. In our case, this proves that the assumption we are introducing is valid. The validity of the introduction of the first assumption is proved using the tactic *asm_prove_tac*, a powerful tactic that uses the assumptions in an automatic proof procedure. Next, after introducing the first condition explained above in the list of assumptions, we use forward chaining again to state the fact that the alphabet of Y is a.

The next step introduces the fact that the set to which Y belongs is in fact a set of REL_PRED. The proof of the validity of this assumption uses ProofPower-Z's proof context *z_sets_ext*, an aggressive complete proof context for manipulating Z set expressions. The last assumption that is needed is the fact that the pair composed by the alphabet a and the set to which Y belongs, is indeed

```
SML
set_goal([], ⌜∀ F : REL_FUNCTION;
      Y : REL_PRED
      | Y ∈ dom F
          ∧ (F(Y) ⊑_R Y = True_R∅)
      • μ_R(F) ⊑_R Y = True_R∅ ⌝);
a (rewrite_tac[]);
a (REPEAT z_strip_tac);
a (all_asm_fc_tac[z_get_spec ⌜μ_R⌝]);
a (asm_rewrite_tac[]);
a ( (PC_T1 "initial"
     lemma_tac
     ⌜Y ∈ {u : REL_PRED
     | a = u.1 ∧ F u ⊑_R u = True_R{}} ⌝)
   THEN1  (asm_prove_tac[]) );
a (all_asm_fc_tac[]);
```

```
SML
a ( (lemma_tac
     ⌜{u : REL_PRED
       | a = u.1 ∧ F u ⊑_R u = True_R{}}
      ∈ ℙ REL_PRED ⌝)
  THEN1 (PC_T1 "z_sets_ext" asm_prove_tac[]) );
a ( (lemma_tac
     ⌜(a, {u : REL_PRED
          | a = u.1 ∧ F u ⊑_R u = True_R{}})
      ∈ WF_Glb_R_Lub_R ⌝)
   THEN1
   ((rewrite_tac[z_get_spec ⌜WF_Glb_R_Lub_R⌝])
     THEN
     (PC_T1 "z_sets_ext" asm_prove_tac[])) );
a (apply_def REL_lower_bound_thm
     ⌜(a≙a, u≙Y,
       us≙{u : REL_PRED
           | a = u.1 ∧ F u ⊑_R u = True_R{}}) ⌝);
```

Fig. 3. Proof script for the weakest fixed point theorem

of type $WF\_Glb_R\_Lub_R$, which contains all set of pairs (a, bs), in which every binding in the set bs has a as its alphabet. Its proof rewrites the conclusion using the Z definition of $WF\_Glb_R\_Lub_R$, and then, uses the tactic *asm_prove_tac* in the *z_sets_ext* proof context. Finally, we use a tactic defined by us, *apply_def*, to instantiate the theorem *REL_lower_bound_thm* with the given values. The tactic *apply_def* instantiates the given theorem with the values given as arguments, and tries to rewrite the conclusion, using this instantiation.

ProofPower-Z has provided us with facilities that resulted in a rather short proof, for a quite complex theorem. Some of the facilities we highlight are forward chaining, use of existing and user-defined tactics, proof contexts, and automated proof tactics, such as *asm_rewrite_tac*.

4.3 Okay and Designs

The UTP theory of pre and postcondition pairs (designs) introduces an extra observational variable *okay*: it indicates that a program has started, and *okay'* indicates that the program has terminated. In our theory *utp-okay*, we define *okay* as an undashed name ($okay : NAME \mid okay \in undashed$) ranging over the booleans. We restrict the type *BINDING* by determining that *okay* and *okay'* are only associated with boolean values.

$$\forall b : BINDING \mid \{okay, dash\ okay\} \subseteq \mathrm{dom}\ b \bullet \{b\ okay, b(dash\ okay)\} \subseteq BOOL\_VAL$$

We could have introduced this restriction when we first defined *BINDING*, but as we intend to have modular independent theories, we postponed the restriction on observational variables used by specific theories.

Designs are defined in the theory *utp-des*. The set *ALPHABET_DES* is the set of all alphabets that contain *okay* and *okay'*. First we define *DES_PRED*, the set of relations u, such that $u.1 \in ALPHABET\_DES$. Designs with precondition p and postcondition q are written $p \vdash q$ and defined as $okay \wedge p \Rightarrow okay' \wedge q$.

The expression *okay* is the equality $okay =_a true$, which is mechanised in our work as $=_R (a, okay, Val(Bool(true)))$. For a given alphabet a, name n, and expression e, such that $n \in a$ and the free-variables of e are in a, the function $=_R (a, n, e)$ returns a relational predicate (a, bs), in which for every binding b in bs, $b\ n = Eval(b, e)$. A design is defined as follows.

$$\begin{array}{|l}
_ \vdash_D _ : WF_DES_PRED_PAIR \rightarrow REL_PRED \\
\hline
\forall d : WF_DES_PRED_PAIR \bullet \\
\quad d.1 \vdash_D d.2 = (=_R (d.1.1, okay, Val(Bool(true))) \wedge_R d.1) \Rightarrow_R \\
\qquad\qquad (=_R (d.1.1, dash\ okay, Val(Bool(true))) \wedge_R d.2)
\end{array}$$

The members of *WF_DES_PRED_PAIR* are pairs of relations (r_1, r_2) from *DES_PRED* with the same alphabet. The turnstile is used by both ProofPower-Z and the UTP. The former uses it to give names to theorems, and the later uses it to define designs. In our work, we have kept both of them, but we underscore the UTP design turnstile with a D.

The most important result for designs, which is the motivation for its definition, has also been proved in our mechanisation: the left-zero law for $True_R$.

In this new setting, new definitions for Π_R and assignment are needed. The skip for designs Π_D is defined in terms of the relational skip Π_R as follows.

$$\begin{array}{|l}
\Pi_D : WF_Skip_D \rightarrow REL_PRED \\
\hline
\forall a : WF_Skip_D \bullet \Pi_D\ a = True_R\ a \vdash_D (\Pi_R\ a)
\end{array}$$

The type WF_Skip_D is formed by all the homogeneous alphabets that contain *okay* and *okay'*. The new definition of assignment uses the relation assignment in a very similar way and is omitted here.

Designs are also characterised by two healthiness conditions. The first, $H1$, guarantees that observations cannot be made before the program starts. We define $H1(d) = okay \Rightarrow d$ as $H1(d) = (=_R (\{okay\}, okay, Val(Bool(true)))) \Rightarrow_R d$. The set of relations that satisfy a healthiness condition h is the set of relations r such that $h(r) = r$. For instance, $H1\_healthy = \{d : REL\_PRED \mid H1(d) = d\}$.

An *H2_healthy* relation does not require non-termination. In previous research [3], we presented a way of expressing $H2$ in terms of an idempotent function: $H2(P) = P; J$, where $J \mathrel{\widehat=} (okay \wedge okay' \Rightarrow v' = v)$. We express $v' = v$ as the relational skip Π_R on the alphabet containing the names in the lists v and v'. We define J as a function that takes an alphabet a' containing only dashed variables, and yields the relation presented below, where $A = a \cup a'$, and a is obtained by undashing all the names in a'.

$$(okay =_A true \Rightarrow_R okay' =_A true) \wedge_R \Pi_R(A \setminus \{okay, okay'\})$$

Our definition of the function $H2$ is presented below.

$$\begin{array}{|l}
H2 : REL_PRED \twoheadrightarrow REL_PRED \\
\hline
\forall d : REL_PRED \mid dash\ okay \in d.1 \bullet H2\ d = (d ;_R (J(out_a\ d.1)))
\end{array}$$

The function $H2$ is partial because J defines a relation that includes *okay* and *okay*′ in its alphabet, and hence, the alphabet of a relation d that can be made *H2_healthy* must contain *okay*′ in order to be *composable* with $J\,(out\_a\; d.1)$. In order to reuse our previous results [3], we use this definition for $H2$.

More than thirty laws from previous work [9, 3], involving design and their healthiness conditions, have been included in our theory of designs. Their proofs do not expand any definition in the relations theory. Many laws were included in the relations theory, in order to carry out proofs in the designs theory.

4.4 WTR and Reactive Processes

The behaviour of reactive processes cannot be expressed only in terms of their final states; interactions with the environment (events) need to be considered. Besides *okay*, in the theory of reactive processes we have the observational variables *tr*, *wait*, and *ref*. The variable *wait* records whether the process has terminated or is interacting with the environment in an intermediate state. Since it is a boolean, the definition of *wait* is similar to that of *okay*. The variable *tr* records the sequence of events in which the process has engaged; it has type *SEQ_EVENT_VAL*. The variable *ref* is a set of events in which the process may refuse to engage; its type is *SET_EVENT_VAL*. The definitions of these variables are in the theory *utp-wtr*. In the theory *utp-rea*, we define *REA_PRED*, the set of relations whose alphabet is a member of *ALPHABET_REA*. This is the set of alphabets that contain *okay*, *tr*, *wait*, *ref*, and their dashed counterparts.

As for designs, healthiness conditions characterise the reactive processes. The first healthiness condition $R1$ states that the history of interactions of a process cannot be changed, therefore, the value of *tr* can only get longer. Our definition uses a function $\leq_R$ (sequence prefixing), which, is the Z prefixing relation lifted to *VAL*ues.

$$\begin{array}{|l}
_ \leq_R _ : VAL \leftrightarrow VAL \\
\hline
(_ \leq_R _) = \{s1, s2 : SEQ_VAL \mid ((Seq^{\sim})\, s1)\; prefix_Z\; ((Seq^{\sim})\, s2)\}
\end{array}$$

The type *SEQ_VAL* is defined as the $\{s : \mathrm{seq}\; VAL \mid Seq(s)\}$ and the Z sequence prefixing $prefix_Z$ is defined in *utp-z-library*. Furthermore, in Z, $^{\sim}$ stands for the relational inverse operator.

The definition of $R1$ below mechanises the function $R1(P) = P \wedge tr \leq tr'$.

$$\begin{array}{|l}
R1 : REL_PRED \rightarrow REL_PRED \\
\hline
\forall\, r : REL_PRED \bullet \\
\quad R1\; r = r \wedge_R (=_{+R} (\{tr, dash\; tr\}, \\
\qquad\qquad Rel((_ \leq_R _), Var(tr), Var(dash\; tr)), \\
\qquad\qquad Val(Bool(true))))
\end{array}$$

In order to transform the expression $tr \leq tr'$ into a relational predicate, we assert that the expression $Rel((\_ \leq_R \_), Var(tr), Var(dash\; tr))$ is equals to

$Val(Bool(true))$. We adopt the same strategy to lift all needed Z relational operators ($\in, \notin, \subseteq, \ldots$) and functions (using Fun_1 and Fun_2) to relational predicates.

The second healthiness condition establishes that a reactive process should not rely on events that happened before it started. We mechanise the formulation $R2(P(tr, tr')) = P(\langle\rangle, tr' - tr)$ [3]; this requires that P is not changed if tr is taken to be the empty sequence, and tr' is taken to be $tr' - tr$, the sequence obtained from tr' by removing its prefix tr. The notation $P(\langle\rangle, tr' - tr)$ is implemented using substitution; $R2$ is defined as $R2(P) = P[\langle\rangle/tr][tr' - tr/tr']$.

The final healthiness condition $R3$ defines the behaviour of a process that is still waiting for another process to finish: it should not start. In UTP [9], $R3$ is defined as $R3(P) = \Pi_{REA} \lhd wait \rhd P$, and is mechanised in our work as follows.

$$
\begin{array}{|l}
R3 : REA\_PRED \to REA\_PRED \\
\hline
\forall r : REA\_PRED \mid r.1 \in WF\_Skip_{REA} \bullet \\
\quad R3\, r = (\Pi_{REA}\, r.1) \lhd_R (=_R (\{wait\}, wait, Val(Bool(true)))) \rhd_R r
\end{array}
$$

This definition of $R3$ uses a conditional and the reactive skip Π_{REA}. Conditionals are defined only if both branches have the same alphabet and Π_{REA} is only defined for *homogeneous* reactive alphabets (WF_Skip_{REA}). For this reason, our definition reveals that $R3$ is not a total function: it can only be applied to *homogeneous* reactive relations.

A reactive process is a relation with a reactive alphabet a, which is $R\_healthy$; the function R is defined as $R(r) = R1(R2(R3(r)))$. Based on these definitions, more than sixty laws, including those we presented previously [3], are part of our theory of reactive processes. Among other properties, they prove that the healthiness conditions for reactive processes are idempotent and commutative, and the closure of some of the program operators with relation to the healthiness conditions. They also explore relations between healthiness conditions for reactive processes and designs.

4.5 CSP Processes

Our mechanisation of the CSP theory is based on our earlier research [3]. Basically, CSP processes are reactive processes that satisfy two other healthiness conditions; they can all be expressed as reactive designs: the result of applying R to a design. The first healthiness condition states that the only guarantee in the case of divergence ($\neg\, okay$) is that the trace can only be extended. It is mechanised as $CSP1\, r \mathrel{\widehat{=}} r \lor (\neg\, okay \land tr \leq tr')$.

The second healthiness condition is a recast of $H2$, presented in Section 4.3, with an extended reactive alphabet. The mechanisation of $CSP2$ in ProofPower-Z reveals, as it does for $H2$, that this function is not total: it is only applicable to relational predicates which contain $okay'$, tr', $wait'$, and ref' in their alphabet.

$$
\begin{array}{|l}
CSP2 : REL\_PRED \to REL\_PRED \\
\hline
\forall r : REL\_PRED \mid \{dash\ okay, dash\ tr, dash\ wait, dash\ ref\} \subseteq r.1 \\
\qquad \bullet\ CSP2\, r = r ;_R J(out\_a\, r.1)
\end{array}
$$

A *CSP_PROCESS* is a *CSP1_healthy* and *CSP2_healthy* reactive process.

The *SKIP* process terminates immediately. The initial value of *ref* is irrelevant, and it is quantified in the definition of *SKIP*.

$$SKIP : CSP\_PROCESS$$
$$SKIP = R(\exists_R(\{ref\}, \Pi_{REA}\, ALPHABET\_CSP))$$

The *ALPHABET_CSP* contains only *okay*, *tr*, *wait*, *ref*, and their dashed counterparts. The existential quantification does not remove *ref* from the alphabet, as opposed to that used in the definition, for instance, of variable blocks.

Besides the definition for simple prefixing ($e \rightarrow_{CSP} SKIP$, where e is an event) originally given by the UTP, we mechanise a simpler definition which was proven equivalent: $e \rightarrow_{CSP} SKIP = R(true \vdash do_C\ e)$. The following function is a simplified version of do_A presented in the UTP.

$$do_C\ e \mathrel{\widehat=} tr' = tr \land e \notin ref' \lhd wait' \rhd tr' = tr \frown \langle e \rangle$$

The simplification was possible because we express prefixing as a reactive design. An event has either not happened, and the trace has not changed and the process is willing to engage in e, or it has happened and the trace has been extended.

By expressing all operators as reactive designs, we bring uniformity to proofs, and foster reuse of existing results. All of our CSP theorems [3] and Hoare and He's UTP theorems [9] are part of our *utp-csp* theory. It is currently being used as a basis of a *Circus* theory.

5 Conclusions

In this paper we give a set-based model to relations, and use it as a basis for the development of four theories: relations, designs, reactive processes, and CSP. For us, a relation is a pair, whose first element is a set that represents its alphabet and whose second element is a set of functions from names to values.

This is not the only possible model for relations. Our choice was based on the fact that any restriction that applies to the relations has a direct impact on the complexity of the proofs. Our model imposes a simple restriction: the domain of the bindings must be equal to the alphabet. This restriction results in simpler definitions, and hence proofs. For instance, in [4], we defined a relation as a pair formed by an alphabet and a set of pairs of bindings: for every pair (b_1, b_2) of bindings in a relation, the domain of b_1 has only undashed names and that of b_2 only dashed names. Such a restriction has to be enforced by the definition of every operator. There is, however, an isomorphism between our model and this one. By joining and splitting the sets of bindings, we can move from one model to another; our concern is only with the practicality of mechanical theorem proving.

We also could have used bindings whose domains could be different from the relation alphabet. However, the alphabet is the set of names about which the relation describes something. Hence, the alphabet a of a relation would have to be either a subset or equal to the domain of each binding b. Values of names that were not in the alphabet would actually have no meaning. We chose bindings whose domain is the alphabet because, by taking the other approach, we have a more complex definition for alphabet extension: bindings for names that are not in the alphabet need to be removed before being left unrestricted. Alphabet extension is at the heart of the definitions of conjunction and disjunction.

If, in the hope to find simplifications in other points, we accepted the more complex definition of alphabet extension, then we would need to determine how to handle the names that are not in the alphabet of the relation. For example, bindings could be total functions which map these names to an undefined value $\perp$; or we could leave these names unrestricted. These restrictions on relations are in fact more complex than that in our model, and lead to more complex definitions and proofs. We also have an isomorphism between our model and each of these; by applying a domain restriction to the bindings in these models and extending our model's bindings, we can change the representations.

As an industrial theorem prover, ProofPower-Z proved to be powerful (and helpful). The support provided by hundreds of built-in tactics and theories, as libraries for Z constructs and set theory, made our work much simpler. The axiomatisation of the theorems proved in our work in other theorem provers, like Z/Eves [17], and the development of new theories based on these axioms makes the use of our results in different theorem provers possible. In ProofPower-Z, the tactics that can be created are more powerful than in Z/Eves; however, the level of expertise needed for initial users of Z/Eves is not as high as for ProofPower-Z.

The discussion above of alternative models is based on our experience with ProofPower-Z; some of them could make proofs easier in another theorem prover. An investigation of alternative theorem provers is a topic for future research.

Nuka and Woodcock [11] formalised the alphabetised relational calculus in Z/EVES. We extend that work by including many other operations, such as sequencing, assignment, refinement, and recursion. The hierarchical mechanisation of the theories of designs, reactive processes, and CSP is also a contribution of our work that provides a powerful tool for further investigations on them.

Hoare and He [9], although dealing with alphabetised predicates, often leave it quite implicit. For example, *true* is often seen unalphabetised, while in fact, it is alphabetised. This abstraction simplifies things, but is not suitable for theorem provers. With the obligation to deal with alphabets, our work gives more details on how the alphabets are handled within the UTP.

The alphabet extension used in the UTP constrains the values of the new variables: they cannot be changed. However, our set-based model for relations needed a different alphabet extension that leaves their values unconstrained. Furthermore, in the UTP, existential quantifications are used in two different ways: in the definition of variable blocks, the authors explicitly state that the quantified variables are removed from the alphabet; and in the definition of the reactive *SKIP*, the alphabet is, implicitly, left unchanged. Our implementation defines two existential and two universal quantifications: one of them removes the quantified variables from the alphabet, and the other one does not. We also redefined some of the UTP definitions in order to facilitate our proofs.

Our work also reveals details that are left implicit in the UTP regarding the domain of the healthiness conditions. By mechanising the healthiness conditions, $R3$ for instance, we make it explicit that $R3$, and consequently R, is a partial function that can only be applied to *homogeneous* reactive processes.

We expressed the language constructors as functions. For this reason, they can be simply extended without loosing the previous proofs; the syntax of expressions was abstracted by using three simple definitions. Furthermore, the strategy that we adopted for lifting Z functions and relations to relational predicates, for instance $\leq_R$, makes the Z toolkit directly available in our theory. Our work provides a mechanical support not only to *Circus*, but to any other work theoretically based on any of the UTP theories.

The current number of laws on sequential composition may need to be increased to allow users of our theory of relation not to expand its definition in the proof of theorems. The proof of more laws on sequential composition that will make this possible is an important piece of future work.

We aim at providing a mechanisation of the UTP that can support the development of other languages theoretically based on the UTP; *Circus* is such a language. Our next step is to mechanise the *Circus* theory, which will be based on the CSP theory, and will mechanise not only the final version of the semantics of *Circus*, but also all the refinement laws proposed so far. This will provide *Circus* with a mechanised refinement calculus that can be used in the formal development of State-Rich Reactive Programs.

Acknowledgements

We are grateful for the financial support of QinetiQ and the Royal Society. Philip Clayton, Rob Arthan, Roger Bishop Jones, Mark Adams, and Will Harwood provided valuable advice for our work.

References

1. ProofPower. At http://www.lemma-one.com/ProofPower/index/index.html.
2. A. L. C. Cavalcanti, A. C. A. Sampaio, and J. C. P. Woodcock. A refinement strategy for *Circus*. *Formal Aspects of Computing*, **15**(2–3):146–181, 2003.
3. A. L. C. Cavalcanti and J. C. P. Woodcock. A tutorial introduction to CSP in Unifying Theories of Programming. In *Proceedings of the Pernambuco Summer School on Software Engineering: Refinement 2004*, 2004.
4. A. L. C. Cavalcanti and J. C. P. Woodcock. Angelic nondeterminism and Unifying Theories of Programming. Technical Report 13-04, Computing Laboratory, University of Kent, June 2004.
5. C. Fischer. CSP-OZ: A combination of Object-Z and CSP. In H. Bowmann and J. Derrick, editors, *Formal Methods for Open Object-Based Distributed Systems (FMOODS'97)*, volume **2**, pages 423–438. Chapman & Hall, 1997.
6. M. Gordon, R. Milner, and C. Wadsworth. *Edinburgh LCF*. volume **78** of *LNCS*. Springer-Verlag, 1979.

7. M. J. C. Gordon and T. F. Melham, editors. *Introduction to HOL: A Theorem Proving Environment for Higher Order Logic.* Cambridge University Press, 1993.
8. C. A. R. Hoare. *Communicating Sequential Processes.* Prentice-Hall, 1985.
9. C. A. R. Hoare and H. Jifeng. *Unifying Theories of Programming.* Prentice-Hall, 1998.
10. C. Morgan. *Programming from Specifications.* Prentice-Hall, 1994.
11. G. Nuka and J. C. P. Woodcock. Mechanising the alphabetised relational calculus. In *WMF2003: 6th Braziliam Workshop on Formal Methods*, volume **95**, pages 209–225, Campina Grande, Brazil, October 2004.
12. M. V. M. Oliveira. *Formal Derivation of State-Rich Reactive Programs using Circus – Additional Material*, 2006. At http://www.cs.york.ac.uk/circus/refinement-calculus/oliveira-phd/.
13. M. V. M. Oliveira and A. L. C. Cavalcanti. From *Circus* to JCSP. In J. Davies *et al.*, editor, *Sixth International Conference on Formal Engineering Methods*, volume **3308** of *LNCS*, pages 320–340. Springer-Verlag, November 2004.
14. M. V. M. Oliveira, A. L. C. Cavalcanti, and J. C. P. Woodcock. Refining industrial scale systems in *Circus*. In Ian East, Jeremy Martin, Peter Welch, David Duce, and Mark Green, editors, *Communicating Process Architectures*, volume **62** of *Concurrent Systems Engineering Series*, pages 281–309. IOS Press, 2004.
15. S. C. Qin, J. S. Dong, and W. N. Chin. A semantic foundation of TCOZ in Unifying Theories of Programming. In K. Araki, S. Gnesi, and D. Mandrioli, editors, *FME 2003: Formal Methods*, volume **2805** of *LNCS*, pages 321–340. Springer-Verlag, September 2003.
16. A. W. Roscoe, J. C. P. Woodcock, and L. Wulf. Non-interference through Determinism. In D. Gollmann, editor, *ESORICS 94*, volume **1214** of *LNCS*, pages 33–54. Springer-Verlag, 1994.
17. M. Saaltink. The Z/EVES System. In J. P. Bowen, M. G. Hinchey, and D. Till, editors, *ZUM'97: The Z Formal Specification Notation*, volume **1212** of *LNCS*, pages 72–85, Reading, April 1997. Springer-Verlag.
18. A. Sherif and H. Jifeng. Towards a time model for *Circus*. In C. George and H. Miao, editors, *Formal Methods and Software Engineering: 4th International Conference on Formal Engineering Methods, ICFEM 2002*, volume **2495** of *LNCS*, pages 613–624. Springer-Verlag, June 2002.
19. K. Taguchi and K. Araki. The state-based CCS semantics for concurrent Z specification. In M. Hinchey and Shaoying Liu, editors, *International Conference on Formal Engineering Methods*, pages 283–292. IEEE, 1997.
20. H. Treharne and S. Schneider. Using a process algebra to control B operations. In K. Araki, A. Galloway, and K. Taguchi, editors, *Proceedings of the 1st International Conference on Integrated Formal Methods*, pages 437–456. Springer, June 1999.
21. J. C. P. Woodcock and A. L. C. Cavalcanti. *Circus*: a concurrent refinement language. Technical report, Oxford University Computing Laboratory, Wolfson Building, Parks Road, Oxford OX1 3QD UK, July 2001.
22. J. C. P. Woodcock and J. Davies. *Using Z—Specification, Refinement, and Proof.* Prentice-Hall, 1996.
23. J. C. P. Woodcock and A. Hughes. Unifying Theories of Parallel Programming. In H. Miao C. George, editor, *Formal Methods and Software Engineering: 4th International Conference on Formal Engineering Methods, ICFEM 2002*, volume **2495** of *LNCS*, pages 24–37. Springer-Verlag, June 2002.

Termination of Real-Time Programs: Definitely, Definitely Not, or Maybe

Ian J. Hayes

School of Information Technology and Electrical Engineering, The University of Queensland, Brisbane, 4072, Australia

Abstract. Real-time control programs are often used in contexts where (conceptually) they run forever. Repetitions within such programs (or their specifications) may either (i) be guaranteed to terminate, (ii) be guaranteed to never terminate (loop forever), or (iii) may possibly terminate. In dealing with real-time programs and their specifications, we need to be able to represent these possibilities, and define suitable refinement orderings.

A refinement ordering based on Dijkstra's weakest precondition only copes with the first alternative. Weakest liberal preconditions allow one to constrain behaviour provided the program terminates, which copes with the third alternative to some extent. However, neither of these handles the case when a program does not terminate. To handle this case a refinement ordering based on relational semantics can be used. In this paper we explore these issues and the definition of loops for real-time programs as well as corresponding refinement laws.

1 Introduction

Consider the program in Fig. 1, that detects when an input *sensor* goes above a *critical* level and sets an output *alarm*. It makes use of auxiliary timing variables, *curr* and *prev*, to ensure that successive samples of the sensor are at most *limit* time units apart. If the sensor is continuously above the critical level for at least *limit* time units, the loop is guaranteed to terminate and set the alarm within *limit* time units from the time at which the previous sample (which was less than the critical level) was taken. If the sensor is transiently above the critical level for less than *limit* time units, the loop may or may not detect this and may or may not terminate, but if it does terminate it does so within *limit* time units of the time at which the previous sample was taken. If the sensor is never above the critical level, the loop is guaranteed to execute forever, conceptually at least, because no implementation can achieve this in practice.

Within the program the deadlines are (rather special) commands, that guarantee to terminate by the given deadline when execution of the program reaches the deadline command [4, 8]. If execution of a program does not reach a deadline command, the deadline has no effect (just like any other command that is not reached). In the example in Fig. 1, the final deadline has no effect if the loop never terminates.

There are two significant points from this discussion that need to be handled by the semantics we give to real-time programs:

- deadlines are treated as commands within a program (rather than some external constraint imposed on a program), and

S. Dunne and W. Stoddart (Eds.): UTP 2006, LNCS 4010, pp. 141–154, 2006.

$curr := \tau;$
$alarm := off;$
repeat
  $curr, prev := \tau, curr;$
  $level :$ **read**$(sensor);$
  deadline $prev + limit$
until $level \geq critical;$
$alarm := on;$
deadline $prev + limit$

Fig. 1. Program to set alarm when sensor goes above critical

- loops may be required to terminate in some circumstances, required not to terminate in others, and allowed to either terminate or not terminate in yet others.

In Sect. 2 we discuss a number of issues about modelling real-time programs as relations, including healthiness conditions on the relations. Sect. 3 formalises a model of real-time programs and Sect. 4 gives the semantics of basic commands. These sections expand on the issues discussed in an earlier paper on a predicative semantics for real-time refinement [7], which is itself a generalisation of an earlier real-time refinement calculus, that did not handle nonterminating programs [9]. In Sect. 5 we discuss the semantics of loops in a real-time context, in particular, the case of a nonterminating loop that iterates an infinite number of times, and in Sect. 6 we discuss refinement laws for such loops. These last two sections give an overview of earlier work on reasoning about real-time repetitions [6].

2 Modelling Real-Time Programs

Time. To model real-time programs, we need to model time. One simple way to do this is to add a special time variable, τ, representing the "current" time [11]. All commands need to ensure that time does not go backwards, which we represent by

$$\tau_0 \leq \tau \qquad (1)$$

where τ_0 represents the start time of a command and τ its finish time. In general, we model commands as relations between their *before* state and their *after* state, which are represented respectively by zero-subscripted variables and unsubscripted variables. For real-time control programs, we need to allow for commands that execute forever, which we do by allowing τ to take on the value infinity (∞). Real-time control applications may involve variables that vary continuously over time, and hence we model time by real numbers plus infinity (but for other applications discrete time could be used). Some behaviours we might want to specify are:

- termination is required if condition RT holds, i.e., $RT \Rightarrow \tau < \infty$,
- nontermination is required if NRT holds, i.e., $NRT \Rightarrow \tau = \infty$,

- termination is allowed only if AT holds, i.e., $\tau < \infty \Rightarrow AT$, and
- nontermination is allowed only if ANT holds, i.e., $\tau = \infty \Rightarrow ANT$.

For example, to specify the task for which the repeat loop in Fig. 1 provides an implementation, we require that following hold.

- If the sensor never strays above critical, the loop must not terminate:

  $$(sensor < critical) \ \mathbf{over} \ [\tau_0 \ldots \infty) \Rightarrow \tau = \infty,$$

  where $(sensor < critical)$ **over** $[\tau_0 \ldots \infty)$ means

  $$(\forall i : Time \bullet \tau_0 \leq i < \infty \Rightarrow sensor(i) < critical).$$

- The loop is allowed to terminate only if the sensor strays above critical, but should do so within *limit* time units:

  $$\tau < \infty \Rightarrow (\exists t : Time \bullet \tau_0 \leq t \wedge sensor(t) \geq critical \wedge \tau \leq t + limit).$$

- The loop must terminate by the end of the earliest time interval over which the sensor remains critical for *limit* time units, if such an interval exists:

  $$\begin{array}{l} \mathbf{let}\ crit\_times \mathrel{\widehat{=}} \{t : Time \mid \tau_0 \leq t \wedge (sensor \geq critical) \ \mathbf{over} \ [t \ldots t + limit]\} \bullet \\ \quad crit\_times \neq \{\} \Rightarrow \tau \leq inf(crit\_times) + limit \end{array}$$

  where $inf(crit\_times)$ gives the infimum (greatest lower bound) of the set $crit\_times$. If the set is empty then its infimum is ∞. In addition, arithmetic involving infinity gives $\infty + limit = \infty$, and hence the constraint becomes $\tau \leq \infty$, which is no constraint at all. This allows one to drop "$crit\_times \neq \{\} \Rightarrow$" from the above formula without changing its meaning.

Two common forms of program correctness are total and partial correctness. These can be encoded in postconditions by making use of the time variable. For *total correctness* the program is guaranteed to terminate and establish some condition Q; we can use a postcondition of the form: $\tau < \infty \wedge Q$. For *partial correctness*, if the program terminates, then condition Q is guaranteed to hold (but the program isn't guaranteed to terminate); we can use a postcondition of the form: $\tau < \infty \Rightarrow Q$.

Inputs and outputs. Real-time programs are reactive: their behaviour over time is significant, not just the final value of their variables when they terminate. This is particularly the case for programs that execute forever, because they have no final state for their local variables. To model the reactive behaviour of real-time programs, external inputs and outputs can be modelled as traces over time, i.e., functions from time to their value at that time. We consider inputs to be traces over all time. This allows one to write assumptions about the future values of inputs, e.g., assume upper/lower bounds on their values or their rates of change. For example, the sensor in the example in Fig. 1 may have its rate of change limited:

$$\forall t : Time \bullet (deriv(sensor))(t) \leq max\_rate$$

where $deriv(sensor)$ gives the derivative of the function $sensor$ with respect to is argument, time. At time τ an output, o, is modelled by a trace whose domain is the set of times up until τ, i.e.,

$$dom(o) = \{t : Time \mid t \leq \tau\}. \tag{2}$$

If a command does not terminate, the domain of its outputs is given by the set *Time* (which does not include ∞). Commands cannot change past values of outputs. If o_0 represents the initial value of an output trace (with domain up to τ_0) at the start of the execution of a command, and o represents its final value, then o_0 must be a prefix of o:

$$o_0 \subseteq o \tag{3}$$

Because for all times, t, in the domain of o_0 we have $o_0(t) = o(t)$, in specifications and refinement laws we do not need to refer explicitly to o_0, because we can always refer to o instead; the underlying semantics ensures o_0 is a prefix of o.

Local variables. In addition to input and output variables, which are externally observable, we would like to model local variables, whose values are not externally observable. For commands we model local variables via their before and after values. A special case applies when the command does not terminate. In this case there is no final state for the locals. Hence if R is a relation representing a command with locals v, then if R does not terminate, it should not constrain the final values of v:

$$\tau = \infty \Rightarrow (R \Leftrightarrow (\forall v \bullet R)) \tag{4}$$

Sequential composition. As in other theories that model commands as relations, sequential composition of commands is modelled by relational composition. However, care needs to be taken if the first command, C_1, in a sequential composition, "$C_1;\ C_2$" does not terminate. In this case the behaviour of the sequential composition should be the same as the behaviour of C_1.

For a sequential composition, "$C_1;\ C_2$", the final state of the locals for C_1 corresponds to the initial state of the locals for C_2. This intermediate state is hidden in the sequential composition so that only the initial and final values of the whole sequential composition are available for further composition. This is quite different to the case for outputs where the whole trace of an output is observable, including its intermediate values between the start and finish times of the command. The final value of the output trace extends its initial value.

For a sequential composition "$C_1;\ C_2$", the initial time for C_2 will be the same as the final time for C_1, but if C_1 does not terminate, this time will be infinity. In this case, for C_2 we have that $\tau_0 = \infty$, but, for any command, we have $\tau_0 \leq \tau$ and hence $\tau = \infty$ for C_2. If C_1 does not terminate, then for any output o, for C_2, $\mathrm{dom}(o_0) = Time$. However, we also have $\tau = \infty$ and hence $\mathrm{dom}(o) = Time$, and hence $o_0 = o$ because o_0 and o have the same domain and by (3), $o_0 \subseteq o$. Note that when $\tau_0 = \infty$, by (1) we have $\tau = \infty$, and hence by (4) the final values of the local variables are not constrained.

Abort versus nontermination. In a control application, the desired behaviour of a control program may be to monitor an input and control an output in response, forever.

We would like to distinguish such behaviour from a program that aborts, because, say, of a division-by-zero (or in general because its precondition is not satisfied). For this reason we can't use a semantics that identifies abort and nontermination, such as Dijkstra's weakest preconditions [2]. Dunne [3] has investigated the notion of generalised correctness, which allows one to specify not only that a program should terminate, but also that a program should never terminate. While general correctness generalises Dijkstra's approach, it does not allow one to distinguish nontermination from abortion, as we require here.

One way to distinguish aborting behaviour is to add a boolean variable, *ok*, to represent a normal nonaborted state iff it is true. The variable name *ok* is borrowed from Hoare and He [12] where it represents normal termination. However, in their semantics nontermination and abort are equated, which is not the case here. We have that

- $ok \wedge \tau < \infty$ represents a normal, terminated state,
- $ok \wedge \tau = \infty$ represents a normal, nonterminated state, and
- $\neg\, ok$ represents an abnormal (i.e., aborted) state.

A command has both a before and after value for *ok*, represented by ok_0 and *ok*, respectively. If ok_0 holds then the program has not yet aborted when the command is commenced, and if *ok* holds, the command did not abort.

For a sequential composition "$C_1;\ C_2$", if C_1 neither aborts nor terminates then, for C_2, ok_0 is true and $\tau_0 = \infty$. In this case, the whole sequential composition should not abort, and hence *ok* should also hold for C_2. That is, for C_2

$$ok_0 \wedge \tau_0 = \infty \Rightarrow ok. \tag{5}$$

Once a program aborts, no guarantees can be given about its behaviour from that point of time onwards, other than that time increases (1) and the previous values of the outputs can't be changed (3). Hence for a sequential composition, "$C_1;\ C_2$", if C_1 aborts then, for C_2, ok_0 is false, and if R_2 is the relation representing C_2, we have

$$\neg\, ok_0 \Rightarrow (R_2 \Leftrightarrow \tau_0 \leq \tau \wedge o1_0 \subseteq o1 \wedge \ldots \wedge om_0 \subseteq om), \tag{6}$$

where $o1, \ldots, om$ are the outputs of the program. Note that no constraints are placed on *ok*, the final values of the local variables, or the values of the outputs beyond time τ_0. Similarly, if C_1 does not terminate, then, for C_2, $\tau_0 = \infty$, and R_2 should have no effect other than to ensure $\tau = \infty$, the outputs are unchanged, and nonabortion is maintained:

$$\tau_0 = \infty \Rightarrow (R_2 \Leftrightarrow \tau = \infty \wedge o1_0 = o1 \wedge \ldots \wedge om_0 = om \wedge (ok_0 \Rightarrow ok)). \tag{7}$$

3 Formalisation of the Model

Fig. 2 formalises the semantic domains used in our model of real-time programs. *Time* is modelled by the nonnegative real numbers, with the time variable also allowed to take on the value infinity. We interpret a program in the context of an environment, ρ, which gives the names of the program inputs, $\rho.input$, outputs, $\rho.output$, and local variables, $\rho.local$. The values of local variables are modeled by a function that for each

Let ρ and ρ' be environments, such that $\rho.input = \rho'.input$ and $\rho.output = \rho'.output$. For a schema value σ with component loc, the notation $\sigma\,[loc\backslash v]$ stands for the schema value σ but with the value of the component loc replaced by v.

$$
\begin{aligned}
Time &\mathrel{\widehat=} \mathbb{R}_+ \\
Time_\infty &\mathrel{\widehat=} Time \cup \{\infty\} \\
Local_\rho &\mathrel{\widehat=} \rho.local \rightarrow VAL \\
In_\rho &\mathrel{\widehat=} \rho.input \rightarrow (Time \rightarrow VAL) \\
Out_\rho &\mathrel{\widehat=} \rho.output \rightarrow (Time \mathrel{+\!\!\!\rightarrow} VAL) \\
\Sigma_\rho &\mathrel{\widehat=} [ok : Boolean;\ \tau : Time_\infty;\ loc : Local_\rho;\ out : Out_\rho \mid \\
&\qquad\qquad \forall\, o : \mathrm{dom}(out) \bullet \mathrm{dom}(out(o)) = \{t : Time \mid t \leq \tau\}] \\
Pred_\rho &\mathrel{\widehat=} In_\rho \times \Sigma_\rho \rightarrow Boolean \\
Rel_{\rho,\rho'} &\mathrel{\widehat=} In_\rho \times \Sigma_\rho \times \Sigma_{\rho'} \rightarrow Boolean \\
Healthy_{\rho,\rho'} &\mathrel{\widehat=} (\lambda\,\sigma_0 : \Sigma_\rho;\ \sigma : \Sigma_{\rho'} \bullet \sigma_0.\tau \leq \sigma.\tau \wedge (\sigma_0.ok \wedge \sigma_0.\tau = \infty \Rightarrow \sigma.ok) \wedge \\
&\qquad (\forall\, o : \rho.output \bullet \sigma_0.out(o) \subseteq \sigma.out(o))) \\
Command_{\rho,\rho'} &\mathrel{\widehat=} \{R : Rel_{\rho,\rho'} \mid \forall\, in : In_\rho;\ \sigma_0 : \Sigma_\rho;\ \sigma : \Sigma_{\rho'} \bullet \\
&\qquad \left(R(in,\sigma_0,\sigma) \Leftrightarrow \left(\begin{array}{l} Healthy_{\rho,\rho'}(\sigma_0,\sigma) \wedge \\ (\sigma_0.ok \wedge \sigma_0.\tau < \infty \Rightarrow R(in,\sigma_0,\sigma)) \end{array} \right) \right) \wedge \\
&\qquad (\sigma.\tau = \infty \Rightarrow (R(in,\sigma_0,\sigma) \Leftrightarrow (\forall\, v : Local_\rho \bullet R(in,\sigma_0,\sigma\,[loc\backslash v])))))\}
\end{aligned}
$$

Fig. 2. Semantic domains

local variable name gives its value. Inputs and outputs are modelled similarly, but their values are traces over time. The set of possible program states, Σ_ρ, is modelled by a Z schema[1] containing the boolean component, *ok*, the "current" time, τ, the values of the local variables, and the values of the traces of the output variables up until τ (see (2)).

Single-state predicates, $Pred_\rho$, are boolean functions on the inputs and program state, whereas *relational predicates* (or *relations* for short) are boolean functions on the inputs plus a before state and an after state. To allow for program primitives that allocate/deallocate local variables, we allow the before and after environments to be different. Hence we use of Σ_ρ for the before state, and $\Sigma_{\rho'}$ for the after state. The notation we used in Sect. 2 is an abbreviation for that used in the semantics, for example, ok_0 stands for $\sigma_0.ok$, ok stands for $\sigma.ok$, and o stands for $\sigma.out(o)$.

Commands are relations that satisfy the conditions outlined in Sect. 2. The predicate *Healthy* puts together three constraints that all commands must satisfy:

- time does not go backwards (1),
- if the initial state has time infinity and isn't aborted (i.e., the program before the command did not terminate or abort) then the command preserves the nonaborted state (5), and
- the past value of outputs is preserved (3).

[1] A Z schema is like a record, but with the ability to specify a constraint on its components.

A relation, R, representing a command must satisfy

$$R(in, \sigma_0, \sigma) \Leftrightarrow (Healthy_{\rho,\rho'}(\sigma_0, \sigma) \wedge (\sigma_0.ok \wedge \sigma_0.\tau < \infty \Rightarrow R(in, \sigma_0, \sigma))).$$

This ensures $R(in, \sigma_0, \sigma)$ implies $Healthy_{\rho,\rho'}(\sigma_0, \sigma)$. In addition, if either $\sigma_0.\tau = \infty$ or $\neg\, \sigma_0.ok$, it ensures $R(in, \sigma_0, \sigma) \Leftrightarrow Healthy_{\rho,\rho'}(\sigma_0, \sigma)$, as required by (6) and (7). That is, if the initial state is an abort state or has time infinity, then the relation puts no further constraint on the program variables, other than the healthiness constraints listed above.

If the command does not terminate there is no final state for the local variables and hence the command relation is independent of the values of the final state of the local variables (4).

4 Semantics of Commands

The semantics of a command, C, is given by a function $\mathcal{M}_\rho(C)$ that for an environment ρ gives the relation representing C. A command, C_1, is refined by another command, C_2, written $C_1 \sqsubseteq C_2$, if the relation corresponding to C_1 contains that of C_2, that is,

$$\begin{array}{l} C_1 \sqsubseteq_\rho C_2 \mathrel{\widehat{=}} \forall\, in : In_\rho, \sigma_0 : \Sigma_\rho, \sigma : \Sigma_{\rho'} \bullet \\ \qquad\qquad \mathcal{M}_\rho(C_2)(in, \sigma_0, \sigma) \Rightarrow \mathcal{M}_\rho(C_1)(in, \sigma_0, \sigma) \end{array}$$

In general the final environment of a command, ρ', may differ from the initial environment, ρ. This allows one to treat variable allocation (which extends the environment)

Let ρ, ρ', and ρ'' be environments; $P \in Pred_\rho$, such that P is independent of ok; $Q \in Rel_{\rho,\rho}$, such that Q is independent of ok_0 and ok and the final values of the local variables in the case of nontermination; a vector, $\vec{x}$, of local variables and outputs within ρ; $C_1, C_2, C_i \in Command_{\rho,\rho'}$ for $i \in S$; $C' \in Command_{\rho,\rho'}$; $C'' \in Command_{\rho',\rho''}$; $\vec{no}$ be the vector of outputs in $\rho.output$ that are not in the frame $\vec{x}$; and $\vec{nx}$ be the vector of local variables in $\rho.local$ that are not in $\vec{x}$.

$$\begin{array}{rl}
\text{Command } C & \mathcal{M}_\rho(C) \\
\{P\} & \lambda\, in \in In_\rho, \sigma_0, \sigma \in \Sigma_\rho \bullet Healthy_{\rho,\rho}(\sigma_0, \sigma) \wedge \\
& \quad (\sigma_0.ok \wedge \sigma_0.\tau < \infty \wedge P(in, \sigma_0) \Rightarrow \\
& \qquad \sigma.ok \wedge \sigma_0.\tau = \sigma.\tau \wedge (\forall\, v : \rho.local \bullet \sigma_0.loc(v) = \sigma.loc(v))) \\
\infty\vec{x}\colon [Q] & \lambda\, in \in In_\rho, \sigma_0, \sigma \in \Sigma_\rho \bullet Healthy_{\rho,\rho}(\sigma_0, \sigma) \wedge \\
& \quad (\sigma_0.ok \wedge \sigma_0.\tau < \infty \Rightarrow \\
& \qquad \sigma.ok \wedge Q(in, \sigma_0, \sigma) \wedge stable(\vec{no}, [\sigma_0.\tau \ldots \sigma.\tau]) \wedge \\
& \qquad (\sigma.\tau < \infty \Rightarrow (\forall\, v : \vec{nx} \bullet \sigma_0.loc(v) = \sigma.loc(v)))) \\
C';\ C'' & \mathcal{M}_\rho(C') \fatsemi \mathcal{M}_{\rho'}(C'') \\
C_1 \sqcap C_2 & \mathcal{M}_\rho(C_1) \cup \mathcal{M}_\rho(C_2) \\
\bigsqcap_{i:S} C_i & \bigcup_{i:S} \mathcal{M}_\rho(C_i)
\end{array}$$

Fig. 3. Semantics of basic commands

and deallocation (which contracts the environment). Assumption and specification commands have the same before and after environments. In Fig. 3 we define the following commands.

- An assumption, $\{P\}$, that for a single-state predicate, P, has no effect (is a null operation) if P holds, but aborts if P does not hold. P must be independent of ok.
- A specification command, $\infty\vec{x}\colon [Q]$, that for a vector of outputs and local variables, $\vec{x}$, and a relation, Q, guarantees to establish the relation Q and modify only the variables in its *frame* $\vec{x}$. The outputs not in the frame ($\vec{no}$) are stable for the duration of the command, and, provided the command terminates, the final values of the local variables not in the frame ($\vec{nx}$) are the same as their initial values. Q must be independent of ok_0 and ok, and in the case of nontermination, independent of the final values of the local variables.
- Sequential composition of commands. For relations $R_1 : Rel_{\rho,\rho'}$ and $R_2 : Rel_{\rho',\rho''}$, their relational composition is defined by

$$R_1 \mathbin{⨾} R_2 \mathrel{\widehat{=}} (\lambda\, in : In_\rho;\ \sigma_0 : \Sigma_\rho;\ \sigma : \Sigma_{\rho''} \bullet (\exists\, \sigma' : \Sigma_{\rho'} \bullet R_1(in, \sigma_0, \sigma') \wedge R_2(in, \sigma', \sigma))) \tag{8}$$

- Demonic nondeterministic choice between commands, both binary and over a set of commands. Union of relations is given by pointwise disjunction of relations.

In the following definitions, Q is a relation; d is a time-valued expression; i is a natural number; and C is a command, that has the same before and after environments. An empty frame on a specification command is represented by $\varnothing$.

$$\begin{aligned}
\mathbf{skip} &\mathrel{\widehat{=}} \infty\varnothing\colon [\tau_0 = \tau] \\
\mathbf{idle} &\mathrel{\widehat{=}} \infty\varnothing\colon [\tau < \infty] \\
\mathbf{boneidle} &\mathrel{\widehat{=}} \infty\varnothing\colon [\tau = \infty] \\
\mathbf{abort} &\mathrel{\widehat{=}} \{\mathit{false}\} \\
\mathbf{magic} &\mathrel{\widehat{=}} \infty\varnothing\colon [\mathit{false}]
\end{aligned}$$

$$\begin{aligned}
\vec{x}\colon [Q] &\mathrel{\widehat{=}} \infty\vec{x}\colon [Q \wedge \tau < \infty] \\
[Q] &\mathrel{\widehat{=}} \varnothing\colon [Q \wedge \tau_0 = \tau] \\
\mathbf{deadline}\, d &\mathrel{\widehat{=}} [\tau \le d] \\
C^0 &\mathrel{\widehat{=}} \mathbf{skip} \\
C^{i+1} &\mathrel{\widehat{=}} C;\ C^i \\
C^* &\mathrel{\widehat{=}} \bigsqcap_{i:\mathbb{N}} C^i
\end{aligned}$$

Fig. 4. Additional commands

Given these basics, Fig. 4 gives the definition of some additional useful commands:

skip – a command that does nothing and takes no time; **skip** is the unit of sequential composition: **skip**; $C = C = C$; **skip**.

idle – a command that does nothing, but may take time but must terminate.

boneidle – a command that never does anything and never terminates.

abort – a command that guarantees nothing. It is the zero of nondeterministic choice and a left zero of sequential composition:

$$\mathbf{abort} \sqcap C = \mathbf{abort} = C \sqcap \mathbf{abort}$$
$$\mathbf{abort};\ C = \mathbf{abort}$$

It is not a right zero of sequential composition because the command preceding it may not terminate, e.g., **boneidle**; **abort** = **boneidle** . In addition, it is not a right zero because the behaviour up until the time of abort is preserved.

magic – an infeasible command that refines anything (and hence can not be implemented). **magic** is the unit of nondeterministic choice and a left zero of sequential composition:

$$\mathbf{magic} \sqcap C = C = C \sqcap \mathbf{magic}$$
$$\mathbf{magic};\ C = \mathbf{magic}$$

It is not a right zero of sequential composition because the command preceding it may not terminate or may abort, e.g.,

$$\mathbf{abort};\ \mathbf{magic} = \mathbf{abort}$$
$$\mathbf{boneidle};\ \mathbf{magic} = \mathbf{boneidle}$$

$\vec{x}\colon \lceil Q \rceil$ – a terminating specification command.

$\lceil Q \rceil$ – a test (or coercion) that acts like **skip** if Q is true and **magic** if Q is false.

deadline d – a test that guarantees to meet the deadline d.

iteration of commands – both to a particular natural number, C^i, and any finite number of iterations, C^*, including zero [1, 14, 10].

To be well defined, commands used in iterations must have the same before and after environments. The iterated commands are used to define the semantics for loops, but in order to do that we also need to define the iteration of a relation an infinite number of times. To define infinite iteration we use an infinite sequence of intermediate states. For a relation, $R \in Rel_{\rho,\rho}$,

$$\begin{aligned} R^{\infty} \mathrel{\widehat{=}} (\lambda\, in : In_{\rho};\ \sigma_0, \sigma : \Sigma_{\rho} \bullet \\ &(\exists\, tr : \mathbb{N} \rightarrow \Sigma_{\rho} \bullet tr(0) = \sigma_0 \wedge \\ &\quad (\forall\, i : \mathbb{N} \bullet R(in, tr(i), tr(i+1)) \wedge tr(i).\tau < \infty \wedge \\ &\qquad (\forall\, o : \rho.output \bullet tr(i).out(o) \subseteq \sigma.out(o))) \wedge \\ &\quad ((\forall\, i : \mathbb{N} \bullet tr(i).ok) \Rightarrow \sigma.ok) \wedge \\ &\quad \sigma.\tau = sup(\{i : \mathbb{N} \bullet tr(i).\tau\}))) \end{aligned} \tag{9}$$

Successive states in the sequence are related by R. As we are considering an infinite repetition, we only consider terminating behaviour of R on every iteration. The final value of an output contains the output of every iteration as a prefix — it is the limit of the values of the outputs. If all iterations don't abort, the infinite repetition does not abort. The termination time of the infinite repetition is the supremum (least upper bound) of the termination times of all iterations. If there is some strictly positive time, d, such that every iteration takes at least d time units — as is the case in practice — then the supremum will be infinity. If the relation R is well founded and terminates then R^{∞} is the empty relation. Note that, while R^{∞} constrains the final values of the outputs as well as ok and τ, it does not put any constraints on the final values of the local variables.

In an environment ρ, the semantics of infinite iteration of a command, C, is given by the infinite iteration of the relation representing C:

$$\begin{aligned} \mathcal{M}_{\rho}(C^{\infty}) \mathrel{\widehat{=}} (\lambda\, in : In_{\rho};\ \sigma_0, \sigma : \Sigma_{\rho} \bullet Healthy_{\rho,\rho}(\sigma_0, \sigma) \wedge \\ &(\sigma_0.ok \wedge \sigma_0.\tau < \infty \Rightarrow ((\mathcal{M}_{\rho}(C))^{\infty})(in, \sigma_0, \sigma))). \end{aligned}$$

5 Modelling a Loop

To model a loop, **do** $B \rightarrow C$ **od**, we need to consider both the case when it executes a finite number of iterations and the case when it executes an infinite number of iterations. We start with a simple model that ignores timing aspects. We can model a single iteration of the loop by a test (or coercion) $\lceil B \rceil$ followed by the command C. Any finite number of iterations can then be modelled by

$$(\lceil B \rceil \; ; \; C)^*.$$

From the definition of Kleene star this is equivalent to

$$\sqcap_{i:\mathbb{N}}(\lceil B \rceil \; ; \; C)^i.$$

Recall that a test whose predicate is false is equivalent to **magic**, which is the unit of nondeterministic choice. Hence if after i iterations the guard B becomes false, all iterations higher than i will be equivalent to **magic** and will not contribute to the nondeterministic choice.

The loop terminates if the guard is false. We can model this by

$$(\lceil B \rceil \; ; \; C)^*; \; \lceil \neg B \rceil.$$

If after i iterations the guard is still true, that element of the nondeterministic choice will be equivalent to **magic** and not contribute to the choice. Note that if, on the ith iteration, C does not terminate, the guard will not be reached and hence the behaviour will be equivalent to $(\lceil B \rceil \; ; \; C)^i$.

The other case in which the loop does not terminate is if it iterates an infinite number of times, which we can model as

$$(\lceil B \rceil \; ; \; C)^\infty.$$

Hence a loop can be modelled as

$$((\lceil B \rceil \; ; \; C)^*; \; \lceil \neg B \rceil) \sqcap (\lceil B \rceil \; ; \; C)^\infty.$$

To adapt this definition to the real-time context we need to handle the following issues:

1. the loop guard may contain a reference to an output, o, which needs to be interpreted as the value of the output at the current time, $o(\tau)$;
2. evaluation of the loop guard and the branch back to the start of the loop may take time; and
3. each iteration of the loop takes some minimum time.

The first of these we handle by introducing the notation $B@\tau$ to stand for the expression B with every occurrence of each output, o, replaced by $o(\tau)$.

The second we model by introducing **idle** commands in the definition of a single iteration. Instead of $\lceil B \,@\, \tau \rceil \; ; \; C$, we use

$$\lceil B \,@\, \tau \rceil \; ; \; \mathbf{idle}; \; C; \; \mathbf{idle}.$$

We require that the loop guard, B, is *idle stable*, that is, its value does not change just with the passage of time. If B is idle stable, then

$$\lceil B @ \tau \rceil \ ; \ \mathbf{idle} = \mathbf{idle}; \ \lceil B @ \tau \rceil \ .$$

To ensure the third condition, i.e., that every iteration takes a minimum amount of time, d, we introduce a fresh auxiliary local variable [5]. The auxiliary variable, s, captures the start time of the command, and a test at the end of an iteration ensures it takes at least d time units. A single iteration becomes

$$ITER \mathrel{\widehat{=}} [\![\ \mathbf{aux}\, s : Time; \ s := \tau; \ \lceil B @ \tau \rceil \ ; \ \mathbf{idle}; \ C; \ \mathbf{idle}; \ \lceil s + d \leq \tau \rceil \ ]\!] .$$

Our real-time loop is then defined as a nondeterministic choice over all strictly positive times d, of either a finite number of iterations of the loop followed by a false guard or an infinite number of iterations.

$$\mathbf{do}\, B \rightarrow C \ \mathbf{od} \quad \mathrel{\widehat{=}} \bigsqcap d : Time \mid d > 0 \bullet (ITER^{*}; \ \lceil \neg B @ \tau \rceil \ ; \ \mathbf{idle}) \sqcap ITER^{\infty}$$

Note that the requirement that every single iteration take at least d time units both ensures that the termination time of an infinite number of iterations is infinity and also avoids Zeno-like behaviour, where, for example, each iteration takes half the execution time of the previous iteration. The nondeterministic choice over all strictly positive times d allows the definition to be machine independent. We could arbitrarily use a time for d of one yoctosecond (10^{-24} seconds) which should be more than small enough for the foreseeable future, but the machine independent approach seems cleaner.

6 Refinement Laws for Loops

Jones presents a law for the refinement of a specification command to a loop that involves both a loop invariant, I, which is a single-state predicate, and a well-founded relation R [13]. Using the refinement calculus notation, in which "$\sqsubseteq$" stands for "is refined by", the law can be phrased as follows.

$$\{I\}; \ x\!: \lceil I \wedge \neg B \wedge R^{*} \rceil \sqsubseteq \mathbf{do}\, B \rightarrow \{I \wedge B\}; \ x\!: \lceil I \wedge R \rceil \ \mathbf{od} \tag{10}$$

When executed in a state satisfying both the invariant and the guard, the body of the loop terminates and re-establishes the invariant as well as establishing the relation R between the before and after states of the loop body. Given this loop body, the above rule states that, if the loop is executed in a state satisfying the invariant, it is guaranteed to terminate in a state satisfying the invariant, the negation of the guard, and the reflexive transitive closure of the relation (R^{*}). Termination of the loop is guaranteed by the fact that the relation R is well founded; i.e., there is no infinite sequence of values such that successive pairs elements in the sequence are related by R.

This law has been generalised to handle real-time, possibly-nonterminating loops [6]. The generalisation also makes use of an invariant and a relation, but it does not require the relation to be well founded in order to allow for nonterminating loops. We consider a loop body that either,

- terminates and maintains an invariant I and establishes the relation R between its before and after states, or
- fails to terminate and establishes the relation Q.

The general repetition law allows for the following three behaviours of a loop.

Termination after a finite number of iterations. On termination the negation of the guard, the invariant, and the reflexive transitive closure, R^*, of the relation hold, as for Jones's law (10).

Body nontermination: The loop fails to terminate because the loop body fails to terminate on an iteration. The loop establishes the composition of R^* and Q, i.e., $R^* \fatsemi Q$. The R^* represents a finite number of iterations (zero or more) that terminate, and the Q represents the final nonterminating iteration.

Infinite iteration: Even though the loop body terminates on every iteration, the loop fails to terminate because the the loop guard is always true. We can make use of the infinite iteration of a relation, R^∞ (9). We also need to define the equivalent of the invariant in this case. For a loop that iterates infinitely many times, if the loop's body terminates and maintains an invariant, I, then that invariant and the guard of the loop, B, are true infinitely many times. Hence for any time τ', there exists a later time at which the invariant, the guard, and R^* hold.

$$
\begin{aligned}
I' &\mathrel{\widehat=} (B \mathbin{@} \tau \wedge I \wedge R^*)\\
I'_\infty &\mathrel{\widehat=} (\lambda\, in : In_\rho;\ \sigma_0, \sigma : \Sigma_\rho \bullet\\
&\qquad\qquad (\forall\, \tau' : \mathit{Time} \bullet (\exists\, \sigma : \Sigma_\rho \bullet \tau' \leq \sigma.\tau \wedge I'(in, \sigma_0, \sigma))))
\end{aligned}
$$

Infinite iteration of the loop establishes both I'_∞ and R^∞.

In the real-time case, if an invariant, I, holds before the start of a loop, it is not guaranteed to still hold after guard evaluation because the invariant may be time dependent and the invariant could become false in the time it takes to evaluate the guard. Similarly, if the invariant held at the end of one iteration, it isn't guaranteed to still hold after the guard evaluation for the next iteration. To avoid these problems, we require the loop invariant to be *idle-invariant*, that is, it must satisfy,

$$\{I\};\ \mathbf{idle} \sqsubseteq \mathbf{idle};\ \{I\}.$$

For the same reasons the relation, Q, must be *pre-idle-invariant*, that is,

$$\infty x\colon \left[Q\right] \sqsubseteq \mathbf{idle};\ \infty x\colon \left[Q\right],$$

and the relation, R, must be both pre- and post-idle-invariant, that is,

$$\infty x\colon \left[R\right] \sqsubseteq \mathbf{idle};\ \infty x\colon \left[R\right];\ \mathbf{idle}.$$

We can now give the most complex form of the rule for introducing a repetition.

Law 1 (Repetition). *Given an idle-stable, boolean-valued expression, B; a pre-idle-invariant relation, Q; an idle-invariant, single-state predicate, I; and a pre- and post-idle-invariant relation, R; let $I' \mathrel{\widehat=} (B \mathbin{@} \tau \wedge I \wedge R^*)$, then*

$$
\begin{aligned}
&\{I\};\ \infty x\colon \left[\begin{array}{c}(\tau < \infty \wedge \neg\, B \mathbin{@} \tau \wedge I \wedge R^*) \vee\\ (\tau = \infty \wedge ((I'_\infty \wedge R^\infty) \vee (R^* \fatsemi Q)))\end{array}\right]\\
&\sqsubseteq \mathbf{do}\, B \rightarrow \{B \mathbin{@} \tau \wedge I\};\ \infty x\colon \left[(\tau < \infty \wedge I \wedge R) \vee (\tau = \infty \wedge Q)\right]\ \mathbf{od}
\end{aligned}
$$

The above law can be specialised in a number of ways. If the loop body is guaranteed to terminate, i.e., Q is false, that alternative for the loop and the loop body can be eliminated.

Law 2 (terminating body).

$$\begin{array}{l} \{I\};\ \infty x\colon \left[(\tau < \infty \wedge \neg\, B @ \tau \wedge I \wedge R^*) \vee (\tau = \infty \wedge (I'_\infty \wedge R^\infty))\right] \\ \sqsubseteq \mathbf{do}\, B \rightarrow \{B @ \tau \wedge I\};\ \infty x\colon \left[\tau < \infty \wedge I \wedge R\right] \mathbf{od} \end{array}$$

If the loop body terminates, i.e., Q is false, and the relation R is well founded, i.e., R^∞ is false, then only the terminating behaviour remains and the law is that of Jones [13].

Law 3 (terminating). *Provided R is well founded,*

$$\begin{array}{l} \{I\};\ \infty x\colon \left[\tau < \infty \wedge \neg\, B @ \tau \wedge I \wedge R^*\right] \\ \sqsubseteq \mathbf{do}\, B \rightarrow \{B @ \tau \wedge I\};\ \infty x\colon \left[\tau < \infty \wedge I \wedge R\right] \mathbf{od} \end{array}$$

If the guard is just *true* then the terminating case of the loop can't occur.

Law 4 (true guard).

$$\begin{array}{l} \{I\};\ \infty x\colon \left[\tau = \infty \wedge ((I'_\infty \wedge R^\infty) \vee (R^* \fatsemi Q))\right] \\ \sqsubseteq \mathbf{do}\, \mathit{true} \rightarrow \{I\};\ \infty x\colon \left[(\tau < \infty \wedge I \wedge R) \vee (\tau = \infty \wedge Q)\right] \mathbf{od} \end{array}$$

If in addition to the guard being *true*, if the body of the loop terminates, i.e., Q is false, then the only behaviour allowed is infinite iteration.

Law 5 (infinite iteration).

$$\begin{array}{l} \{I\};\ \infty x\colon \left[\tau = \infty \wedge I'_\infty \wedge R^\infty\right] \\ \sqsubseteq \mathbf{do}\, \mathit{true} \rightarrow \{I\};\ \infty x\colon \left[\tau < \infty \wedge I \wedge R\right] \mathbf{od} \end{array}$$

7 Conclusions

Providing a semantics for real-time programs is a subtle process. We need to handle:

- specifying timing constraints on behaviours,
- specifying reactive behaviour where the intermediate values of outputs are significant (not just their final values), and
- allowing nonterminating (eternal) programs as normal behaviour (rather than equating nontermination and aborting behaviour).

In this paper, we have summarised the issues involved in coming up with a suitable semantics, and given a formalisation that handles these issues. The exposition on the healthiness constraints for commands in Sect. 2 and the way they are formalised in Sect. 3 is new in this paper.

To define loops that may not terminate we need to model not only finite numbers of iterations of the loop, but also an infinite number of iterations. This can be done by introducing an infinite iteration operator as well as using the conventional Kleene star operator to handle a finite number of iterations.

The refinement law for loops generalises that given by Jones [13], which makes use of not only a loop invariant but a relation, R, between the before and after states of a single iteration. The general law allows for not only the terminating case of Jones's law, but nontermination due to either infinite iteration or because the loop body does not terminate.

Acknowledgments. This research was supported by Australian Research Council (ARC) Discovery Grant DP0558408, *Analysing and generating fault-tolerant real-time systems.* I would like to thank Jeremy Gibbons and Larissa Meinicke for feedback on earlier drafts of this paper.

References

[1] E. Cohen. Hypotheses in Kleene algebra. Technical report TM-ARH-023814, Bellcore, 1994.

[2] E. W. Dijkstra. *A Discipline of Programming*. Prentice-Hall, 1976.

[3] S.E. Dunne. Recasting Hoare and He's unifying theory of programs in the context of general correctness. In A. Butterfield, G. Strong, and C. Pahl, editors, *Proceedings of the 5th Irish Workshop in Formal Methods, IWFM 2001*, Workshops in Computing. British Computer Society, 2001. http://ewic.bcs.org/conferences/2001/5thformal/papers.

[4] C. J. Fidge, I. J. Hayes, and G. Watson. The deadline command. *IEE Proceedings—Software*, 146(2):104–111, April 1999.

[5] I. J. Hayes. Real-time program refinement using auxiliary variables. In M. Joseph, editor, *Proc. Formal Techniques in Real-Time and Fault-Tolerant Systems*, volume 1926 of *LNCS*, pages 170–184. Springer, 2000.

[6] I. J. Hayes. Reasoning about real-time repetitions: Terminating and nonterminating. *Science of Computer Programming*, 43(2–3):161–192, 2002.

[7] I. J. Hayes. A predicative semantics for real-time refinement. In A. McIver and C. C. Morgan, editors, *Programming Methodology*, pages 109–133. Springer Verlag, 2003.

[8] I. J. Hayes and M. Utting. Coercing real-time refinement: A transmitter. In D. J. Duke and A. S. Evans, editors, *BCS-FACS Northern Formal Methods Workshop (NFMW'96)*, Electronic Workshops in Computing. Springer, 1997.

[9] I. J. Hayes and M. Utting. A sequential real-time refinement calculus. *Acta Informatica*, 37(6):385–448, 2001.

[10] I.J. Hayes. Programs as paths: An approach to timing constraint analysis. In Jin Song Dong and Jim Woodcock, editors, *Formal Methods and Software Engineering: Proc. 5th Int. Conf. on Formal Engineering Methods (ICFEM 2003)*, volume 2885 of *Lecture Notes in Computer Science*, pages 1–15. Springer Verlag, 2003.

[11] E. C. R. Hehner. Termination is timing. In J.L.A. van de Snepscheut, editor, *Mathematics of Program Construction*, volume 375 of *Lecture Notes in Computer Science*, pages 36–47. Springer, June 1989.

[12] C. A. R. Hoare and He Jifeng. *Unifying Theories of Programming*. Prentice Hall, 1998.

[13] C. B. Jones. Program specification and verification in VDM. Technical Report UMCS-86-10-5, Department of Computer Science, University of Manchester, 1986.

[14] Dexter Kozen. Kleene algebra with tests. *ACM Transactions on Programming Languages and Systems*, 19(3):427–443, May 1997.

Hierarchical Organisation of Predicate-Semantic Models

Yifeng Chen

Department of Computer Science, University of Durham,
Durham DH1 3LE, UK
Yifeng.Chen@dur.ac.uk

Abstract. This paper introduces techniques to organise predicate-semantic models in a hierarchical structure so that a new model can inherit the laws of the existing ones. Generic composition is used to simplify the manipulation of predicates. Necessary restrictions are imposed on the definition of each model so that the inheritance relation can be established by checking a few conditions on the healthiness conditions and the commands. Much of the checking can be supported by laws of generic composition. The techniques also help simplify the proof of well-definedness of program combinators (i.e. their closure in the semantic space) so that we no longer need to prove it (in predicate calculus) for every new model.

1 Introduction

One of the aims of Unifying Theories of Programming (UTP) [4] is to support systematic semantic studies. The main techniques include healthiness conditions and normal forms. A number of semantic models have been introduced for a variety of computational models. The process of semantic modelling for each language consists of several steps including the identification of observables, the definition of the semantic space (by identifying the healthiness conditions), the proof that all operators are closed in the space, the identification of the laws, the definition of normal form, and the proof that the laws are complete with respect to the normal form. From an application point of view, the identified laws are of the most importance, as they represent our knowledge about the language.

This paper follows the above approach but introduces further restrictions on the well-formedness of healthiness conditions. We are interested in the conditions under which one semantic model can inherit the laws (and other properties) of another model. If a number of existing models are placed in a hierarchical structure, it then becomes much easier to develop a new model extending the existing ones, as many laws can be inherited, with various proof obligations alleviated.

In UTP, each program or specification is represented as a predicate. Program combinators become the operators on predicates. To simplify the manipulation of predicates, we use a notation called *generic composition* [2]. A generic composition is a relational composition with a designated interface consisting of several

S. Dunne and W. Stoddart (Eds.): UTP 2006, LNCS 4010, pp. 155–172, 2006.

logical variables. Generic composition has an inverse operator. With the help of the two operators, we no longer need the existential and universal quantifiers. Healthiness conditions defined with generic composition can then be manipulated with the higher-level laws of generic composition.

Section 2 introduces generic composition. Section 3 defines the idempotence and commutativity of predicate functions in general and identifies the necessary disciplines of semantic definitions. Section 4 formalises the conditions for inheritance between semantic models. Section 5 introduces the set-theoretic model of predicate calculus, a model with alphabetic restriction and a model of binary relations.

2 Generic Composition

As a convention we let $x, y, z, r, s, t, x_0, y_0, \cdots$ denote individual variables and $u, v, w, u_0, v_0, \cdots$ denote variable lists. A variable x can be decorated as $\overline{x}$, x' and so on. Decorating a list of variables preserves the order of the list. For example, if $v \mathrel{\widehat{=}} x, y, z$ then $v' = x', y', z'$. For convenience, we use $\{v\}$ to denote the set $\{x, y, z\}$ of variables

We accept two classes of logical variables: non-overlined variables such as $x, y, z, x', y' \cdots$ and overlined ones such as $\overline{x}, \overline{y}, \overline{z}, \overline{x'}, \overline{y'}, \cdots$. Overlining is only used to associate corresponding logical variables syntactically. We assume that overlining can only be applied once. Thus $\overline{\overline{x}}$ is not considered a logical variable. A generic composition is a relational composition with a designated interface of non-overlined variables.

Definition 1. $P :_v R \mathrel{\widehat{=}} \exists v_0 \cdot P[v_0/v] \wedge R[v_0/\overline{v}]$.

A *fresh* variable list v_0 is used to connect the list v of P and the list $\overline{v}$ of R with the interface v_0 hidden by the existential quantifier. Generic composition is a restricted form of relational composition. It relates two predicates on only some of their logical variables. For example, the following composition relates two predicates on only x (and $\overline{x}$ for the second predicate):

$$(x = 10 \wedge y = 20) :_x (\overline{x} \leqslant x \wedge z = 30) \;=\; (10 \leqslant x \wedge y = 20 \wedge z = 30).$$

The existential quantifier $\exists x \cdot P$ is simply represented as $P :_x \mathit{true}$, and variable substitution $P[e/x]$ as $P :_x (\overline{x} = e)$. A generic composition with an empty interface becomes a conjunction: $P : R = P \wedge R$.

Generic composition has an inverse operator denoted by $P /_v R$, which is the weakest predicate X such that $X :_v R \subseteq P$. It can be defined by a Galois connection.

Definition 2. $X \subseteq P /_v R$ *iff* $X :_v R \subseteq P$ *for any predicate* X .

Generic composition and its inverse satisfy a property:

$$P /_v R \;=\; \neg(\neg P :_v R^{\cup}) \;=\; \forall v_0 \cdot (R[v_0/v, v/\overline{v}] \Rightarrow P[v_0/v])$$

where $R^{\cup} \mathrel{\widehat{=}} R[\overline{v}/v, v/\overline{v}]$ is the converse of R for the variable v. Universal quantifier $\forall v \cdot P$ can then be written as $P /_v \mathit{true}$. Negation $\neg P$ becomes false / P with an empty interface. Implication $P \Rightarrow Q$ becomes Q / P with an empty interface. Disjunction $P \vee Q$ is a trivial combination of negation and implication. Thus all connectives, substitution and quantifiers become special cases of generic composition and its inverse [2]. The above theorem shows the expressiveness of generic composition for predicate manipulation.

Theorem 1. *Generic composition and its inverse are complete in the sense that any predicate that does not contain overlined free variables can be written in terms of generic composition and its inverse using only the constant predicates and predicate letters.*

Generic composition and its inverse form a Galois connection and satisfy the algebraic laws of strictness, distributivity and associativity.

Laws 1

(1) $A \subseteq (A :_v R) /_v R$	(2) $(A /_v R) :_v R \subseteq A$
(3) $\mathit{false} :_v R = \mathit{false}$	(4) $\mathit{true} /_v R = \mathit{true}$
(5) $A :_v (R \vee S) = (A :_v R) \vee (A :_v S)$	(6) $(A \vee B) :_v R = (A :_v R) \vee (A :_v R)$
(7) $A /_v (R \vee S) = (A /_v R) \wedge (A /_v S)$	(8) $(A \wedge B) /_v R = (A /_v R) \wedge (A /_v R)$
(9) $(A :_v R) :_v S = A :_v (R :_v S)$	(10) $(A /_v R) /_v S = A /_v (S :_v R)$.

The notation is especially useful when the interfaces of the operators in a predicate are not identical. For example, in the following law we assume that x, y and z are three different logical variables, $A = \exists z \cdot A$ (independence of the variable z) and $C = \exists \overline{y} \cdot C$ (independence of the variable $\overline{y}$).

Laws 2. $(A :_{(y,x)} B) :_{(x,z)} C \; = \; A :_{(y,x)} (B :_{(x,z)} C)$.

Generic composition and its inverse can be used to define modalities. These properties make the composition a useful technical tool for linking temporal logics. Generic composition has also been applied to define a variety of healthiness conditions and parallel compositions. The above laws and a series of other laws can be found in [2].

3 Predicative Semantics

3.1 Set-Theoretic Predicate Calculus

Any semantic space studied in this thesis is a complete lattice (closed under arbitrary lub and glb, refer to Proposition 3). Our mathematical foundation is set theory. However, if we define predicates as sets we can then hide set-theoretic operators and use predicate calculus directly in our later semantic studies. Predicate calculus is the most primitive model in our hierarchy and provides the basis for other semantic models.

Let ν denote the set of all (non-overlined) variables used in semantic models, and $\mathbb{T}$ be a set of all constants. An *observation* a is a total function $a \in \nu \to \mathbb{T}$.

A predicate (or 'program') is a set of observations. Note that the set ν is also used if a list is expected where the variables in ν are assumed to be ordered alphabetically.

Let $\text{PRED}(\nu) \mathrel{\hat{=}} \mathcal{P}(\nu \to \mathbb{T})$ denote the set of all predicates where $\mathcal{P}(\mathrm{X})$ denotes the powerset of a set X. It is a complete lattice ordered by $\supseteq$, the lub is $\cap$, the glb is $\cup$, the top is the empty set $\emptyset$, and the bottom is $(\nu \to \mathbb{T})$.

The following table lists all the predicate commands. They are defined as sets and operators on sets. In the definition $e(u)$ is an expression, x is a variable, and u is a list of variables.

Command	Set-theoretic definition	Explanation
$true$	$\hat{=} (\nu \to \mathbb{T})$	bottom
$false$	$\hat{=} \emptyset$	top
$p(u)$	$\hat{=} \{a : \nu \to \mathbb{T} \mid p \circ a(u) = 1\}$	pre-defined Boolean function
$P[e(u)/x]$	$\hat{=} \{b : \nu \to \mathbb{T} \mid e \circ b(u) = a(x),$ $a \in P,\ b \dagger \{x \mapsto a(x)\}\}$	substitution of $e(u)$ for x in P
$\neg P$	$\hat{=} (\nu \to \mathbb{T}) \setminus P$	negation
$\exists x \cdot P$	$\hat{=} \{a \oplus \{x \mapsto t\} \mid a \in P,\ t \in \mathbb{T}\}$	existential quantification
$\forall x \cdot P$	$\hat{=} \neg \exists x \cdot \neg P$	universal quantification
$P \vee Q$	$\hat{=} P \cup Q$	disjunction
$P \wedge Q$	$\hat{=} P \cap Q$	conjunction
$P \Rightarrow Q$	$\hat{=} \neg P \vee Q$	implication
$\mu_\perp f$	$\hat{=} \bigcup \{P \mid P \subseteq f(P)\}$	the weakest fixpoint of monotonic f

Evidently all laws of predicate calculus are true in $\text{PRED}(\nu)$ and hence complete in the sense that the equivalence between two predicates (without recursion) can be proved in finitely many steps using the laws of predicate calculus. Note that the syntax of any predicate must be finite, although we allow universal union $\bigcup$ and intersection $\bigcap$ in set theory.

3.2 Healthiness Conditions and Predicate Functions

In a predicative semantics the denotation of each (generalised) program P is a predicate, thought of as a binary relation describing the set of behaviors of P. For example, a predicate $x' = x + 1$ (or equivalently a relation $\{(x, x+1) \mid x \in S\}$ where S is the state space) denotes a sequential program $x := x + 1$ that increases x by 1. The syntax of the predicate is no longer of primary importance: two predicates are considered the same if they describe the same relation. This style of semantics has the substantial advantage of employing only elementary widely-known mathematics, rendering the resulting theory accessible to most computer scientists. Technically, its advantages are firstly that it makes available the set-theoretic operators like universal union and intersection for specifications; and secondly that it enables semantic denotations to be characterised using some fixpoint equations called *healthiness conditions*. One semantic model is more concrete than another model if it satisfies a stronger healthiness condition. A healthiness condition is normally written $A = H(A)$ where H is a predicate function.

Healthiness conditions provide the key to our hierarchical approach. The relationships between semantic spaces, the closure of commands and the inheritance of laws are all closely related to the idempotence and commutativity of predicate functions. For example, a predicate representing a sequential computation satisfies a disjunctive healthiness condition that if the program has not started properly, its behaviour is chaotic.

HC 1 (*Hok*) $\quad A = ok \Rightarrow A$

We use $Hok(X) \mathrel{\widehat{=}} ok \Rightarrow X$ to denote the corresponding predicate function.

Some other healthiness conditions in UTP can be re-defined as fixpoints of predicate functions. The healthiness condition $A[false/ok'] \Rightarrow A[true/ok']$ describes the upward closure of ok'. It is equivalent to a fixpoint equation:

HC 2 (*Hok′*) $\quad A = A :_{ok'} (\overline{ok}' \Rightarrow ok')$.

A stronger healthiness condition $A = A \mathbin{;} (ok \Rightarrow (ok' \wedge v = v'))$ describes the divergent behaviour of non-terminating sequential programs and can be re-defined as a fixpoint equation:

HC 3 (*Hdev*) $\quad A = A :_{(ok', v')} (\overline{ok}' \Rightarrow (ok' \wedge \overline{v'} = v'))$.

It can be shown that any *Hdev*-healthy predicate P (satisfiying $P = Hdev(P)$) is also *Hok′*-healthy (satisfiying $P = Hok'(P)$).

Another healthiness condition $A = \bigsqcap_s A[s/tr,\ s^\frown(tr' - tr)/tr]$ describes the prefix independence of a trace specification and can be re-defined as fixpoint equation:

HC 4 (*Htr*) $\quad A = A :_{(tr, tr')} (\overline{tr'} - \overline{tr} = tr' - tr)$.

The idempotence of the above healthiness functions is a result of generic composition's associativity. More examples of healthiness conditions including some higher-order ones can be found in Chen [2].

Defining predicate transformer H to equal the right-hand side there, that identity becomes $A = H(A)$. Thus the predicates we wish to call healthy are the fixed points of the transformer H. But for idempotent H (i.e. satisfying $H \circ H = H$) the set of fixed points equals the range of H. Since H is also monotonic, that range is a complete sublattice of predicates (though in the general case, with differing glb and lub). Such a predicate transformer transforms any unhealthy predicate to a healthy one. If the healthiness condition of a semantic model is expressed as the combination of several small healthiness conditions, we must show that the composition of the healthiness transformers is also idempotent and monotonic.

The type of an n-ary predicate function is $\textsc{Pred}(\nu)^n \to \textsc{Pred}(\nu)$.

Definition 3 (Pointwise commutativity). *1-ary functions f and g commute for predicative argument P, written $(f \bowtie g)(P)$, iff $f \circ g(P) = g \circ f(P)$.*

In the case that g is a n-ary function $(f \bowtie g)(P_1, P_2, \cdots, P_n)$ denotes the commutativity of f and g for the predicates $P_1, P_2, \cdots, P_n$. If f commutes with 1-ary function g for any predicative argument P, we simply write $f \bowtie g$.

Definition 4 (Idempotence). *A 1-ary function f is idempotent for predicative argument P, written $\Diamond f(P)$, iff $f \circ f(P) = f(P)$.*

If function f is idempotent for any predicate, we simply write $\Diamond f$.

Definition 5 (Closure). *A function f is closed with regard to another function g iff $g \bowtie (f \circ g)$.*

Definition 6 (Distributivity). *A function g distributes through another function f iff $g \bowtie (g \circ f)$.*

3.3 Basic Predicate Functions

We are particularly interested in two basic forms of predicate functions: the disjunctive ones $H_{\vee R}$ and the generic ones $H_{:_v S}$ where $R \in \textsc{Pred}$, while S may contain overlined free variables. A predicate function is called *common* if it is the composition of predicate functions in these these forms.

Definition 7.
$$H_{\vee R}(A) \ \widehat{=}\ A \vee R$$
$$H_{:_v S}(A) \ \widehat{=}\ A :_v S$$

Many predicate functions are common. For example, the conjunctive predicate function $H_{\wedge R}(X) = X :_v R$ is a special generic one when the predicate R does not have free overlined variables. The constant predicate function $H_{@P}(A) \ \widehat{=}\ H_{\wedge P} \circ H_{\vee true}$ is a composition of a conjunctive function and a disjunctive one. The following theorem shows the generality of common predicate functions:

Theorem 2. *A predicate function L is common, iff it satisfies universal disjunctivity such that $L(\bigvee \mathrm{M}) = \bigvee \{L(P) \mid P \in \mathrm{M}\}$ for any $\mathrm{M} \subseteq \textsc{Pred}(\nu)$.*

Proof. The disjunctivity of a common predicate function directly follows the disjunctivity of disjunction and generic composition. On the other hand, any universally disjunctive predicate function L can be represented as $H_{\vee S} \circ H_{:_\nu R}$ where $S = L(\mathit{false})$ and $R = \bigvee \{(\overline{\nu} = a \wedge \nu \in L(\{a\})) \mid a \in \nu \to \mathbb{T}\}$. □

The following table lists the conditions for idempotence of common predicate functions. They can be proved using the laws of generic composition in Section 2.

Function	Condition for Idempotence
$H_{\vee R}$	*true*
$H_{:_v R}$	$R = R :_v R$
$H_{\vee S} \circ H_{:_v R}$	$(S :_v R) \Rightarrow S$ and $R = R :_v R$
$H_{:_v S} \circ H_{\vee R}$	$S = (S :_v S)$
$H_{:_v S} \circ H_{:_v R}$	$(R :_v S) = (R :_v S :_v R :_v S)$

The following table lists the conditions for commutativity of predicate functions:

Function	Function	Condition for Commutativity
$H_{\vee R}$	$H_{\vee S}$	*true*
$H_{\vee R}$	$H_{:_v S}$	$R = R :_v S$
$H_{\vee R}$	$H_{:_v S} \circ H_{\vee R}$	$R \Rightarrow R :_v S$
$H_{:_v R}$	$H_{:_v S}$	$(R :_v S) = (S :_v R)$

Unification of semantic models becomes more systematic if we adopt these disciplines, which need to be strong enough to allow inheritance but flexible enough to incorporate various computational models.

3.4 Semantic Spaces

In this paper each semantic space is a set of predicates satisfying a healthiness condition. The healthiness condition is defined by a fixpoint equation $A = H(A)$ in which H is a *healthiness function*, i.e. a monotonic and idempotent predicate function:

Definition 8. *A set* $H(\text{PRED}(\nu))$ *of predicates is a semantic space if* H *is a healthiness function.*

Since a semantic space is characterises by a healthiness function, we can study the properties of semantic spaces by only considering their corresponding healthiness functions.

Proposition 3. *Any semantic space is a complete lattice.*

Proof. Let $f : \mathrm{S} \to \mathrm{S}$ be a monotonic and idempotent function on a complete lattice S. Let $\mathrm{T} \mathrel{\widehat{=}} f(\mathrm{S})$. $\sqcap_\mathrm{S}$ and $\sqcap_\mathrm{T}$ denote the lub s of S and T respectively. Apparently $\mathrm{T} \subseteq \mathrm{S}$. Then for any $\mathrm{E} \subseteq \mathrm{T}$, E is a set of fixpoints of f and $f(\mathrm{E}) = \mathrm{E}$. Thus $\sqcup_\mathrm{S} f(\mathrm{E}) = \sqcup_\mathrm{S}\mathrm{E} \in \mathrm{S}$ and $f(\sqcup_\mathrm{S}\mathrm{E}) \in \mathrm{T}$. For any $e \in \mathrm{E}$, $f(e) = e \sqsubseteq \sqcup_\mathrm{S}\mathrm{E}$ and $e = f(e) = f^2(e) \sqsubseteq f(\sqcup_\mathrm{S}\mathrm{E})$, or $f(\sqcup_\mathrm{S}\mathrm{E})$ is an upper bound of E in T. Let $t \in \mathrm{T}$ be an upper bound of E, i.e. for any $e \in \mathrm{E}$, $f(e) \sqsubseteq t = f(t)$ and $\sqcup_\mathrm{S}\mathrm{E} = \sqcup_\mathrm{S} f(\mathrm{E}) \sqsubseteq t$. Thus $f(\sqcup_\mathrm{S}\mathrm{E}) \sqsubseteq f(t) = t$, or $f(\sqcup_\mathrm{S}\mathrm{E}) = \sqcup_\mathrm{T}\mathrm{E}$. Glb is the dual of lub. Thus T is also a complete lattice. □

3.5 Commands and Programs

A command is called a *primitive command* or simply a *primitive*, if it is a predicate in the semantic space. For example assignment statements are primitives. A command is called a *compositional command* or simply a *composition*, if it is an n-ary predicate function closed in the semantic space. For example, the sequential composition of any two healthy predicates of semantic space must also be in the space.

Definition 9. *An n-ary composition f is closed in a semantic space* M *if for any* $P_1, P_2, \cdots, P_n \in \mathrm{M},\ f(P_1, P_2, \cdots P_n) \in \mathrm{M}$.

Proposition 4. *A composition f is closed in a semantic space $H(\mathrm{PRED}(\nu))$ iff the function f is closed with regard to the healthiness function H.*

A *program letter* is an arbitrary predicate in a semantic space. A *command tree* is a finite tree whose leaf nodes are either primitives or program letters and non-leaf nodes are compositions. For example, $x' = x + 1 \sqcap P$ is a command tree in which $x' = x + 1$ is a primitive command, P is program letter, and $\sqcap$ is the composition between them. We can represent a command tree f as a generalised predicate function:

$$f(P_1, \cdots, P_n \,;\, Q_1, \cdots, Q_m)$$

where each P_i is a primitive command and each Q_j is a program letter. A *program* is a command tree without program letters.

A command directly defined in its parent model is called *basic*. A command defined as the combination of a finite number of basic commands is called *derived*.

3.6 Laws

An algebraic law is an equation between two command trees, each of which may include some *program letters*. For example, $P \vee Q = Q \vee P$ is an algebraic law in predicate calculus. P and Q are program letters. The equation must hold for any program letters in the semantic space. A refinement law is an inequation between two programs. The refinement order $A \sqsubseteq B$ means B always implies A. For example, $P \sqsubseteq P \wedge Q$ is a refinement law. It holds for any program letters P and Q. In general a refinement law $P \sqsubseteq Q$ can be expressed algebraically as $P = P \sqcap Q$.

Definition 10. $f(P_1, \cdots, P_n \,;\, Q_1, \cdots, Q_m) = g(P'_1, \cdots, P'_{n'} \,;\, Q'_1, \cdots, Q'_{m'})$ *is a law in a semantic space $H(\mathrm{PRED}(\nu))$, if* $P_1, \cdots, P_n, P'_1, \cdots, P'_{n'} \in H(\mathrm{PRED}(\nu))$ *and the equation holds for any* $Q_1, \cdots, Q_m, Q'_1, \cdots, Q'_{m'} \in H(\mathrm{PRED}(\nu))$.

3.7 Normal Form and Completeness

Normal form is a general technique used to show the adequacy (or *completeness*) of a set of algebraic laws. The normal form of a language is a sub-language with more restricted syntax. It is easier to compare two programs in the same normal form. If any program of the model can be reduced to a normal form in finitely many steps using just the algebraic laws, the laws are considered 'complete' for the normal form [3].

3.8 Semantic Models

We can now formalise semantic models.

Definition 11. *A quadruple* $(H, \mathcal{P}, \mathcal{C}, \mathcal{L})$ *is a semantic model, if*

1. H *is a healthiness function;*
2. $\mathcal{P}$ *is a set of primitives s.t.* $\mathcal{P} \subseteq H(\textrm{PRED}(\nu))$*;*
3. $\mathcal{C}$ *is a set of compositions, each* $C \in \mathcal{C}$ *of which is closed with regard to* H*;*
4. $\mathcal{L}$ *is a set of laws that always hold for any program letters in* $H(\textrm{PRED}(\nu))$*, and each law consists of only primitives in* $\mathcal{P}$ *and compositions in* $\mathcal{C}$*.*

Note that we $H(\textrm{PRED}(\nu))$ to denote the image of the predicate set $\textrm{PRED}(\nu)$ through the healthiness function H. A quadruple $(H, \mathcal{P}_1, \mathcal{C}_1, \mathcal{L}_1)$ is a *reduced* model of $(H, \mathcal{P}_2, \mathcal{C}_2, \mathcal{L}_2)$ if $\mathcal{P}_1 \subseteq \mathcal{P}_2$, $\mathcal{C}_1 \subseteq \mathcal{C}_2$ and $\mathcal{L}_1 \subseteq \mathcal{L}_2$.

4 Semantic Inheritance

The main purpose of hierarchical semantics is reuse, and the main technique to achieve so is inheritance. Disciplines are needed to support inheritance. The inheritance of a semantic model includes the inheritance of its healthiness conditions, commands (including primitives and compositions) and laws (including recursions).

4.1 Inheritance of Healthiness Functions

The inheritance of a semantic space is the same as the inheritance of its healthiness function.

Definition 12. *Let* H_1 *and* H_2 *be healthiness functions.* H_2 *inherits* H_1 *iff* $H_2 = H_2 \circ H_1$*.*

For example, we can apply a new healthiness function H to the healthiness function H_1 of semantic space $H_1(\textrm{PRED}(\nu))$. If their composition $H \circ H_1$ is idempotent, it becomes a healthiness function that inherits H_1. This function characterises a new semantic space $H \circ H_1(\textrm{PRED}(\nu))$ where H is called an *additional healthiness function.* This has been our standard technique. To inherit the healthiness function of an existing semantic space, we apply a new additional healthiness function to it and then prove the idempotence of their composition.

4.2 Inheritance of Commands

The commands of an abstract model can be inherited by a more concrete model. However, primitives and compositions are treated differently.

A primitive P of an abstract model M is a constant predicate healthy in terms of H_{M}. It can be unconditionally inherited as $H_{\mathrm{N}}(P)$ by any concrete model N where H_{N} forces the command to be healthy in the model N. That means the inherited primitive is no longer the original predicate! For example, assignment statement $x := x+1$ is denoted by a predicate $x' = x+1$. To model termination, [4] introduced a healthiness condition $A = ok \Rightarrow A$ where ok is a fresh variable denoting the proper start of a computation. The assignment statement is then inherited as $ok \Rightarrow x' = x+1$, which is clearly different from its original definition.

A composition is a function closed in the semantic space of a model. We require a composition to be inherited exactly as its original definition. Not meeting this requirement will inevitably lead to unnecessary complexity in later semantic studies. For example sequential composition should always be relational composition. To enable inheritance, we need to prove its closure in the model inheriting it. In some cases syntactic restrictions are needed to ensure that a composition is closed in the new semantic space.

The following proposition helps decompose the closure of a composition f into its closure with regard to the individual healthiness functions g and h respectively.

Proposition 5 (Inheritance of compositions). *If H_1 and H_2 are healthiness functions, the composition f is closed with regard to H_1 and H_2, and H_2 is closed with regard to H_1, then the composition f is closed in regard to $H_2 \circ H_1$.*

Proof.

$H_2 \circ H_1 \circ f \circ \underline{H_2 \circ H_1}$

$=$ {$H_1 \bowtie H_2 \circ H_1$ and idempotence of H_1}

$H_2 \circ \underline{H_1 \circ f \circ H_1} \circ H_2 \circ H_1$

$=$ {$H_1 \bowtie f \circ H_1$ and idempotence of H_1}

$H_2 \circ f \circ \underline{H_1 \circ H_2 \circ H_1}$

$=$ {$H_1 \bowtie H_2 \circ H_1$ and idempotence of H_1}

$\underline{H_2 \circ f \circ H_2} \circ H_1$

$=$ {$H_2 \bowtie f \circ H_2$ and idempotence of H_2}

$f \circ H_2 \circ H_1$

$=$ {idempotence of H_1 and H_2}

$f \circ H_2 \circ \underline{H_2 \circ H_1 \circ H_1}$

$=$ {$H_1 \bowtie H_2 \circ H_1$}

$f \circ H_2 \circ \underline{H_1 \circ H_2 \circ H_1}$

thus, the composition f is closed with regard to $H_2 \circ H_1$. □

4.3 Inheritance of Laws

The following theorem identifies an easy-to-check condition under which a law can be inherited.

Theorem 6 (Inheritance of laws). *If the additional healthiness function of a new model commutes with any composition for its arguments in a law, then that law can be inherited by the new model.*

Proof. Let $f(P_1, \cdots, P_n\ ;\ Q_1, \cdots, Q_m) = g(P'_1, \cdots, P'_{n'}\ ;\ Q'_1, \cdots, Q'_{m'})$ be a law in an abstract model $H_1(\textsc{Pred}(\nu))$, which is inherited by a concrete model $H \circ H_1(\textsc{Pred}(\nu))$ where H is an additional healthiness function, which commutes with any composition for its arguments. Then H commutes with f and g for their arguments respectively:

$$\begin{aligned} & f(H(P_1), \cdots, H(P_n)\ ;\ H(Q_1), \cdots, H(Q_m)) \\ = \ & g(H(P'_1), \cdots, H(P'_{n'})\ ;\ H(Q'_1), \cdots, H(Q'_{m'}))\,. \end{aligned}$$

Consequently,

$$\begin{aligned} & f(H(P_1), \cdots, H(P_n)\ ;\ Q_1, \cdots, Q_m) \\ = \ & g(H(P'_1), \cdots, H(P'_{n'})\ ;\ Q'_1, \cdots, Q'_{m'}) \end{aligned}$$

must be a law in $H(\textsc{Pred}(\nu))$, because any program letter Q_i in $H(\textsc{Pred}(\nu))$ is a fixpoint of H and any primitive P_i is inherited with H automatically applied to it. □

Example: The following law needed to be re-proved in [4] (section 3.1) when new healthiness conditions for termination/nontermination were added:

$$v := e\ ⨟\ P \lhd b \rhd Q \ = \ (v := e\ ⨟\ P) \lhd b \circ e \rhd (v := e\ ⨟\ Q)\,.$$

To inherit such laws systematically, we need to identify some general conditions for the inheritance. According to Theorem 6, a new healthiness function must commute with (⨟) for its two arguments in the law: $v := e$ and an arbitrary program letter. We also need to show that the new healthiness function commutes with $\lhd b \rhd$ (see Theorem 14). □

Theorem 7. *A law without primitives can be inherited directly by a a new model with an additional healthiness function, if the additional healthiness function is closed with regard to the original healthiness function.*

Corollary 8. *A law of* $\textsc{Pred}(\nu)$ *without primitives can be inherited directly by any semantic model.*

Example: The equation $P \vee Q = Q \vee P$ is a valid law in a model if the composition $\vee$ is closed in the semantic space. Any healthiness function commutes with a closed composition for any healthy arguments. □

4.4 Inheritance of Semantic Models

A semantic model can be inherited if its healthiness function, commands and laws can be inherited.

Definition 13. *Let* $M_1 \mathrel{\widehat{=}} (H_1, \mathcal{P}_1, \mathcal{C}_1, \mathcal{L}_1)$ *and* $M_2 \mathrel{\widehat{=}} (H_2, \mathcal{P}_2, \mathcal{C}_2, \mathcal{L}_2)$ *be two semantic models.* M_2 *inherits* M_1, *if* $H_2 \circ H_1 = H_2$, $H_2(\mathcal{P}_1) \subseteq \mathcal{P}_2$, $\mathcal{C}_1 \subseteq \mathcal{C}_2$ *and* $\mathcal{L}_1 \subseteq \mathcal{L}_2$.

Proposition 9. *If* M_2 *is a reduced model of* M_1, *then* M_2 *inherits* M_1.

The following theorem summarises the conditions of inheritance of semantic models.

Theorem 10 (Inheritance of semantic models). *Let* $M_1 \mathrel{\widehat{=}} (H_1, \mathcal{P}_1, \mathcal{C}_1, \mathcal{L}_1)$ *and* $M_2 \mathrel{\widehat{=}} (H_2, \mathcal{P}_2, \mathcal{C}_2, \mathcal{L}_2)$ *be two semantic models.* M_2 *inherits* M_1, *if*

1. *there exists an additional healthiness function* H, *s.t.* $H_2 = H \circ H_1$;
2. *for any* $C \in \mathcal{C}_1$, C *is closed with regard to* H, *i.e.* $H \bowtie C \circ H$;
3. *for any* $L \in \mathcal{L}$, H *commutes with any composition* C *for its arguments in the law* L, *i.e.* $(H \bowtie C)(A_1, A_2, \cdots, A_n)$.

4.5 Inheritance of Fixpoints

According to Tarski's theorem [5], any monotonic function f on a complete lattice (or a domain) has a weakest fixpoint, denoted by $\mu_\perp f$. The theorem reveals that we can recursively apply the function to the bottom element $\perp$:

$$\perp \supseteq f(\perp) \supseteq f^2(\perp) \supseteq \cdots \supseteq f^\omega(\perp) \supseteq f^{\omega+1}(\perp) \supseteq \cdots \supseteq f^\iota(\perp) \supseteq \cdots$$

where $f^\iota(\perp) \mathrel{\widehat{=}} f(\bigsqcup\{f^\kappa(\perp) \mid \kappa \text{ is an ordinal}, \kappa \prec \iota\})$ and $\mu_\perp f$ is formally defined by:

$$\bigsqcup\{f^\iota(\perp) \mid \iota \text{ is an ordinal}\}.$$

We first look at the inheritance of Tarski's weakest fixpoint $\mu_\perp f$. A fixpoint of a recursive function f is a primitive command, and hence must be transformed to the corresponding fixpoint in a more concrete model by an additional healthiness function H. A major theorem in [4] (section 4.1) showed that under certain sufficient conditions, a healthiness function transforms a weakest fixpoint to the weakest fixpoint in a more concrete model. However, those results are not very applicable in practice. In fact, function f may contain primitive commands, which may be changed by additional healthiness functions. That means the corresponding function in a more concrete model is in general not the same as the original recursive function (refer to section 4.2 for an example)!

The following theorem solves the above problem by treating a recursive function as a command tree.

Theorem 11 (Inheritance of weakest fixpoint). *If the additional healthiness function* H *of a new model commutes with any composition for its arguments in a recursive function* $f(X)$ *where* X *is any predicate in the original model, then*

$$H(\mu_\perp f) = \mu_{H(\perp)}(H \circ f).$$

Proof. According to assumption, H commutes with any composition for its arguments in $f(X) \mathrel{\widehat{=}} F(P_1, \cdots, P_n \,;\, X)$ where F is a command tree, each P_i is a primitive, and X is a program letter of the abstract model. Thus $H \circ f = H \circ f \circ H$ where

$$H \circ f(X) = F(H(P_1), \cdots, H(P_n), H(X)).$$

We then need to show that $H(\mu_\bot f) = \mu_{H(\bot)} H \circ f$. This can be done by induction on ordinals:

1. $H(\bot) = H(\bot)$;
2. if $H \circ f^\kappa(\bot) = (H \circ f)^\kappa \circ H(\bot)$,
   then $H \circ f^{\kappa+1}(\bot) = H \circ f \circ H \circ f^\kappa(\bot) = (H \circ f)^{\kappa+1} \circ H(\bot)$.

$f^\kappa(\bot)$ and $(H \circ f)^{\kappa+1}(H(\bot))$ reach their weakest fixpoints before exhausting the elements of their semantic space respectively. Thus $H(\mu_\bot f) = \mu_{H(\bot)}(H \circ f)$.□

It is not surprising that the inheritance of recursions is similar to the inheritance of laws. Indeed a recursion $\mu_\bot f = F$ can be considered a law in which F is a primitive and $\mu_\bot f$ is an infinite command tree. For example the recursive program $\mu_\bot X \cdot (v := e \,\S\, X)$ is inherited as $\mu_{H(\bot)} X \cdot (H(v := e) \,\S\, H(X))$ in a derived model with an additional healthiness function H. The strongest fixpoint can be treated similarly by reversing the order of the complete lattices.

5 Basic Semantic Models

5.1 Predicate Calculus

Simple commands of programming languages can be directly derived from predicate calculus in PRED(ν).

$\bot$	$\widehat{=}$	*true*	chaos (the bottom)
$\top$	$\widehat{=}$	*false*	magic (the top)
$P \sqcap Q$	$\widehat{=}$	$P \vee Q$	glb, nondeterministic choice
$P \sqcup Q$	$\widehat{=}$	$P \wedge Q$	lub
$P \lhd b \rhd Q$	$\widehat{=}$	$(b \sqcup P) \sqcap (\neg b \sqcup Q)$	binary conditional

Note that, in general, the glb and lub in a predicate-semantic space are not the logical conjunction and disjunction unless $\sqcap$ and $\sqcup$ are closed in the space. This is guaranteed by the requirement of their inheritance.

Nondeterministic choice commutes with any conjunctive, disjunctive and generic predicate functions and their composition. Thus $\sqcap$ is closed in common semantic spaces and hence can be directly inherited.

Theorem 12 (Inheritance of glb). *For any R and S, $H_{\vee R}$ and $H_{;_v S}$ commute with nondeterministic choice $\sqcap$.*

Lub $\sqcup$ is closed with regard to any weakening idempotent generic predicate function. It also commutes with any conjunctive and disjunctive predicate function. If the healthiness function of a model is a composition of disjunctive, conjunctive and generic predicate functions, Proposition 5 guarantees the closure of $\sqcup$.

Theorem 13 (Inheritance of lub). *For any R, S and T, if T is idempotent $T = T :_v T$ and weakening $T \sqsubseteq (\overline{v} = v)$, then $\sqcup$ is commutative with $H_{\vee R}$ and closed with regard to $H_{:_v T}$.*

Proof. $\sqcup$'s commutativity with $H_{\vee R}$ is trivial. To prove its closure with regard to $H_{:_v T}$, we first need to check a condition where v_0 and v_1 are 'fresh' variables:

$$
\begin{array}{ll}
T(v_0, v) \wedge T(v_1, v) & \\
= & \\
(T(v_0, v) \wedge T(v_1, v)) :_v \overline{v} = v & \\
\sqsupseteq & T \text{ is weakening, i.e. } T \sqsubseteq \overline{v} = v \\
(T(v_0, v) \wedge T(v_1, v)) :_v T & \\
\sqsupseteq & \text{property of relational compositions} \\
(T(v_0, v) :_v T) \wedge (T(v_1, v) :_v T) & \\
= & \text{idempotence } T = T :_v T \\
T(v_0, v) \wedge T(v_1, v). &
\end{array}
$$

Thus, $T(v_0, v) \wedge T(v_1, v) = (T(v_0, v) \wedge T(v_1, v)) :_v T$, and for any pair of P and Q, we have:

$$
\begin{array}{ll}
H_{:_v T}(P) \sqcup H_{:_v T}(Q) & \\
= & \text{definition of generic predicate function} \\
P :_v T \sqcup Q :_v T & \\
= & \text{definition of generic composition} \\
\exists v_0 v_1 \cdot P_0 \wedge Q_1 \wedge T(v_0, v) \wedge T(v_1, v) & \\
= & \\
(\exists v_0 v_1 \cdot P_0 \wedge Q_1 \wedge T(v_0, v) \wedge T(v_1, v)) :_v T & \\
= & \text{definition of generic predicate function} \\
H_{:_v T}(H_{:_v T}(P) \sqcup H_{:_v T}(Q)) &
\end{array}
$$

where $P_0 \mathrel{\widehat{=}} P[v_0/v]$, $Q_1 \mathrel{\widehat{=}} Q[v_1/v]$, and $T(v_a, v_b) \mathrel{\widehat{=}} T[v_a, v_b/\overline{v}, v]$. □

Binary conditional $\lhd b \rhd$ commutes with any conjunctive and disjunctive predicate functions. It also commutes with any generic predicate function $H_{:_v} T$ if b does not depend on the interface v. This means, with some minor restriction, binary conditional is closed in a common semantic space.

Theorem 14 (Inheritance of conditional). *For any R, S and T, if $b = \exists v \cdot b$, then $H_{\vee R}$ and $H_{:_v T}$ commute with binary conditional $\lhd b \rhd$.*

Basic Laws I. The basic laws of glb, lub, conditional and recursions are listed as follows:

Laws 3 (1) $\bot \sqcap P = \bot$ (2) $\top \sqcap P = P$
(3) $\bot \sqcup P = P$ (4) $\top \sqcup P = \top$

Laws 4
(1) $P \sqcap P = P$ (2) $P \sqcup P = P$
(3) $P \sqcap Q = Q \sqcap P$ (4) $P \sqcup Q = Q \sqcup P$
(5) $(P \sqcap Q) \sqcap R = P \sqcap (Q \sqcap R)$
(6) $(P \sqcup Q) \sqcup R = P \sqcup (Q \sqcup R)$
(7) $(P \sqcap Q) \sqcup R = (P \sqcup R) \sqcap (Q \sqcup R)$
(8) $(P \sqcup Q) \sqcap R = (P \sqcap R) \sqcup (Q \sqcap R)$

Laws 5
(1) $P \lhd b \rhd P = P$ (2) $P \lhd \mathit{true} \rhd Q = P$
(3) $P \lhd b \rhd Q = Q \lhd \neg b \rhd P$ (4) $P \lhd \mathit{false} \rhd Q = Q$
(5) $P \lhd a \rhd (Q \lhd b \rhd R) = (P \lhd a \rhd Q) \lhd a \vee b \rhd R$
(6) $P \lhd a \rhd (Q \lhd b \rhd R) = (P \lhd a \rhd Q) \lhd b \rhd (P \lhd a \rhd R)$
(7) $(P \sqcap Q) \lhd b \rhd R = (P \lhd b \rhd R) \sqcap (Q \lhd b \rhd R)$
(8) $P \lhd b \rhd (Q \sqcap R) = (P \lhd b \rhd Q) \sqcap (P \lhd b \rhd R)$

Laws 6
(1) $f(\mu_\perp f) = \mu_\perp f$
(2) $X \sqsupseteq f(X) \;\Leftrightarrow\; X \sqsupseteq \mu_\perp f$

A healthiness function is monotonic and transforms bottom and top to the bottom and top respectively in a new model. Note that any semantic space here is a complete lattice, and thus Laws 3 is inherited directly by any semantic model. Laws 4 and 5 do not contain primitives. Thus:

Lemma 15. *Laws 4 and 5 are inherited by a semantic model in which* $\sqcap$, $\sqcup$ *and* $\lhd b \rhd$ *are closed.*

The inheritance of Laws 6 is guaranteed by Theorem 11.

Theorem 16. Basic Laws I *are inherited by a semantic model if all basic commands are inherited.*

5.2 Alphabets

Model ALPHA(w) is a sub-model of PRED(ν) where w is a list of logical variables. It adds the healthiness condition of alphabetic restrictions to PRED(ν). An *alphabet* w is a set of variables without overlines. An alphabetically-restricted predicate does not depend on any variable outside the alphabet. Note that healthiness condition for alphabet is nothing more than a mathematical representation of the alphabet (or similarly the frame). A predicate observes a certain alphabetical restriction if it satisfies the following healthiness condition.

HC 5 (*Ha*) $A \;=\; A :_\nu (\overline{w} = w)$

All commands of PRED are inherited by ALPHA(w). The only restriction is that the parameter expression e in substitution should not contain any variable outside of w and no new variable is introduced by generic composition.

5.3 Binary Relations

Model $\text{REL}(v)$ is a sub-model of $\text{ALPHA}(w)$. The alphabet w is partitioned into two lists v and v' of variables such that $w = \{v, v'\}$. The list v of variables, called the *input alphabet* consisting of all undashed variables and records the observation at the start of a computation; the list v', called the *output alphabet*, consists of all dashed variables and records the observation at the end of the computation.

+ what is a sub-model?

$\text{REL}(v)$ inherits the following commands from $\text{ALPHA}(w)$. Note that b in $\lhd b \rhd$ must satisfy $b = \exists v' \cdot b$ and a recursive function f contains only commands of $\text{REL}(v)$.

$\bot$	$\top$	$\sqcap$	$\sqcup$	$\lhd b \rhd$	$\mu_\bot f$

A couple of new basic commands are introduced in $\text{REL}(v)$. In the following table we assume that $\{s, t\} \subseteq \{v\}$, and e is a list of expressions, each of which is a total function and can be calculated in finitely many steps.

$s := e(t)$	total assignment statement
$P \,;\, Q$	sequential composition

Definition 14. $s := e(t) \;\widehat{=}\; (s' = e(t) \wedge u = u')$ *where* $u = v \setminus \{s\}$.

Definition 15. $P \,;\, Q \;\widehat{=}\; \exists v_0 \cdot (P[v_0/v'] \wedge Q[v_0/v])$ *where* v_0 *is a list of new variables.*

No new variables are introduced outside of the alphabet, and hence all commands are closed. Some commands can be derived from the abstract ones.

$\mathbf{II}$	$\widehat{=}$	$v := v$	skip, no operation
$(b)_\top$	$\widehat{=}$	$\mathbf{II} \lhd b \rhd \top$	conditional magic ($b = \exists v' \cdot b$)

Basic Laws II. The basic laws involving assignment statements and sequential composition are as follows:

Laws 7
(1) $(s, s, t := e, f, g) \;=\; (s, t := e, g \lhd e = f \rhd \top)$
(2) $s := e \;=\; s, t := e, t \qquad (s \diamond t)$
(3) $s, t := e, f \;=\; t, s := f, e$
(4) $u, s, t := e, f, g \;=\; s, t, u := f, g, e$
(5) $(s := e \,;\, s := f) \;=\; (s := f \circ e)$
(6) $s := e \,;\, (b)_\top \;=\; (b \circ e)_\top \,;\, s := e$
(7) $(a)_\top \,;\, (b)_\top \;=\; (a \wedge b)_\top$

Laws 8
(1) $\top \,;\, P \;=\; \top$ (2) $\bot \,;\, v := e \;=\; \bot$
(3) $v := f \,;\, \top \;=\; \top$ (4) $v := e \,;\, \bot \;=\; \bot$
(5) $\mathbf{II} \,;\, P \;=\; P \,;\, \mathbf{II} \;=\; P$
(6) $P \,;\, (Q \,;\, R) \;=\; (P \,;\, Q) \,;\, R$
(7) $P \,;\, (Q \sqcap R) \;=\; (P \,;\, Q) \sqcap (P \,;\, R)$
(8) $(P \sqcap Q) \,;\, R \;=\; (P \,;\, R) \sqcap (Q \,;\, R)$

Laws 9 (1) $P \lhd b \rhd Q \;=\; ((b)_\top \,{}_9^{\circ}\, P) \sqcap ((\neg b)_\top \,{}_9^{\circ}\, Q)$
(2) $s := e \,{}_9^{\circ}\, P \lhd b \rhd Q \;=\; (s := e \,{}_9^{\circ}\, P) \lhd b \circ e \rhd (s := e \,{}_9^{\circ}\, Q)$
(3) $(P \lhd b \rhd Q) \,{}_9^{\circ}\, R \;=\; (P \,{}_9^{\circ}\, R) \lhd b \rhd (Q \,{}_9^{\circ}\, R)$

If a REL(v) program is composed of a finite number of the following commands

$\top$	$\sqcap$	$\lhd b \rhd$	$s := e(t)$	$({}_9^{\circ})$

then it can be reduced to the following normal form N in finitely many steps [3]:

$$N \;=\; \textstyle\bigsqcap_{i \leqslant n} ((b_i)_\top \,{}_9^{\circ}\, v := e_i(v))$$

Any finite non-recursive program in REL(v) can be reduced to the above normal form in finitely many steps using the basic laws. This (relative) completeness theorem can be found in [3, 4].

5.4 Sequential Programming

Sequential programming with recursion requires additional observables ok and ok' to represent termination and nontermination. Most commands of binary relations except the lub operator are inherited. Note that the variable ok must not appear as a program variable in any sequential program. The model of sequential programs SEQ(w) is a subset of REL(v) where $\{w, ok\} = \{v\}$. The healthiness condition is $A = Hdev \circ Hok \circ Ha(A)$. The additional healthiness function is defined: $Hseq \mathrel{\widehat{=}} Hdev \circ Hok$.

The question is which laws of binary relations can be inherited by sequential programming. The challenge is that, in general, the additional healthiness function $Hseq$ does not commute with sequential composition. In fact the commutativity only holds when the first argument of a sequential composition always terminates from any initial state. We introduce a new conjunctive healthiness condition (hence also a generic one):

HC 6 (Htm) $A \;=\; A \wedge (ok = ok') \;=\; A :_{(ok,\, ok')} (ok = ok')$.

A predicate represents a terminating computation if it is a fixpoint of the healthiness function Ht where $Ht \mathrel{\widehat{=}} Hseq \circ Htm \circ Ha$. The following theorem shows that, in a sequential composition, if the first program always terminates and the second program is a normal sequential computation, then $Hseq$ commutes with the sequential composition. Note that $Hseq$ is idempotent.

Theorem 17. *The healthiness function $Hseq$ commutes sequential composition ${}_9^{\circ}$ on Ht and $Hseq$, i.e. $Hseq(Ht(P) \,{}_9^{\circ}\, Hseq(Q)) \;=\; Ht(P) \,{}_9^{\circ}\, Hseq(Q)$.*

Given that the first arguments of all sequential compositions in **Basic Laws II** are Ht-healthy, we conclude that all the laws can be inherited.

6 Conclusion

This paper has introduced techniques to organise various predicate-semantic models in a hierarchical structure so that the construction of a semantic model can be based on the reuse of more abstract models. The restrictions in this paper are more strict than those of the original theory of UTP. For example, the precondition for the inheritance of fixpoints is stronger than the sufficient conditions originally identified. Although the additional restrictions might exclude some well-defined theoretical models, they do admit common real languages. The combination of disjunctive and generic healthiness functions is general enough to represent any healthiness function that distributes universal disjunction (i.e. observation-based and relational). Non-trivial healthiness conditions such as H2 and R2 in UTP are typical generic healthiness conditions. Some healthiness conditions such as convexity in probabilistic models require the second-order (or high-order) generic composition. An extension to this work is needed for those models.

The advantage of more disciplined models is that many tedious proof obligations related to well-definedness of the combinators (i.e. the closure in the semantic space) and the laws can be reduced to straightforward checking of simple conditions. The use of generic composition helps lift the level of reasoning up to a level similar to modal/temporal logics. Indeed generic composition can be regarded as a two-ary modality. The power of generic composition for writing healthiness condition has been demonstrated in a previous paper [2].

Acknowledgement

This paper partly arose from the D.Phil. thesis [1] of the author who would like to thank his PhD supervisor J.W. Sanders for discussions and advice.

References

1. Y. Chen. *Formal Methods for Global Synchrony.* PhD thesis, Oxford University Computing Laboratory, 2001.
2. Y. Chen. Generic composition. *Formal Aspects of Computing*, 14(2):108–122, 2002.
3. C. A. R. Hoare and et al. Laws of programming. *Communications of the ACM*, 30(8):672–686, 1987.
4. C. A. R. Hoare and J. He. *Unifying Theories of Programming.* Prentice Hall, 1998.
5. A. Tarski. A lattice-theoretical fixpoint theorem and its applications. *Pacific Journal of Mathematics*, 5:285–309, 1955.

Unifying Probability

Jifeng He and J. W. Sanders

East China Normal University, Shanghai
and
Programming Research Group, Oxford

Abstract. We demonstrate a new unification of probability with standard computation in which a nonzero chance of disaster is treated as disaster. Laws and a Galois connection with the more traditional probabilistic model are provided. Reversibility in the probabilistic guarded-command language is discussed. Finally the formalism is applied to unify quantum computation and cryptography within the probabilistic method.

1 Introduction

In the world at large, probabilism offers a simple, fast and unbiased choice between alternatives. So it is in programming where the probability, instead of being constant, may be state dependent. Its use therefore provides an alternative to a time or space intensive computation for resolving a choice. For not only is its use efficient in both those senses, but it may provide a symmetrical algorithm where no (efficient) non-probabilistic symmetric algorithm exists. However the price to be paid for these worthwhile benefits is that some probabilistic algorithms meet their ideal specifications with only high probability.

Probabilistic techniques have been used in mathematics for over two centuries. A popular example consists of Buffon's method of estimating π by using a physical process of dropping needles on a grid. A less commonly appreciated application establishes that certain properties hold almost everywhere (i.e. with probability 1) in spite of the fact that individual examples are unknown or very hard to establish (for example in number theory). However only in 1955 was the foundation laid for probabilistic algorithms, in the form of probabilistic Turing machines. In the 1970s Monte Carlo methods (e.g. primality testing) became popular, particularly in numerical mathematics. Since then the use of probabilism has burgeoned in Computing Science. It has been used, for example: to defeat an input adversary and hence to improve average-case efficiency (e.g. quicksort with randomly-chosen pivot); to overcome difficulties due to symmetry (e.g. randomised backoff); in efficient symmetrical distributed algorithms (e.g. choice coordination); and in quantum algorithms (e.g. Shor's algorithm). More recently the foundation has been extended to embrace the nondeterminism inherent in the contemporary more abstract treatment of algorithms, so that a refinement calculus is now in place [MM05]. It is that work which we exploit in this paper.

S. Dunne and W. Stoddart (Eds.): UTP 2006, LNCS 4010, pp. 173–199, 2006.

One approach to using formal methods to reason about probabilistic programs or systems would be to use a standard (non-probabilistic) method to reason about the non-probabilistic aspects of the program or system and then to use probability theory to 'graft on' an argument about the probabilistic behaviour. We follow the alternative approach championed in [MM05, H04] which extends a standard formal method to embrace probability, thus achieving a homogeneous, unified method. This unification is sensible only if the resulting method is not appreciably more complex than its original standard basis. All case studies so far point overwhelmingly to that being the case.

We take as implicit that programs and systems are specified and verified either by step-wise derivation from their specification or by verification establishing refinement. The basis in either case is of course the same: a 'refinement' relation $\sqsubseteq$ on the space of computations that includes both operation and data refinement. An implementation is simply a refinement that is expressed in a restricted subset of computations decreed to represent executable computations or (abstract) 'code'.

We promote the use of laws, as distinct from semantic reasoning, wherever possible. Both approaches are consistent with *unifying theories of programming* [HH98] and are interdependent. A semantic model shows a set of laws to be sound; a set of laws encapsulates properties of a semantic model. And the Galois connection that shows one semantic model to be a refinement of its coarser approximation does the same for the two corresponding sets of laws. But laws are more readily automated, more easily appreciated by practitioners, and build on existing algebraic facility in a which semantics tends not to.

In this paper we broach three topics involving probability. The first topic concerns a weaker model than that used to date to augment functional behaviour with probability. In the standard program calculus, **abort** $\sqcap A =$ **abort**: if a program may (nondeterministically) fail it is assumed actually to do so. The reason is that we want our design calculus to be 'conservative' in the sense that its products are *always* valid, not just (nondeterministically) sometimes so. By equating nondeterministically possible abortion with abortion we ensure that if the system might not fail then it will not.

One of the motivations for introducing probabilism into a formal method is to enable that decision to be revised and refined. A program or system that behaves (demonic-) nondeterministically like either A or B, $A \sqcap B$, can be refined to behave like a probabilistic choice between them. For example the equi-likely choice is written $A\ {}_{\frac{1}{2}}\!\oplus B$, so that $A \sqcap B \ \sqsubseteq\ A\ {}_{\frac{1}{2}}\!\oplus B$ and in fact the refinement is strict. The same remains true of any probability p in place of $\frac{1}{2}$. The resulting language (in our case *pGCL*: the guarded-command language plus probability) enables a far weaker statement to be made than merely that the nondeterminism is resolved to either A or B. It specifies the probability with which it is to be resolved.

In particular $\mathbf{abort}_{\frac{1}{2}}\!\oplus A$ is quite distinct from **abort** because it has probability only $\frac{1}{2}$ of aborting. In particular probabilism is non-strict, like the conditional it generalises:

$$B \lhd b \rhd A \ =\ B\,{}_b\!\oplus A\,.$$

(wherein we have identified predicate b on state space with a 0 or 1-valued function). And frequently (but not probably) that is exactly what we wish to describe. But early in the design process it may be premature and we might wish to adhere to the original conservative principle that even a positive chance of abortion should be abortion. That is the model we consider here. Probabilism, $\oplus$, becomes strict:

$$\forall p : (0, 1] \cdot \textbf{abort}\ {}_p\!\oplus A \;=\; \textbf{abort}\,.$$

It might be thought that since the model is coarser than *pGCL* we would construct a new model and present its laws. But we benefit from the *unifying theories* approach by simply embedding the new model in *pGCL* via a well-behaved Galois connection, strong enough for us to be able to infer the laws we seek from those in *pGCL*.

Our second topic, reversibility, arose during the workshop. The stimulating paper [SZL06] surveyed the notion of reversible computation from its original physical origins to more recent work on *pGCL*. Here we present a complementary approach for comparison with the one taken in that paper. There the approach to reversibility allows extra state to be added to enable a computation, either *en bloc* or step-by-step, to be reversed. Here we are more stringent and investigate reversibility in which no extra state is permitted. We call it *strict* reversibility and show that in *pGCL* it reduces to *GCL* where it is equivalent to bijective assignment.

Our third topic, quantum computation, is a topic of considerable current interest. Apart from providing an introduction to it from the viewpoint of formal methods, we make the case that both sequential and distributed quantum computations can be unified in the probabilistic method. In this section we discuss work in progress, and concentrate on expressing the quantum algorithms and protocols in *pGCL*. The challenge remaining pertains to the stepwise derivation of the algorithms using data refinement in *pGCL*. Progress and difficulties are surveyed.

2 Probabilistic Guarded Commands

Before recalling the probabilistic guarded-command language *pGCL* we recall the standard guarded-command language and introduce some convenient notation within it.

2.1 The Guarded-Command Language

The guarded-command language with its refinement relation $(GCL, \sqsubseteq)$ provides a convenient forum for the calculus of procedural programming. Its combinators are recalled in Figure 1. The binary conditional $A \lhd b \rhd B$ is read, and stands for, *A if b else B*. The other combinators, and the laws they satisfy, 'need no introduction'. When we wish to emphasise that the underlying state space is X

skip	no op
abort	divergent computation
magic	unenabled computation
$x := e$	assignment
$A \lhd b \rhd B$	binary conditional
$A \fatsemi B$	sequential composition
μF	recursion
var $y : Y \cdot A$ **rav**	local variable
$A \sqcap B$	nondeterministic choice
$A \sqcup B$	angelic choice
$A \sqsubseteq B$	refinement: $A \sqcap B = A$

Fig. 1. Syntax for our variant of the guarded-command language $(GCL(X), \sqsubseteq)$

we write $GCL(X)$, and then assignments are to $x : X$. In this paper we assume state space X to be finite.

Operationally, a computation is *deterministic* if from each initial state it is enabled and terminates in a single (initial-state dependent) final state. It is *predeterministic* if from each initial state it is enabled but either fails to terminate or terminates in a single final state. Formally, a computation is deterministic if it is $\sqsubseteq$-maximal amongst enabled computations.

Programs in *GCL* are those *GCL* computations that are enabled at each initial state and whose nondeterminism is bounded. As usual, in expressing algorithms we use iteration when it is convenient. But we prefer to take recursion as primitive, for its generality and for the theoretical convenience of least fixed points.

Although we express algorithms as programs, we need the extension to programs provided by angelic choice. Thus $(GCL(X), \sqsubseteq)$ forms not only a complete partial order with least element **abort** but also a complete lattice with greatest element **magic**. In spite of claims sometimes made to the contrary it is not a quantale (at least not in both the relational and transformer models), since in general only these refinements hold:

$$\sqcup\{A \fatsemi B \mid A \in \mathcal{A}\} \sqsubseteq (\sqcup\mathcal{A}) \fatsemi B$$
$$\sqcup\{A \fatsemi B \mid B \in \mathcal{B}\} \sqsubseteq A \fatsemi (\sqcup\mathcal{B}) .$$

(In the relational model, intersection only sub-distributes sequential composition of relations from either side.) With the reversed order one of those refinements becomes an equality (the one in which the demonic choice occurs at the same point—first—on both sides)

$$\sqcap\{A \fatsemi B \mid A \in \mathcal{A}\} = (\sqcap\mathcal{A}) \fatsemi B$$
$$\sqcap\{A \fatsemi B \mid B \in \mathcal{B}\} \sqsupseteq A \fatsemi (\sqcap\mathcal{B}) .$$

The refinement is an equality in the relational model (since union distributes sequential composition of relations) but not in the transformer model. The lack of symmetry between $\sqcup$ and $\sqcap$ may be explained by neither of the first two refinements offering a situation in which the angelic choice is offered at the same point—last—on both sides. With probabilism, even greater subtleties arise.

2.2 Fibres

It will be convenient to have notation that enables us to reason algebraically in a way that is normally achieved semantically; particularly since, as we have just seen, the relational and transformer models differ in fundamental ways.

We define the fibre of computation A at initial state x_0 to be the computation that aborts off x_0, where it behaves like A. In other words the fibre of A at x_0 consists of the assertion $x = x_0$ followed by A.

Definition (fibres). For $A : GCL(X)$ and $E \subseteq X$, the fibre of A at E is defined

$$A \bullet E \;\widehat{=}\; (A \lhd x \in E \rhd \textbf{abort}\ ).$$

For simplicity, $A \bullet \{x_0\}$ is written $A \bullet x_0$.

Fibres are distributed by the combinators of GCL. The routine proof follows directly from the laws of GCL.

Lemma (fibre distribution). For $A, B : GCL(X)$, $x_0, x_1 : X$ and predicate b on X,

$$\begin{aligned}
\textbf{abort} \bullet x_0 &= \textbf{abort} \\
(A \lhd b \rhd B) \bullet x_0 &= (A \bullet x_0) \lhd b \rhd (B \bullet x_0) \\
(A \,⨟\, B) \bullet x_0 &= (A \bullet x_0) \,⨟\, B \\
(A \sqcap B) \bullet x_0 &= (A \bullet x_0) \sqcap (B \bullet x_0) \\
(A \sqcup B) \bullet x_0 &= (A \bullet x_0) \sqcup (B \bullet x_0) \\
(A \bullet x_0) \bullet x_1 &= (A \bullet x_0) \lhd x_0 = x_1 \rhd \textbf{abort} \\
&= (A \bullet x_1) \bullet x_0 .
\end{aligned}$$

Theorem (fibre normal form). A computation is the bundle of its fibres: for each $A : GCL(X)$,

$$A \;=\; \sqcup\{A \bullet x_0 \mid x_0 \in X\}$$

(in spite of the fact that the right-hand side does not form a directed set).

2.3 The Probabilistic Guarded-Command Language

With those preliminaries, we recall that the probabilistic guarded-command language $(pGCL, \sqsubseteq)$ consists of the guarded-command language augmented by a binary combinator for probabilistic choice: for $A, B : GCL(X)$ and $0 \leq p \leq 1$,

$$A \;{}_p\!\oplus B$$

equals A with probability p and B with probability $1-p$. Henceforth we write $\overline{p} \mathrel{\widehat{=}} 1-p$. The probability p is an expression over state. Recall that we are assuming here that state space X is finite.

The refinement relation $\sqsubseteq$ removes nondeterminism as in GCL but now also increases likelihood[1]. As expected from the introduction, for example, for any p

$$A \sqcap B \ \sqsubseteq\ A \,{}_p{\oplus}\, B\,.$$

Indeed one of the laws will confirm that there is no more to nondeterminism than the combination of all possible probabilistic choices.

2.4 Features of $pGCL$

The calculus $(pGCL, \sqsubseteq)$ incorporates several design decisions that it is worth pointing out to allay confusion.

Firstly, although there is a difference between certain termination and termination with probability 1, the two are identified in $(pGCL, \sqsubseteq)$. For example this program in $pGCL(\mathbb{B})$ does not always terminate.

$$\begin{array}{l} b := 1\ ; \\ \textbf{do}\ b \rightarrow \\ \qquad (b := \neg b)\ {}_{\frac{1}{2}}{\oplus}\ \textbf{skip} \\ \textbf{od} \end{array}$$

It diverges if the right-hand probabilistic choice is taken on each iteration; but that occurs with probability 0 (the infinite product of the constant $\frac{1}{2}$).

To highlight the subtle interaction between probabilism and nondeterminism we observe that in $pGCL$ disjoint assignments need not commute! For with state $(x, y) : \mathbb{B} \times \mathbb{B}$ and computations

$$\begin{aligned} A &\mathrel{\widehat{=}} (y := 0)\ {}_{\frac{1}{2}}{\oplus}\ (y := 1) \\ B &\mathrel{\widehat{=}} (x := 0) \sqcap (x := 1)\,, \end{aligned}$$

merely $A \,;\, B \ \sqsubset\ B \,;\, A$. (To see that the refinement is strict, consider the probability with which each finally achieves $x = y$. The left-hand side does so with probability 0 since although A assigns y to its two values with equal likelihood, the nondeterministic choice in B acts to minimise the possibility of achieving the postcondition $x = y$ which it does with $x \neq y$. By comparison, on the right B assigns x to either of its two values (a nondeterministic choice does not have prescience) and then the probabilistic choice in A assigns y with equal likelihood to its two possible values, a choice which coincides with the value of x with probability $\frac{1}{2}$. Thus the left-hand side achieves the postcondition with probability 0 whilst the right-hand side achieves it with probability $\frac{1}{2}$; and so although $\sqsubseteq$ increases likelihood, equality fails.)

[1] We use 'likelihood' as synonymous with, but slightly less formal than, 'probability', choosing to ignore any alternative technical interpretation.

The operational intuition is that the demon resolving the nondeterminism acts early on the right-hand side and so by embodying fewer possible behaviours than the later version on the left-hand side yields a more refined computation.

Finally we observe that, as a consequence,

$$A \mathbin{;} (x := 0 \sqcap x := 1) \;\sqsubseteq\; (A \mathbin{;} x := 0) \sqcap (A \mathbin{;} x := 1)\,.$$

(For possible strictness, with A as above we have already seen that the left-hand side has probability 0 of finally achieving $x = y$. Now each of the two terms on the right-hand side achieves it with probability $\frac{1}{2}$, and therefore so too does the nondeterministic choice on the right.)

Thus even in a relational model for *pGCL* we cannot expect nondeterminism to distribute sequential composition on the left. Although neither side explicitly mentions probabilism, the anomaly is explained by the implicit appearance of probabilism in nondeterminism (as already mentioned and as about to appear in one of the laws).

Programs in *pGCL* consist, like those in *GCL*, of *pGCL* computations that are enabled at each initial state and exhibit bounded nondeterminism and probabilism.

2.5 Laws of *pGCL* Programming

Laws for probabilism alone are anticipated by calculating the probability with which each computation occurs on each side.

$$\begin{aligned}
A \,{}_1\!\oplus B &= A \\
A \,{}_p\!\oplus B &= B \,{}_{\overline{p}}\!\oplus A \\
A \,{}_p\!\oplus A &= A \\
(A \,{}_p\!\oplus B) \,{}_q\!\oplus C &= A \,{}_{pq}\!\oplus (B \,{}_r\!\oplus C)\,, \quad r = \overline{p}q/\overline{pq}
\end{aligned}$$

Laws relating probabilism to conditional and sequential composition are

$$\begin{aligned}
A \,{}_p\!\oplus (B \lhd b \rhd C) &= (A \,{}_p\!\oplus B) \lhd b \rhd (A \,{}_p\!\oplus C) \\
(A \,{}_p\!\oplus B) \mathbin{;} C &= (A \mathbin{;} C) \,{}_p\!\oplus (B \mathbin{;} C) \\
(A \mathbin{;} B) \,{}_p\!\oplus (A \mathbin{;} C) &\sqsubseteq A \mathbin{;} (B \,{}_p\!\oplus C)
\end{aligned}$$

As expected, the first follows from the last law for probabilism alone.

The laws relating probabilism and nondeterminism are, as we have seen, the most subtle. Since the demon resolving nondeterminism has memory but not prescience, early nondeterminism offers fewer behaviours and hence refines later nondeterminism.

$$\begin{aligned}
A \sqcap B &= \sqcap\{A \,{}_p\!\oplus B \mid 0 \le p \le 1\} \\
&\sqsubseteq A \,{}_p\!\oplus B \\
(A \sqcap B) \,{}_p\!\oplus C &= (A \,{}_p\!\oplus C) \sqcap (B \,{}_p\!\oplus C) \\
(A \sqcap C) \,{}_p\!\oplus (B \sqcap C) &\sqsubseteq (A \,{}_p\!\oplus B) \sqcap C \\
(A \sqcap B) \mathbin{;} C &= (A \mathbin{;} C) \sqcap (B \mathbin{;} C) \\
A \mathbin{;} (B \sqcap C) &\sqsubseteq (A \mathbin{;} B) \sqcap (A \mathbin{;} C)
\end{aligned}$$

The fact that the refinements may be strict means that, in performing data refinements to derive designs from their specifications, care must be exercised to ensure that the simulation refinements work in the right direction (when such care may not be required in *GCL*). We return to this in Section 5.8.

2.6 Convexity in *pGCL*

The probabilistic-choice combinator is exact: $A\ {}_p\oplus\ B$ chooses its arguments with probabilities p and $\overline{p}$. But in many situations p is known only to lie in some interval, $a \le p \le b$. The infinite nondeterministic statement for that,

$$\sqcap\{A\ {}_p\oplus\ B \mid a \le p \le b\},$$

is evidently a *pGCL* computation; but is it code? The following theorem shows that it is. Its corollary deals with the important special case in which A occurs with probability *at least* p (and B with probability at most $\overline{p}$).

The convexity principle embodied in this theorem is usually justified 'geometrically' using the relational semantics to be introduced in the next section. Here we choose show that it is a simple consequence of the laws.

Theorem (convexity for ***pGCL*****).** If $0 \le a \le b \le 1$ then

$$\sqcap\{A\ {}_p\oplus\ B \mid a \le p \le b\} \;=\; (A\ {}_a\oplus\ B) \sqcap (A\ {}_b\oplus\ B).$$

Proof. We reason from the right-hand side:

$$(A\ {}_a\oplus\ B) \sqcap (A\ {}_b\oplus\ B)$$

$=$ first law in the previous table

$$\sqcap\{(A\ {}_a\oplus\ B)\ {}_p\oplus\ (A\ {}_b\oplus\ B) \mid 0 \le p \le 1\}$$

$=$ 'associativity' law

$$\sqcap\{A\ {}_{ap}\oplus\ (B\ {}_{\frac{p(1-a)}{1-ap}}\oplus\ (A\ {}_b\oplus\ B)) \mid 0 \le p \le 1\}$$

$=$ skew symmetry law

$$\sqcap\{A\ {}_{ap}\oplus\ (B\ {}_{\frac{p(1-a)}{1-ap}}\oplus\ (B\ {}_{1-b}\oplus\ A)) \mid 0 \le p \le 1\}$$

$=$ 'associativity' law

$$\sqcap\{A\ {}_{ap}\oplus\ ((B\ {}_{\frac{p(1-a)}{p(b-a)+1-b}}\oplus\ B)\ {}_{\frac{p(b-a)+1-b}{1-ap}}\oplus\ A) \mid 0 \le p \le 1\}$$

$=$ idempotence law

$$\sqcap\{A\ {}_{ap}\oplus\ (B\ {}_{\frac{p(b-a)+1-b}{1-ap}}\oplus\ A) \mid 0 \le p \le 1\}$$

$=$ skew symmetry law

$$\sqcap\{A\ {}_{ap}\oplus\ (A\ {}_{\frac{b(1-p)}{1-ap}}\oplus\ B) \mid 0 \le p \le 1\}$$

$=$ 'associativity' law

$$\sqcap\{(A\ {}_{\frac{ap}{ap+b(1-p)}}\oplus\ A)\ {}_{ap+b(1-p)}\oplus\ B \mid 0 \le p \le 1\}$$

$=$ idempotence law

$$\sqcap\{A\ {}_{ap+b(1-p)}\oplus\ B \mid 0 \le p \le 1\}$$

$=$ arithmetic

$\sqcap\{A\ {}_s\!\oplus B \mid a \leq s \leq b\}$.

In particular, with $b = 1$,

Corollary. $\sqcap\{A\ {}_p\!\oplus B \mid a \leq p \leq 1\} \;=\; A \sqcap (A\ {}_a\!\oplus B)$.

2.7 Relational Semantics of *pGCL*

The operational intuition concerning the demon in *pGCL* is sufficiently tenuous to demand a semantic model. Here we sketch the idea behind the relational model [HSM97]; for further details, for the transformer model and for the (Galois) connection between the two models see [MM05].

Definition (subdistributions). A *subdistribution* on a finite set X is a function from X to the real interval [0,1] whose sum is at most 1:

$$f : X \to [0,1] \cdot \sum\{f.x \mid x \in X\} \leq 1 .$$

For any $x_0 : X$, the *point mass at* x_0 is the subdistribution $\hat{x_0}$ that is 1 at x_0 and 0 elsewhere. Subdistributions are ordered pointwise:

$$f \sqsubseteq g \quad \hat{=} \quad \forall x : X \cdot f.x \leq g.x .$$

From any initial state x_0 a nonprobabilistic deterministic program A terminates in a single final state x_1. In the (probabilistic) relational model that final state is represented by the point-mass $\hat{x_1}$. The (solid) triangle in Figure 2 represents the set of all subdistributions on the set $\mathbb{B}$ of two values, 0 and 1. The point masses $\hat{0}$ and $\hat{1}$ account for two of its extreme points; the third is the (constant) zero function $\mathbf{0}$. Any other element of the triangle is a convex combination of extreme points. For example the mid-point of the diagonal is a $\frac{1}{2}$-convex combination of $\hat{0}$ and $\hat{1}$. All points on the diagonal represent subdistributions whose sum is 1: each is maximal in the $\sqsubseteq$-ordering.

In Figure 2 are shown, therefore, the relational semantics of the assignments $x := 0$ and $x := 1$ in $pGCL(\mathbb{B})$. Each is particularly simple because it is independent of initial state; and each is an extreme point and maximal in the ordering on subdistributions, as is to be expected.

From any initial state x_0 the $pGCL(\mathbb{B})$ computation $x := 1\ {}_{\frac{1}{2}}\!\oplus x := 0$ terminates with a single subdistribution that is $\frac{1}{2}$ at each of 0 and 1. Thus it is a $\frac{1}{2}$-convex combination of the point masses $\hat{0}$ and $\hat{1}$; see Figure 2. All such convex combinations—probabilistic assignments to either 0 or 1—lie on the diagonal line. And so they are all $\sqsubseteq$-maximal and hence deterministic in $pGCL(\mathbb{B})$. (It bears emphasis that determinism is $\sqsubseteq$-maximality. In other areas, like physics and quantum computation, such probabilistic choices are called nondeterministic. We shall call them probabilistic or nonstandard, but shall reserve 'nondeterminism' for the sense conveyed by $\sqsubseteq$ and $\sqcap$ on which the entire calculus is based.)

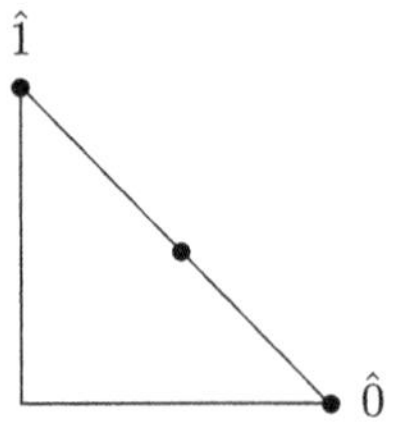

Fig. 2. The relational semantics of three deterministic computations

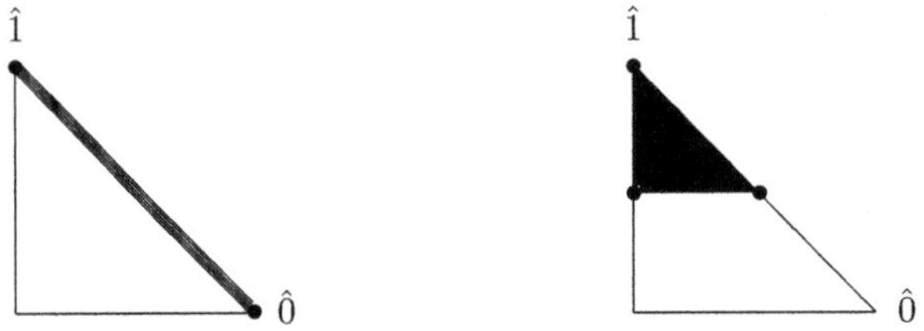

Fig. 3. The relational semantics of two nondeterministic computations

Thus a deterministic computation is represented, from each initial state, by a singleton set of subdistributions. A nondeterministic computation is represented (from each initial state) by a larger set of distributions.

For example the nondeterministic combination of the two deterministic assignments $x := 0$ and $x := 1$,

$$x := 0 \sqcap x := 1 \quad = \quad \sqcap \{ (x := 0 \,_p\!\oplus x := 1) \mid 0 \leq p \leq 1 \} ,$$

is represented by the set of all convex combinations of the two point masses $\hat{0}$ and $\hat{1}$. See the left-hand side of Figure 3.

Abortion is treated as extreme nondeterminism. The computation **abort** is thus represented by a set of subdistributions that contains the constant subdistribution $\mathbf{0}$ (assigning probability 0 to each final state) and is $\sqsubseteq$-upclosed. It thus contains every subdistribution and so is represented by the entire triangle in the figures. Alternatively it is the convex hull of the three subdistributions $\mathbf{0}$, $\hat{0}$ and $\hat{1}$.

The computation that is equally likely to diverge or to assign 1 to x,

$$\textbf{abort} \;_{\frac{1}{2}}\!\oplus\; x := 1 ,$$

is represented by the $\sqsubseteq$-upclosure of the set containing just the subdistribution

$$\frac{1}{2} \times \hat{1} + \frac{1}{2} \times \mathbf{0} \quad = \quad \frac{1}{2} \times \hat{1} .$$

Its extreme points are $\frac{1}{2} \times \hat{1}$, $\hat{1}$ and $\frac{1}{2}\hat{0} + \frac{1}{2}\hat{1}$; see the right-hand side of Figure 3.

The intuition '$\sqsubseteq$ increases likelihood' is represented in the relational semantics by fibrewise containment. As an exercise the reader may like to envisage the semantics of the predeterministic program **abort** ${}_{\frac{1}{8}}\oplus$ $(x := 0 \ {}_{\frac{2}{7}}\oplus \ x := 1)$ in Figure 3 and thereby to see that it refines **abort** ${}_{\frac{1}{2}}\oplus$ $x := 1$. A more interesting exercise is to invisage the semantics of the nondeterministic program

$$\textbf{abort} \ {}_{\frac{1}{6}}\oplus \ (x := 0 \ {}_{\frac{2}{5}}\oplus \ x := 1) \ \sqcap \ \textbf{abort} \ {}_{\frac{1}{6}}\oplus \ (x := 0 \ {}_{\frac{1}{5}}\oplus \ x := 1)\,,$$

again a refinement.

The set of subdistributions representing a fibre of a *pGCL* program is an $\sqsubseteq$-upclosed, convex hull of a (nonempty) finite set of extreme points. For *pGCL* computations more generally, the sets are just convex, $\sqsubseteq$-upclosed subsets. (And if state space X is infinite then they must also be assumed to be (topologically) closed in the product space $[0,1]^X$.)

The semantic model we have sketched is called relational, although the reason can scarcely be apparent since we have not touched upon the semantics of sequential composition. For that, each initial state is identified with its point mass and linearity used to extend our state-wise definitions to distributions; for details we refer to [MM05].

3 Reversing Probabilism

A stimulating paper by Stoddart *et al* [SZL06] in this proceedings, surveys reversible computations in models ranging from the original physical model of Landauer [L61] to Zuliani's treatment [Z01] in *pGCL* and to their own treatment in UTP designs. The context is one in which computation consisting of reversible steps may be expected to be more efficient. But in order to render a computation reversible it is sometimes necessary to augment it with extra state whose sole purpose is to facilitate reversibility. Indeed that is the approach taken previously by Zuliani in *pGCL*, motivated by the concerns of quantum computation.

Here we consider an alternative interpretation of reversibility by asking the much stricter question: given state space X, which computations in $pGCL(X)$ are reversible in $pGCL(X)$ in the sense that they have a right reverse in $pGCL(X)$ (with respect to sequential composition)? Thus no state may be added in order to facilitate reversibility.

Definition (strict reversibility). A computation A over state space X is *strictly reversible* iff there is a computation B also with state space X for which $A \mathbin{;} B = \textbf{skip}$.

Although that definition is general, our interest here is primarily in the spaces $GCL(X)$ and $pGCL(X)$.

Examples of strictly reversible computations are well known. For example over the state space of integers, addition is reversible:

$$x := x + n \qquad \text{has reverse} \qquad x := x - n$$

and that fact may be used to interchange two variables in three assignments but without the luxury of a third temporary variable. However by using additive inverse it fails on bounded subsets in particular implementations (when addition fails to have a total inverse). An example which works both in theory and practice takes for state space the Booleans and, for operation, exclusive-or. Operation

$$x := x \oplus y$$

is actually self inverse (and the interchanging of two variables can be achieved with three assignment statements having identical expressions).

Those examples are typical in the sense that an assignment $x := e$ is reversible over the same state space iff its expression e is bijective as a function of state x in the usual sense: $e(x) = e(x')$ implies $x = x'$.

Lemma (reversibility in *GCL*). The space of strictly reversible computations in $GCL(X)$ contains bijective assignments and is closed under sequential composition but not (in general) under conditional, nondeterminism or iteration.

Proof. The claim for total bijective assignments follows from the fact that the inverse assignment (well defined by assumption) acts as a right inverse. The claim for composition is routinely proved: assuming that A and B have right inverses A' and B' respectively (we need make no claim about their uniqueness), $A \fatsemi B$ has right inverse $B' \fatsemi A'$ since

$(A \fatsemi B) \fatsemi (B' \fatsemi A')$

$=$ $\quad$ $\fatsemi$ associative and B' a right inverse for B

$A \fatsemi \mathbf{skip} \fatsemi A'$

$=$ $\quad$ associativity, **skip** the identity for $\fatsemi$ and A' a right inverse for A

skip .

Although both **skip** and negation over Booleans are reversible (indeed both are self inverse) the conditional $(x := \neg x) \lhd x \rhd \mathbf{skip}$ is irreversible, being equivalent to $x := \mathit{false}$. Similarly for the iteration: $\mathbf{do}\ x \rightarrow \neg x\ \mathbf{od}$. For nondeterminism, we reason that were the computation $\mathbf{skip} \sqcap (x := \neg x)$, constructed from reversible arguments, to have a right inverse A' then

$(\mathbf{skip} \sqcap (x := \neg x)) \fatsemi A' = \mathbf{skip}$

$\Leftrightarrow$ $\quad$ *GCL* law

$(\mathbf{skip} \fatsemi A') \sqcap ((x := \neg x) \fatsemi A') = \mathbf{skip}$

$\Leftrightarrow$

$A' \sqcap ((x := \neg x) \fatsemi A') = \mathbf{skip}$

$\Rightarrow$ $\quad$ **skip** deterministic

$A' = \mathbf{skip}$

which would be inconsistent with the definition of A'. □

Theorem (reversibility for ***GCL*****).** A *GCL* computation is strictly reversible iff it is a bijective assignment.

Proof. By the lemma it remains to show that a strictly reversible computation in *GCL*(X) is a bijective assignment. Let A be a strictly reversible computation with right inverse $A' \in GCL(X)$ and let x_0 be an arbitrary initial state. Then, presaging the fibre notation of section 4,

$$\begin{array}{ll} \mathbf{skip} \bullet x_0 & \\ = & \text{definition of } A' \\ (A \fatsemi A') \bullet x_0 & \\ = & \text{fibre-distribution law} \\ (A \bullet x_0) \fatsemi A' & \end{array}$$

We infer not only that A cannot abort from x_0 (since **abort** is a left zero for sequential composition) but, following the reasoning of the lemma, that it is deterministic at x_0. So we continue to reason

$$\begin{array}{ll} (A \bullet x_0) \fatsemi A' & \\ = & \text{reasoning above} \\ (x := e) \bullet x_0 \fatsemi A' . & \\ = & \\ (x := e) \bullet x_0 \ \fatsemi \ A' \bullet e(x_0) . & \end{array}$$

Thus from initial state $e(x_0)$ the computation A' terminates in final state x_0. Since x_0 was arbitrary, expression e is a bijective function of state, as required. □

Before considering *pGCL* we observe that if A and B are deterministic computations then so too is the probabilistic choice $A \ {}_p\!\oplus B$, in spite of its commonly (and perfectly reasonably, outside the refinement calculus) being called a nondeterministic choice (particularly by quantum physicists). Of course in our terms, to be deterministic is to be maximal with respect to the refinement ordering $\sqsubseteq$ (see [MM05], section 8.3).

We next observe that strictly reversible computations in *pGCL* are not closed under probabilism.

Lemma (reversibility in ***pGCL*****).** The space of strictly reversible computations in *pGCL*(X) is not (in general) closed under probabilism.

Proof. Consider the state space of Booleans. Were the computation $\mathbf{skip} \ {}_p\!\oplus (x := \neg x)$, constructed from reversible arguments, to have a right inverse $A' \in pGCL(\mathbb{B})$ then

$$\begin{array}{l} (\mathbf{skip} \ {}_p\!\oplus (x := \neg x)) \fatsemi A' \ = \ \mathbf{skip} \\ \Leftrightarrow \\ A' \ {}_p\!\oplus ((x := \neg x) \fatsemi A') \ = \ \mathbf{skip} \end{array}$$

$$\Rightarrow \qquad \textbf{skip} \text{ an extreme point}$$

$$A' \;=\; (x := \neg x) \mathbin{;} A' \;=\; \textbf{skip}$$

which would be inconsistent with the definition of A'. □

The main result of this section is therefore that strict reversibility in $pGCL$ reduces to that in GCL.

Theorem (reversibility for $pGCL$**).** An element of $pGCL(X)$ is strictly reversible iff it is a bijective assignment.

It might be thought that a richer notion of reversibility for $pGCL$ might be obtained by replacing the requirement 'a right inverse composes to give **skip**' by the far weaker but more probabilistic requirement 'a right inverse composes to give the uniform distribution' (over finite state space). However that is too weak: any terminating computation would be reversible in that sense, with right inverse the assignment having uniform distribution (i.e. each member of state space is equally likely to be assigned).

Extending computations to include miracles and angelic choice adds nothing to the theory. Indeed a computation miraculous at some initial state has no right inverse restoring the initial state, in view of the law: $\textbf{magic} \mathbin{;} A \;=\; \textbf{magic}$; and reversibility is readily shown not to be closed under angelic choice.

4 Possible Failure is Failure

In this section we explore the model in which a positive probability of failure is deemed equivalent to failure.

4.1 $(\mathcal{N}, \sqsubseteq)$

Definition $(\mathcal{N})$**.** The space of probabilistic computations that abort if they have a positive probability of aborting is defined fibre-wise: for each initial state x_0 if the fibre $A \bullet x_0$ has a positive probability of aborting then it aborts certainly.

$$\begin{aligned}\mathcal{N}(X) \;\widehat{=}\; \{A : pGCL(X) \mid \forall x_0 : X \cdot \forall p : (0,1) \cdot \forall B : pGCL(X) \cdot \\ (A \bullet x_0 \;=\; (\textbf{abort} \;{}_p{\oplus}\; B) \bullet x_0) \Rightarrow\; B \bullet x_0 = \textbf{abort}\;\}\end{aligned}$$

The ordering of $(\mathcal{N}(X), \sqsubseteq)$ is as for $(pGCL(X), \sqsubseteq)$.

4.2 Relational Semantics of $\mathcal{N}$

The advantage of presenting the definition of $\mathcal{N}$ fibre-wise is that its relational semantics is readily appreciated. For any $A : \mathcal{N}(X)$ and any initial state $x_0 : X$, the set of distributions of the fibre $A \bullet x_0$ is either the whole region

$$\Delta \;\widehat{=}\; \{f : X \to [0,1] \mid \sum f \leq 1\}$$

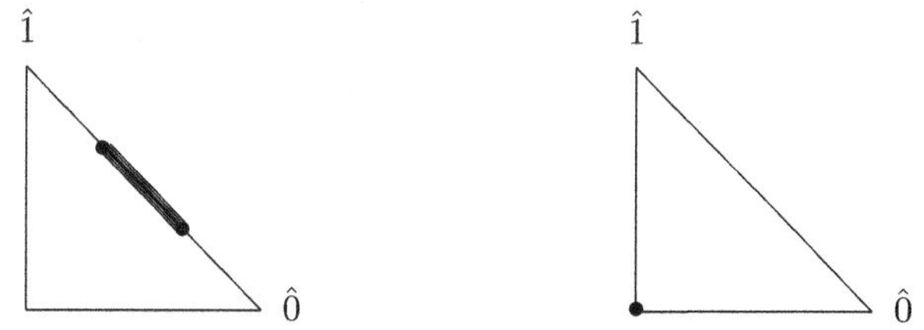

Fig. 4. The relational semantics of two computations in $\mathcal{N}$

(for example at any initial state other than x_0) or a subset of its face

$$\{f : X \to [0,1] \mid \sum f = 1\}\,.$$

The relationally healthy subsets are thus the nonempty, convex, closed subsets of the region which, if they contain a subdistribution that sums to less than 1, equal the whole region Δ.

For example the nondeterministic choice

$$\begin{array}{l} (x := 0 \;{}_{\frac{2}{3}}\!\oplus\; x := 1) \;\sqcap\; (x := 0 \;{}_{\frac{1}{3}}\!\oplus\; x := 1) \\ = \\ \sqcap\{(x := 0 \;{}_{p}\!\oplus\; x := 1) \mid \frac{1}{3} \le p \le \frac{2}{3}\} \end{array}$$

is depicted on the left-hand side of Figure 4 and is just as it would be in *pGCL*. On the other hand the program (**abort** ${}_{\frac{1}{2}}\!\oplus$ **skip**) is represented from each initial state by the set Δ of all subdistributions; it is the entire triangle on the right-hand side of Figure 4: the upclosure of the subdistribution **0**.

We thus see, in case it was not already obvious either semantically or algebraically, that from an initial state x_0 a *pGCL* computation is converted to a $\mathcal{N}$ computation by the closure operation which on a set of subdistributions F is defined

$$\Delta \;\lhd\; \exists f{:}F \cdot \Sigma f < 1 \;\rhd\; F\,.$$

In other words, if the set F meets the interior of Δ then it equals all of Δ, but otherwise it remains unchanged on the face of Δ. We formalise the adjoint, an embedding, of that operation and reclaim the closure operation as the relational semantics of its Galois projection.

4.3 Laws

As usual, the advantage of a Galois connection between a new space and a well-studied space is that it may be used to infer new laws from old.

Theorem (Galois connection). The space $(\mathcal{N}, \sqsubseteq)$ is a complete subspace of $(pGCL, \sqsubseteq)$, interposed between $(GCL, \sqsubseteq)$ and $(pGCL, \sqsubseteq)$ by Galois connections whose embeddings are the natural insertions

$$\begin{array}{ll} \varepsilon 0 : (GCL, \sqsubseteq) \to (\mathcal{N}, \sqsubseteq)\,, & \varepsilon 0.A \;\hat{=}\; A \\ \varepsilon 1 : (\mathcal{N}, \sqsubseteq) \to (pGCL, \sqsubseteq)\,, & \varepsilon 1.B \;\hat{=}\; B\,. \end{array}$$

Recall that if $(X, \leq_X)$ and $(Y, \leq_Y)$ are say complete lattices then a function $\phi : X \to Y$ is *universally* $(\vee_X, \vee_Y)$*-junctive* if for any subset E of X

$$\phi . \vee_X E \;=\; \vee_Y \{\phi . e \mid e \in E\} .$$

Similarly, or dually, for *universally* $(\wedge_X, \wedge_Y)$*-junctivity.* If the spaces are complete then the embedding in a Galois connection is universally $(\vee, \vee)$-junctive and the projection is universally $(\wedge, \wedge)$-junctive. With little more work we have:

Corollary (junctivity). The embeddings $\varepsilon 0$ and $\varepsilon 1$ are both injective, universally $(\sqcap, \sqcap)$-junctive, universally $(\sqcup, \sqcup)$-junctive and preserve $\fatsemi$.
The projections $\nu = \pi 1$ and $\pi 0$ are both surjective, universally $(\sqcap, \sqcap)$-junctive, preserve $\fatsemi$ and ν is weakening: $\nu . A \sqsubseteq A$.

In spite of that corollary, ν is not universally $\sqcup$-junctive. Indeed

$$\begin{array}{l}
\nu . \sqcup \{\mathbf{abort}\ {}_p\!\oplus\ \mathbf{skip} \mid 0 < p \leq 1\} \\
= \\
\nu . \mathbf{skip} \\
\sqsupset \\
\mathbf{abort} \\
= \\
\sqcup \{\nu . (\mathbf{abort}\ {}_p\!\oplus\ \mathbf{skip}) \mid 0 < p \leq 1\} ,
\end{array}$$

although $\nu . \mathbf{abort} \;=\; \mathbf{abort}$.

Corollary (laws for $\mathcal{N}$). For $A, B : \mathcal{N}$, predicate b on state space and probability p,

$$\begin{array}{rcl}
\nu . \mathbf{skip} & = & \mathbf{skip} \\
\nu . \mathbf{abort} & = & \mathbf{abort} \\
\nu . (x := e) & = & (x := e \lhd \mathit{def} . e \rhd \mathbf{abort}\ ) \\
\nu . (A \fatsemi B) & = & (\nu . A) \fatsemi (\nu B) \\
\nu . (A \sqcap B) & = & (\nu . A) \sqcap (\nu . B) \\
\nu . (A \lhd b \rhd B) & = & \nu . A \lhd b \rhd \nu . B \\
\nu . (A\ {}_p\!\oplus B) & = & (\nu . A\ {}_p\!\oplus \nu . B) \\
 & & \lhd \left(\begin{array}{l} \nu . A = \mathbf{abort}\ \vee \nu . B = \mathbf{abort} \\ \Rightarrow \\ p = 0 \vee p = 1 \end{array} \right) \rhd \\
 & & \mathbf{abort}\ .
\end{array}$$

4.4 Characterisation

Although the definition given of $\mathcal{N}$ was convenient for visualising its relational semantics, it has a simpler fibre-free characterisation.

Theorem ($\mathcal{N}$ characterisation). $A \in \mathcal{N}$ iff

$$\forall p : (0,1) \cdot \forall B : \mathcal{N} \cdot (A = (\textbf{abort}\ {}_p\!\oplus B)) \Rightarrow B = \textbf{abort}\ .$$

Proof. The replacement of $B{:}pGCL(X)$ by $B{:}\mathcal{N}$ is justified simply

$\textbf{abort}\ {}_p\!\oplus (\textbf{abort}\ {}_q\!\oplus B)$

$=$ 'associativity' law

$(\textbf{abort}\ {}_r\!\oplus \textbf{abort})\ {}_s\!\oplus B$

$=$ idempotence; $s \in (0,1)$ since $p, q \in (0,1)$

$\textbf{abort}\ {}_s\!\oplus B\,.$

For the equivalence we reason in each direction.
($\Rrightarrow$) Substitution gives

$$\forall x_0 : X \cdot B \bullet x_0 \ = \ \textbf{abort}$$

and so the result follows by the normal-form theorem.
($\Lleftarrow$) We reason using the fibre-distribution lemma: for any state x_0,

$A \bullet x_0 \ = \ (\textbf{abort}\ {}_p\!\oplus B) \bullet x_0$

$\Rightarrow$ fibre-distribution lemma

$A \bullet x_0 \ = \ (\textbf{abort} \bullet x_0)\ {}_p\!\oplus (B \bullet x_0)$

$\Rightarrow$ fibre-distribution lemma

$A \bullet x_0 \ = \ \textbf{abort}\ {}_p\!\oplus (B \bullet x_0)$

$\Rightarrow$ hypothesis applied to $A \bullet x_0$ and $B \bullet x_0$

$B \bullet x_0 \ = \ \textbf{abort}$

which completes the proof. □

4.5 Domain and Range

The notion of 'terminating set' makes sense for *GCL* computations. For if a computation may nondeterministically terminate or abort from some given state then, as discussed in the Introduction, the computation actually aborts. Thus there is no conflict deciding whether the state should be in the 'terminating set' of the computation or not. But for *pGCL* computations the situation is more complex, since from a given state a computation may abort with some positive probability and terminate with some positive probability; should that state lie in the 'terminating set' or not?

For the space $\mathcal{N}$ those difficulties disappear, and the notions of 'terminating set' and 'range' make sense as subsets of state space (rather than distributionally).

Definition ($\mathcal{N}$). For a computation $A{:}\mathcal{N}$, *domain* of A, *pre.A*, consists of all states x_0 from which A has no (positive) chance of aborting:

$$pre.A \ \widehat{=} \ \{x_0{:}X \mid A \bullet x_0 \neq \textbf{abort}\}\,.$$

The range of A, $erp.A$, consists of all states which have a (positive) chance of occurring from an execution begun in $pre.A$:

$$erp.A \mathrel{\widehat{=}} \{x_1 : X \mid \exists\, x_0 : pre.A \cdot \exists\, p > 0 \cdot \exists\, B : \mathcal{N} \cdot A \bullet x_0 \sqsubseteq (x := x_1 \,{}_p\!\oplus B) \bullet x_0\}\,.$$

We observe that the definition of $\mathcal{N}$ ensures those concepts are well defined, but do not pursue those ideas here.

5 Quantum Computation

In this section we propose to substantiate the claim that the various kinds of computation proposed by the quantum model, sequential and distributed, can be captured by probabilistic formal methods. We refer to the thorough text [NC00] for a general exposition of quantum computation.

Sequential quantum computation corresponds to computation, with the usual control structures, executed on a device bound by the laws of quantum mechanics: possessing quantum state operated on by unitary updates. In principle that enables an exponential amount of standard work to be done in one quantum operation, as all 2^n states of a standard register are updated. The problem in designing a quantum algorithm is utilising that work in the finalisation (or observation) operation. Perhaps that is why there are so few quantum algorithms, and not many that achieve an exponential speedup over the best standard algorithm for the same problem.

Distributed quantum computation, so far largely cryptographic as if to make amends for the effect of Shor's quantum factorisation algorithm on RSA, consists of processes interacting again subject to the quantum model. But the quantum features relevant to this paradigm of computation turn out to be a little different. Communication must ensure that if an arbitrary quantum state is output then no copy of it remains; for that would violate unitarity of the output operation. It is quite possible to achieve such output in a process-algebraic model using quantum teleportation, but here we choose to model distributed computations *and* sequential computations in *pGCL*.

5.1 Sequential Quantum Computation

Figure 5 depicts the quantum state corresponding to a bit—a *qubit*. It is a complex number of length 1 (though we show only the first quadrant). The qubit represents the bit 0 by being (purely) real: by $\hat{0}$; it represents the bit 1 by being purely imaginary: by $\hat{1}$. But it is initialised, for the purpose of (almost every) quantum computation, to be midway between those two (see the left-hand side of Figure 5): by $(\hat{0}+\hat{1})/\sqrt{2}$. Each (unitary) quantum evolution step moves that state vector around the unit circle in the complex plane. Finalisation returns a (standard) bit: it is 0 with probability equal to the length of the projection of the state vector onto the horizontal axis and it is 1 with the complementary

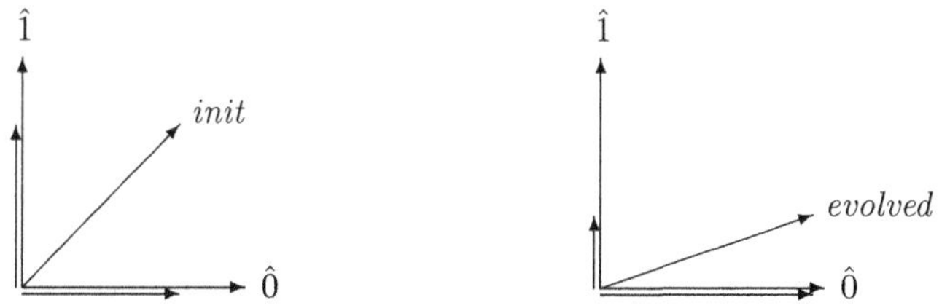

Fig. 5. A quantum bit, its initialisation, evolution and finalisation

probability, which equals the length of the state vector projected onto the vertical axis. Those two numbers sum to 1 since the state vector stays on the unit circle (and by Pythagorus).

Thus initialisation places the qubit in a state which, were it to be finalised immediately, would result in either 0 or 1 with equal likelihood. Quantum state can be revealed only by finalisation. But finalisation with respect to any orthonormal basis is possible, in which case the outcome is determined with probability given by the projections onto that basis. So whilst Figure 5 considers only the standard basis, Figure 7 shows also the standard basis rotated by 45 degrees.

But finalisation is a little more involved than we have admitted so far: it returns a bit as well as leaving the qubit in a corresponding state. We follow standard practice and acknowledge von Neumann's contribution to quantum mechanics by referring to the former as the eigenvalue and the latter as the eigenvector.

In summary, for a single quantum bit, we introduce $q.\mathbb{B}$ for the space of qubits and χ for a typical element:

quantum state	$\chi : q.\mathbb{B}$
initialisation	$\chi := 2^{-\frac{1}{2}}(\hat{0} + \hat{1})$
evolution	$\chi := U(\chi)$ where U is unitary
finalisation	$Fin_{[\xi,\eta]}(\chi, x) \;\widehat{=}\; \chi, x \;:=\; \xi \;{}_p\!\oplus\; \eta,\; 0 \;{}_p\!\oplus\; 1$ where $p = \lvert\langle\chi, \xi\rangle\rvert^2$.

We have used multiple assignment to describe finalisation and will return to that shortly. For now we observe that $z := a \;{}_p\!\oplus\; b$ is shorthand for $(z := a) \;{}_p\!\oplus\; (z := b)$, designed specifically to enable us to write probabilistic multiple assignments as readily as standard multiple assignments.

The definition of quantum state, which we need in the next section for registers larger than a single bit, is a simple extension of the qubit case. For a type $\mathbb{T}$ its quantum analogue is

$$q.\mathbb{T} \;\widehat{=}\; \{\chi : \mathbb{T} \to \mathbb{C} \mid \sum\{|\chi(x)|^2 \mid x : \mathbb{T}\} \;=\; 1\}\,.$$

The only fact we need about q concerns its modularity: the quantum analogue of a direct product is the tensor product of the quantum analogues of the components:

$$q.(\mathbb{T}\times\mathbb{U}) \;=\; (q.\mathbb{T}) \otimes (q.\mathbb{U})\,.$$

Finalisation is a procedure with value-result parameter χ (the eigenvector) and result parameter x (the eigenvalue) which depends on the orthonormal basis $[\xi, \eta]$; there $p = |\langle\chi, \xi\rangle|^2$ is the length of the projection of state vector χ onto ξ and $\overline{p} = |\langle\chi, \eta\rangle|^2$ is the length of the projection of χ onto η . As a procedure, finalisation is a multiple probabilistic assignment. If the orthonormal basis is standard, we omit it and write just $Fin(\chi, x)$. Finalisation of $\chi : q.\mathbb{B}^n$ with respect to a given basis results in χ equalling each element of the basis with probability equal to the length of χ projected onto that element (and corresponding bitstring for x).

Thus in a quantum computation, probabilism arises only in finalisation (although a uniform choice is required in the standard part of Shor's algorithm). In physics the resulting probabilistic state is called a *mixed state.* Nondeterminism arises from errors that give rise to a range of probabilities. As we have already seen from the convexity principle, that is readily expressed in the *pGCL* programming language

$$\sqcap\{A\ {}_p\!\oplus B \mid a \leq p \leq b\} \;=\; (A\ {}_a\!\oplus B) \sqcap (A\ {}_b\!\oplus B)\,.$$

5.2 Quantum Programming: Grover's Algorithm

The case has been made elsewhere [SZ00] that sequential quantum computation can be incorporated into the approach of formal methods and as a result raised from the level of 'gate chasing' in hardware design to that expected in contemporary Computer Science of 'specified, verified design'. In fact [SZ00] provides a derivation in the refinement calculus of the Deutsch-Jozsa algorithm from its nondeterministic specification. Together with verified compilation [Z05], the claim is made that the result is not mere quantum computation, but quantum programming.

Here we provide a taste by specifying and describing Grover's *point search* algorithm [G96] as a quantum program. The problem it solves is:

given an array f of 2^n bits containing a single 1, locate it.

(More sophisticated versions deal with multiple 1s, but this suffices to make our point.) However it is not always sure to give the correct result and so its specification is formalised by saying that the program always terminates with some value for the index i, and with probability at least λ it returns the index i at which f is high.

var $i : 0\,..\,2^n \cdot$
  $i := f^{\sim}.1 \ {}_{\geq\lambda}\!\oplus\ i :\in 0\,..\,2^n$
rav

There $f^{\sim}$ denotes the converse of array f considered as a function, so that $i := f^{\sim}(1)$ assigns to i the unique value at which f is high; and $i :\in E$ denotes and arbitrary assignment to i from E . The value λ is n-dependent and is also related to the number N of iterations performed by the quantum implementation; we overlook the details here.

In describing Grover's algorithm in *pGCL* we use a register $\mathbb{B}^n$ of n bits. Its quantum version, $q.\mathbb{B}^n$ $(= q.(\mathbb{B}^n))$, extends the case $n = 1$ by consisting of the unit sphere in n-dimensional complex space; the state vector χ is thus a point on that sphere which finalisation projects, in this case, to one of the standard axes. The eigenvalue x returned by finalisation is the binary representation of the index i which is obtained from x by the 'decoding' function *num*. Initialisation of χ is written $In(\chi)$ and puts χ, as for the qubit case, in a state which if finalised would lead with equal probability to each element of the register $\mathbb{B}^n$. As expected, the program consists of initialisation, unitary evolution and finalisation.

var $\chi : q.\mathbb{B}^n,\ x : \mathbb{B}^n,\ i : [0, 2^n) \cdot$
  $In(\chi)$ ⨟
  do N times $\rightarrow$
    $\chi := T_f.\chi$ ⨟
    $\chi := M.\chi$
  od ⨟
  $Fin\,(\chi, x)$ ⨟
  $i := num(x)$
rav

Each evolution steps involves two transformations. The first, $T_f : q.\mathbb{B}^n \rightarrow q.\mathbb{B}^n$, acts coordinate-wise on χ by inverting in the origin just the coordinate corresponding to the index i at which f is high

$$T_f.i \ \widehat{=}\ (-\chi.i) \lhd f.i \rhd \chi.i\,.$$

The second, $M : q.\mathbb{B}^n \rightarrow q.\mathbb{B}^n$, inverts each coordinate of χ about the average value of χ's coordinates: $\chi - \overline{\chi} = \overline{\chi} - M\chi$, where $\overline{\chi}$ denotes the average of χ. Thus

$$M.\chi.i \ \widehat{=}\ 2\,(2^{-n} \sum \{\chi.j \mid j \in \mathbb{B}^n\}) - \chi.i\,.$$

Each transformation is readily seen to be unitary. A correctness proof of Grover's algorithm in the expectation-transformer semantics of *pGCL* appears in [BH99]. We expect that it is possible to give an algebraic derivation, starting from a non-quantum but probabilistic algorithm and using refinement steps (as in the derivation of the Deutsch-Josza algorithm in [SZ00]). For interest we observe that the asymptotic efficiency of Grover's algorithm is $\Theta(\sqrt{n})$; and with $n = 2^7$, the error bound λ is about 99.6%.

But let us consider a distributed quantum algorithm.

5.3 Distributed Quantum Computation

Initialisation, (unitary) evolution and finalisation in the sequential case ensure that a quantum program thus expressed conforms to the tenets of the quantum model. But in the case of a distributed algorithm just a little more care is required. Unitary evolution forbad something that in the distributed case might be taken for granted: the copying and output of a quantum state. Unfortunately it has long been known thatcopying an arbitrary quantum state is inconsistent with quantum theory [WZ82]. The proof is trivial but relies on the putative cloning operation acting on the quantum version of product space (one space for the value before and one space for the copied value after) which, by the previous law for q, is a tensor product.

Theorem (no-cloning). An arbitrary unknown quantum state cannot be copied without alteration.

Proof. Were a cloning operation T to exist it would be a unitary transformation (hence linear) on $H \otimes H$. But

$$
\begin{array}{l}
T.(x \otimes 0) + T.(y \otimes 0) \\
= \\
x \otimes x \ + \ y \otimes y \\
\neq \\
x \otimes x \ + \ x \otimes y \ + \ y \otimes x \ + \ y \otimes y \\
= \\
(x+y) \otimes (x+y) \\
= \\
T.((x+y) \otimes 0) .
\end{array}
$$

□

5.4 Quantum Key Distribution

The distributed quantum algorithm we consider is due to Bennett and Brassard [BB84] and enables, with reasonable likelihood, agents Alice A and Bob B to share a secure key. The context is this.

Since Shor's algorithm makes factorisation feasible, *albeit* on a quantum computer, public-key encryption using RSA becomes less secure than originally anticipated. So the old technique of a shared secure (i.e. private) key between pairs of agents regains importance. Fortuitously quantum computation provides a way to establish such a key; as someone has said: 'what the quantum model takes with one hand it returns with the other'.

The idea of the algorithm is that A and B are in touch by two different kinds of channel: a quantum channel and a standard channel (Figure 6). Eavesdropper E has access to both, and to the protocol employed by A and B. But, as we have seen, in the quantum model she is able to determine its quantum state only by finalisation: no copying of the state is possible (though of course she can perform a unitary operation on it in an attempt to confound A and B; but that provides her with no information about the state).

Rather than communicating bits, A and B communicate bases. To describe their protocol, we need a little more notation.

5.5 Conjugate Bases and Encoding

On a quantum channel, A sends a qubit to B initialised using one of two orthonormal bases (but see [BB92] for a one-basis variant and [G99], Section 6.2, for a comparison and background discussion). B guesses which basis was used.

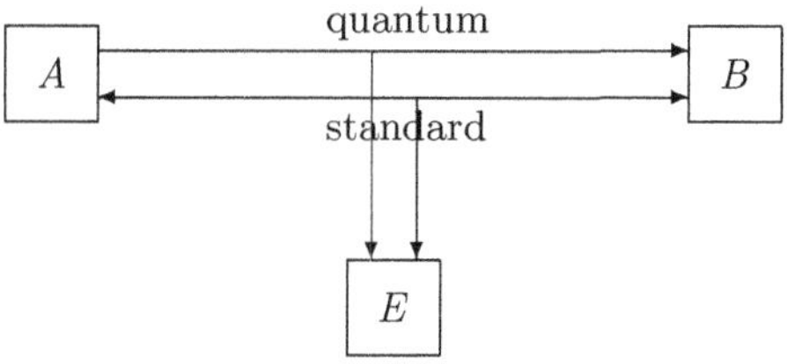

Fig. 6. Alice A and Bob B communicate on quantum and standard channels in the presence of an eavesdropper E in an attempt to gain a secure key

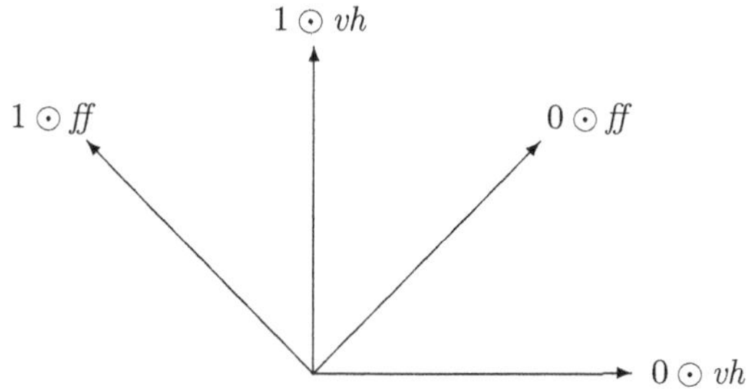

Fig. 7. Conjugate bases: the standard vertical-horizontal basis vh and its forty-five-degree rotation ff. Bit b encoded with respect to basis m is written $b \odot m$.

The two bases are as in Figure 7. The first we have already seen in Figure 5: the standard basis is now denoted vh. The second, ff, consists of vh rotated by 45 degrees anticlockwise. The two bases are chosen to have the property, called *conjugacy*, that if either vector of one basis is finalised with respect to the other basis then the two outcomes, 0 and 1, are equally likely. That property is evident from Figure 7.

For the set of bases we write $\mathbb{M} = \{vh, \mathit{ff}\}$ and we record the fact that each basis is involute (or conjugate, literally) to the other: $vh^* = \mathit{ff}$ and $\mathit{ff}^* = vh$.

Before, we wrote $\hat{b}$ for the encoding of bit b with respect to the basis vh. Now that we have two bases we must be a little more discriminating. So for the encoding of bit b with respect to basis m we write $b \odot m$. The quantum encoding function is thus:

$$\begin{aligned} &\odot : \mathbb{B} \times \mathbb{M} \to q\mathbb{B} \\ &0 \odot vh = \hat{0} \\ &1 \odot vh = \hat{1} \\ &0 \odot \mathit{ff} = 2^{-\frac{1}{2}}(\hat{0} + \hat{1}) \\ &1 \odot \mathit{ff} = 2^{-\frac{1}{2}}(\hat{0} - \hat{1}) . \end{aligned}$$

Quantum finalisation acts as a decoding function,

$$\begin{aligned} &\ominus : q\mathbb{B} \times \mathbb{M} \to \mathbb{B} \\ &\chi \ominus m = \mathit{Fin}_{[m]}(x) , \end{aligned}$$

(assuming the finalisation procedure *Fin* returns just the eigenvalue x) inverting $\odot$ by conjugacy:

$$(b \odot m) \ominus l \;=\; \begin{cases} b & \text{if } m = l \\ 0 \;{}_{\frac{1}{2}}\!\oplus 1 & \text{if } m = l^*. \end{cases}$$

5.6 BB84

A sends qubits to B, each encoded with one of the two bases, on the quantum channel. In bursts, eavesdropper E either finalises with respect to one of the bases, inflicts some unitary evolution on the quantum state of the channel, or is quiescent. There is also some chance of qubits being corrupted in the channel. As the qubits reach B he finalises them with respect to his choices of basis.

If E finalises a qubit with respect to the same basis that A used to encode her bit (probability $\frac{1}{2}$), then she observes the bit A sent and leaves the quantum state unaltered for B to observe. But if she finalises with respect to the conjugate of the basis A used, E is equally likely to observe either 0 or 1, in which case she leaves the channel in a state from which B is equally likely to observe 0 or 1 regardless of whether he uses the same basis as A or not.

Thus if A and B choose the same basis and B observes a bit other than the one A encoded, then they know that E has interfered. But if they choose the same basis and B observes the same bit that A encoded then they can infer E has not interfered only with probability $\frac{1}{4}$ (in the complementary case, with probability $\frac{1}{2}$ E chose the same basis as A and so observed the same bit; with probability $\frac{1}{4}\times\frac{1}{4}$ she chose the wrong basis and perchance observed the right bit). So in the next stage of the protocol, A and B confer to compare bases and bits.

B uses a standard channel to tell A the sequence of bases he used in finalisation and she replies confirming which were the same as hers. Of those, B chooses a subsequence and tells A, again on a standard channel, which bits he observed; and again she replies, confirming which were correct. All this E can observe but not distort. If an acceptable proportion of bits in the subsequence are correct, taking into account corruption and bursty intrusion by E, then A and B assume that E was quiescent and that the remaining bits, those not in the declared subsequence, are secure. The probability with which they are deluded is $\frac{3}{4}$ for each bit. (In fact there is a method for amplifying the security from the remaining bits; see [BBR88].) An example run is shown in Figure 8.

5.7 Simplification

We consider a simplification of just one iteration of that algorithm (strange as it might seem without the explanation above). To model the distributed algorithm in *pGCL* (rather than probabilistic process algebra) we need to 'partition' variables amongst agents. We do so by determining which variables each agent can write and can read (although a qubit can be 'read' only by finalisation); but first the meaning of the variables.

A's bits a	0	1	1	0	1	1	0	0	1	0	1	1
A's bases k	*ff*	*vh*	*ff*	*vh*	*vh*	*vh*	*vh*	*vh*	*ff*	*ff*	*vh*	*ff*
A's qubits $a \odot k$	45	90	135	0	90	90	0	0	135	45	90	135
B's bases κ	*vh*	*ff*	*ff*	*vh*	*vh*	*ff*	*ff*	*vh*	*ff*	*vh*	*ff*	*ff*
B's observed bits α	1		1		1	0	0	0		1	1	1
B reports κ's	*vh*		*ff*		*vh*	*ff*	*ff*	*vh*		*vh*	*ff*	*ff*
A confirms κ's	$\neg c$		c		c	$\neg c$	$\neg c$	c		$\neg c$	$\neg c$	c
potentially secure bits			1		1			0				1
B reveals some α's					1							
A confirms					d							
shared secure bits			1					0				1

Fig. 8. A tiny sequence of communications between A and B, demonstrating their choice of bases, publicly declared bases and bits, and the remaining secure bits. Gaps correspond to corrupted communications; Booleans c and d if high mean 'equal'.

A chooses bit $a : \mathbb{B}$ and basis $k : \mathbb{M}$ and encodes the former using the latter to produce qubit χ. Then (we choose her to eavesdrop) E chooses basis $e : \mathbb{M}$ and finalises χ with respect to it to observe bit x. B chooses basis κ and finalises χ to observe bit b. A reads κ and b and writes Boolean d saying whether or not both coincide with her choices. If not, the run is aborted. But if so, then A and B both believe their shared bit b $(= a)$ to be secure. (In this one-loop version of the protocol we choose not to distinguish the basis and bit's being concealed from their being publicised in the way depicted in Figure 8.)

With that mapping from variables to reality we see that A writes to variables $\{a, k, \chi, d\}$ and reads from variables $\{a, k, b, \kappa\}$; B writes $\{\kappa, , b\}$ and reads $\{d, \chi\}$; and E writes just $\{\chi, x\}$ but reads $\{\chi, \kappa, \alpha, d\}$.

The specification concerns the variables $x, b, d : \mathbb{B}$: the bit E observes, the bit B observes, and whether A and B chose the same bit and basis. Firstly, it ensures that the shared bit b is equally likely to be 0 or 1 (otherwise E would have an advantage in determining it). Secondly, since d is high iff A and B jointly believe b to be secure (when in fact E has finalised the state of the quantum channel and so with probability $\frac{3}{4}$ has obtained x equal to a), the specification must ensure that the probability of $(x = a) \wedge d$ (which equals the probability of $(x = b) \wedge d$) is bounded away from 1. For then the probability that A and B are deluded can be made realistically small by (independent) iteration. An acceptable value would be $\frac{1}{2}$; in fact by the above the algorithm achieves $\frac{3}{4} \times \frac{1}{2} = \frac{3}{8}$.

$$
\begin{array}{l}
\textbf{var } x, b, d : \mathbb{B} \cdot \\
\quad b \;=\; 0 \,{}_{\frac{1}{2}}\!\oplus 1 \\
\quad (b = x) \wedge d \;=\; 0 \,{}_{\geq \frac{3}{8}}\!\oplus 1 \\
\textbf{rav}
\end{array}
$$

The implementation uses all the extra variables discussed above to achieve that specification

$$
\begin{array}{l}
\textbf{var } a, b, x, d : \mathbb{B},\ k, e, \kappa : \mathbb{M},\ \chi : q.\mathbb{B}\ \cdot \\
\quad a\,, k := 0 \ {}_{\frac{1}{2}}\!\oplus 1\,, vh \ {}_{\frac{1}{2}}\!\oplus \mathit{ff}\ ; \\
\quad \chi := a \odot k\ ; \\
\quad e :\in \mathbb{M}\ ; \\
\quad \mathit{Fin}_{[e]}(\chi, x)\ ; \\
\quad \kappa := vh \ {}_{\frac{1}{2}}\!\oplus \mathit{ff}\ ; \\
\quad \mathit{Fin}_{[\kappa]}(\chi, b)\ ; \\
\quad d := ((k = \kappa) \wedge (a = b))\ ; \\
\quad \textbf{skip} \lhd d \rhd \textbf{abort} \\
\textbf{rav}
\end{array}
$$

5.8 Challenge

We have demonstrated a way in which a distributed quantum algorithm can be specified and described in *pGCL*. In one sense that suffices to show that such computations are unified within the Formal Methods framework. But far more satisfactory would be an incremental, step-wise, derivation of the implementation from its specification. Presumably the first step would provide a probabilistic non-quantum algorithm.

We are experimenting with probabilistic coin tossing [H92] (the structure underlying the simplification described above) and the use of data refinement to derive a quantum implementation. The aim is to convert an abstract, probabilistic, algorithm into a concrete, quantum, one step-by-step using a simulation between the two computations.

References

[BB84] C. H. Bennett and G. Brassard. Quantum cryptography: public key distribution and coin tossing. *Proc. IEEE Conference on Computers, Systems and Signal processing*, Bangalore, pp. 175–179, 1984.

[BBR88] C. H. Bennett, G. Brassard and J.-M. Robert. Privacy amplification by public discussion. *SIAM Journal of Computing*, **17**(2):210–229, 1988.

[BB92] C. H. Bennett. Quantum cryptography using any two nonorthogonal states. Physical Review Letters, **68**(21):3121–3124, 1992.

[BH99] M. J. Butler and P. Hartel. Reasoning about Grover's quantum search algorithm using probabilistic *wp*. *ACM Transactions on Programming Languages and Systems*, **21**(3):417–430, 1999.

[G96] L. Grover. A fast quantum mechanical algorithm for database search. *Proceedings of 28th ACM STOC*, 212–219, 1996.

[G99] J. Gruska. *Quantum Computing.* McGraw-Hill International (UK), Advanced Topics in Computer Science, 1999.

[H92] D. Harel. *Algorithmics: The Spirit of Computing*, second edition. Addison Wesley, 1992.

[HSM97] He, Jifeng, K. Seidel and A. K. McIver. Probabilistic models for the guarded command language. *Science of Computer Programming*, **28**:171–192, 1997.

[H04] E. R. Hehner. Probabilistic predicative programming. *Mathematics of Program Construction*, Stirling Scotland, LNCS **3125**:169–185, Springer-Verlag, 2004.

[HH98] C. A. R. Hoare and He, Jifeng. *Unifying Theories of Programming.* Prentice Hall, 1998.

[L61] R. Landauer. Irreversibility and heat generated in the computing process. *IBM Journal of Research and Development*, **5**, 1961.

[MM05] A. K. McIver and C. C. Morgan. *Abstraction, Refinement and Proof for Probabilistic Systems.* Springer Monographs in Computer Science, 2005.

[NC00] M. A. Nielsen and I. L. Chuang. *Quantum Computation and Quantum Information.* Cambridge University Press, 2000.

[SZ00] J. W. Sanders and P. Zuliani. Quantum Programming. *Mathematics of Program Construction, 2000*, edited by J. N. Oliviera and R. Backhouse, Springer-Verlag LNCS **1837**:80–99, 2000.

[SZL06] W. J. Stoddart, F. Zeyda and R. Lynas. A design-based model of reversible computation. This proceedings.

[WZ82] W. K. Wootters and W. H. Zurek. A single quantum cannot be cloned, *Nature*, **299**(5886):802–803, 1982.

[Z01] P. Zuliani. Logical reversibility. *IBM Journal of Research and Development*, **45**(6):807–818, 2001.

[Z05] P. Zuliani. Compiling Quantum Programs. *Acta Informatica*, **41**(7-8): 435–474, 2005.

Pointers and Records in the Unifying Theories of Programming

Ana Cavalcanti[1], Will Harwood[2,*], and Jim Woodcock[1]

[1] University of York
Department of Computer Science
York, UK
[2] Citrix Systems (R & D) Ltd
Venture House, Cambourne Business Park
Cambourne, Cambs, UK

Abstract. We present a theory of pointers and records that provides a representation for objects and sharing in languages like Java and C++. Our approach to pointers is based on Paige's entity groups, which give an abstract view of storage as equivalence classes of variables that share the same memory location. We first define our theory as a restriction of the general theory of relations, and, as a consequence, it does not distinguish between terminating and non-terminating programs. Therefore, we link it with the theory of designs, providing a foundation for reasoning about total correctness of pointer-based sequential programs. Our work is a step towards the semantics of an object-oriented language that also integrates constructs for specifying state-rich and concurrent systems.

Keywords: semantics, refinement, relations, object models.

1 Introduction

Interest in reasoning about pointer programs is not recent [3], and has been renewed by the importance of sharing in object-oriented languages [1, 11]. Most semantic models of pointers use indexes to represent memory locations or embed a heap [8, 15]. Modern object-oriented languages, however, do not encourage or directly support manipulation of the memory.

In this paper, we present a theory for pointers based on the model of entity groups presented in [13] to formalise rules of a refinement calculus for Eiffel [10]. In that work, the complications of an explicit model of the memory are avoided; instead, each entity (variable) is associated with the set of variables that share its location (entity group). Using this model, the Eiffel semantics for object creation, reference assignment, and call is formalised.

Our long-term goal is to provide a pointer semantics for an object-oriented language for refinement that supports the development of state-rich, concurrent programs. In particular, we are interested in the language *OhCircus* presented

* Also, a Visiting Research Fellow at the University of Kent Computing Laboratory, Canterbury Kent, UK.

S. Dunne and W. Stoddart (Eds.): UTP 2006, LNCS 4010, pp. 200–216, 2006.

in [4]; it is a combination of Z [20] and CSP [16], with object-oriented constructs in the style of Java, including inheritance, subtyping, and null values. Since *OhCircus* combines constructs from several programming theories, the UTP is a very appropriate choice for its semantic model.

Following the UTP style, we are concentrating on the individual aspects of the *OhCircus* semantics separately. The theory that we present here provides a reference semantics for a language with variables whose values are objects: recursive records. It will be integrated to the copy semantics of *OhCircus*.

The program in Figure 1 illustrates the sort of concepts in which we are interested. This program compacts a list l, by sharing references to equal values. The type $List$ of l can be defined as: $List ::= (label : \mathbb{Z};\ next : List)$. This is a recursive labelled record with two fields: $label$ and $next$. The assignments in Figure 1 are pointer assignments, and the equalities are value equalities. In this example we use a reasonably standard programming notation involving **while** and **if** commands, but in our theory we use the notation adopted in the UTP.

```
var p • p := l;
  while p ≠ null do
    var q • q := p.next;
      while q ≠ null do
        if q.label = p.label then q.label := p.label fi;
        q := q.next
      od;
      p := p.next
  od
```

Fig. 1. Compacting a list l

We assume that all values, including primitive values, have a location; variables are names of locations. We are not interested in the particular locations of variables and values, but on whether two (or more) variables are different names for the same location or not. A healthiness condition guarantees that variables that denote the same location have the same value.

In the next section we present our theory: its alphabet and its healthiness conditions. Section 3 revisits the semantics of assignment and variable blocks, and establishes the closedness of our theory. In Section 4 we explore the link to the theory of designs; the combined theory supports reasoning about total correctness of pointer programs. Finally, in Section 5 we summarise our results, and consider some related and future work.

2 Relational Pointer Theory

In our work, we consider recursive data types d_i defined by a set of recursive equations of the form $d_i = \langle\!\langle f_1 : d_1, ..., f_n : d_n \rangle\!\rangle \mid null$ or $d_i = s$, where s is a simple set and the f_j's are field names. We define the predicate $\mathsf{field}(f, d_i)$ to mean that f is a field of the data type d_i. In our example, the definition of $List$

is a shorthand for $List = \langle\langle label : Z;\ next : List \rangle\rangle \mid null$. These recursive records are enough to model object values in a language like Java.

As with the general theory of relations of the UTP, the alphabet of our theory of pointer relations includes the programming variables and their dashed counterparts. Their values, however, are elements of recursive data types.

If the value of a variable x is a record with a field called y, we can use the name $x.y$ to refer to the value of this field: the dot notation is a field selector. If $x.y$ is again a record, we can refer to its z field as $x.y.z$, and so on. We refer to both simple names (of programming variables) and such compound names formed using the field selector, as paths; the set *Path* contains all paths.

Our theory also includes two extra variables pg and pg'; they are path groups: sets of groups (sets) of paths. Two paths that share the same location are in the same group. Path groups correspond to the entity groups in [13].

In the next section, we introduce additional notation related to paths. Later on, in Section 2.2, we define the healthiness conditions of our theory.

2.1 Paths

Given an observational variable x, we use $'x$ to refer to its name. References to x itself are interpreted to stand for the value of x, as usual in the UTP.

We use meta variables p and q to refer to paths; we use subscripts if we need extra variables. Given a path p, its root is p itself, if p is a simple name, or $'x$, if it is of the form $'x.q$. In this latter case, q is called the extension of p. We refer to these as $\mathsf{root}(p)$ and $\mathsf{ext}(p)$. The extension of a variable is empty.

In general, for paths p and q, we call $p.q$ an extension of p by q. The path $p.q$ is said to be a descendant of p. For any two paths p and q, we write $p \prec q$ when p is a descendant of q. Given a set of paths π we define the set of its descendants as follows.

$$\mathsf{desc}(\pi) \mathrel{\widehat=} \{\, p \mid \exists\, q : \pi \bullet p \prec q \,\}$$

We introduce two meta functions: θ and δ. The function θ is inspired by the Z θ-notation. Given an alphabet A, and a path p, $\theta_A(p)$ gives the value of p, if its root $'x$ is in A and p is an appropriate reference to a field of x.

$$\theta_A('x) = x, \ \textbf{provided}\ 'x \in A$$

$$\theta_A(p.f) = v.f, \ \textbf{provided}\ \theta_A(p) = v \wedge v \in d_i \wedge \mathsf{field}(f, d_i)$$

We also introduce decorated versions of θ. For example θ'_A is defined as follows.

$$\theta'_A('x) = x', \ \textbf{provided}\ 'x \in A$$

$$\theta_A(p.f) = v.f, \ \textbf{provided}\ \theta'_A(p) = v \wedge v \in d_i \wedge \mathsf{field}(f, d_i)$$

Other decorations can also be used. The important point is that the domain of θ is always a set of undecorated variable names, along with some of their descendants, whether θ is decorated or not. If we decorate θ, however, these paths are associated to the value of the similarly decorated path. Of course, the decoration of a path is reflected in its root; for example $(x.y)' = x'.y$.

The set $\delta_{A,i}(p)$ includes all paths for p with i extra field selectors. A path for another path p is either p itself or a descendant of p, and, most importantly, it has a value, as defined by θ.

$$\delta_{A,0}(p) = \{\, p \,\}, \textbf{ provided } p \in \operatorname{dom}\theta.$$

$$\delta_{A,n+1}(p) = \{\, q.f \mid q \in \delta_{A,n}(p) \land \theta_A(q) \in d_i \land \mathsf{field}(f, d_i) \,\}$$

In general, $\delta_A(x)$ is the set of all paths for x.

$$\delta_A(x) = \bigcup_i \delta_{A,i}(x)$$

Given a set π of paths, $\Delta(\pi)$ is the set of paths for the paths in π.

$$\Delta_A(\pi) = \{\, p \mid \exists\, x : \pi \bullet p \in \delta_A(x) \,\}$$

In summary, the descendants of a variable x are all path names that can be built using $'x$ as a root. The paths for x, on the other hand, are x itself, and all descendants that can be meaningfully used to access a component of the record value of x, if any. Both notions generalise to paths in general.

Generally, we will drop the alphabet subscript from the above functions when they can be inferred from context.

2.2 Healthiness Conditions

We need healthiness conditions to establish the relationship between the values of the variables and the path groups in pg and pg'. First of all, we have a healthiness condition **HP1** to guarantee that the path group pg partitions all paths of the variables of the program.

$$\textsf{\textbf{HP1}} \quad P = P \land pg \text{ partition } \Delta(var\alpha P)$$

In the UTP, the set $in\alpha P$ includes all the undashed variables in the alphabet of P. We define $var\alpha P = in\alpha P \setminus \{\, pg \,\}$ to include all the undecorated programming variables in the alphabet of P.

We use **HP1** to name the function $\textbf{HP1}(P) \mathrel{\widehat{=}} P \land pg \text{ partition } \Delta(var\alpha P)$ as well. The **HP1**-healthy relations are the fixed points of **HP1**. As usual in the UTP, we adopt the same sort of convention in relation to the definitions of the other healthiness conditions in the sequel.

The second property we require is that the path group is well structured, so that if any group contains a pair of paths p_1 and p_2, then if these paths are extended in the same way, there is a group containing both extensions.

$$\begin{aligned}\textsf{\textbf{HP2}} \quad P = P \land \forall\, g_1 : pg;\ p_1, p_2 : g_1;\ p : Path \mid \{\, p_1.p, p_2.p \,\} \subseteq \Delta(var\alpha P) \bullet \\ (\exists\, g_2 : pg \bullet \{\, p_1.p, p_2.p \,\} \subseteq g_2)\end{aligned}$$

This reflects the fact that if p_1 and p_2 are different names for the same location, then accesses to their components are also accesses to the same location.

Finally, all paths in the same group must have the same value.

HP3 $P = P \wedge \forall g : pg;\ p_1, p_2 : g \bullet \theta_{var\alpha P}\ p_1 = \theta_{var\alpha P}\ p_2$

We use the θ function to determine the values of the paths p_1 and p_2. The θ function is partial: it is only defined for valid applications of the field selector operator. For example, $\theta(x.f)$ is not defined if the value of x is *null*. Therefore, by requiring that p_1 and p_2 have the same image under θ, we not only require that they have the same value, but also that they are valid paths.

The healthiness conditions HP1, HP2 and HP3 impose conditions on the input path group pg; HP4, HP5, and HP6 below impose the same conditions on the output path group pg'.

HP4 $P = P \wedge pg'$ partition $\Delta(var\alpha P)$

It is a consequence of **HP4** that pg', in the same way as pg, includes only undecorated variable names. This is important to avoid the need to change the definition of a sequence $P;\ Q$ to match the value of pg' defined by P to the value of pg used by Q.

HP5 $P = P \wedge \forall g_1 : pg';\ p_1, p_2 : g_1;\ p : Path \mid \{ p_1.p, p_2.p \} \subseteq \Delta(var\alpha P) \bullet$
$(\exists g_2 : pg' \bullet \{ p_1.p, p_2.p \} \subseteq g_2)$

HP6 $P = P \wedge \forall g : pg';\ p_1, p_2 : g \bullet \theta'_{\alpha P}\ p_1 = \theta'_{\alpha P}\ p_2$

In the definition of **HP6**, we use a decorated version of θ. The paths in pg' are not decorated, but θ' gives the values of the primed variables.

The set of healthiness conditions can be simplified by noting that conditions **HP3-6** can be replaced by the condition below.

HP7 $P;\ I\!I_p = P$

The program $I\!I_p$ is the **HP1-3**-healthy identity relation, which we denote by $I\!I_r$ to avoid confusion.

$I\!I_p \mathrel{\widehat{=}}$ **HP1** $\circ$ **HP2** $\circ$ **HP3**$(I\!I_r)$

The theorems below establish that the two sets of healthiness conditions are indeed interchangeable.

Theorem 1. *Every relation R that is* **HP1-3**-*healthy and* **HP7**-*healthy is also* **HP4-6**-*healthy.*

Theorem 2. *Every relation R that is* **HP1-6**-*healthy is also* **HP7**-*healthy.*

A yet more concise way of characterising the healthy pointer relations is justified by the following theorem. It establishes that we can use just the healthiness condition below.

HP8 $P = I\!I_p;\ P;\ I\!I_p$

Theorem 3. *A pointer relation R is healthy if, and only if, it is* **HP8**-*healthy.*

This result is a consequence of the fact that our healthiness conditions are restrictions on the initial and after state of a relation, but not on the transitions that they describe.

This also allows us to prove a further useful theorem.

Theorem 4. *For any pointer relation P, **HP8**(P) is the weakest healthy pointer relation characterised by P: $P \sqsubseteq I\!I_p;\ P;\ I\!I_p$, and for every healthy Q such that $P \sqsubseteq Q$, we have $I\!I_p;\ P;\ I\!I_p \sqsubseteq Q$.*

Proof

$$P \sqsubseteq Q \qquad \textit{monotonicity of sequence}$$
$$\Rightarrow I\!I_p;\ P;\ I\!I_p \sqsubseteq I\!I_p;\ Q;\ I\!I_p \qquad \textit{healthiness of } Q$$
$$= I\!I_p;\ P;\ I\!I_p \sqsubseteq Q \qquad \square$$

This justifies the specification of pointer relations by defining unhealthy relations and using **HP8** to make it healthy.

3 Programming Constructs

In this section, we revisit the semantics of (value) assignment already in the UTP, and introduce a new form of assignment: pointer assignment. For each form of assignment, there is a corresponding notion of equality.

3.1 Equality

Our two notions of equality are standard equality $\_ =_p \_$ and pointer equality $\_ ==\_ \_$. Standard equality equates values and pointer equality equates storage locations.

Value equality is defined in terms of the θ function.

$$p_1 =_p p_2 \mathrel{\widehat{=}} \theta(p_1) = \theta(p_2)$$

The paths p_1 and p_2 are required to be valid, that is, in the domain of θ, and have the same value.

Pointer equality is defined with respect to the path group which models storage.

$$p_1 ==_{pg} p_2 \mathrel{\widehat{=}} \exists\, g : pg \bullet \{ p_1, p_2 \} \subseteq g$$

These two equalities reflect the same distinction found in Lisp, where EQUAL compares values and EQ compares pointers. On the other hand, this is slightly in contrast with Java, where $\_ == \_$ compare values, but the values of objects are locations. In our language, every value has a location, and we assume that literal values have fresh locations. To write the Java expression $e_1 == e_2$ in our language, we have to determine the type(s) of e_1 (and e_2). If they have primitive types, we write $e_1 = e_2$; if not, we keep the $\_ == \_$.

In our theory, if either of x or y is a primed name, then $x == y$ is going to be false, whether the extra parameter is pg or pg'. This is because, as already mentioned, they only hold undashed names.

3.2 Assignment

The first form of assignment $p_1 := p_2$ that we consider is that already available in the UTP, which assigns the value of p_2 to p_1, and, consequently, to all other paths in its group. The second is $p_1 :== p_2$, which makes p_1 to become another name for the location of p_2; in our context, this assignment alters the storage model by merging the path groups containing p_1 and p_2.

Both assignments are alphabetised; they take a set A of programming variables as a parameter.

$$\alpha(p_1 :=_A p_2) = \alpha(p_1 :=_A p_2) = A \cup A' \cup \{ pg, pg' \}$$

Alphabets are left implicit whenever convenient.

Value assignment. As already said, the value assignment $p_1 := p_2$ has the side effect of altering the value of all paths that share the storage location of p_1. As a consequence, the value of all their descendants are also changed. No other paths have their value changed.

In terms of memory usage, there are two issues. Firstly, if a component $x.f$ of x shares location with a path p, and we assign a new value p_2 to x, then $x.f$ takes on a new value as well, that of $p_2.f$, if this is well defined. Therefore, $x.f$ and p cease to share their location. This means that all the descendants of x have to be eliminated from the path groups in which they are.

Secondly, a value assignment duplicates a value and potentially requires extra storage. For example, the assignment $x.f := y$ makes the value of $x.f$, and of all the paths that share its location, to become that of y; the locations of $x.f$ and y, however, are not changed. Moreover, if the value of y is itself a record, with a field g, then $x.f.g$ and $y.g$ have the same value, but different locations. If the location $x.f.g$ did not exist before, because, for example, $x.f$ had value *null* before the assignment, a new location is created.

We define this behavior by defining a general notion of assignment and then making it healthy using **HP8**.

$$\begin{array}{l} \mathsf{assignV}(p_1, p_2, A) \mathrel{\widehat=} \\ \quad \forall\, q : \mathsf{group}(p_1, pg) \bullet \mathsf{update}(\mathsf{root}(q), \mathsf{root}(q)', \mathsf{ext}(q), p_2) \land \\ \quad \forall\, n : A \mid (\neg\, \exists\, p : \mathsf{group}(p_1, pg) \bullet n =_n \mathsf{root}(p)) \bullet n' = n \land \\ \quad pg' = \mathsf{remove}(pg, \mathsf{group}(p_1, pg)) \cup \\ \qquad\qquad \{ q_1 : \Delta(p_2);\ q_2 : Path \mid q_1 =_n p_2.q_2 \bullet \{ q_3 : \mathsf{group}(p_1, pg) \bullet q_3.q_2 \} \} \end{array}$$

The function $\mathsf{group}(x, pg)$ selects the path group of pg that contains x.

$$\mathsf{group}(x, pg) \mathrel{\widehat=} \iota\, g : pg \mid x \in g$$

The ι expression $\iota\, o : S \mid p(o)$ gives a definite description of an object o of a set S that satisfies a constraint $p(o)$; it is defined only when o exists and is unique. It is identical to the Z μ operator; we do not use μ to avoid confusion with the least fixed point operator of the UTP.

The first conjunct in the definition of $\mathsf{assignV}(p_1, p_2, A)$ defines the new value of all the paths in the group of p_1. For each of them, including p_1 itself, we change the value of the variable at its root. This is because, changing the value of $x.f$ really corresponds to changing the value of x: its f field takes on a new value, and all the others keep the same value.

The operator $\mathsf{update}(x, y, p, q)$ defines the value of y as the result of updating the value of x to change the value of its component $x.p$ to be that of the path q. All the other components of y have the same value of the corresponding component of x.

$$\begin{array}{l} \mathsf{update}(x, y, p, q) \mathrel{\widehat=} \\ \quad \forall\, p_1 : \Delta(x) \bullet (p_1 =_n x.p \Rightarrow y.p =_p q) \land \\ \qquad\qquad ((p_1 \neq_n x.p \land \neg\, (p_1 \prec x.p)) \Rightarrow y.\mathsf{ext}(p_1) =_p p_1) \end{array}$$

To define $\mathsf{update}(x, y, p, q)$, we consider each of the descendant paths p_1 of x. For the descendant $x.p$, the corresponding value of $y.p$ is that of q. For the other descendants p_1, if they are not descendants of $x.p$, the value of the corresponding component of y is that of p_1 itself, which is a component of x. If they are a descendant of $x.p$, by defining $y.p$, we have already defined its value.

The equality operator $\_ =_n \_$ compares paths for syntactic equality. In the case of simple names, it compares the names of the variables, instead of their values.

The second conjunct in the definition of $\mathsf{assignV}(p_1, p_2, A)$ defines the value of the variables that are not affected by the assignment: those that are not roots of paths in the group of p_1. As already said, the value of the paths in the group of p_1 is defined by the update function. In doing so, we also determine the value of all the descendants of the roots of those paths, as explained above.

The third conjunct in the definition of $\mathsf{assignV}(p_1, p_2, A)$ defines the value of pg'. The function $\mathsf{remove}(pg, \pi)$ defines the set of path groups obtained by removing all descendants of the paths in π from the groups in pg. If a group of pg contains only descendants of π, it becomes empty, and should be excluded.

$$\mathsf{remove}(pg, \pi) \mathrel{\widehat=} \{\, g : pg \mid \neg\, g \subseteq \mathsf{desc}(\pi) \bullet g \setminus \mathsf{desc}(\pi) \,\}$$

The use of $\mathsf{remove}(pg, \mathsf{group}(p_1, pg))$ accounts for the first issue discussed above in relation to memory usage in the behaviour of the assignment $p_1 := p_2$; namely, the sharing information about all the descendants of the assigned path changes. The duplication of the assigned value is taken into account by requiring that pg' includes new path groups $\{\, q_3 : \mathsf{group}(p_1, pg) \bullet q_3.q_2 \,\}$, for each extension q_2 of the descendants of p_2.

Finally, the definition of assignment is as follows.

$$p_1 :=_A p_2 \mathrel{\widehat=} \mathbf{HP8}(assignV(p_1, p_2, A))$$

An interesting observation is that we only need to compose II_p on the left of $assignV(p_1, p_2, A)$ to make it healthy.

Theorem 5. $p_1 :=_A p_2 = \mathit{II}_p;\ \mathit{assignV}(p_1, p_2, A)$.

This is because the path group pg' defined by $\mathsf{assignV}$ satisfies the requirements of our healthiness conditions. What it does not enforce is that pg is suitable.

Pointer assignment. The second form of assignment, $p_1 :==_A p_2$, makes p_1 to share the location of p_2. As a consequence, the value of p_1 is also changed to that of p_2. Moreover, by changing the location of p_1 to that of p_2, we implicitly change the location of all descendants of p_1, and their values. In our model, we remove them all from their current path groups, and, for each well defined descendant of p_2, we insert a corresponding descendant of p_1 in its group. We use the same style of construction as for value assignment, using **HP8** to ensure healthiness.

$$\begin{array}{l} p_1 :==_A p_2 \mathrel{\widehat{=}} \mathbf{H8}(p_1' =_p p_2 \land (\forall p : \bigcup pg' \mid pg \notin \Delta(p_1) \bullet p' =_p p) \land \\ \qquad\qquad pg' = \mathsf{add}(p_1, p_2, \mathsf{purge}(p_1, pg))) \end{array}$$

The first conjunct of this definition determines the new value of p_1, and implicitly that of all its descendants. It also establishes that the value of all other paths are not changed.

The second conjunct of the above definition determines the new value of pg. We use a strengthened remove operator to state that both p_1 and all its descendants need to be removed from the original path groups.

$$\mathsf{purge}(p, pg) \mathrel{\widehat{=}} \{\, g : pg \mid \neg\, g \subseteq (\mathsf{desc}(p) \cup \{\, p \,\}) \bullet g \setminus (\mathsf{desc}(p) \cup \{\, p \,\}) \,\}$$

Next, we use a function add to define that p_1 itself and its descendants need to be inserted back into the corresponding groups of p_2 and its descendants.

$$\begin{array}{l} \mathsf{add}(p_1, p_2, pg) \mathrel{\widehat{=}} \\ \{\, g : pg \bullet g \cup \{\, p : g;\ q : \mathit{Path} \mid p =_n p_2.q \bullet p_1.q \,\} \cup \{\, p : g \mid p =_n p_2 \bullet p_1 \,\} \,\} \end{array}$$

Again, our use of **HP8** in the definition of $p_1 :==_A p_2$ is required only to enforce that assignments are only defined for healthy path groups pg.

3.3 Variable Blocks

The declaration of a variable requires its inclusion in the set of path groups: new singleton groups containing the new variable and its descendants should be defined. Also, ending the scope of a variable entails in removing it and its descendants from the path groups. Therefore, we redefine **var** x and **end** x.

$$\mathbf{var}_A\ x \mathrel{\widehat{=}} \mathbf{HP8}(\forall n : A \bullet n' =_p n \land pg' = pg \cup \{\, p : \Delta('x) \bullet \{\, p \,\} \,\})$$

The alphabet of the variable declaration includes the new variable.

$$\alpha(\mathbf{var}_A\ x) = A \cup A' \cup \{\, x' \,\} \cup \{\, pg, pg' \,\}$$

This is just as in the UTP definition for the alphabet of **var**, except for the extra observational variables pg and pg'.

To define **end** x, we use the function purge introduced in the previous section.

$$\mathbf{end}_A\ x \mathrel{\widehat{=}} \mathsf{HP8}(\forall n : A \bullet n' =_p n \wedge pg' = \mathsf{purge}(x, pg))$$

The alphabet definition is similar to that of **var** x.

$$\alpha(\mathbf{end}_A\ x) = A \cup \{ x \} \cup A' \cup \{ pg, pg' \}$$

The proof of laws is in our agenda for future work.

3.4 Closure Properties

In this section, we prove that the programming operators are closed. In other words, when applied to healthy relations, they result in healthy relations.

Theorem 6. *If the relations P and Q are healthy, then so is $P;\ Q$.*

Proof

$$\begin{array}{ll} \mathit{II}_p;\ P;\ Q;\ \mathit{II}_p & \textsf{P and Q are healthy} \\ = \mathit{II}_p;\ \mathit{II}_p;\ P;\ \mathit{II}_p;\ \mathit{II}_p;\ Q;\ \mathit{II}_p;\ \mathit{II}_p & \mathit{II}_p;\ \mathit{II}_p = \mathit{II}_p \\ = P;\ Q & \square \end{array}$$

Theorem 7. *If the relations P and Q are healthy, then so is $P \vee Q$.*

Proof

$$\begin{array}{ll} \mathit{II}_p;\ (P \vee Q);\ \mathit{II}_p & \textsf{property of sequence and } \vee \\ = \mathit{II}_p;\ P;\ \mathit{II}_p \vee \mathit{II}_p;\ Q;\ \mathit{II}_p & \textsf{P and Q are healthy} \\ = P \vee Q & \square \end{array}$$

Theorem 8. *If the relations P and Q are healthy, then so is $P \wedge Q$.*

Proof

$$\begin{array}{ll} \mathit{II}_p;\ (P \wedge Q);\ \mathit{II}_p & \textsf{property of } \mathit{II}_p \\ = \mathit{II}_p;\ P;\ \mathit{II}_p \wedge \mathit{II}_p;\ Q;\ \mathit{II}_p & \textsf{P and Q are healthy} \\ = P \wedge Q & \square \end{array}$$

Theorem 9. *If relations P and Q are healthy, then so is $P \lhd b \rhd Q$.*

Proof

Essentially the same. □

The set of healthy pointer relations is a complete lattice, since it is the image of monotonic and idempotent healthiness conditions [7].

Theorem 10. *If F is built out of conjunctions, disjunctions, and sequences applied to healthy pointer relations, then*

$$\mu_p X \bullet F(X) = \mathbf{HP8}(\mu X \bullet F(X))$$

where $\mu_p X \bullet F(X)$ is the least fixed point of F in the lattice of healthy pointer relations.

Proof. Follows from the closure theorems above, and from the fact that **HP8** is a monotonic idempotent that semi-commutes with the programming constructors [7]. □

This result states that a recursion is a healthy pointer relation, if its body is built out of pointer relations itself.

4 Pointer Designs

The theory of pointer relations does not distinguish between terminating and non-terminating programs. This distinction is made in the UTP by defining *designs*, a subclass of relations that satisfy two healthiness conditions (**H1** and **H2**). All design relations can be split into precondition/postcondition pairs, making them similar to specification statements in the refinement calculus.

In this section, we combine the theories of designs and pointers, thereby providing a foundation for a theory of total correctness for pointer-based sequential programs. First, we reproduce the definitions of the design theory that we need, then we define a Galois connection between our theory and designs. Finally, we introduce an extra healthiness condition of the combined theory.

4.1 Designs

The theory of designs include two extra boolean observational variables to record the start and the termination of a program: ok and ok'. The monotonic idempotents used to define the healthiness conditions for designs can be defined as follows, where P is a relation with alphabet $\{ok, ok', v, v'\}$.

$$\mathbf{H1}(P) \mathrel{\widehat{=}} ok \Rightarrow P$$

$$\mathbf{H2}(P) \mathrel{\widehat{=}} P \,;\, J, \text{ where } J \mathrel{\widehat{=}} (ok \Rightarrow ok') \wedge v' = v$$

The variable ok records the observation that the program has been started; the variable ok' records the observation that the program terminated. If P is **H1**-healthy, then it makes no restrictions on the final value of variables before it starts. If P is **H2**-healthy, then termination must be a possible outcome from every initial state. The composition of **H1** and **H2** is named **H**.

The above formulation of **H2** is different from that in [7], but in [19], we prove that it is equivalent.

4.2 Pointer Relations and Designs

The theory of pointer relations is stronger than the theory of designs. This is because on abortion, a design provides no guarantees; however, a pointer relation still requires the properties of *pg* to hold. This seems to be compatible with the reality of pointer programs: the information held in *pg* (and *pg′*) is related to the physical constraints over variables that share locations, and these constraints are not suspended when the program aborts. In this case, the final values of the variables are arbitrary, but those that share the same location will still have the same value, for instance.

Therefore, to combine the theories of pointers and designs, we follow the approach used to combine the theory of reactive processes and designs. We take **HP8** as a link that maps a design to a pointer relation; the range of **HP8** characterises a subset of pointer relations: *pointer designs*. This is our proposed theory for total correctness of pointer programs.

First of all, for insight, we consider $\mathbf{HP8}(\neg\, ok)$; this program is strictly stronger than $\neg\, ok$, which is the top of the lattice of designs. This property prevents **H1** from commuting exactly with **HP8**. In general, we have the following result.

$$
\begin{array}{ll}
\mathbf{HP8} \circ \mathbf{H1}(P) & \mathbf{H1} \\
= \mathbf{HP8}(ok \Rightarrow P) & \textit{propositional calculus, } \mathbf{HP8} \textit{ disjunctive} \\
= \mathbf{HP8}(\neg\, ok) \vee \mathbf{HP8}(P) & \mathbf{HP8}(\neg\, ok) \neq \neg\, ok \\
\neq \neg\, ok \vee \mathbf{HP8}(P) & \mathbf{H1} \\
= \mathbf{H1} \circ \mathbf{HP8}(P) & \Box
\end{array}
$$

For this reason, the theory of pointer relations is disjoint from the theory of designs: a pointer relation cannot be a design, and *vice versa*. Instead, there is an approximate relationship between the two theories:

$$\mathbf{HP8} \circ \mathbf{H}(P) \sqsubseteq P$$

for pointer relation P. This relationship is a property of a Galois connection that translates between the two theories. In particular, it allows us to embed the theory of designs and its refinement calculus in the world of pointers.

Galois connection. Let $\mathbf{S}$ and $\mathbf{T}$ both be partial orders; let L be a function from $\mathbf{S}$ to $\mathbf{T}$; and let R be a function from $\mathbf{T}$ to $\mathbf{S}$. The pair (L, R) is a *Galois connection* if, for all $X \in \mathbf{S}$ and $Y \in \mathbf{T}$

$$Y \sqsubseteq L(X) \quad \textbf{iff} \quad R(Y) \sqsubseteq X$$

L and R are known as the left and right adjoints, respectively.

Our proof of the existence of a Galois connection relies on two simple lemmas about our healthiness conditions and refinement. First, a lemma concerning **H1**.

Lemma 1 (H1-refinement). *For any two relations P and Q with ok and ok′ in their alphabets,*

$$\mathbf{H1}(P) \sqsubseteq \mathbf{H1}(Q) \quad \textit{iff} \quad \mathbf{H1}(P) \sqsubseteq Q$$

Proof

$$
\begin{aligned}
& \mathbf{H1}(P) \sqsubseteq \mathbf{H1}(Q) && \textit{refinement}\\
={}& [\,\mathbf{H1}(Q) \Rightarrow \mathbf{H1}(P)\,] && \mathbf{H1}\\
={}& [\,(ok \Rightarrow Q) \Rightarrow (ok \Rightarrow P)\,] && \textit{propositional calculus}\\
={}& [\,Q \Rightarrow (ok \Rightarrow P)\,] && \mathbf{H1}\\
={}& [\,Q \Rightarrow \mathbf{H1}(P)\,] && \textit{refinement}\\
={}& \mathbf{H1}(P) \sqsubseteq Q && \square
\end{aligned}
$$

This lemma lets us cancel an application of **H1** on the right-hand side of the refinement relation. This works because **H1**(P) is a disjunction, and the cancelation strengths the implementation. Something similar can be done with **HP8**, but since **HP8**(P) is a conjunction, the cancelation takes place on the specification side.

Lemma 2 (HP8-refinement). *For any two relations P and Q with pg and pg′ in their alphabets,*

$$P \sqsubseteq \mathbf{HP8}(Q) \quad \textit{iff} \quad \mathbf{HP8}(P) \sqsubseteq \mathbf{HP8}(Q)$$

Proof

$$
\begin{aligned}
& P \sqsubseteq \mathbf{HP8}(Q) && \textit{refinement}\\
={}& [\,\mathbf{HP8}(Q) \Rightarrow P\,] && \mathbf{HP8}\\
={}& [\,\mathit{II}_P \,;\, Q \,;\, \mathit{II}_P \Rightarrow P\,] && \textit{sequence}\\
={}& [\,(\exists\, v_0, v_1 \bullet \mathit{II}_P[v_0/v'] \wedge Q[v_0, v_1/v, v'] \wedge \mathit{II}_P[v_1/v]) \Rightarrow P\,] && \\
& && \textit{predicate calculus}\\
={}& [\,\mathit{II}_P[v_0/v'] \wedge Q[v_0, v_1/v, v'] \wedge \mathit{II}_P[v_1/v] \Rightarrow P\,] && \textit{predicate calculus}\\
={}& [\,\mathit{II}_P[v_0/v'] \wedge Q[v_0, v_1/v, v'] \wedge \mathit{II}_P[v_1/v] && \mathit{II}_P\textit{, Leibnitz}\\
& \quad \Rightarrow \mathit{II}_P[v_0/v'] \wedge P \wedge \mathit{II}_P[v_1/v]\,] && \\
={}& [\,\mathit{II}_P[v_0/v'] \wedge Q[v_0, v_1/v, v'] \wedge \mathit{II}_P[v_1/v] && \textit{sequence}\\
& \quad \Rightarrow \mathit{II}_P[v_0/v'] \wedge P[v_0, v_1/v, v'] \wedge \mathit{II}_P[v_1/v]\,] && \\
={}& [\,\mathit{II}_P \,;\, Q \,;\, \mathit{II}_P \Rightarrow \mathit{II}_P \,;\, P \,;\, \mathit{II}_P\,] && \mathbf{HP8}\\
={}& [\,\mathbf{HP8}(Q) \Rightarrow \mathbf{HP8}(P)\,] && \textit{refinement}\\
={}& \mathbf{HP8}(P) \sqsubseteq \mathbf{HP8}(Q) && \square
\end{aligned}
$$

Applications of the above lemmas justify the main result of this section.

Theorem 11. *There is a Galois connection between designs and pointer relations, where* **HP8** *is the right adjoint and* **H** *is the left one.*

$$D \sqsubseteq \mathbf{H}(P) \quad \textit{iff} \quad \mathbf{HP8}(D) \sqsubseteq P$$

Here, D is a design whose alphabet contains pg and pg'; and P is a pointer relation whose alphabet contains ok and ok'.

Proof

$$\begin{array}{ll} D \sqsubseteq \mathbf{H1}(P) & \mathbf{H1}\textit{-refinement} \\ = D \sqsubseteq P & P \textit{ is } \mathbf{HP8} \\ = D \sqsubseteq \mathbf{HP8}(P) & \mathbf{HP8}\textit{-refinement} \\ = \mathbf{HP8}(D) \sqsubseteq \mathbf{HP8}(P) & P \textit{ is } \mathbf{HP8} \\ = \mathbf{HP8}(D) \sqsubseteq P & \square \end{array}$$

Proof of closedness of the programming operators in this new theory is simple.

4.3 Healthy Pointer Designs

The variables *ok* and *ok'* describe observations about initiation and termination of designs; they are certainly not program variables, and so must never be mentioned in program texts. In order to avoid confusion, a pointer design should isolate *ok* in its own partition in *pg* and *pg'*. This is a healthiness condition of our combined theory.

$$\mathbf{HD} \quad P = P \wedge \#group(ok, pg) = 1 \wedge \#group(ok, pg') = 1$$

Further exploration of the laws of this theory is left as future work.

5 Conclusions

We have presented a UTP theory for programs involving variables whose record values and their components may share locations. With this theory, we capture an abstract memory model of a modern object-oriented language.

In this work, we do not consider, for instance, the issues of classes and visibility in object-oriented languages, because our aim is the isolation of programming concepts. On the other hand, we do not have an explicit memory model that allows the definition of allocation and deallocation operations, because these are not needed to reason about object-oriented programs.

In order to reason about total correctness, we have investigated the theory that combines pointer relations and UTP designs. We established a formal link to translate between the two theories.

Recursive records have also been considered by Naumann in the context of higher-order imperative programs and a weakest precondition semantics [12]. In that work, many of the concerns are related to record types, and the possibility of their extension, as achieved by class inheritance in object-oriented languages. Here, we are only concerned with record values. We propose to handle the issue of inheritance separately, in a theory of classes with a copy semantics [17].

Hoare & He present a theory of pointers and objects using an analogy with process algebras [6]. They use a model of graphs based on a traces semantics [5], where a graph describes a snapshot of the entire heap during the execution of an object-oriented program. The heap is represented by a set of sets of traces: each set of traces describing the paths that may be used to access a particular object; this corresponds to our path groups. The main operator for updating the heap is known as *pointer swing*, and it updates the target of a pointer; this corresponds to our pointer assignment. In our work, we consider a model of pointers in the unified context of programming language models. We also handle the correspondence between the values of record variables and the sharing structure of these variables and their components. To manage complexity, we use healthiness conditions to factor out basic properties from definitions.

The idea of avoiding the use of locations to model pointers and sharing was first considered in [2] for an Algol-like language. The motivation was the definition of a fully abstract semantics, which does not distinguish programs that allocate variables to different positions in memory. In that work, groups are represented by functions in which each variable is associated with the set of variables that share its location. A healthiness condition ensures that variables in the same location have the same value: this corresponds to our **HP3**. A stack of functions is used in [2] to handle nested variable blocks and redeclaration. We do not consider the scope issues of redeclaration, but we handle the presence of record variables, and sharing between record components, not only variables.

The refinement calculus for object systems (rCOS) [9] is based on a UTP semantics for a relational object-oriented programming language that contains sub-typing, type casting, visibility, inheritance, dynamic binding, and polymorphism. Values in the language are drawn from primitive types or an infinite set of object references, augmented by information essential to the resolution of dynamic typing. By using object identities, the model refers explicitly to storage in an implementation-oriented way, and as a result is not fully abstract.

A UTP reference semantics for an object-oriented language has also been considered in [14]. In this case, we have a language that combines Object-Z [18], CSP, and timing constructs. Again, object values have identities which are abstract records of their location in memory.

For the kind of language in which we are interested, we believe that these identities are not needed, and the simpler model of the theory of path groups is enough. As already mentioned, our long-term goal is the definition of a reference semantics for *OhCircus*: an object-oriented language that also combines Z and CSP. Our approach, however, is based on the combination of models of isolated features of this rather rich language.

In the short term, we plan to investigate refinement laws of our theory, and explore its power to reason about pointer programs in general, and data structures and algorithms typically used in object-oriented languages in particular. After that, we want to go a step further in our combination of theories and consider a theory of reactive designs with pointers.

Acknowledgments

The authors are grateful to Richard Paige for detailed comments on a draft version of this paper; anonymous referees have also contributed with important suggestions. The work of Ana Cavalcanti is partially supported by the Royal Society and QinetiQ. Jim Woodcock also acknowledges QinetiQ's support.

References

1. R. J. Back, X. Fan, and V. Preoteasa. Reasoning about Pointers in Refinement Calculus. In *10th Asia-Pacific Software Engineering Conference (APSEC 2003)*, page 425. IEEE Computer Society, 2003.
2. S. D. Brookes. A Fully Abstract Semantics and a Proof System for an Algol-like Language with Sharing. In A. Melton, editor, *Mathematical Foundations of Programming Semantics*, volume 239 of *Lecture Notes in Computer Science*, pages 59 – 100. Springer-Verlag, 1985.
3. R. M. Burstall. Some techniques for proving correctness of programs which alter data structures. *Machine Intelligence*, 7:23–50, 1972.
4. A. L. C. Cavalcanti, A. C. A. Sampaio, and J. C. P. Woodcock. Unifying Classes and Processes. *Software and System Modelling*, 4(3):277 – 296, 2005.
5. C. A. R. Hoare. *Communicating Sequential Processes.* Prentice-Hall International, 1985.
6. C. A. R. Hoare and H. Jifeng. A trace model for pointers and objects. pages 223–245, 2003.
7. C. A. R. Hoare and He Jifeng. *Unifying Theories of Programming.* Prentice-Hall, 1998.
8. Samin Ishtiaq and Peter W. O'Hearn. BI as an assertion language for mutable data structures. In *POPL*. ACM Press, 2001.
9. Z. Liu, J. He, and X. Li. rCOS: Refinement of Component and Object Systems. In F. .S. de Boer, M. M. Bonsangue, S. Graf, and W.-P. de Roever, editors, *Proceedings of Formal Methods for Components and Objects: FMCO 2004*, volume 3657 of *Lecture Notes in Computer Science.* Springer Verlag, 1994.
10. B. Meyer. *Eiffel: the language.* Prentice-Hall, 1992.
11. B. Meyer. Towards practical proofs of class correctness. In *ZB 2003: Formal Specification and Development in Z and B*, volume 2651 of *Lecture Notes in Computer Science*, pages 359 – 387. Springer-Verlag, 2003.
12. D. A. Naumann. Predicate Transformer Semantics of a Higher Order Imperative Language with Record Subtypes. *Science of Computer Programming*, 41(1):1–51, 2001.
13. R. F. Paige and J. S. Ostroff. ERC – An object-oriented refinement calculus for Eiffel. *Formal Aspects of Computing*, 16(1):5, 2004.
14. S. Qin, J. S. Dong, and W. N. Chin. A Semantic Foundation for TCOZ in Unifying Theories of Programming. In K. Araki, S. Gnesi, and D. Mandrioli, editors, *FME2003: Formal Methods*, volume 2805 of *Lecture Notes in Computer Science*, pages 321 – 340, 2003.
15. John C. Reynolds. Intuitionistic reasoning about shared mutable data structure. In *Millenial Perspectives in Computer Science.* Palgrave, 2001.
16. A. W. Roscoe. *The Theory and Practice of Concurrency.* Prentice-Hall Series in Computer Science. Prentice-Hall, 1998.

17. T. L. V. L. Santos, A. L. C. Cavalcanti, and A. C. A. Sampaio. Object-orientation in the UTP. In *UTP'06*, Lecture Notes in Computer Science. Springer-Verlag, 2006. To appear.
18. G. Smith. *The Object-Z Specification Language.* Kluwer Academic Publishers, 1999.
19. J. C. P. Woodcock and A. L. C. Cavalcanti. A Tutorial Introduction to CSP in Unifying Theories of Programming. In *Pernambuco Summer School on Software Engineering 2004: Refinement*, Lecture Notes in Computer Science. Springer-Verlag, 2005. To appear.
20. J. C. P. Woodcock and J. Davies. *Using Z—Specification, Refinement, and Proof.* Prentice-Hall, 1996.

Mechanising a Unifying Theory

Gift Nuka[1] and Jim Woodcock[2]

[1] Computing Laboratory, University of Kent,
Canterbury, Kent CT2 7NF, UK
G.S.Nuka@kent.ac.uk
[2] Computer Science Dept, University of York,
York, UK
jim@cs.york.ac.uk

Abstract. In this paper, we present a formalisation of a subset of the *unifying theories of programming* (*UTP*). In *UTP*, the alphabetised relational calculus is used to describe and relate different programming paradigms, including functional, imperative, logic, and parallel programming.

We develop a verification framework for *UTP*; we give a formal semantics to an imperative programming language, and use our definitions to create a deep embedding of the language in *Z*. We use ProofPowerZ, a theorem prover for *Z* to provide mechanised support for reasoning about programs in the unifying theory.

1 Introduction

Hoare and He [16] propose a relational approach to defining the semantics of a variety of programming constructs including sequential and concurrent programming notation, thus providing a unified framework for different programming paradigms.

This approach takes specifications, designs and programs as predicates [15, 12, 13, 24, 8]. Consequently, a specification can be seen as a less deterministic program with respect to a defined alphabet. The signature of a specification language might include some non-implementable constructs, but can be transformed to an executable program by using well defined refinement rules. This approach allows for program statements and specification statements to be mixed freely.

The unifying theories of programming (*UTP*) are an important mathematical framework for unifying the science of programming. Alphabetised relational calculus (*ARC*) is the logical basis of *UTP*. In the unifying theory, programs, specifications, and designs are all represented as predicates defining relations between an initial observation involving undashed variables, and a later observation involving dashed variables as in *Z*'s schemas [33].

In this paper, we extend the formalisation of the alphabetised relational calculus [26], to include appropriate signature, and formalise an imperative programming language for writing specifications and programs in *UTP*. We formalise the

S. Dunne and W. Stoddart (Eds.): UTP 2006, LNCS 4010, pp. 217–235, 2006.

language in *Z* and use ProofPowerZ, a conventional *Z* theorem prover to reason about *UTP* programs and verify its algebraic laws.

The aim of the formalisation is twofold: to get a precise representation of the programming notation in a theorem prover for mechanical support in reasoning about theoretical aspects of the language and to provide a formal framework for mechanical verification of the development of concrete applications. In general mathematical proofs tend to be involving even for a small sized program, such that correct analysis of a system requires the high level of precision provided by formalisation. Programs can be proved to be well defined mechanically with respect to the specification context. Programs can also be constructed in a stepwise fashion and at each step the correctness of the refinement can be proved with respect to the specification. This calls for a refinement calculus which is a major research theme [30, 2, 22].

This paper is organised as follows. We present an overview of the alphabetised relational calculus in the next section. Section 3 presents an introduction to ProofPowerZ. In Section 4 we present the formalisation of the theory of predicates and in Section 5 we present the formalisation of the specification language. Section 6 deals with operators for program correctness. Section 7 summarises the algebraic properties proved with respect to our formalisation. We present related research in Section 8 and make conclusions in Section 9.

2 Overview of ARC

Relational calculus is a very useful framework for the study of mathematics and theory of computer science. It presents a formalism, which can be used to represent many phenomena in computer science and has been a basis for analysing and modelling some computer science problems including program specification, refinement, verification and database design.

The study of the calculus of relations was pioneered by De Morgan, Pierce, and Schröder and was axiomatised by Tarski [31] in the 1940s. The theory of relational algebras evolved from the axiomatisation of the calculus of relations by Tarski. Recently, Maddux [18] has presented a historical study of relational algebras and axiomatisations of the calculus of relations in a modern context.

ARC is based on Tarski's calculus, but free variables appearing in the predicate do play a major role, and are used to identify sub-theories. An *alphabetised relation* is a pair $(\alpha p, p)$, where predicate p is the predicate containing no free variables other than those in the alphabet, αp. In general, a relational calculus provides a useful tool for concise and precise formal reasoning. Furthermore, a relational formalisation provides a calculational approach to program correctness and refinement. This makes calculations simpler, a property that is valuable in reasoning about programs and in program development.

The alphabet of the relation is a set of observational names and contains undashed and dashed variable names; the undashed names (input alphabet) are disjoint from the dashed ones (output alphabet).

Predicates are used to describe the behaviour of a program. A predicate may consist only of a set of (in)equations, which can be composed using the relational algebraic operators in the standard way.

The undashed variables represent an initial observation and the dashed variables represent the final observation. In some cases the relation is homogeneous; that is, all the final global variables in a program are all the initial variables primed.

$$out\alpha(p) = in\alpha'(p)$$

The predicate models observation of programs. For example, consider a simple program, a program that increments the value of variable x by 1, with state variables x and y,

$$x := x + 1$$

One model of this program is the following observation

$$x = 5 \wedge x' = 6 \wedge y' = y$$

The calculation of program correctness is a major feature of *UTP*. The refinement relation is defined in terms of the universal closure of an implication. A program P is a refinement of a specification S, $S \sqsubseteq P$, if every observation in P is possible in S

$$S \sqsubseteq P \mathrel{\widehat{=}} [P \Rightarrow S]$$

An important consequence of this relation is that refinement can be presented in terms of non-determinism.

$$S \sqsubseteq P \mathrel{\widehat{=}} S \sqcap P = S$$

The signature of the calculus consists of primitive operators as well as those defined in terms of the primitive ones. These include negation, disjunction and existential quantification. General properties of many of calculus operators include commutativity, associativity, idempotence, and absorption. Other operators can always be added to the calculus as necessary for greater expressiveness or convenience and are derived from the primitive ones.

The relation **true** is primitive, and denotes a universal relation that is a bottom of the predicate lattice with respect to the refinement ordering above. It describes all possible observations with respect to the alphabet in context. Therefore for all programs, P

$$P = P \wedge \mathbf{true}$$

Its dual, the relation **false**, is the empty relation, which is the top of the lattice. All programs allow empty observation.

$$P = P \vee \mathbf{false}$$

Theories in *UTP* are identified by their alphabets, signature and healthiness conditions. Alphabets are sets of observational names that characterise a relation. The signature is the syntactical universe; the set of operators for denoting objects in the given theory. The healthiness conditions model the essential properties of the theory.

Special variables are used to model extra observational information that characterises a given theory: designs use *okay* to signify that a program has started execution, in concurrency theories *tr* and *ref* model some aspects of event sequences and refusal sets respectively, while in reactive systems, *wait* models stability of the program.

In this paper we focus on presenting the formalisation of imperative programming notation and proving the algebraic laws of the language.

3 ProofPowerZ

ProofPower is a specialised HOL prover and was developed from the HOL system with the proof infrastructure strengthened to support particular applications, mainly to support the specification language *Z*. ProofPower supports the same logic as other HOL systems [21, 27] but has a different proof infrastructure. ProofPowerZ is an embedding of a *Z* theory on top of ProofPower and employs higher order logic as the underlying proof engine for the *Z* notation. We will refer to ProofPower as the collection of tools including ProofPowerZ in the rest of the paper.

ProofPower's implementation is in ML and follows the LCF paradigm for interactive theorem proving. The LCF strategy means that users can only perform valid logical inferences. ProofPower provides an environment in which you can easily extend built in theories and also provides tactics (ML functions) which you apply to construct proof.

Theory Development

Working with ProofPower starts with the development of a theory which is basically a collection of types, functions and theorems. Terms and theorems are ML datatypes. A user can extend theories by using axioms or can derive theorems by formal proof; thus, providing a consistent way to formalisation. This style is referred to as conservative extension. A user can use the HOL logic meta-language (*ML*) to build new theorems from existing ones in a forward proof style or can do goal directed proofs. A forward proof search also referred to as forward chaining is mainly done in simpler proofs. Forward proof is constructed by applying ML functions (which represent inference rules) to axioms or theorems that have previously been proved. The three main primitive rules used in forward proof are assumption introduction, implication introduction and implication elimination.

Assumption introduction (*asm_rule*) gets a term and returns a theorem.

$$\frac{}{t \ \vdash \ t}$$

Implication elimination $\Rightarrow$ *_elim* is popularly known as Modus Ponens and gets an implicative theorem and a theorem that is α convertible to the antecedent.

$$\frac{\Gamma_1 \vdash t_1 \Rightarrow t_2 \quad \Gamma_2 \vdash t_1}{\Gamma_1 \cup \Gamma_2 \quad \vdash \quad t_2}$$

Implication introduction $\Rightarrow$ *_intro* proves an implicative theorem. That is

$$\frac{\Gamma \quad \vdash \quad t_1}{\Gamma - \{t_1\} \vdash t_1 \Rightarrow t}$$

An inference rule can be a derived rule and an important derived rule in ProofPower is the *rewrite_rule*, which takes a list of theorems. It repeatedly (unless qualified) replaces instances of the left hand side of an equation by the corresponding instance of the right hand side until no further changes occur.

Variations of the rewrite rule include *once_rewrite_rule*, *asm_rewrite_rule* and *pure_rewrite_rule*, where an inference rule is applied once, or the theorem rewritten will include assumptions or no default rewriting will be done respectively.

Most often goal-oriented proofs are undertaken. In this style a conjecture is set up as a goal and users apply tactics to reduce the goal to a simpler subgoal. This is done recursively until all the subgoals from the main goal are resolved; thus, solving the main goal. Tactics are ML functions that decompose a goal into subgoals and keep track of why discharging subgoals is equivalent to proving the main goal. A tactic discharges a goal when it generates an empty list of subgoals.

4 The Embedding

We present an embedding of *ARC* and an imperative programming notation in *Z*. An embedding is an encoding of some specialised logic or language into a different formal system for the purpose of providing proof support and reasoning in it. A user sees the syntax of the specialised language and sometimes this is mixed with the syntax of the host language. The host system provides the underlying proof support. Embedding can be shallow or deep, but most mechanisation lie between the two extremes.

Shallow Embedding. In a shallow embedding a translation of the semantics of the object language is developed and implemented into the host-language. Such mechanisation does not implement the syntax and structure of the object language. This approach is usually simpler and if the host language is powerful enough you can reason about applications of the language using the host language logic. However, such translation can be problematic in reasoning about the object language, for example, a proposition referring to the object language may not be expressible in the host logic. This can be seen in reasoning about Z schemas in Bowen's embedding of Z into HOL [3, 4] where reasoning about schema conjunction in the translated HOL theory was not possible. This happens because the axioms and rules are theorems of the host language and may not be expressible for meta-reasoning on the object language.

$Pred ::=$	$true_A$	truth
$\mid$	$false_A$	falsity
$\mid$	$\mathcal{N}\ compOp_A\ Term$	prim. predicate expression
$\mid$	$\neg Pred$	negation
$\mid$	$Pred\ binPredOp\ Pred$	binary operators
$\mid$	$\exists\, n \bullet Pred$	existential quantifier
$\mid$	$\forall\, n \bullet Pred$	universal quantifier
$\mid$	$Pred[e/x]$	substitution

Fig. 1. The syntax of a predicate

Deep Embedding. A different approach would be to carefully implement the syntax of the object language into the host language as well, such that meta-theoretic reasoning about the object language can be possible. Deep embedding has been the approach of Maharaj [19] in the implementation of *Z*-Schemas into a type theory, Melham [20] in mechanising π-calculus into HOL, and Camilleri [7] in formalising CSP in higher order logic.

We take this latter approach in our work, where both the syntax and semantics of the language are implemented into *Z*, and thereby allowing us to prove theorems on the language itself.

4.1 The Theory of Predicates

We now define the syntax and the semantics of *ARC*, using the embedding approach we have chosen. The syntax for predicates is similar to that of the classical predicate calculus.

We assume an infinite set of names denoting variables and an infinite set of values, given as $\mathcal{N}$ and *Value* respectively. We present the syntax of predicates in Figure 1, where variables x, n and m range over $\mathcal{N}$, e is an expression and A is a set of names over the domain *Values.*

Predicates are formed in the standard way, but in our embedding the primitive predicates carry alphabets. The constants $true_A$ and $false_A$ carry a particular alphabet A. An atomic predicate, for example $n \ =_A \ e$, carries alphabet A. The (in)equality operators *compOp* are used to construct atomic predicates. In practice the alphabet may be omitted if it can be calculated from the context.

The unary predicate operator ($\neg$) negates a predicate. *binPredOp* represents the binary predicate operators: disjunction ($\vee$), conjunction ($\wedge$), implication ($\Rightarrow$). Quantification follows standard notation with implicit typing. Substitution, $p[e/x]$, is a substitution of expression e for variable x in predicate p.

Encoding the Syntax

The implementation of the syntax in a logic depends on the type of embedding chosen. We implement a deep embedding, so the grammar of *ARC* is explicitly represented allowing for structural induction on the format of the relational logic which is amenable to meta-theoretic reasoning.

The set of names $\mathcal{N}$ and values *Value* are encoded as given types. The syntax of *ARC* is encoded as a data type. *Z* provides *free type* style definitions which allow embedding inductive and non-inductive data types into the logic. The predicate type *Pred* is defined recursively as a *Z free type* with appropriate constructors corresponding to the predicate constants and expression operators described in Figure 1. For example, consider the predicate $true_A$, where A is the alphabet, *true* is constructed as a function defined on a set of names as follows.

$$true : \alpha \rightarrow Pred$$

The unary operator, negation, is a function from predicates to predicates

$$neg : Pred \rightarrow Pred$$

Likewise the binary infix operators are defined similarly; for example, conjunction.

$$conj : Pred \times Pred \rightarrow Pred$$

For clarity of notation, we shall present the syntax using the conventional predicate syntax, as opposed to using the formalised operator names. For example we shall abbreviate $conj(p, q)$ to $p \wedge q$. In some cases, where necessary, we shall explicitly distinguish the formalised operators.

4.2 Semantics

We present the denotational semantics of the relational calculus, using the approach put forward by Scott and Strachey. In denotational semantics the meaning of each predicate is derived from the meaning of its direct constituents using a mathematical function.

The semantics of the predicates are given in the form of the Herbrand interpretations and models, where the meaning of the predicates corresponds to the observation relation that is a minimal model of the predicate.

We define three predicate meaning functions: β, which interprets predicates to their models (observations), $\mathcal{V}$, which interprets the value expressions to their values, and α which calculates the alphabet of a predicate. These semantic functions are implemented in the theorem prover ProofPowerZ.

Alphabets. Each predicate in *ARC* has an associated alphabet which is made explicit in the predicate or can be calculated. The variables of the predicate can be grouped into either free names and bound names. An alphabet, α, denotes the free names that have been introduced by the predicate. We represent it as a function from predicates to sets of names.

$$\alpha : Pred \rightarrow \mathbb{P}\,\mathcal{N}$$

Some predicates have their alphabet explicitly marked with them. For example the alphabet of predicates *true*, *false*, and primitive predicate expressions are always specified. Negating a predicate p does not change its alphabet, such that

$$\alpha(p) = \{n, m\} \Rightarrow \alpha(\neg p) = \{n, m\}$$

The alphabet of a binary predicate expression is the union of the alphabets of the operands. Quantification removes a variable from the alphabet: we can no longer observe its value.

$$\alpha(\exists\, n \bullet p) = \alpha(p) \setminus \{n\} \qquad \alpha(\forall\, n \bullet p) = \alpha(p) \setminus \{n\}$$

For example, if p is the predicate $\forall\, n \bullet m =_{\{m\}} 1 \wedge n =_{\{n\}} 2$, then $\alpha(p) = \{m\}$.

Substitution $p[e/x]$ allows an expression e to be systematically substituted for free occurrences of the name x. It removes the variable x from the alphabet, but introduces the names of expression e, $\alpha_e(e)$ instead. If x is bound to some quantifier in predicate p then substitution does not change the alphabet since $x \notin \alpha(p)$

$$\alpha(p[e/x]) = (\alpha(p) \setminus \{x\}) \cup \alpha_e(e)\} \;\lhd\; occurs(x, p) \;\rhd\; \alpha(p))$$

We say that a variable x *occurs* in predicate p, if $x \in \alpha p$

$$occurs(x, p) \equiv x \in \alpha(p)$$

Substitution may cause name capture. In the sequel we discuss the methods we use to avoid name capture.

Decoration. The alphabet of a program consists of two sets of variables, the input alphabet, referred to as undashed variables (such as x, y, n, m) and output alphabet which refers to decorated variables (such as x', y', n', m'). We model variable decoration using the total injection *dash*

$$dash : \mathcal{N} \rightarrowtail \mathcal{N}$$

Bound Variables. The semantic function σ defines the set of bound variables in a predicate, and is a set of names disjoint from the alphabet of the predicate. We need to distinguish between bound and free variables occurring in a predicate so that we can reason about substitution and quantifiers.

$$\sigma : Pred \rightarrow \mathbb{P}\,\mathcal{N}$$

Predicates $true_A$, $false_A$, and primitive expressions ($e.g. n =_a e$) do not have any bound variables. All variables that appear in them are free. The bound variables of the negation of a predicate are the same as those bound variables of the predicate itself. The set of bound variables of conjunction, disjunction, implication, equivalence are the union of the respective bound variables of the two constituent predicates.

Quantification introduces a bound variable, the one quantified.

$$\sigma(\exists\, n \bullet p) = \sigma(p) \cup \{n\}$$
$$\sigma(\forall\, n \bullet p) = \sigma(p) \cup \{n\}$$

Substitution in semantics that avoid name clashes, does change the bound variable set. Whenever a new variable would make an already existing variable become bound, then the original variable is renamed.

4.3 Observations

An observation of a particular program can be expressed by a predicate. This can be represented by a set of pairs where the first element in each pair is a variable from the alphabet of the predicate and the other element is a constant value assigned to the particular variable. We represent an observation as a partial function, *Binding*.

$$Binding == \mathcal{N} \pfun Value$$

We model it as a partial function since some variables from the alphabet set may not be associated with any particular value or the alphabet of the predicate may not be the entire name set. Observations expressed by a predicate are defined by the semantic function β: a set of observations. Given a predicate p we can calculate the set of observations (bindings) denoted by the predicate by applying the β function.

$$\beta : Pred \longrightarrow \mathbb{P}\, Binding$$

The set of observations of a predicate p are similar to the Z schema bindings. We use the terms observations and bindings interchangeably in this paper. The set of bindings for $true_A$ are all the pairs involving alphabet A. The bindings of $true_A$ represent the universal function set with respect to alphabet A. The predicate $false_A$ gives no observations and its set of bindings is empty. Given term t, a set of names A and $n \in Name$

$$\begin{aligned} &\beta(true_A) = \{\, b : Binding \mid \operatorname{dom} b = A \,\} \\ &\beta(false_A) = \emptyset \end{aligned}$$

For predicate expressions involving terms, the set of bindings depends on the expression *compOp* operator. For example if $\odot$ is one of the expression operators, then

$$\begin{aligned} \beta(m \odot_A t) \;=\; &\{\, b : Binding \mid \operatorname{dom} b = A \wedge \\ &m \in \operatorname{dom} b \wedge b(m) \odot \mathcal{V}(t) \,\} \end{aligned}$$

where $\mathcal{V}(t)$ gives the value after evaluation of term t. Negating a predicate p gives a set of bindings that are not in the set of *bindings* for p. This set of observations is represented as the set difference between the observations of $true_{\alpha p}$ and bindings of p.

$$\beta(\neg p) = \beta(true_{\alpha(p)}) \setminus \beta(p)$$

Extension set. Disjoining and conjoining of predicates results in extending the observations described by one predicate to the possible observations from the alphabet of the other predicate. To model the bindings of such predicates we use an extend function. Given a set of observations $s \in \mathbb{P}\, Binding$ we can extend this set to a new set by enlarging the domain of every element in s.

$$extend : \mathbb{P}\, Binding \times \mathbb{P}\, \mathcal{N} \times \mathbb{P}\, \mathcal{N} \rightarrow \mathbb{P}\, Binding$$

$$\forall\, s : \mathbb{P}\, Binding;\ \alpha_1, \alpha_2 : \mathbb{P}\, \mathcal{N};\ b : Binding \bullet$$
$$b \in extend(s, \alpha_1, \alpha_2) \Leftrightarrow \alpha_1 \lhd b \in s \wedge \operatorname{dom} b = \alpha_1 \cup \alpha_2$$

An extension set $extend(s, \alpha_1, \alpha_2)$ gives a map extension for observations in s. Consider a bindings set for a predicate p, $\beta(p)$, extending this set from $\alpha(p)$ to a set of variables a where $a \in \mathbb{P}\, \mathcal{N}$, can be represented as $\beta(p)_{+A}$. That is for every predicate p and $A \in \mathbb{P}\, \mathcal{N}$

$$\beta(p)_{+A} \mathrel{\widehat{=}} extend(\beta(p), \alpha(p), A)$$

Substitution. The embedding we have implemented forces us to deal with the complex issue of substitution. In a shallow embedding this can easily be taken care of by the host logic. But in a deep embedding we have to provide for substitution. In the substitution, $p[e/x]$ every occurrence of x is replaced by e. In general this can be formalised as

$$\beta(p[e/x]) \mathrel{\widehat{=}} \beta(p \wedge (x = e))_{-x}) \lhd occurs(x, p) \rhd \beta(p)$$

This has to be done in a way that avoids capture. For the predicates that are not quantified the substitution is straight forward.

Formalisation of the capture avoiding substitution semantics requires performing an appropriate renaming (using fresh variables) on the bound variables. We define a function that creates fresh free variables that do not clash with either the free variables or the bound variables in the predicate terms. The function *fname* changes the variable x, in a way that it is no longer a member of A.

$$fname(x, A) \neq x \wedge$$
$$finite(A) \Rightarrow fname(x, A) \notin A$$

We assume our source of names is infinite as otherwise we would run out of fresh names to generate.

Now we can define the semantics of substitution, where any quantified predicate has appropriate variable renaming.

$$\beta(\exists\, y \bullet p[e/x]) = \beta(\exists\, z \bullet p[z/y][e/x]$$
$$\beta(\forall\, y \bullet p[e/x]) = \beta(\forall\, z \bullet p[z/y][e/x]$$

where $z = fname(y, names(p))$ and $names(p) = \alpha(p) \cup \sigma(p)$.

Substitution is a complex operation and if dealing with logical syntax and in avoiding name capture and need for alpha conversion de Bruijn scheme [5] is sometimes used. De Bruijn scheme uses an indexing technique where numbers are used instead of names. However we choose the renaming scheme as it is intuitive and still not very difficult. Gabbay and Pitts [10] formalises most of the ideas in the renaming scheme in the nominal logic [28] using freshness and swapping and partly justifies our choice.

$$\beta(p \vee q) = \beta(p)_{+\alpha(q)} \cup \beta(q)_{+\alpha(p)}$$

$$\beta(p \wedge q) = \beta(p)_{+\alpha(q)} \cap \beta(q)_{+\alpha(p)}$$

$$\beta(\exists\, n \bullet p) = \beta(p)_{-n}$$

$$\beta(\forall\, n \bullet p) = \beta(true(\alpha(p) \setminus \{n\})) \setminus \beta(\neg p)_{-n}$$

$$\beta(p \Rightarrow q) = \beta(\neg p \vee q)$$

$$\beta(p \Leftrightarrow q) = \beta((p \Rightarrow q) \wedge (q \Rightarrow p))$$

$$\beta(p \bigtriangledown q) = \beta(\neg(p \Leftrightarrow q))$$

Fig. 2. Semantics of some predicate terms

$P ::=$	$\mathbb{I}$	*skip*
$\mid$	$\bot$	*abort*
$\mid$	$\top$	*miracle*
$\mid$	$P \lhd P \rhd P$	conditional
$\mid$	$P;\ P$	sequential composition
$\mid$	$n := e$	assignment
$\mid$	$P \sqcap P$	non deterministic choice
$\mid$	$\{p\}Q\{r\}$	Hoare triple
$\mid$	$c_{\bot}$	assertion
$\mid$	$c^{\top}$	assumption
$\mid$	$wp(p, r)$	weakest precondition
$\mid$	**var** x	variable declaration
$\mid$	**end** x	variable undeclaration
$\mid$	$b * P$	iteration

Fig. 3. The syntax of a *UTP* program

Other predicates. We can now present the semantics of the rest of the predicate operators. For a detailed account refer to [26]. Bindings of implications are defined in terms of the bindings of disjunction. And those of equivalence in terms of conjunction and implication, with exclusive-or defined in terms of the negation of equivalence.

5 The Specification Language

The operators of the language cover conventional programming concepts.

The notation consist of the standard imperative programming operators including assignment, conditional, sequential composition, variable declaration and iteration. It also includes program correctness operators such as Hoare triples, Floyd's assertions, assumptions and weakest preconditions.

We now present the formalisation of the operators in detail.

Assignment. Assignment is a primitive operator for many programming languages. An assignment ($x := e$) updates the value of x to the value e. Values for any of the variables not mentioned remain unchanged. Expression e may not contain any dashed variables. Let $A = \{x, y, z, x', y', z'\}$, and let $\alpha(e) \subseteq A$ then

$$x :=_A e \mathrel{\widehat=} (x' = e \wedge y' = y \wedge z' = z)$$
$$\alpha(x :=_A e) \mathrel{\widehat=} A$$

A special assignment predicate denoted by II (*skip*) does not change any observations. Skip is marked with its alphabet.

$$II_a \mathrel{\widehat=} (\bar{v} = \bar{v}'), \quad \textit{where } a = (\bar{v}, \bar{v}')$$
$$\alpha(II_a) \mathrel{\widehat=} a$$

The Conditional. A common programming construct is the conditional with its general notation

if b **then** p **else** q

meaning that depending on the evaluation of the predicate condition b the program may choose to execute p or execute q. We present the conditional in the compact notation of [16].

$$\beta(p \lhd b \rhd q) \mathrel{\widehat=} \beta((b \wedge p) \vee (\neg b \wedge q)), \quad \textit{if } \alpha(b) \subseteq \alpha(p) = \alpha(q)$$
$$\alpha(p \lhd b \rhd q) \mathrel{\widehat=} \alpha(p)$$

A condition in this case is some predicate that has an alphabet without output variables, it represents a predicate term that always terminates after evaluation. In other theories this can be relaxed and output variables can be allowed.

In a conditional the set of bound variables is the set of bound variables in the predicates. For every predicate b, p and q

$$\sigma(p \lhd b \rhd q) = \sigma(p) \cup \sigma(b) \cup \sigma(q)$$

Sequential Composition. The composition of two relations produces an intermediary state which is not observable. For predicate p and q where $out\alpha(p) = \bar{v}'$ and $in\alpha(Q) = \bar{v}$. The representation $p(v)$ represents substitution.

$$\beta(p(\bar{v});\ q(\bar{v})) \mathrel{\widehat=} \beta(\exists\, \bar{v}_0 \bullet p(\bar{v}_0) \wedge q(\bar{v}_0)), \textit{ if } out\alpha(p) = in\alpha'(q) = \bar{v}$$
$$\alpha(p(\bar{v}');\ q(\bar{v})) \mathrel{\widehat=} in\alpha(p) \cup out\alpha(q)$$

where $in\alpha$ and $out\alpha$ of the composition are defined as follows

$$in\alpha(p(\bar{v}');\ q(\bar{v})) \mathrel{\widehat=} in\alpha(p)$$
$$out\alpha(p(\bar{v}');\ q(\bar{v})) \mathrel{\widehat=} out\alpha(q)$$

The final state of the composition is the final state of q. The alphabet of a composition is therefore the input alphabet of p and the output alphabet of q.

Sequential composition is associative and distributes over the conditional.

Non-determinism. Non-determinism is modelled by a choice operator. Given a program with two components, the program may non-deterministically choose one component from the other. Choice is define in terms of disjunction

$$\beta(p \sqcap q) \mathrel{\widehat{=}} \beta(p \vee q), \quad \textit{if } \alpha(p) = \alpha(q)$$
$$\alpha(p \sqcap q) \mathrel{\widehat{=}} \alpha(p)$$

The choice operator is associative, symmetric as well as idempotent. The dual of disjunction is conjunction

$$\beta(p \sqcup q) \mathrel{\widehat{=}} \beta(p \wedge q)$$
$$\alpha(p \sqcup q) \mathrel{\widehat{=}} \alpha p \cup \alpha q$$

We represent a program that has been made less deterministic by the implication law

$$[p \Rightarrow (p \sqcap q)]$$

where the square braces mean that the predicate is everywhere quantified, i.e., it is quantified on every variable in the alphabet of the predicate. A bottom element, usually represented as $(\bot)$, of such an implication ordering represents a program that is unpredictable. This is referred to as *Abort.*

$$\beta(\bot_a) \mathrel{\widehat{=}} \beta(\mathbf{true})$$
$$\alpha(\bot_a) \mathrel{\widehat{=}} a$$

On the other end of the ordering we have the strongest element, $(\top)$, which represent a program that can not be used and whose power is miraculous. This predicate implements every specification. We denote this predicate as a *miracle*

$$\beta(\top_a) \mathrel{\widehat{=}} \beta(\mathbf{false})$$
$$\alpha(\top_a) \mathrel{\widehat{=}} a$$

Variable declaration. New variables can be introduced into scope at any point within the program. A variable block marks the scope of the new variables and the new variables are free within the scope. The program statement **var** x marks the start of the variable block and program statement **end** x marks the end of the block.

$$\beta(\mathbf{var}\, x) \mathrel{\widehat{=}} \beta(\exists\, x \bullet \mathit{\Pi})$$
$$\beta(\mathbf{end}\, x) \mathrel{\widehat{=}} \beta(\exists\, x' \bullet \mathit{\Pi})$$

A program variable x has observational variables x and x'. We assume that x and x' belong to the alphabet in context. For example, if the alphabet in the context is A, then the alphabet of the variable declaration is defined as follows

$$\alpha(\mathbf{var}\, x) \mathrel{\widehat{=}} A \setminus \{x\}$$
$$\alpha(\mathbf{end}\, x) \mathrel{\widehat{=}} A \setminus \{x'\}$$

Consequently we have

$$\beta(\mathbf{var}\, x;\ p) = \beta(\exists\, x \bullet p)$$

$$\beta(p;\ \mathbf{end}\, x) = \beta(\exists\, x' \bullet p)$$

Iteration. Before we define the implementation of iteration, we require the theory of fixed points defined elsewhere. The refinement relation has been defined already. We employ the fixpoint theorem for complete lattices to define the semantics of recursion.

Proposition 1. *Consider a set of predicates $\mathcal{P}$ with an ordering as defined before. Then the following are equivalent*

1. *$\mathcal{P}$ is a complete lattice*
2. *$\mathcal{P}$ satisfies the following (healthiness) conditions if $\alpha P \subseteq A$*
   (a) $P \sqcup \mathit{true}_A = P$
   (b) $P \sqcap \mathit{false}_A = P$

where $\sqcup$ and $\sqcap$ are the meet and join lattice operators.

It is straight forward to show that the refinement relation is a partial order (i.e. it is reflexive, antisymmetric and transitive. We also show that arbitrary joins and meets exist for $\mathcal{P}$ and that the bottom of the lattice is $\bot_A$ and the top of the lattice is $\top_A$.

Since the alphabetised predicates form a complete lattice, every continuous function has a fixed point, a result by Tarski. Considering that any continuous function is also monotonic and that $\sqsubseteq$ is a complete partial order and a complete lattice, we can now use the *Knaster-Tarski* fixed point theorem to define recursion. The weakest fixed point for functions on $\mathcal{P}$ is defined as

$$\mu(f) = (\sqcap\{x : \mathcal{P} \mid \mathit{fixedPoint}(x)\})$$

where a pre-fixed point for a function f, $f(x) \sqsubseteq x$, would give the same result.

The semantics of the while loop then can be defined in term of the weakest fixed point.

$$\beta(b * P) \mathrel{\widehat{=}} \beta(\mu\, X \bullet ((P;\ X) \lhd b \rhd I\!I))$$

6 Program Correctness

A major theme in automation is proving correctness of programs. The correctness theories of Hoare-style calculus [14], Floyd's assertions [9] and Dijkstra's weakest precondition calculus [8] are well known. The key concepts are the use of conditions (assumptions and assertions) to annotate programs. These become the basis for formal proof of the correctness of the programs.

Assertions and Assumptions. Assumptions are program properties that we assume to hold at some point.

$$\beta(c^{\top}) \mathrel{\widehat{=}} \beta(\mathit{II} \lhd c \rhd \top)$$

If the condition c is true, the program skips, otherwise it behaves miraculously. An assertion is a predicate inserted at particular points in program statements that is expected to hold at that point.

$$\beta(c_{\bot}) \mathrel{\widehat{=}} \beta(\mathit{II} \lhd c \rhd \bot)$$

It is defined as follows: if c is true, it behaves as skip, otherwise the program aborts.

Using assertions and assumptions can help in an effective way, improve observability, localisation of design analysis for correctness. They provide functional checks at critical points inside a program block or internal and external interfaces.

Assertions in code serve as internal invariants, control flow invariants or pre-post conditions. Most modern programming languages (e.g in Java 2 Platform, C/C++) support such constructs. Some programming languages like Eiffel [17] encourage developers to use assertions by design ("Design by Contract").

Hoare triple. Hoare logic provides a system of logical rules to reason about program correctness. The key feature is the Hoare triple. A Hoare triple is specification statement that was designed to help provide for partial and total correctness mechanisms in Hoare logic. A statement $\{p\}Q\{r\}$, is a predicate that says: whenever the property p holds before a run of the program Q, then Q is guaranteed to terminate and on termination it will satisfy the post condition r.

$$\beta(\{p\}Q\{r\}) \mathrel{\widehat{=}} \beta([Q \Rightarrow (p \Rightarrow r')])$$

Here p is the precondition of Q and r is the post condition of program statement Q. Alternatively, this can be expressed using the refinement ordering.

$$\{p\}Q\{r\} = (p \Rightarrow r') \sqsubseteq Q$$

Weakest precondition. Dijikstra's weakest precondition calculus [8] has been used to assign meaning to programs. It is also used for correctness calculation in program analysis. A weakest precondition identifies an initial condition that will guarantee proper termination of a program. For example, given a program p, and a post condition r for the program. the weakest precondition is the condition that has to hold for program p to satisfy the postcondition r.

$$\beta(wp(p, r)) \mathrel{\widehat{=}} \beta(\neg(p;\ \neg r))$$

Weakest precondition and Hoare triples are related. The problem of calculating the weakest precondition reduces to calculating the precondition p in the triple $\{p\}Q\{r\}$ i.e. $[p \Rightarrow wp(Q, r)]$.

7 Algebraic Laws

The predicate operators implemented in this paper do enjoy several algebraic properties as a consequence of their definitions. We will not list a complete list of these properties in this paper but a complete list of the algebraic laws can be found in [16, 23, 26].

We have proved a number of laws concerning the basic properties of predicates and programs [26], including the following.

Basic laws. Laws for idempotence, commutativity, associativity and absorption of the operators for conjunction and disjunction of predicates.

Laws concerning Quantifiers. Laws of idempotence, commutativity, associativity of existential and universal quantifiers.

Laws for the Specification language. The programming operators have several properties including distributivity over certain operators, idempotence.

Lattice properties. We have proved that the refinement ordering, $\sqsubseteq$, is a partial order (i.e. it is reflexive, antisymmetric and transitive). Subsequently, we have shown that the set of alphabetised predicates with a defined alphabet, A under the refinement relation $\sqsubseteq_A$ is a complete lattice. We have shown that the top of the lattice is $\top_A$ and the bottom of the lattice is $\bot_A$.

Many of the theorems can be proved from the definitions and the sets and relation theories of the *Z* library of ProofPower.

8 Related Work

In our earlier work [26] we implemented the semantics of *ARC* in the theorem prover Z/EVES [29]. This work is similar to the one presented here, but the Z/EVES tool is different from the proof environment of ProofPowerZ in many respects. Importantly, Z/EVES is not a flexible environment that can be easily extended to build your own theories. It is most suited to reasoning about software specification as opposed to implementation of specification languages. ProofPower on the other hand offers a deeper embedding of Z and offers much more flexibility in choice of actions and tactics to use than Z/EVES. It also offers a much easier way to build theories and offers ways of merging your own theories with built in theories as it uses the LCF paradigm for interactive theorem proving.

A relational approach to specification and programming has been at the heart of many formalisms including the *Z* specification language. However, the *UTP* approach is special and significant as it allows and uses several useful ideas from different theories and presents an integrated mathematical framework for describing programs. The formalisation of *UTP* is therefore in itself useful.

Formalisation of the semantics of programming languages was pioneered by Gordon [11]. Gordon explores the mechanisation of a software verification by deriving the rules of the Hoare logic for a simple programming language with while statements. Based on this mechanisation he develops a verification condition generator.

Similar encodings of programming languages have been done, notably the work of Nipkow [25] in formalising part of a programming textbook and Back et al. [1] in formalising Back's refinement calculus [2]. Nipkow implements the semantics of a textbook "Formal Semantics of Programming Languages" by Winskel [32] and proves completeness and soundness of a simple program verifier. He presents the operational, axiomatic and denotational semantics and proves their equivalence. Back et al. formalises a refinement calculus in higher order logic. They embed both the predicates and the command notation of the calculus and define the semantics in terms of the weakest preconditions. This work is ongoing and presently have developed a refinement calculator [6], a useful tool to ensure that proper abstraction and modularity is preserved in program construction.

Our formalisation in general is related to all these. However, there are some differences. We implement *UTP* in first order logic using a *Z* theorem prover. This is of course not a very common approach for embeddings even though first order theorem proving is popular and indeed all the above mentioned research is done in higher order logic. We are also motivated to reuse *Z* theories since *UTP* has some similarities with *Z* we are therefore prepared to use a less expressive logic. We also treat the different subtheories in a unified way, where programs and the associated assertion language are all defined in the relational frame using denotational semantics and we implement a deep embedding.

9 Conclusions

We have presented a theory of the alphabetised relational calculus and its formal definition in the *Z* notation. Our approach has been to embed both the syntax and the semantics into *Z* so that we can be able to reason and prove theorems on the language. An alternative approach could have been direct translation of the semantics into equivalent *Z* denotations. In this approach the syntax of the language is not implemented in the host language and thus making it difficult to reason and make reference to propositions on the whole language.

We have presented various definitions of the imperative programming constructs of a subset of *UTP* and formalised their denotational semantics in *Z* using ProofPowerZ. We have also derived the rules of Hoare logic from their semantic definitions and thus can apply the Hoare laws to calculation of program correctness. A verification condition generator which we develop elsewhere nicely handles such calculations. Several algebraic laws for *UTP* have been proved and can used for proving correctness of refinement steps.

This formalisation is done conservatively, using definition of existing concepts to define new concepts. Therefore, the theory is guaranteed to be consistent. The formalisation we have presented forms the basis on which further mechanisation of *UTP* and program correctness analysis can be done.

References

1. Ralph-Johan Back and Joakim von Wright. Refinement concepts formalised in higher order logic. *Formal Asp. Comput.*, 2(3):247–272, 1990.
2. Ralph-Johan J. Back, Abo Akademi, and J. Von Wright. *Refinement Calculus: A Systematic Introduction.* Springer-Verlag New York, Inc., Secaucus, NJ, USA, 1998.
3. J. P. Bowen and M. J. C. Gordon. A shallow embedding of Z in HOL. *Information and Software Technology*, 37(5–6):269–276, May–June 1995.
4. Jonathan P. Bowen and Michael J. C. Gordon. Z and HOL. In J. P. Bowen and J. A. Hall, editors, *Z User Workshop, Cambridge 1994*, Workshops in Computing, pages 141–167. Springer-Verlag, 1994.
5. N.G. De Bruijn. Lambda Calculus Notation with Nameless Dummies: A Tool for Automatic Formula Manipulation, with Application to the Church-Rosser Theorem. *Indag Math*, 34:381–392, 1972.
6. Michael Butler, Jim Grundy, Thomas Långbacka, Rimvydas Rukšėnas, and Joakim von Wright. The refinement calculator: Proof support for program refinement. In Lindsay Groves and Steve Reeves, editors, *Formal Methods Pacific'97: Proceedings of FMP'97*, Discrete Mathematics and Theoretical Computer Science, pages 40–61, Wellington, New Zealand, July 1997. Springer-Verlag.
7. A.J. Camilleri. Mechamising CSP Trace Theory in Higher Order Logic. *IEEE Transactions on SoftwareEngineering*, 16(9):pages 88–118, September 1990.
8. E.W. Dijkstra. *A Discipline of Programming.* Prentice Hall, 1976.
9. R. W. Floyd. Assigning meaning to programs. In J. T. Schwartz, editor, *Mathematical aspects of computer science: Proc. American Mathematics Soc. symposia*, volume 19, pages 19–31, Providence RI, 1967. American Mathematical Society.
10. Murdoch Gabbay and Andrew Pitts. A new approach to abstract syntax involving binders. In *LICS '99: Proceedings of the 14th Annual IEEE Symposium on Logic in Computer Science*, page 214, Washington, DC, USA, 1999. IEEE Computer Society.
11. M.J.C. Gordon. Mechanizing programming logics in higher-order logic. In G.M. Birtwistle and P.A. Subrahmanyam, editors, *Current Trends in Hardware Verification and Automatic Theorem Proving (Proceedings of the Workshop on Hardware Verification)*, pages 387–439, Banff, Canada, 1988. Springer-Verlag, Berlin.
12. Eric C. R. Hehner. Predicative programming part i. *Commun. ACM*, 27(2): 134–143, 1984.
13. Eric C. R. Hehner. Predicative programming part ii. *Commun. ACM*, 27(2): 144–151, 1984.
14. C. A. R. Hoare. An axiomatic basis for computer programming. *Commun. ACM*, 12(10):576–580, 1969.
15. C.A. Hoare. *Programs are predicates.* Prentice Hall, 1984.
16. C.A.R. Hoare and Jifeng He. *Unifying Theories of Programming.* Prentice Hall, 1998.
17. Jean-Marc Jezequel. *Object-oriented software engineering with Eiffel.* Addison Wesley Longman Publishing Co., Inc., Redwood City, CA, USA, 1996.
18. R.D. Maddux. The origin of relation algebras in the development and axiomatization of the calculus of relations. *Studia Logica*, 6(9):423–455, 1991.
19. Savi Maharaj. Enconding Z-style schemas in type theory. In *Types '93: Types for Proofs and Programs*, Lecture Notes in Computer Science. Springer-Verlag, 1994.

20. Thomas F. Melham. A Mechanized Theory of the π-calculus in HOL. *Nordic Journal of Computing*, 1(1):50–76, 1994.
21. R. Milner M.J.C. Goldon. *Introduction to HOL: A Theorem proving Environment for Higher Order Logic.* Cambridge University Press, 1993.
22. Carroll Morgan. *Programming from specifications.* Prentice-Hall, Inc., Upper Saddle River, NJ, USA, 1990.
23. C.C. Morgan and J.W. Sanders. *Laws of the Logical calculi. Technical Report PRG-78.* Programming Research group, Oxford, England, 1989.
24. Greg Nelson. A Generalization of Dijkstra's calculus. *ACM Trans. Program. Lang. Syst.*, 11(4):517–561, 1989.
25. Tobias Nipkow. Winskel is (almost) right: Towards a mechanized semantics textbook. In *Proceedings of the 16th Conference on Foundations of Software Technology and Theoretical Computer Science*, pages 180–192, London, UK, 1996. Springer-Verlag.
26. Gift Nuka and Jim Woodcock. Mechanising the alphabetised relational calculus. *Electr. Notes Theor. Comput. Sci.*, 95:209–225, 2004.
27. L.C. Paulson. *Isabelle - A generic Theorem Prover.* Springer-Verlag, 1994.
28. Andrew M. Pitts. Nominal logic, a first order theory of names and binding. *Information and Computation*, 186(2):165–193, 2003.
29. Mark Saaltink. The Z/EVES system. In J. P. Bowen, M. G. Hinchey, and D. Till, editors, *ZUM'97: Z Formal Specification Notation*, volume 1212 of *Lecture Notes in Computer Science*, pages 72–85. Springer-Verlag, 1997.
30. Augusto Sampaio, Jim Woodcock, and Ana Cavalcanti. Refinement in Circus. In Lars-Henrik Eriksson and Peter Alexander Lindsay, editors, *FME2002: Formal Methods - Getting it Right (Proc. Intl. Symposium of Formal Methods Europe, Copenhagen, Denmark, July 2002)*, volume 2391, pages 451–470. Springer-Verlag, 2002.
31. A. Tarski. On the calculus of relations. *Journal of Symbolic Logic*, 6(9):73–89, 1941.
32. Glynn Winskel. *The formal semantics of programming languages: an introduction.* MIT Press, Cambridge, MA, USA, 1993.
33. Jim Woodcock and Jim Davies. *Using Z Specification, Refinement, and Proof.* Prentice Hall, 1996.

Modal Design Algebra

Walter Guttmann[1] and Bernhard Möller[2]

[1] Abteilung Programmiermethodik und Compilerbau, Fakultät für Informatik, Universität Ulm, D-89069 Ulm, Germany
walter.guttmann@uni-ulm.de
[2] Institut für Informatik, Universität Augsburg, D-86135 Augsburg, Germany
moeller@informatik.uni-augsburg.de

Abstract. We give an algebraic model of the designs of UTP based on a variant of modal semirings, hence generalising the original relational model. This is intended to exhibit more clearly the algebraic principles behind UTP and to provide deeper insight into the general properties of designs, the program and specification operators, and refinement. Moreover, we set up a formal connection with general and total correctness of programs as discussed by a number of authors. Finally we show that the designs form a left semiring and even a Kleene and omega algebra. This is used to calculate closed expressions for the least and greatest fixed-point semantics of the demonic while loop that are simpler than the ones obtained from standard UTP theory and previous algebraic approaches.

1 Introduction

The Unifying Theories of Programming (UTP), developed in [13], model the termination behaviour of programs using two special variables *ok* and *ok*′ that express whether a program has been started and has terminated, respectively. Specifications and programs are identified with predicates relating the initial values v of variables to their final values v'; moreover, *ok* and *ok*′ may occur freely in predicates. Using these variables, Hoare and He introduce a special class of predicates that reflect an assumption/commitment style of specification. These *designs* have the form

$$P \vdash Q \;\;\Leftrightarrow_{df}\;\; ok \wedge P \Rightarrow ok' \wedge Q \;,$$

with *ok* and *ok*′ not occurring in P or Q. The informal meaning is: if a computation allowed by the design has started in a state that satisfies the precondition P it will eventually terminate in a state that satisfies the postcondition Q.

In the general case, UTP allows the precondition P to involve both initial and final values of the program variables. A subclass that is interesting for a number of reasons is that of *normal* designs in which P is a *condition*, i.e., is only allowed to depend on input values of variables. Originally [13] these were called *(H3)* designs and characterised by a healthiness condition; the term "normal" is due to [10]. A yet smaller subclass, the *feasible* or *(H4)* designs models programs that cannot "recover" from nontermination.

S. Dunne and W. Stoddart (Eds.): UTP 2006, LNCS 4010, pp. 236–256, 2006.

The aims and results of the present paper are the following:

1. We model normal designs in a more general class of algebras than pure relation algebra. This is intended to exhibit more clearly the algebraic principles behind UTP and to provide deeper insight into the general properties of designs, the program and specification operators, and refinement.
2. We set up a formal connection between UTP and the theories of general (e.g., [2, 3, 9, 19, 21]) and total (e.g., [1, 5, 6, 8, 20]) correctness of programs (the latter also being known as demonic semantics).
3. We show that the designs form a left semiring and even a Kleene and omega algebra. This is used to calculate closed expressions for the least and greatest fixed-point semantics of the demonic while loop that are simpler than the ones obtained from standard UTP theory and previous algebraic approaches.

To achieve this we model normal designs as pairs (a, t) where a corresponds to a state transition relation and condition t characterises the input states from which termination is guaranteed. The structure from which a and t are taken is that of an idempotent semiring which is an algebraic abstraction of the basic operations of choice and sequential composition, as detailed in the next section.

2 The Basis: Choice and Composition

A *semiring* is a structure $(S, +, 0, \cdot, 1)$ such that

- $(S, +, 0)$ is a commutative monoid,
- $(S, \cdot, 1)$ is a monoid,
- operation $\cdot$ distributes over $+$ in both arguments
- and 0 is a left and right annihilator, i.e., $0 \cdot x = 0 = x \cdot 0$.

A semiring is *idempotent* if $+$ is, i.e., if $x + x = x$. Then $+$ can be interpreted as (angelic) choice, with 0 modelling the most partial program with no transition possibilities at all, and $\cdot$ as sequential composition, where 1 models the program skip. In this case, the relation $x \leq y \Leftrightarrow x + y = y$ is a partial order, called the *natural order* on S. It has 0 as its least element. Moreover, $+$ and $\cdot$ are isotone w.r.t. $\leq$ and $x + y$ is the least upper bound or join of x and y w.r.t. $\leq$.

An idempotent semiring is *Boolean* if it also has a greatest lower bound or meet operation $\wedge$, such that $+$ and $\wedge$ distribute over each other, and an operation $\bar{\ }$ that satisfies de Morgan's laws as well as $x \wedge \overline{x} = 0$ and $x + \overline{x} = \top$, where $\top = \overline{0}$ is the greatest element. In other words, a Boolean semiring is a Boolean algebra with a sequential composition operation. To save parentheses we use the convention that $\wedge$ binds tighter than $+$ but less tight than $\cdot$ does. We we use $\wedge$ rather than $\sqcap$ for the meet to avoid a clash of notation between semiring theory and the theory of UTP. To disambiguate the formulas we use a larger $\bigwedge$ for meta-logical conjunction.

An important, even Boolean, semiring is $\text{REL}(M) = \mathcal{P}(M \times M)$, the algebra of binary relations under union and composition over a set M, of which the predicates of UTP form a special instance. The greatest element is $\top = M \times M$.

Next to that, we have the Boolean semiring TRC(A) of sets of traces (i.e., finite strings) over alphabet A under union as $+$ and trace concatenation (i.e., fusion product) as the $\cdot$ operation. TRC(A) is isomorphic to the path algebra described in detail in [7]; in the present paper it will mainly be used for counterexamples to properties that hold in REL(M) but not necessarily in general semirings.

3 Modelling Conditions

Elements of REL(M), denoted by predicates relating pre- and post-states, can be used to describe the input/output behaviour of programs. To keep the framework uniform one wants to encode also assertions about the program variables, i.e., to characterise subsets $N \subseteq M$ of states, as special predicates or relations. There are three basic methods to do this:

1. Use predicates that do not depend on the output values of variables, corresponding to *right-universal* relations $N \times M$. In a semiring with $\top$ they are abstractly characterised as *right ideals*, i.e., as elements a with $a \cdot \top = a$.
2. Use predicates that do not depend on the input values of variables, corresponding to *left-universal* relations $M \times N$. In a semiring with $\top$ they are abstractly characterised as *left ideals*, i.e., as elements a with $\top \cdot a = a$.
3. Use sub-predicates of skip corresponding to *partial identity* relations of the form $\{(s,s) : s \in N\}$. In an idempotent semiring they are abstractly characterised as elements a with $a \leq 1$.

Each of these approaches has its advantages and disadvantages. Classical UTP uses variant 1, while variant 3 is used in test and modal semirings. Since we are going to import some results from the latter framework, we will show some connections between variants 1 and 3 (we do not need variant 2 in the present paper, but the treatment for it would be symmetrical).

1. A *test semiring* [15] is a pair $(S, \mathsf{test}(S))$, where S is an idempotent semiring and $\mathsf{test}(S) \subseteq [0,1]$ is a Boolean subalgebra of the interval $[0,1]$ of S such that $0, 1 \in \mathsf{test}(S)$ and join and meet in $\mathsf{test}(S)$ coincide with $+$ and $\cdot$. This fits well with the notation in switching and lattice theory and is the reason why $+$ is used for general choice in semiring notation. In general, $\mathsf{test}(S)$ may be a proper subset of the elements below 1 in S. The negation of test p, i.e., its complement relative to 1 in $\mathsf{test}(S)$, is denoted by $\neg p$. We have the correspondences *false* $\leftrightarrow 0$ and *true* $\leftrightarrow 1$. In a test semiring, for $p \in \mathsf{test}(S)$ and $a \in S$, the products $p \cdot a$ and $a \cdot p$ are the *input* and *output restrictions* of a to those pre-/post-states that satisfy p. An important example is REL(M) with the partial identities as tests.
2. A *(right) pre-condition-semiring* is a pair $(S, \mathsf{cond}(S))$, where S is an idempotent semiring with a greatest element $\top$ and $\mathsf{cond}(S) \subseteq S$ is a Boolean subalgebra of S with $0, \top \in \mathsf{cond}(S)$ satisfying the following properties: the join operation in $\mathsf{cond}(S)$ coincides with $+$ and for every element $a \in S$ and every condition $t \in \mathsf{cond}(S)$ the meet $t \wedge a$, i.e., their greatest lower bound w.r.t. $\leq$, exists and satisfies $(t+u) \wedge a = (t \wedge a) + (u \wedge a)$ as well as

$t \wedge (a+b) = t \wedge a + t \wedge b$. The meet $t \wedge a$ is also called the *input restriction of a by t*. We have the correspondences *false* $\leftrightarrow 0$ and *true* $\leftrightarrow \top$. The negation of t, i.e., its complement relative to $\top$ in $\mathsf{cond}(S)$, is denoted by $\overline{t}$. Finally, S is called a *(right) condition semiring* if all elements of $\mathsf{cond}(S)$ are right ideals. An example is again $\mathrm{REL}(M)$, with the right-universal relations as conditions.

We will use the letters $a, b, c, \ldots$ for semiring elements, $p, q, r, \ldots$ for tests and $s, t, u, \ldots$ for conditions. It should be noted that 0 and $\top$ are always right (and left) ideals. For 0 this follows from its left annihilation property, while for $\top$ we get, using neutrality of 1 and isotony, $\top = \top \cdot 1 \leq \top \cdot \top \leq \top$, which, together with antisymmetry of $\leq$ shows the claim.

In a pre-condition-semiring there is no reasonable definition of output restriction. However, as we will see below, for condition semirings there is.

Using input restriction we can define conditionals by setting, respectively,

$$a \lhd p \rhd b \ =_{df}\ p \cdot a + \neg p \cdot b\ , \qquad a \lhd v \rhd b \ =_{df}\ v \wedge a + \overline{v} \wedge b\ .$$

Moreover, we have the following correspondence for input restriction:

Lemma 3.1. *[16] In every test semiring S with greatest element $\top$, for all $p \in \mathsf{test}(S)$ and $a \in S$ the meet $p \cdot \top \wedge a$ exists and $p \cdot a = p \cdot \top \wedge a$.*

By associativity of $\cdot$ and $(p \cdot \top) \cdot \top = p \cdot (\top \cdot \top) = p \cdot \top$ the element $p \cdot \top$ is indeed a right ideal. In fact it is easy to show that the right ideals in a semiring S with $\top$ are exactly the products $a \cdot \top$ for $a \in S$.

Now we look at condition semirings. We obtain the representation

$$t = (t \wedge 1) \cdot \top\ , \qquad \text{(crep)}$$

and $t \wedge a = (t \wedge 1) \cdot a$, the analogue of Lemma 3.1, by specialising the

Lemma 3.2. $(t \wedge a) \cdot b = t \wedge (a \cdot b)$ *for a condition t.*

Proof. ($\leq$) By isotony, $(t \wedge a) \cdot b \leq a \cdot b$ and $(t \wedge a) \cdot b \leq t \cdot b \leq t \cdot \top = t$ since, as a condition, t is a right ideal.
($\geq$) By Boolean algebra and the first inequality, $t \wedge (a \cdot b) = t \wedge ((t \wedge a) \cdot b + (\overline{t} \wedge a) \cdot b) \leq t \wedge ((t \wedge a) \cdot b + \overline{t} \wedge (a \cdot b)) = t \wedge ((t \wedge a) \cdot b) \leq (t \wedge a) \cdot b$. □

Corollary 3.3. *In a condition semiring, $t \wedge 1 \leq u \wedge 1 \Leftrightarrow t \leq u$.*

Proof. ($\Leftarrow$) follows by isotony of meet.
($\Rightarrow$) $t \underset{\text{(crep)}}{=} (t \wedge 1) \cdot \top \underset{\text{(assump., isot.)}}{\leq} (u \wedge 1) \cdot \top \underset{\text{(crep)}}{=} u$. □

So $\mathsf{cond}(S)$ and the set $\mathrm{CS}(S) =_{df} \{t \wedge 1 : t \in \mathsf{cond}(S)\}$ of *condition subidentities* are order-isomorphic. Hence also $\mathrm{CS}(S)$ is a Boolean algebra with

$$\begin{aligned} t \wedge 1 + u \wedge 1 &= (t+u) \wedge 1\ , \\ (t \wedge 1) \wedge (u \wedge 1) &= (t \wedge 1) \cdot (u \wedge 1)\ , \\ \neg(t \wedge 1) &= \overline{t} \wedge 1\ . \end{aligned}$$

Altogether we have the

Corollary 3.4. *Every condition semiring S can be made into a test semiring by setting* $\mathsf{test}(S) =_{df} \mathrm{CS}(S)$ *and choosing the operations as above.*

By these results, in a condition semiring we can define the *output restriction of a by t* as $a \cdot (t \wedge 1)$.

4 Domain and Modal Operators

The domain of a semiring element a is intended to characterise the set of possible input states of a, i.e., the states from which corresponding output states may be reached under a. Again, such sets can be modelled by tests or by conditions.

A simple equational axiomatisation for the case of test semirings has been presented in [7]. We give a corresponding axiomatisation for the case of pre-condition-semirings here. Both cases are compared side-by-side in [12].

The domain operation $\ulcorner : S \to \mathsf{cond}(S)$ has the axioms

$$
\begin{aligned}
a &\le \ulcorner a \wedge a && \text{(cd1)}\\
\ulcorner(t \wedge a) &\le t && \text{(cd2)}\\
\ulcorner(a \cdot (\ulcorner b \wedge 1)) &\le \ulcorner(a \cdot b) && \text{(cd3)}
\end{aligned}
$$

Actually, (cd1) and (cd3) can be strengthened to equations (see Lemma 4.1 below). By reasoning as in [7] we obtain that (cd1) $\wedge$ (cd2) is equivalent to

$$\ulcorner a \le t \Leftrightarrow a \le t \wedge a \Leftrightarrow a \le t \,. \qquad \text{(GCc)}$$

This property has the form of a Galois connection that corresponds to the one for test semirings with $\top$ (see [7] for details). Moreover, by shunting, (cd1) $\wedge$ (cd2) is equivalent to $\ulcorner a \le t \Leftrightarrow \bar{t} \wedge a \le 0$. By the Galois connection, the domain operation is unique if it exists. Moreover, one obtains the following consequences.

Lemma 4.1.

$$
\begin{array}{rrclrrcl}
1. & \ulcorner a \le 0 & \Leftrightarrow & a \le 0\,, & 6. & a & = & \ulcorner a \wedge a\,,\\
2. & \ulcorner(a+b) & = & \ulcorner a + \ulcorner b\,, & 7. & \ulcorner(t \wedge a) & = & t \wedge \ulcorner a\,,\\
3. & a \le b & \Rightarrow & \ulcorner a \le \ulcorner b\,, & 8. & \ulcorner(a \cdot b) & \le & \ulcorner(a \cdot \ulcorner b)\,,\\
4. & \ulcorner t & = & t\,, & 9. & \ulcorner(a \cdot \top) = \ulcorner a & \Leftrightarrow & \ulcorner b = \ulcorner b \cdot \top\,,\\
5. & \ulcorner(\ulcorner a) & = & \ulcorner a\,, & 10. & \ulcorner(a \cdot b) \le \ulcorner a & \Leftrightarrow & \ulcorner c = \ulcorner c \cdot \top\,.
\end{array}
$$

Of these, properties 9. and 10. again show the special importance of using condition semirings rather than pre-condition-semirings. See [12] for the proofs.

By 9. and (crep), in a condition semiring the third axiom simplifies to

$$\ulcorner(a \cdot \ulcorner b) \le \ulcorner(a \cdot b) \,. \qquad \text{(cd3)}$$

Moreover, we have $\ulcorner 1 \underset{9.}{=} \ulcorner(1 \cdot \top) = \ulcorner\top \underset{4.}{=} \top$.

Now we make the connection with the relational case more explicit. Call a semiring S with $\top$ *ideal-closed*, briefly *id-closed*, if its set $\mathrm{RI}(S)$ of right ideals is a Boolean algebra. The relation semiring $\mathrm{REL}(M)$ is id-closed whereas the trace semiring $\mathrm{TRC}(A)$ is not.

Lemma 4.2.

1. *Consider an id-closed semiring S. Then the pair $(S, \mathrm{RI}(S))$ can uniquely be made into a domain semiring by setting $\ulcorner a =_{df} a \cdot \top$.*
2. *In this case we have $\ulcorner a \cdot \top = a \cdot \top$.*

Proof. 1. We show that $\ulcorner$ satisfies the domain axioms.
(cd1) $\ulcorner a \wedge a = a$, since $a = a \cdot 1 \leq a \cdot \top$.
(cd2) $\ulcorner(t \wedge a) \underset{(\text{def.})}{=} (t \wedge a) \cdot \top \underset{(\text{Lemma 3.2})}{=} t \wedge a \cdot \top \leq t$.
(cd3) $\ulcorner(a \cdot \ulcorner b) \underset{(\text{def., assoc.})}{=} a \cdot b \cdot \top \cdot \top = a \cdot b \cdot \top \underset{(\text{def.})}{=} \ulcorner(a \cdot b)$.
2. $\ulcorner a \cdot \top = a \cdot \top \cdot \top = a \cdot \top$. □

Based on domain we can define forward modal operators by

$$\langle\!\langle a \rangle\!\rangle t =_{df} \ulcorner(a \cdot t) \;, \qquad [\![a]\!] t =_{df} \overline{\langle\!\langle a \rangle\!\rangle \overline{t}} \;.$$

Thus $\langle\!\langle a \rangle\!\rangle t$ and $[\![a]\!] t$ characterise those states for which *some* and *all* a-successor states satisfy t, respectively; $[\![a]\!] t$ is the abstract counterpart of the wlp operator [19]. The special case corresponding to $\mathrm{REL}(M)$ is immediate from Lemma 4.2:

Corollary 4.3. *Over an id-closed semiring $\langle\!\langle a \rangle\!\rangle t = a \cdot t$ and $[\![a]\!] t = \overline{a \cdot \overline{t}}$.*

From the general definitions it straightforward to prove the following properties:

$$\begin{array}{rclrcl}
\langle\!\langle a \rangle\!\rangle 0 &=& 0 \;, & [\![a]\!] \top &=& \top \;, \\
\langle\!\langle 0 \rangle\!\rangle t &=& 0 \;, & [\![0]\!] t &=& \top \;, \\
\langle\!\langle a \rangle\!\rangle (t + u) &=& \langle\!\langle a \rangle\!\rangle t + \langle\!\langle a \rangle\!\rangle u \;, & [\![a]\!] (t \wedge u) &=& [\![a]\!] t \wedge [\![a]\!] u \;, \\
\langle\!\langle a + b \rangle\!\rangle t &=& \langle\!\langle a \rangle\!\rangle t + \langle\!\langle b \rangle\!\rangle t \;, & [\![a + b]\!] t &=& [\![a]\!] t \wedge [\![b]\!] t \;, \\
\langle\!\langle t \wedge a \rangle\!\rangle u &=& t \wedge \langle\!\langle a \rangle\!\rangle u \;, & [\![t \wedge a]\!] u &=& \overline{t} + [\![a]\!] u \;, \\
\langle\!\langle 1 \rangle\!\rangle t &=& t \;, & [\![1]\!] t &=& t \;, \\
\langle\!\langle a \cdot b \rangle\!\rangle t &=& \langle\!\langle a \rangle\!\rangle \langle\!\langle b \rangle\!\rangle t \;, & [\![a \cdot b]\!] t &=& [\![a]\!] [\![b]\!] t \;.
\end{array}$$

Hence $\langle\!\langle a \rangle\!\rangle$ and $[\![a]\!]$ are isotone. Moreover, the diamond is isotone and the box is antitone in its first argument, respectively.

Because of the importance of modal operators, we call a test or condition semiring with domain *modal.*

5 Designs, Commands and Correctness

To stay in line with the treatment in [13], we now restrict ourselves to modelling sets of states by conditions rather than tests. Assume a modal condition semiring S. As mentioned in the introduction, then the set of *commands* [19, 18] over S is $\mathrm{COM}(S) =_{df} S \times \mathsf{cond}(S)$. In a command (a, t) the element $a \in S$ describes the state transition behaviour and $t \in \mathsf{cond}(S)$ characterises the states with guaranteed termination; all states characterised by $\overline{t}$ have the "result" of looping besides any proper states that may be reached from them under a. The command (a, t) is synonymous both for the normal designs $t \vdash a$ of [13] and the normal prescriptions $t \Vdash a$ of Dunne [10]. The difference is reflected in the refinement relations on commands that will be detailed below. The following definitions and properties are adaptations of the corresponding ones in [18].

In the command view the weakest (liberal) precondition can be defined as

$$\mathsf{wlp}.(a,t).u =_{df} [\![a]\!]u , \qquad \mathsf{wp}.(a,t).u =_{df} t \wedge \mathsf{wlp}.(a,t).u .$$

This implies Nelson's *pairing condition* for commands k:

$$\mathsf{wp}.k.u = \mathsf{wp}.k.\top \wedge \mathsf{wlp}.k.u .$$

An important auxiliary concept is the *guard* of a command:

$$\mathsf{grd}.(a,t) =_{df} \overline{\mathsf{wp}.(a,t).0} = \bar{t} + {}^{\ulcorner}a .$$

It characterises the set of states that, if non-diverging, allow a transition under a. A command is called *total* if its guard equals top. The above formula links Parnas's condition [21] on termination constraints with totality:

$$\mathsf{grd}.(a,t) = \top \Leftrightarrow t \leq {}^{\ulcorner}a .$$

We will shortly see that this condition characterises exactly the feasible normal designs. Nelson remarks that totality of command k is also equivalent to Dijkstra's law $\mathsf{wp}.k.0 = 0$ of the excluded miracle.

The basic non-iterative commands are defined as

$$\mathsf{fail} =_{df} (0,\top) , \qquad \mathsf{skip} =_{df} (1,\top) , \qquad \mathsf{loop} =_{df} (0,0) ,$$
$$(a,t) [\!] (b,u) =_{df} (a+b, t \wedge u) , \qquad (a,t) ; (b,u) =_{df} (a \cdot b, t \wedge [\![a]\!]u) .$$

Here $t \wedge [\![a]\!]u$ characterises those states for which a is guaranteed to terminate and which under a only lead to guaranteed termination states of b.

The commands form a *left semiring*, i.e., satisfy all semiring laws except for the right annihilation law for the zero element fail.

Theorem 5.1. *The structure* $\mathrm{COM}(S) =_{df} (\mathrm{COM}(S), [\!], \mathsf{fail}, ;, \mathsf{skip})$ *is an idempotent left semiring. The associated natural order on* $\mathrm{COM}(S)$ *is*

$$(a,t) \leq (b,u) \Leftrightarrow a \leq b \wedge t \geq u .$$

The proof, which is a mere transliteration of the corresponding one in [18] for the test semiring case, can be found in [12]. It is essential that semiring S be a semiring and not only a left semiring. The natural order between commands is used in [10]. Its drawback is that it cannot be used as the approximation order for fixed-point semantics; for details see again [18].

By standard order theory, if S is a complete lattice with $\mathsf{cond}(S)$ as a complete sublattice then $\mathrm{COM}(S)$ is again a complete lattice with, for arbitrary I,

$$\bigsqcup\{(a_i,p_i) : i \in I\} = (\bigsqcup\{a_i : i \in I\}, \bigsqcap\{a_i : i \in I\}).$$

Likewise, $\mathsf{chaos} =_{df} (\top, 0)$ is the greatest element of COM(S), whereas $\mathsf{havoc} =_{df} (\top, \top)$ represents the most nondeterministic everywhere terminating program.

As in [13] we say that command k is *(H4)* or *feasible* iff $k \,;\, \mathsf{loop} = \mathsf{loop}$. One calculates, using $[\![a]\!]0 = \overline{\ulcorner a}$ and semiring properties,

$$(a,t) \,;\, \mathsf{loop} = (a \cdot 0, t \wedge [\![a]\!]0) = (0, t \wedge \overline{\ulcorner a}) \ .$$

Corollary 5.2. *Command (a,t) is feasible iff $t \leq \ulcorner a$.*

Therefore loop, skip, havoc and chaos are feasible, whereas fail is not. Moreover, $[\,]$ and ; preserve feasibility.

6 Refinement

Let us now look more closely at the natural order induced on the commands by the left semiring structure. By antitony of box we obtain for commands k, l

$$k \leq l \ \Rightarrow\ \mathsf{wlp}.k \geq \mathsf{wlp}.l \ \ \wedge \ \ \mathsf{wp}.k \geq \mathsf{wp}.l \ ,$$

where on the right hand side $\geq$ is the pointwise order between condition transformers. The second conjunct is the converse of the usual refinement relation. For it we calculate

$$\begin{array}{ll}
 & \mathsf{wp}.(a,t).v \geq \mathsf{wp}.(b,u).v \\
\Leftrightarrow & \quad \{\![\text{ definition }]\!\} \\
 & t \wedge [\![a]\!]v \geq u \wedge [\![b]\!]v \\
\Leftrightarrow & \quad \{\![\text{ universal property of meet }]\!\} \\
 & t \geq u \wedge [\![b]\!]v \ \wedge \ [\![a]\!]v \geq u \wedge [\![b]\!]v \\
\Leftrightarrow & \quad \{\![\text{ shunting in right conjunct }]\!\} \\
 & t \geq u \wedge [\![b]\!]v \ \wedge \ \langle\!\langle b \rangle\!\rangle \overline{v} \geq u \wedge \langle\!\langle a \rangle\!\rangle \overline{v} \\
\Leftrightarrow & \quad \{\![\text{ diamond law }]\!\} \\
 & t \geq u \wedge [\![b]\!]v \ \wedge \ \langle\!\langle b \rangle\!\rangle \overline{v} \geq \langle\!\langle u \wedge a \rangle\!\rangle \overline{v} \\
\Leftarrow & \quad \{\![\text{ isotony }]\!\} \\
 & t \geq u \ \wedge \ b \geq u \wedge a \ .
\end{array}$$

We use the latter formula as the refinement relation between commands:

$$(a,t) \sqsubseteq (b,u) \ \Leftrightarrow_{df}\ u \leq t \ \wedge \ u \wedge a \leq b \ .$$

Due to our generalised setting we only have $k \sqsubseteq l \Rightarrow \mathsf{wp}.k \geq \mathsf{wp}.l$. Equivalence holds if the underlying modal condition semiring S is *extensional*, i.e, if $\langle\!\langle a \rangle\!\rangle \leq \langle\!\langle b \rangle\!\rangle \Rightarrow a \leq b$ (the converse implication holds by isotony). For instance, REL(M) is extensional, whereas TRC(A) is not.

Unlike $\leq$ the relation $\sqsubseteq$ is only a pre-order with associated equivalence relation

$$k \equiv l \ \Leftrightarrow_{df}\ k \sqsubseteq l \ \wedge \ l \sqsubseteq k \ .$$

Componentwise, it works out to $(a,t) \equiv (b,u) \Leftrightarrow t = u \ \wedge \ t \wedge a \leq b \ \wedge \ t \wedge b \leq a$, which further simplifies to

$$(a,t) \equiv (b,u) \Leftrightarrow t = u \ \wedge \ t \wedge a = t \wedge b \ . \qquad \text{(eqc)}$$

This agrees with the behaviour of designs described in [13]. For instance,

$$(t \wedge a, t) \equiv (a,t) \equiv (\bar{t} + a, t) \ .$$

Our relations between commands are put into perspective by

Lemma 6.1.

1. $k \leq l \Rightarrow k \sqsubseteq l \Rightarrow \mathsf{wp}.k \geq \mathsf{wp}.l$.
2. $k \sqsubseteq l \Leftrightarrow k \mathbin{[\!]} l \equiv l$.

Proof.

1. $(a,t) \leq (b,u) \Leftrightarrow u \leq t \ \wedge \ a \leq b \Rightarrow u \leq t \ \wedge \ u \wedge a \leq b \Leftrightarrow (a,t) \sqsubseteq (b,u)$. The second implication has been shown above.
2. By (eqc) and lattice algebra, $(a,t) \mathbin{[\!]} (b,u) \equiv (b,u) \Leftrightarrow (a+b, t \wedge u) \equiv (b,u) \Leftrightarrow t \wedge u = u \ \wedge \ u \wedge (a+b) = u \wedge b \Leftrightarrow u \leq t \ \wedge \ u \wedge a + u \wedge b = u \wedge b \Leftrightarrow u \leq t \ \wedge \ u \wedge a \leq u \wedge b \Leftrightarrow u \leq t \ \wedge \ u \wedge a \leq b \Leftrightarrow (a,t) \sqsubseteq (b,u)$. □

This lemma explains our choice for the direction of the $\sqsubseteq$ relation; in many texts on refinement it is used the other way around.

For calculations to work smoothly the following property is important:

Lemma 6.2.

1. *The operations* $[\!]$ *and* ; *on commands are* $\sqsubseteq$*-isotone.*
2. *The equivalence* $\equiv$ *is a congruence w.r.t.* $[\!]$ *and* ;.

Proof.

1. Assume $(a,t) \sqsubseteq (b,u)$, i.e., $u \leq t \ \wedge \ u \wedge a \leq b$.
   For $[\!]$ we obtain from the definitions and the universal property of meet

   $$\begin{aligned}&(a,t) \mathbin{[\!]} (c,v) \sqsubseteq (b,u) \mathbin{[\!]} (c,v) \Leftrightarrow \\ &\qquad u \wedge v \leq t \wedge v \ \wedge \ u \wedge v \wedge a \leq b + c \ \wedge \ u \wedge v \wedge c \leq b + c \ ,\end{aligned}$$

   and by isotony all three conjuncts are implied by the assumption. Commutativity of $[\!]$ shows $\sqsubseteq$-isotony in its second argument.

   For the first argument of ; we obtain from the definitions and the universal property of meet

   $$\begin{aligned}&(a,t) \,;\, (c,v) \sqsubseteq (b,u) \,;\, (c,v) \ \Leftrightarrow \\ &\qquad u \wedge [\![b]\!]v \leq t \ \wedge \ u \wedge [\![b]\!]v \leq [\![a]\!]v \ \wedge \ u \wedge [\![b]\!]v \wedge a \cdot c \leq b \cdot c \ .\end{aligned}$$

   The first conjunct is implied by the assumption $u \leq t$. The second one transforms by shunting into $[\![b]\!]v \leq \overline{u} + [\![a]\!]v = [\![u \wedge a]\!]v$, which follows from the assumption $u \wedge a \leq b$ and antitony of box. The third one transforms by Lemma 3.2 into $[\![b]\!]v \wedge (u \wedge a) \cdot c \leq b \cdot c$, which follows again from $u \wedge a \leq b$ and isotony of composition.

For the second argument of ; we obtain from the definitions

$$(c, v) ; (a, t) \sqsubseteq (c, v) ; (b, u) \Leftrightarrow v \wedge [\![c]\!]u \leq v \wedge [\![c]\!]t \;\wedge\; v \wedge [\![c]\!]u \wedge c \cdot a \leq c \cdot b\ .$$

The first conjunct is implied by the assumption $u \leq t$ and isotony of $[\![c]\!]$. The second one follows by shunting from $c \cdot a \leq c \cdot b + {}^{\ulcorner}(c \cdot \overline{u})$ which follows from the assumption $a \leq b + \overline{u}$ and isotony of composition and domain.

2. Immediate from 1. □

Finally we look at the lattice structure of commands under $\sqsubseteq$. Note that join and meet can also be defined for pre-orders; they enjoy all the usual properties except that they are unique only up to the associated equivalence relation.

Lemma 6.3.

1. *The join of commands* (a, t) *and* (b, u) *w.r.t.* $\sqsubseteq$ *is*
$$(a, t) \sqcup (b, u) \;=\; (a + b, t \wedge u) \;=\; (a, t) \,[\!]\, (b, u)\ .$$
2. *If the meet* $a \wedge b$ *exists then so does the meet of* (a, t) *and* (b, u) *w.r.t.* $\sqsubseteq$*, viz.*
$$(a, t) \wedge (b, u) \;=\; (a \wedge b + \overline{t} \wedge b + \overline{u} \wedge a + \overline{t} \wedge \overline{u}, t + u)\ .$$

Proof.

1. We use indirect equality. For all (c, v) we have

$$\begin{array}{ll} & (a,t) \sqsubseteq (c,v) \;\wedge\; (b,u) \sqsubseteq (c,v) \\ \Leftrightarrow & \quad \{\!\mid \text{definition} \mid\!\} \\ & v \leq t \;\wedge\; v \wedge a \leq c \;\wedge\; v \leq u \;\wedge\; v \wedge b \leq c \\ \Leftrightarrow & \quad \{\!\mid \text{lattice algebra} \mid\!\} \\ & v \leq t \wedge u \;\wedge\; v \wedge a + v \wedge b \leq c \\ \Leftrightarrow & \quad \{\!\mid \text{distributivity} \mid\!\} \\ & v \leq t \wedge u \;\wedge\; v \wedge (a + b) \leq c \\ \Leftrightarrow & \quad \{\!\mid \text{definition} \mid\!\} \\ & (a + b, t \wedge u) \sqsubseteq (c, v)\ . \end{array}$$

2.
$$\begin{array}{ll} & (c,v) \sqsubseteq (a,t) \;\wedge\; (c,v) \sqsubseteq (b,u) \\ \Leftrightarrow & \quad \{\!\mid \text{definition} \mid\!\} \\ & t \leq v \;\wedge\; t \wedge c \leq a \;\wedge\; u \leq v \;\wedge\; u \wedge c \leq b \\ \Leftrightarrow & \quad \{\!\mid \text{lattice algebra, shunting} \mid\!\} \\ & t + u \leq v \;\wedge\; c \leq \overline{t} + a \;\wedge\; c \leq \overline{u} + b \\ \Leftrightarrow & \quad \{\!\mid \text{lattice algebra} \mid\!\} \\ & t + u \leq v \;\wedge\; c \leq (\overline{t} + a) \wedge (\overline{u} + b)\ , \end{array}$$

so that $(a, t) \wedge (b, u) \;=\; ((\overline{t} + a) \wedge (\overline{u} + b), t + u)$. The form of the expression given in the statement of the lemma results by Boolean algebra. □

In the remainder we will work with the quotient set $\mathrm{C}(S) = \mathrm{COM}(S)/\!\equiv$ most of the time, but still abbreviate the classes $[(a, t)]_{\equiv}$ by their representatives (a, t).

7 Conditionals

To round off the picture, we define a number of conditional commands in terms of the basic ones:

$$t \rightarrow k =_{df} (t \wedge 1, \top) ; k \;, \qquad k \lhd t \rhd l =_{df} (t \rightarrow k) \,[\!]\, (\overline{t} \rightarrow l) \;,$$
$$\mathsf{assert}\, t =_{df} \mathsf{skip} \lhd t \rhd \mathsf{loop} \;, \qquad \mathsf{assume}\, t =_{df} \mathsf{skip} \lhd t \rhd \mathsf{chaos} \;.$$

In particular, these commands are again $\sqsubseteq$-isotone so that $\equiv$ is a congruence w.r.t. them as well. Componentwise, the first two definitions work out to

$$\begin{aligned} t \rightarrow (b, u) &= (t \wedge b, \overline{t} + u) \;, \\ (b, u) \lhd t \rhd (c, v) &= (b \lhd t \rhd c, u \lhd t \rhd v) \;. \end{aligned}$$

For the latter one calculates by Boolean algebra

$$\begin{aligned} (\overline{t} + u) \wedge (t + v) &= \overline{t} \wedge v + t \wedge u + u \wedge v = \overline{t} \wedge v + t \wedge u + t \wedge u \wedge v + \overline{t} \wedge u \wedge v \\ &= t \wedge u + \overline{t} \wedge v = u \lhd t \rhd v \;. \end{aligned}$$

Let us prove two laws for the two-sided conditional. As an abbreviation, let $p =_{df} (t \wedge 1, \top)$, $q =_{df} (\overline{t} \wedge 1, \top)$, and observe that $p \,[\!]\, q = \mathsf{skip}$. Then, first,

$$k \lhd t \rhd k \underset{\text{(defs.)}}{=} p ; k \,[\!]\, q ; k \underset{\text{(dist.)}}{=} (p \,[\!]\, q) ; k \underset{\text{(above)}}{=} \mathsf{skip} ; k \underset{\text{(neut.)}}{=} k \;.$$

Second,

$$(k \lhd t \rhd l) ; m \underset{\text{(defs.)}}{=} (p ; k \,[\!]\, q ; l) ; m \underset{\text{(dist.)}}{=} p ; k ; m \,[\!]\, q ; l ; m \underset{\text{(defs.)}}{=} (k ; m) \lhd t \rhd (l ; m) \;.$$

From these two laws it follows that $k \lhd t \rhd l$ preserves feasibility, whereas $t \rightarrow k$ does this only in the uninteresting case $t = \top$. Therefore also $\mathsf{assert}\, t$ and $\mathsf{assume}\, t$ are feasible.

Moreover, the conditional operators distribute over choice, since

$$(t \rightarrow k) \,[\!]\, (t \rightarrow l) \underset{\text{(defs.)}}{=} p ; k \,[\!]\, p ; l \underset{\text{(dist.)}}{=} p ; (k \,[\!]\, l) \underset{\text{(defs.)}}{=} t \rightarrow (k \,[\!]\, l) \;,$$

and therefore

$$\begin{aligned} (k \lhd t \rhd l) \,[\!]\, (m \lhd t \rhd n) &\underset{\text{(defs.)}}{=} (t \rightarrow k) \,[\!]\, (\overline{t} \rightarrow l) \,[\!]\, (t \rightarrow m) \,[\!]\, (\overline{t} \rightarrow n) \\ &\underset{\text{(above)}}{=} (t \rightarrow (k \,[\!]\, m)) \,[\!]\, (\overline{t} \rightarrow (l \,[\!]\, n)) \underset{\text{(defs.)}}{=} (k \,[\!]\, m) \lhd t \rhd (l \,[\!]\, n) \;. \end{aligned}$$

Finally, we prove a more specialised property that we will need later on.

Lemma 7.1. $(a, t) ; (b, u) \lhd z \rhd (c, v) = (z \wedge a, t \lhd z \rhd \top) ; (b, u) \,[\!]\, (\overline{z} \wedge c, \top \lhd z \rhd v)$.

Proof. First, for arbitrary commands k, l and m,

$$\begin{aligned} & k ; l \lhd z \rhd m \\ = \quad & \{\!\![\text{ Theorem 5.1 }]\!\!\} \end{aligned}$$

$$
\begin{array}{ll}
 & (k \,;\, l \,[]\, \mathsf{fail}) \lhd z \rhd (\mathsf{fail} \,[]\, m) \\
= & \quad \{\!\![\text{ conditional distributes over choice }]\!\!\} \\
 & (k \,;\, l \lhd z \rhd \mathsf{fail}) \,[]\, (\mathsf{fail} \lhd z \rhd m) \\
= & \quad \{\!\![\text{ Theorem 5.1 }]\!\!\} \\
 & (k \,;\, l \lhd z \rhd \mathsf{fail} \,;\, l) \,[]\, (\mathsf{fail} \lhd z \rhd m) \\
= & \quad \{\!\![\text{ composition distributes over conditional }]\!\!\} \\
 & (k \lhd z \rhd \mathsf{fail}) \,;\, l \,[]\, (\mathsf{fail} \lhd z \rhd m).
\end{array}
$$

Componentwise, we therefore have

$$
\begin{array}{ll}
 & (a,t) \,;\, (b,u) \lhd z \rhd (c,v) \\
= & \quad \{\!\![\text{ above calculation }]\!\!\} \\
 & ((a,t) \lhd z \rhd (0,\top)) \,;\, (b,u) \,[]\, ((0,\top) \lhd z \rhd (c,v)) \\
= & \quad \{\!\![\text{ command conditional }]\!\!\} \\
 & (a \lhd z \rhd 0, t \lhd z \rhd \top) \,;\, (b,u) \,[]\, (0 \lhd z \rhd c, \top \lhd z \rhd v) \\
= & \quad \{\!\![\text{ definition of conditional }]\!\!\} \\
 & (z \wedge a, t \lhd z \rhd \top) \,;\, (b,u) \,[]\, (\overline{z} \wedge c, \top \lhd z \rhd v).
\end{array}
$$

□

8 Feasible Normal Designs and Demonic Semantics

We have already seen that command (a,t) is feasible if and only if $t \leq {\ulcorner}a$ and thus define the set of feasible commands as $\mathrm{F}(S) = \{(a,t) | (a,t) \in \mathrm{C}(S) \ \wedge \ t \leq {\ulcorner}a\}$. The aim of the present section is to establish a correspondence between feasible commands and elements of the underlying semiring S. It will be used to define the demonic operators on S and is an abstract version of the mappings $\mathcal{I}_d$ and $\mathcal{H}_d$ on relations defined in [11], and given by

$$
\begin{array}{ll}
E : \mathrm{F}(S) \to S\ , & D : S \to \mathrm{F}(S)\ , \\
E((a,t)) =_{df} t \wedge a\ , & D(a) =_{df} (a, {\ulcorner}a)\ .
\end{array}
$$

We will abbreviate $E((a,t))$ to $E(a,t)$. This function, which would make sense even for arbitrary pairs, describes the demonic view of (a,t) that discards all input states of a for which both termination and nontermination may occur, i.e., all those characterised by $\overline{t} \wedge {\ulcorner}a$. For the resulting semiring element, no extra termination information is needed; this is reflected in the definition of D.

Lemma 8.1. *E and D are inverse to each other, in one case up to $\equiv$.*

Proof. By Lemma 4.1(7), feasibility, and refinement ordering,

$$D(E(a,t)) = D(t \wedge a) = (t \wedge a, {\ulcorner}(t \wedge a)) = (t \wedge a, t \wedge {\ulcorner}a) = (t \wedge a, t) \equiv (a,t).$$

Conversely, by (cd1) we have $E(D(a)) = E(a, {\ulcorner}a) = {\ulcorner}a \wedge a = a$. □

We will give a demonic ordering and demonic operations on S for modelling total correctness. In contrast to [8], where such an ordering and operations are introduced by new definitions, we can derive these using the correspondence from Lemma 8.1. The demonic refinement ordering is

$$a \sqsubseteq b \Leftrightarrow_{df} D(a) \sqsubseteq D(b) \Leftrightarrow (a, \ulcorner a) \sqsubseteq (b, \ulcorner b) \Leftrightarrow \ulcorner b \leq \ulcorner a \ \wedge \ \ulcorner b \wedge a \leq b.$$

By (eqc) and (cd1) $\sqsubseteq$ is antisymmetric, i.e., a partial order. Thus, by Lemma 8.1, the mappings E and D are order isomorphisms between $(\mathrm{F}(S), \sqsubseteq)$ and $(S, \sqsubseteq)$. Since chaos is the greatest element of $\mathrm{COM}(S)$, and therefore also of $\mathrm{F}(S)$, the $\sqsubseteq$-greatest element of S is $E(\mathsf{chaos}) = E(\top, 0) = 0$. In general, however, there is no $\sqsubseteq$-smallest element, since the corresponding least element fail of $\mathrm{COM}(S)$ is not feasible.

The demonic composition is

$$\begin{aligned} a \,\Box\, b &=_{df} E(D(a)\,;D(b)) = E((a, \ulcorner a)\,;(b, \ulcorner b)) = E(a \cdot b, \ulcorner a \wedge [\![a]\!]\ulcorner b) \\ &= \ulcorner a \wedge [\![a]\!]\ulcorner b \wedge a \cdot b = [\![a]\!]\ulcorner b \wedge a \cdot b, \end{aligned}$$

since $a \cdot b \leq \ulcorner(a \cdot b) \leq \ulcorner a$ by (cd1) and Lemma 4.1(10). The unit skip of $\mathrm{COM}(S)$ is feasible, thus $E(\mathsf{skip}) = E(1, \top) = 1$ is also the unit of demonic composition.

The demonic choice (which coincides with the $\sqsubseteq$-join) is

$$\begin{aligned} a \sqcup b &=_{df} E(D(a) \,[\!]\, D(b)) = E((a, \ulcorner a) \,[\!]\, (b, \ulcorner b)) = E(a + b, \ulcorner a \wedge \ulcorner b) \\ &= \ulcorner a \wedge \ulcorner b \wedge (a + b). \end{aligned}$$

The demonic meet, whenever it exists, is, by Lemma 6.3.2,

$$\begin{aligned} a \sqcap b &=_{df} E(D(a) \wedge D(b)) = E((a, \ulcorner a) \wedge (b, \ulcorner b)) \\ &= E(a \wedge b + \overline{\ulcorner a} \wedge b + \overline{\ulcorner b} \wedge a, \ulcorner a + \ulcorner b) \\ &= (\ulcorner a + \ulcorner b) \wedge (a \wedge b + \overline{\ulcorner a} \wedge b + \overline{\ulcorner b} \wedge a) \\ &= a \wedge b + \overline{\ulcorner a} \wedge b + \overline{\ulcorner b} \wedge a, \end{aligned}$$

since $a \wedge b + \overline{\ulcorner a} \wedge b + \overline{\ulcorner b} \wedge a \leq a + b + a = a + b \leq \ulcorner a + \ulcorner b$ by (cd1). The necessary and sufficient condition for its existence is the feasibility of $D(a) \wedge D(b)$, hence,

$$\begin{aligned} & D(a) \wedge D(b) \in \mathrm{F}(S) \\ \Leftrightarrow \quad & \{\![\text{ above calculation, feasibility }]\!\} \\ & \ulcorner a + \ulcorner b \leq \ulcorner(a \wedge b + \overline{\ulcorner a} \wedge b + \overline{\ulcorner b} \wedge a) \\ \Leftrightarrow \quad & \{\![\text{ Lemma 4.1(2,7) }]\!\} \\ & \ulcorner a + \ulcorner b \leq \ulcorner(a \wedge b) + \overline{\ulcorner a} \wedge \ulcorner b + \overline{\ulcorner b} \wedge \ulcorner a \\ \Leftrightarrow \quad & \{\![\text{ shunting and de Morgan }]\!\} \\ & (\ulcorner a + \ulcorner b) \wedge (\ulcorner a + \overline{\ulcorner b}) \wedge (\ulcorner b + \overline{\ulcorner a}) \leq \ulcorner(a \wedge b) \\ \Leftrightarrow \quad & \{\![\text{ Boolean algebra }]\!\} \\ & \ulcorner a \wedge \ulcorner b \leq \ulcorner(a \wedge b), \end{aligned}$$

which is equivalent to $\ulcorner(a \wedge b) = \ulcorner a \wedge \ulcorner b$.

Finally, the demonic conditional is

$$\begin{aligned} E(D(a) \lhd t \rhd D(b)) &= E((a, \ulcorner a) \lhd t \rhd (b, \ulcorner b)) = E(a \lhd t \rhd b, \ulcorner a \lhd t \rhd \ulcorner b) \\ &= (\ulcorner a \lhd t \rhd \ulcorner b) \wedge (a \lhd t \rhd b) = (\ulcorner a \wedge a) \lhd t \rhd (\ulcorner b \wedge b) \\ &= a \lhd t \rhd b \end{aligned}$$

by Boolean algebra and (cd1). Hence we do not introduce a new notation for it.

The solutions to demonic recursions are also derived according to the order isomorphism and the following general lemma.

Lemma 8.2. *1. Let $(A, \leq)$ and $(B, \sqsubseteq)$ be partial orders, $h : A \to B$ an order isomorphism, $f : A \to A$, and $g : B \to B$ such that $h \circ f = g \circ h$. Then f is order preserving if and only if g is order preserving.*
2. Furthermore, let f be order preserving and f° a fixed point of f. Then $h(f^\circ)$ is a fixed point of g.
3. Furthermore, let $f^\perp$ be the least fixed point of f, and $f^\top$ the greatest. Then $h(f^\perp)$ is the least fixed point of g, and $h(f^\top)$ the greatest.

Proof. 1. Assume $x \leq y$. Then

$$f(x) \leq f(y) \Leftrightarrow h(f(x)) \sqsubseteq h(f(y)) \Leftrightarrow g(h(x)) \sqsubseteq g(h(y)) ,$$

which, together with surjectivity of h shows the claim.
2. $g(h(f^\circ)) = h(f(f^\circ)) = h(f^\circ)$.
3. $h(f^\perp)$ and $h(f^\top)$ are fixed points of g by 2. Let g° be a fixed point of g. Swapping the partial orders, 2. states that $h^{-1}(g^\circ)$ is a fixed point of f. Hence, $f^\perp \leq h^{-1}(g^\circ) \leq f^\top$. By order isomorphism, $h(f^\perp) \sqsubseteq g^\circ \sqsubseteq h(f^\top)$. □

Corollary 8.3. *Let $f : S \to S$ be $\sqsubseteq$-preserving. Then the least fixed point of f with respect to $\sqsubseteq$ is $\mu_\sqsubseteq(f) = E(\mu_\sqsubseteq(D \circ f \circ E))$. Analogously, the greatest fixed point is $\nu_\sqsubseteq(f) = E(\nu_\sqsubseteq(D \circ f \circ E))$.*

9 The Kleene Algebra of Commands

A *Kleene algebra* is a structure $(K, {}^*)$ such that K is an idempotent semiring and the star * satisfies the unfold and induction laws

$$\begin{array}{ll} 1 + a \cdot a^* \leq a^* & 1 + a^* \cdot a \leq a^* \\ b + a \cdot c \leq c \Rightarrow a^* \cdot b \leq c & b + c \cdot a \leq c \Rightarrow b \cdot a^* \leq c \end{array}$$

for $a, b, c \in K$ [14]. Hence $a^* \cdot b$ is the least fixed point of the mapping $\lambda x.a \cdot x + b$.

The following Lemma proves a generalisation to condition semirings of the left induction law from Kleene algebra.

Lemma 9.1. *$v \wedge (b + c \cdot a) \leq c \Rightarrow v \wedge b \cdot a^* \leq c$.*

Proof. By Boolean algebra and Lemma 3.2, $v \wedge (b + c \cdot a) = v \wedge b + v \wedge (c \cdot a) = v \wedge b + (v \wedge c) \cdot a = v \wedge b + (v \wedge (c + \overline{v})) \cdot a = v \wedge b + v \wedge ((c + \overline{v}) \cdot a) = v \wedge (b + (c + \overline{v}) \cdot a)$. Hence, by the above calculation, shunting, Kleene star induction and shunting again,

$$\begin{aligned} v \wedge (b + c \cdot a) \leq c &\Leftrightarrow v \wedge (b + (c + \overline{v}) \cdot a) \leq c \Leftrightarrow b + (c + \overline{v}) \cdot a \leq c + \overline{v} \\ &\Rightarrow b \cdot a^* \leq c + \overline{v} \Leftrightarrow v \wedge b \cdot a^* \leq c . \end{aligned}$$

□

Lemma 9.2. *1.* $v \le \llbracket a \rrbracket v \Leftrightarrow a \cdot \overline{v} \le \overline{v}$.
2. $v \le t \wedge \llbracket a \rrbracket v \Rightarrow v \le \llbracket a^* \rrbracket t$.

Proof. 1. By the definition of box, Boolean algebra, and (GCc),

$$v \le \llbracket a \rrbracket v \Leftrightarrow v \le \overline{\ulcorner(a \cdot \overline{v})} \Leftrightarrow \ulcorner(a \cdot \overline{v}) \le \overline{v} \Leftrightarrow a \cdot \overline{v} \le \overline{v}.$$

2.

$$\begin{array}{ll} & v \le t \wedge \llbracket a \rrbracket v \\ \Leftrightarrow & \quad \{\!\mid \text{Boolean algebra} \mid\!\} \\ & v \le t \;\wedge\; v \le \llbracket a \rrbracket v \\ \Leftrightarrow & \quad \{\!\mid \text{Boolean algebra and 1.} \mid\!\} \\ & \overline{t} \le \overline{v} \;\wedge\; a \cdot \overline{v} \le \overline{v} \\ \Leftrightarrow & \quad \{\!\mid \text{Boolean algebra} \mid\!\} \\ & \overline{t} + a \cdot \overline{v} \le \overline{v} \\ \Rightarrow & \quad \{\!\mid \text{Kleene star induction} \mid\!\} \\ & a^* \cdot \overline{t} \le \overline{v} \\ \Leftrightarrow & \quad \{\!\mid \text{(GCc)} \mid\!\} \\ & \ulcorner(a^* \cdot \overline{t}) \le \overline{v} \\ \Leftrightarrow & \quad \{\!\mid \text{Boolean algebra and definition of box} \mid\!\} \\ & v \le \overline{\ulcorner(a^* \cdot \overline{t})} = \llbracket a^* \rrbracket t. \end{array}$$

□

We will now lift the Kleene star from the underlying semiring S to the quotient command semiring $\mathrm{C}(S)$. This is needed to calculate the least fixed point of loops. Since the right annihilation law fails to hold in $\mathrm{C}(S)$ the resulting structure is called a *weak Kleene algebra* [18].

Theorem 9.3. $(a, t)^* = (a^*, \llbracket a^* \rrbracket t)$.

Proof. We first note that if two functions agree in their values up to $\equiv$ then their $\sqsubseteq$-least and $\sqsubseteq$-greatest fixed points are $\equiv$-equivalent, too. So the star axioms characterise the star operation uniquely up to $\equiv$ in $\mathrm{COM}(S)$. Therefore, to prove the claim it suffices to show the star axioms for $(a^*, \llbracket a^* \rrbracket t)$ using arbitrary representatives of the $\equiv$-classes involved.

1. By command operations, properties of box, and the Kleene unfold axiom,

$$\begin{aligned} \mathsf{skip} \;[\!]\; (a,t) \,;\, (a^*, \llbracket a^* \rrbracket t) &= (1, \top) \;[\!]\; (a \cdot a^*, t \wedge \llbracket a \rrbracket \llbracket a^* \rrbracket t) \\ &= (1 + a \cdot a^*, \llbracket 1 \rrbracket t \wedge \llbracket a \cdot a^* \rrbracket t) = (a^*, \llbracket 1 + a \cdot a^* \rrbracket t) = (a^*, \llbracket a^* \rrbracket t). \end{aligned}$$

2. For similar reasons,

$$\begin{aligned} \mathsf{skip} \;[\!]\; (a^*, \llbracket a^* \rrbracket t) \,;\, (a,t) &= (1, \top) \;[\!]\; (a^* \cdot a, \llbracket a^* \rrbracket t \wedge \llbracket a^* \rrbracket t) \\ &= (1 + a^* \cdot a, \llbracket a^* \rrbracket t) = (a^*, \llbracket a^* \rrbracket t). \end{aligned}$$

3. By command operations and ordering,

$$\begin{aligned} (b,u) \;[\!]\; (a,t) \,;\, (c,v) \sqsubseteq (c,v) &\Leftrightarrow (b,u) \;[\!]\; (a \cdot c, t \wedge \llbracket a \rrbracket v) \sqsubseteq (c,v) \\ &\Leftrightarrow (b + a \cdot c, u \wedge t \wedge \llbracket a \rrbracket v) \sqsubseteq (c,v) \\ &\Leftrightarrow v \le t \wedge u \wedge \llbracket a \rrbracket v \;\wedge\; v \wedge (b + a \cdot c) \le c. \end{aligned}$$

By Lemma 9.2.1, $a \cdot \overline{v} \leq \overline{v}$, hence $b + a \cdot (c + \overline{v}) = b + a \cdot c + a \cdot \overline{v} \leq c + \overline{v}$. By Kleene star induction, $a^* \cdot b \leq c + \overline{v}$, thus $v \wedge a^* \cdot b \leq c$ by shunting. Moreover, $v \leq [\![a^*]\!](t \wedge u)$ by Lemma 9.2.2.
By command operations, properties of box, and the last two facts,

$$(a^*, [\![a^*]\!]t) ; (b, u) = (a^* \cdot b, [\![a^*]\!]t \wedge [\![a^*]\!]u) = (a^* \cdot b, [\![a^*]\!](t \wedge u)) \sqsubseteq (c, v).$$

4. By command operations and ordering,

$$\begin{aligned} (b, u) \,[\!]\, (c, v) ; (a, t) \sqsubseteq (c, v) &\Leftrightarrow (b, u) \,[\!]\, (c \cdot a, v \wedge [\![c]\!]t) \sqsubseteq (c, v) \\ &\Leftrightarrow (b + c \cdot a, u \wedge v \wedge [\![c]\!]t) \sqsubseteq (c, v) \\ &\Leftrightarrow v \leq u \;\wedge\; v \leq [\![c]\!]t \;\wedge\; v \wedge (b + c \cdot a) \leq c. \end{aligned}$$

By Lemma 9.1, $v \wedge b \cdot a^* \leq c$. Moreover, $v \leq [\![c]\!]t \leq [\![v \wedge b \cdot a^*]\!]t = \overline{v} + [\![b \cdot a^*]\!]t$ by box properties. By $v \leq u$ and shunting, $v \leq u \wedge [\![b \cdot a^*]\!]t$.
Together, by command operations, and properties of box,

$$(b, u) ; (a^*, [\![a^*]\!]t) = (b \cdot a^*, u \wedge [\![b]\!][\![a^*]\!]t) = (b \cdot a^*, u \wedge [\![b \cdot a^*]\!]t) \sqsubseteq (c, v).$$

□

Corollary 9.4. *Since the designs of UTP are commands over relations, we have a weak Kleene algebra of designs where* $(P \vdash Q)^* = \overline{Q^*; \overline{P}} \vdash Q^*$.

10 The Omega Algebra of Commands

A *weak omega algebra* is a structure $(K, {}^\omega)$ such that K is a weak Kleene algebra and the omega ${}^\omega$ satisfies the unfold and co-induction laws

$$\begin{gathered} a^\omega = a \cdot a^\omega \\ c \leq a \cdot c + b \Rightarrow c \leq a^\omega + a^* \cdot b \end{gathered}$$

for $a, b, c \in K$ [16]. It follows that $a^\omega + a^* \cdot b$ is the greatest fixed point of the mapping $\lambda x.a \cdot x + b$.

In contrast to this definition, an *omega algebra* requires K to be a Kleene algebra but weakens the unfold axiom to $a^\omega \leq a \cdot a^\omega$ [4]. The reverse inequality need not hold in absence of the right annihilation law [16].

For the greatest fixed point of loops, we will now lift the omega operator from the underlying semiring S to the quotient command semiring $\mathrm{C}(S)$. To calculate the weak omega operator we need the analogue of the convergence algebra defined in [18]. The convergence operation $\triangle : S \to \mathsf{cond}(S)$ satisfies the unfold and co-induction laws

$$\begin{gathered} [\![a]\!](\triangle a) \leq \triangle a \\ t \wedge [\![a]\!]u \leq u \Rightarrow \triangle a \wedge [\![a^*]\!]t \leq u \end{gathered}$$

The condition $\triangle a$ characterises the states from which no infinite transition paths emerge. The following lemma states a few properties of convergence.

Lemma 10.1. *1.* $\triangle a \wedge [\![a^*]\!]t$ *is the least (pre-)fixed point of* $\lambda u.t \wedge [\![a]\!]u$.
In particular, $\triangle a$ *is the least (pre-)fixed point of* $[\![a]\!]$.

2. $\overline{\ulcorner a} \leq \triangle a \leq \overline{\ulcorner a^\omega}$ *and hence* $\triangle a \wedge a^\omega = 0$.

3. $\triangle$ *is antitone.*

4. $[\![a^*]\!](\triangle a) = [\![a \cdot a^*]\!](\triangle a) = [\![a]\!](\triangle a) = \triangle a$.

Proof. 1. By box properties, and the Kleene star and convergence unfold laws, $t \wedge [\![a]\!](\triangle a \wedge [\![a^*]\!]t) = t \wedge [\![a]\!](\triangle a) \wedge [\![a]\!][\![a^*]\!]t \leq \triangle a \wedge [\![1 + a \cdot a^*]\!]t = \triangle a \wedge [\![a^*]\!]t$. Hence, by the co-induction axiom, $\triangle a \wedge [\![a^*]\!]t$ is the least pre-fixed point of $\lambda u.t \wedge [\![a]\!]u$. Then, it is also the least fixed point [8].
Choose $t = \top$ for the special case, using $[\![a^*]\!]\top = \top$.

2. By condition semiring properties, the definition of box, and the unfold law,

$$\overline{\ulcorner a} = \overline{\ulcorner(a \cdot \top)} \leq \overline{\ulcorner(a \cdot \overline{\triangle a})} = [\![a]\!](\triangle a) = \triangle a.$$

By definition of box, Lemma 4.1(8), and the omega axioms,

$$[\![a]\!]\overline{\ulcorner a^\omega} = \overline{\ulcorner(a \cdot \ulcorner a^\omega)} \leq \overline{\ulcorner(a \cdot a^\omega)} = \overline{\ulcorner a^\omega}.$$

Hence, $\overline{\ulcorner a^\omega}$ is a fixed point of $[\![a]\!]$, and $\triangle a \leq \overline{\ulcorner a^\omega}$ by 1.

3. By antitony of box and 1, $a \leq b \Rightarrow [\![b]\!] \leq [\![a]\!] \Rightarrow \triangle b \leq \triangle a$.

4. By box properties and 1, $[\![1]\!](\triangle a) = \triangle a = [\![a]\!](\triangle a)$. Moreover, by star and box properties,

$$[\![a]\!][\![a^*]\!](\triangle a) = [\![a \cdot a^*]\!](\triangle a) = [\![a^* \cdot a]\!](\triangle a) = [\![a^*]\!][\![a]\!](\triangle a) = [\![a^*]\!](\triangle a)\ ,$$

so that $[\![a^*]\!](\triangle a)$ is a fixed point of $[\![a]\!]$. The remaining inequalities follow by antitony of the box operator. □

In the special case of REL(M), $\triangle a = \overline{a^\omega}$ can be proved by Corollary 4.3.

Theorem 10.2. $(a, t)^\omega = (a^\omega, \triangle a \wedge [\![a^*]\!]t) \equiv (0, \triangle a \wedge [\![a^*]\!]t)$.

Proof. Using the same observation as in the proof of Theorem 9.3, it suffices to show that $(a^\omega, \triangle a \wedge [\![a^*]\!]t)$ satisfies the weak omega axioms. The claimed $\equiv$-relation then follows by Lemma 10.1.2.

1. By command operations, the fixed-point property of a^ω and Lemma 10.1.1,

$$(a, t)\,;(a^\omega, \triangle a \wedge [\![a^*]\!]t) \;=\; (a \cdot a^\omega, t \wedge [\![a]\!](\triangle a \wedge [\![a^*]\!]t)) \;=\; (a^\omega, \triangle a \wedge [\![a^*]\!]t)\ .$$

2. Assume

$$(c, v) \sqsubseteq (a, t)\,;(c, v) \mathbin{[\,]} (b, u) = (a \cdot c, t \wedge [\![a]\!]v) \mathbin{[\,]} (b, u) = (a \cdot c + b, t \wedge [\![a]\!]v \wedge u),$$

which is equivalent to $w \leq v \;\wedge\; w \wedge c \leq a \cdot c + b$, where $w =_{df} t \wedge u \wedge [\![a]\!]v$. We have to show

$$\begin{aligned}(c, v) \sqsubseteq\; &(a^\omega, \triangle a \wedge [\![a^*]\!]t) \mathbin{[\,]} (a^*, [\![a^*]\!]t)\,;(b, u)\\ =\; &(a^\omega + a^* \cdot b, \triangle a \wedge [\![a^*]\!]t \wedge [\![a^*]\!]t \wedge [\![a^*]\!]u)\\ =\; &(a^\omega + a^* \cdot b, \triangle a \wedge [\![a^*]\!](t \wedge u))\ ,\end{aligned}$$

which by definitions and shunting is equivalent to $x \leq v \ \wedge \ c \leq a^\omega + a^* \cdot b + \overline{x}$, where $x =_{df} \triangle a \wedge [\![a^*]\!](t \wedge u)$.

The first conjunct follows from the first assumption by convergence co-induction. For the second one transforms the second assumption by shunting into $c \leq a \cdot c + b + \overline{w}$. By omega co-induction $c \leq a^\omega + a^* \cdot b + a^* \cdot \overline{w}$, so we are done if we can show $a^* \cdot \overline{w} \leq \overline{x}$.
We have $a^* \cdot \overline{w} \leq \ulcorner(a^* \cdot \overline{w}) = \overline{[\![a^*]\!]w}$, so that it suffices to show $\overline{[\![a^*]\!]w} \leq \overline{x}$, equivalently $x \leq [\![a^*]\!]w$. Now, by box and star properties,

$$\begin{aligned} x \leq [\![a^*]\!]w &\Leftrightarrow x \leq [\![a^*]\!](t \wedge u) \wedge [\![a^*]\!][\![a]\!]v \\ &\Leftrightarrow x \leq [\![a^*]\!](t \wedge u) \ \wedge \ x \leq [\![a^*]\!]v \ . \end{aligned}$$

The first conjunct holds by definition of x. For the second one, since $x \leq v$ as shown above, it suffices by isotony of $[\![a^*]\!]$ to show $x \leq [\![a^*]\!]x$. Now, by disjunctivity of $[\![a^*]\!]$, Lemma 10.1.4 and star properties,

$$\begin{aligned} [\![a^*]\!]x &= [\![a^*]\!](\triangle a \wedge [\![a^*]\!](t \wedge u)) = [\![a^*]\!](\triangle a) \wedge [\![a^*]\!][\![a^*]\!](t \wedge u) \\ &= \triangle a \wedge [\![a^*]\!][\![a^*]\!](t \wedge u) = \triangle a \wedge [\![a^*]\!](t \wedge u) = x \ . \end{aligned}$$ □

Corollary 10.3. *Again, since the designs of UTP are commands over relations, we have a weak omega algebra of designs where* $(P \vdash Q)^\omega = \overline{Q^\omega \vee Q^*; \overline{P}} \vdash \mathit{false}$.

11 The Demonic While Loop

The Kleene and omega algebraic properties of commands finally enable the calculation of the least and greatest fixed points of the function that describes the demonic while loop.

Theorem 11.1.

1. $\mu_\sqsubseteq(\lambda x. a \,\square\, x \lhd t \rhd 1) = [\![(t \wedge a)^*]\!](\overline{t} + \ulcorner a) \wedge (t \wedge a)^* \cdot (\overline{t} \wedge 1)$.
2. $\nu_\sqsubseteq(\lambda x. a \,\square\, x \lhd t \rhd 1) = \triangle(t \wedge a) \wedge \mu_\sqsubseteq(\lambda x. a \,\square\, x \lhd t \rhd 1)$.

Proof. We calculate the fixed points according to Corollary 8.3.

1. For the least fixed point,

$$\begin{aligned} & \mu_\sqsubseteq(\lambda x. a \,\square\, x \lhd t \rhd 1) \\ = & \quad \{\!\![\text{ Corollary 8.3 }]\!\!\} \\ & E(\mu_\sqsubseteq(\lambda(b,u).D(a \,\square\, E(b,u) \lhd t \rhd 1))) \\ = & \quad \{\!\![\text{ demonic conditional: } D(a \lhd t \rhd b) = D(a) \lhd t \rhd D(b)]\!\!\} \\ & E(\mu_\sqsubseteq(\lambda(b,u).D(a \,\square\, E(b,u)) \lhd t \rhd D(1))) \\ = & \quad \{\!\![\text{ demonic composition: } D(a \,\square\, b) = D(a) \,;\, D(b)]\!\!\} \\ & E(\mu_\sqsubseteq(\lambda(b,u).D(a) \,;\, D(E(b,u)) \lhd t \rhd D(E(\mathsf{skip})))) \\ = & \quad \{\!\![\text{ Lemma 8.1 }]\!\!\} \\ & E(\mu_\sqsubseteq(\lambda(b,u).(a, \ulcorner a) \,;\, (b,u) \lhd t \rhd (1, \top))) \\ = & \quad \{\!\![\text{ Lemma 7.1 }]\!\!\} \end{aligned}$$

$$
\begin{aligned}
& E(\mu_{\sqsubseteq}(\lambda(b,u).(t \wedge a, \ulcorner a \lhd t \rhd \top) ; (b,u) \,[]\, (\bar{t} \wedge 1, \top))) \\
= \quad & \{\!|\ \text{definition of conditional and Boolean algebra}\ |\!\} \\
& E(\mu_{\sqsubseteq}(\lambda(b,u).(t \wedge a, \bar{t} + \ulcorner a) ; (b,u) \,[]\, (\bar{t} \wedge 1, \top))) \\
= \quad & \{\!|\ a^* \cdot b \text{ is the least fixed point of } (\lambda x.a \cdot x + b)\ |\!\} \\
& E((t \wedge a, \bar{t} + \ulcorner a)^* ; (\bar{t} \wedge 1, \top)) \\
= \quad & \{\!|\ \text{Theorem 9.3}\ |\!\} \\
& E(((t \wedge a)^*, [\![(t \wedge a)^*]\!](\bar{t} + \ulcorner a)) ; (\bar{t} \wedge 1, \top)) \\
= \quad & \{\!|\ \text{command composition}\ |\!\} \\
& E((t \wedge a)^* \cdot (\bar{t} \wedge 1), [\![(t \wedge a)^*]\!](\bar{t} + \ulcorner a) \wedge [\![(t \wedge a)^*]\!]\top) \\
= \quad & \{\!|\ \text{box properties and definition of } E\ |\!\} \\
& [\![(t \wedge a)^*]\!](\bar{t} + \ulcorner a) \wedge (t \wedge a)^* \cdot (\bar{t} \wedge 1).
\end{aligned}
$$

2. For the greatest fixed point,

$$
\begin{aligned}
& \nu_{\sqsubseteq}(\lambda x.a \,\square\, x \lhd t \rhd 1) \\
= \quad & \{\!|\ \text{calculation as in 1.}\ |\!\} \\
& E(\nu_{\sqsubseteq}(\lambda(b,u).(t \wedge a, \bar{t} + \ulcorner a) ; (b,u) \,[]\, (\bar{t} \wedge 1, \top))) \\
= \quad & \{\!|\ a^* \cdot b + a^\omega \text{ is the greatest fixed point of } (\lambda x.a \cdot x + b)\ |\!\} \\
& E((t \wedge a, \bar{t} + \ulcorner a)^* ; (\bar{t} \wedge 1, \top) \,[]\, (t \wedge a, \bar{t} + \ulcorner a)^\omega) \\
= \quad & \{\!|\ \text{Theorem 10.2 and calculation as in 1.}\ |\!\} \\
& E(((t \wedge a)^* \cdot (\bar{t} \wedge 1), [\![(t \wedge a)^*]\!](\bar{t} + \ulcorner a)) \,[] \\
& \quad (0, \triangle(t \wedge a) \wedge [\![(t \wedge a)^*]\!](\bar{t} + \ulcorner a))) \\
= \quad & \{\!|\ \text{command disjunction}\ |\!\} \\
& E((t \wedge a)^* \cdot (\bar{t} \wedge 1), \triangle(t \wedge a) \wedge [\![(t \wedge a)^*]\!](\bar{t} + \ulcorner a)) \\
= \quad & \{\!|\ 1.\ |\!\} \\
& \triangle(t \wedge a) \wedge \mu_{\sqsubseteq}(\lambda x.a \,\square\, x \lhd t \rhd 1).
\end{aligned}
$$

□

12 Conclusion

The treatment has shown that almost all of the standard theory of normal designs carries over to the general case. One can even prove a generalisation of the fixed point theorem 3.1.6 of [13] that allows an alternative derivation of the omega operator for commands. It should be noted that the operations of complement and meet are not required for all semiring elements but only on the conditions.

By defining refinement as in Section 6 we committed ourselves to total correctness. The branch of general correctness, exemplified by the normal prescriptions of [10], can be explored by taking the natural order of commands given in Theorem 5.1 instead. Since then, however, the connection starting with Lemma 8.1 no longer holds, the loop semantics cannot be calculated in the same way. An alternative treatment using the Egli-Milner order is given in [18]. The treatment of conditions as right ideals has been an interesting exercise but is not as smooth as using tests, not least because of its lack of symmetry.

Finally, we would like to mention that the command semiring can actually be made into a modal semiring itself, so that the general soundness and completeness proof for the associated Hoare logic can directly be applied to commands (see [17] for details).

It is to be hoped that the generalised results will be of use for handling trace semantics and other semantical models by taking algebras like TRC(A) and their properties into account, thus dealing with healthiness conditions such as (R1)–(R3) of UTP in a purely algebraic fashion. The presented method could also serve as a model for the extension by parameters that describe further observations as proposed in [13].

Acknowledgement. We are grateful to Peter Höfner, Kim Solin and the anonymous referees for helpful discussions and remarks.

References

1. R. C. Backhouse, J. van der Woude: Demonic operators and monotype factors. Mathematical Structures in Computer Science 3, 417–433 (1993)
2. R. Berghammer, H. Zierer: Relational algebraic semantics of deterministic and non-deterministic programs. Theoretical Computer Science 43, 123–147 (1986)
3. M. Broy, R. Gnatz, M. Wirsing: Semantics of nondeterministic and non-continuous constructs. In F.L. Bauer, M. Broy (eds.): Program construction. Lecture Notes in Computer Science 69. Springer 1979, 553–592
4. E. Cohen: Separation and reduction. In R. Backhouse, J. Oliveira (eds.): Mathematics of Program Construction. Lecture Notes in Computer Science 1837, Springer 2000, 45–59
5. J. Desharnais, N. Belkhiter, S.B.M. Sghaier, F. Tchier, A. Jaoua, A. Mili, and N. Zaguia: Embedding a demonic semilattice in a relation algebra. Theoretical Computer Science 149, 333–360 (1995)
6. J. Desharnais, A. Mili, T.T. Nguyen: Refinement and demonic semantics. In C. Brink, W. Kahl, G. Schmidt (eds): Relational methods in computer science, Chapter 11. Springer 1997, 166–183
7. J. Desharnais, B. Möller, G. Struth: Kleene algebra with domain. ACM TOCL (to appear)
8. J. Desharnais, B. Möller, F. Tchier: Kleene under a modal demonic star. Journal of Logic and Algebraic Programming 66:2 (Special Issue on Relation Algebra and Kleene Algebra), 127–160 (2006)
9. H. Doornbos: A relational model of programs without the restriction to Egli-Milner-monotone constructs. In E.-R. Olderog (ed.): Programming concepts, methods and calculi. North-Holland 1994, 363–382
10. S. Dunne: Recasting Hoare and He's unifying theory of programs in the context of general correctness. In Butterfield, A., Strong, G., Pahl, C., eds.: 5th Irish Workshop on Formal Methods. EWiC, The British Computer Society, 2001
11. W. Guttmann: Non-termination in Unifying Theories of Programming. In W. MacCaull, M. Winter and I. Düntsch (eds.): Relational Methods in Computer Science. LNCS 3929. Springer 2006, 108–120
12. W. Guttmann, B. Möller: Modal design algebra. Institut für Informatik, Universität Augsburg, Report 2005-15

13. C.A.R. Hoare, J. He: Unifying theories of programming. Prentice Hall 1998
14. D. Kozen: A completeness theorem for Kleene algebras and the algebra of regular events. Information and Computation 110, 366–390 (1994)
15. D. Kozen: Kleene algebra with tests. ACM TOPLAS 19:427–443 (1997)
16. B. Möller: Lazy Kleene algebra. In D. Kozen (ed.): Mathematics of Program Construction. Lecture Notes in Computer Science 3125. Springer 2004, 252–273
17. B. Möller, G. Struth: Modal Kleene algebra and partial correctness. In C. Rattray, S. Maharaj, C. Shankland (eds.): Algebraic methodology and software technology. Lecture Notes in Computer Science 3116. Springer 2004, 379–393. Revised and extended version: B. Möller, G. Struth: Algebras of modal operators and partial correctness. Theoretical Computer Science 351, 221–239 (2006)
18. B. Möller, G. Struth: wp is wlp. In W. MacCaull, M. Winter and I. Düntsch (eds.): Relational Methods in Computer Science. LNCS 3929. Springer 2006, 200–211
19. G. Nelson: A generalization of Dijkstra's calculus. ACM TOPLAS 11, 517–561 (1989)
20. T.T. Nguyen: A relational model of nondeterministic programs. International J. Foundations Comp. Sci. 2, 101–131 (1991)
21. D. Parnas: A generalized control structure and its formal definition. Commun. ACM 26, 572–581 (1983)

Author Index

Lecture Notes in Computer Science

For information about Vols. 1–3915

please contact your bookseller or Springer

Vol. 4039: M. Morisio (Ed.), Reuse of Off-the-Shelf Components. XI, 444 pages. 2006.

Vol. 4027: H.L. Larsen, G. Pasi, D. Ortiz-Arroyo, T. Andreasen, H. Christiansen (Eds.), Flexible Query Answering Systems. XVIII, 714 pages. 2006. (Sublibrary LNAI).

Vol. 4024: S. Donatelli, P. S. Thiagarajan (Eds.), Petri Nets and Other Models of Concurrency - ICATPN 2006. XI, 441 pages. 2006.

Vol. 4011: Y. Sure, J. Domingue (Eds.), The Semantic Web: Research and Applications. XVIII, 723 pages. 2006.

Vol. 4010: S. Dunne, B. Stoddart (Eds.), Unifying Theories of Programming. VIII, 257 pages. 2006.

Vol. 4007: C. Àlvarez, M. Serna (Eds.), Experimental Algorithms. XI, 329 pages. 2006.

Vol. 4006: L.M. Pinho, M. González Harbour (Eds.), Reliable Software Technology – Ada-Europe 2006. XII, 241 pages. 2006.

Vol. 4004: S. Vaudenay (Ed.), Advances in Cryptology - EUROCRYPT 2006. XIV, 613 pages. 2006.

Vol. 4003: Y. Koucheryavy, J. Harju, V.B. Iversen (Eds.), Next Generation Teletraffic and Wired/Wireless Advanced Networking. XVI, 582 pages. 2006.

Vol. 4001: E. Dubois, K. Pohl (Eds.), Advanced Information Systems Engineering. XVI, 560 pages. 2006.

Vol. 3999: C. Kop, G. Fliedl, H.C. Mayr, E. Métais (Eds.), Natural Language Processing and Information Systems. XIII, 227 pages. 2006.

Vol. 3998: T. Calamoneri, I. Finocchi, G.F. Italiano (Eds.), Algorithms and Complexity. XII, 394 pages. 2006.

Vol. 3997: W. Grieskamp, C. Weise (Eds.), Formal Approaches to Software Testing. XII, 219 pages. 2006.

Vol. 3996: A. Keller, J.-P. Martin-Flatin (Eds.), Self-Managed Networks, Systems, and Services. X, 185 pages. 2006.

Vol. 3995: G. Müller (Ed.), Emerging Trends in Information and Communication Security. XX, 524 pages. 2006.

Vol. 3994: V.N. Alexandrov, G.D. van Albada, P.M.A. Sloot, J. Dongarra (Eds.), Computational Science – ICCS 2006, Part IV. XXXV, 1096 pages. 2006.

Vol. 3993: V.N. Alexandrov, G.D. van Albada, P.M.A. Sloot, J. Dongarra (Eds.), Computational Science – ICCS 2006, Part III. XXXVI, 1136 pages. 2006.

Vol. 3992: V.N. Alexandrov, G.D. van Albada, P.M.A. Sloot, J. Dongarra (Eds.), Computational Science – ICCS 2006, Part II. XXXV, 1122 pages. 2006.

Vol. 3991: V.N. Alexandrov, G.D. van Albada, P.M.A. Sloot, J. Dongarra (Eds.), Computational Science – ICCS 2006, Part I. LXXXI, 1096 pages. 2006.

Vol. 3990: J. C. Beck, B.M. Smith (Eds.), Integration of AI and OR Techniques in Constraint Programming for Combinatorial Optimization Problems. X, 301 pages. 2006.

Vol. 3987: M. Hazas, J. Krumm, T. Strang (Eds.), Location- and Context-Awareness. X, 289 pages. 2006.

Vol. 3986: K. Stølen, W.H. Winsborough, F. Martinelli, F. Massacci (Eds.), Trust Management. XIV, 474 pages. 2006.

Vol. 3984: M. Gavrilova, O. Gervasi, V. Kumar, C.J. K. Tan, D. Taniar, A. Laganà, Y. Mun, H. Choo (Eds.), Computational Science and Its Applications - ICCSA 2006, Part V. XXV, 1045 pages. 2006.

Vol. 3983: M. Gavrilova, O. Gervasi, V. Kumar, C.J. K. Tan, D. Taniar, A. Laganà, Y. Mun, H. Choo (Eds.), Computational Science and Its Applications - ICCSA 2006, Part IV. XXVI, 1191 pages. 2006.

Vol. 3982: M. Gavrilova, O. Gervasi, V. Kumar, C.J. K. Tan, D. Taniar, A. Laganà, Y. Mun, H. Choo (Eds.), Computational Science and Its Applications - ICCSA 2006, Part III. XXV, 1243 pages. 2006.

Vol. 3981: M. Gavrilova, O. Gervasi, V. Kumar, C.J. K. Tan, D. Taniar, A. Laganà, Y. Mun, H. Choo (Eds.), Computational Science and Its Applications - ICCSA 2006, Part II. XXVI, 1255 pages. 2006.

Vol. 3980: M. Gavrilova, O. Gervasi, V. Kumar, C.J. K. Tan, D. Taniar, A. Laganà, Y. Mun, H. Choo (Eds.), Computational Science and Its Applications - ICCSA 2006, Part I. LXXV, 1199 pages. 2006.

Vol. 3979: T.S. Huang, N. Sebe, M.S. Lew, V. Pavlović, M. Kölsch, A. Galata, B. Kisačanin (Eds.), Computer Vision in Human-Computer Interaction. XII, 121 pages. 2006.

Vol. 3978: B. Hnich, M. Carlsson, F. Fages, F. Rossi (Eds.), Recent Advances in Constraints. VIII, 179 pages. 2006. (Sublibrary LNAI).

Vol. 3976: F. Boavida, T. Plagemann, B. Stiller, C. Westphal, E. Monteiro (Eds.), Networking 2006. Networking Technologies, Services, and Protocols; Performance of Computer and Communication Networks; Mobile and Wireless Communications Systems. XXVI, 1276 pages. 2006.

Vol. 3975: S. Mehrotra, D.D. Zeng, H. Chen, B. Thuraisingham, F.-Y. Wang (Eds.), Intelligence and Security Informatics. XXII, 772 pages. 2006.

Vol. 3973: J. Wang, Z. Yi, J.M. Zurada, B.-L. Lu, H. Yin (Eds.), Advances in Neural Networks - ISNN 2006, Part III. XXIX, 1402 pages. 2006.

Vol. 3972: J. Wang, Z. Yi, J.M. Zurada, B.-L. Lu, H. Yin (Eds.), Advances in Neural Networks - ISNN 2006, Part II. XXVII, 1444 pages. 2006.

Vol. 3971: J. Wang, Z. Yi, J.M. Zurada, B.-L. Lu, H. Yin (Eds.), Advances in Neural Networks - ISNN 2006, Part I. LXVII, 1442 pages. 2006.

Vol. 3970: T. Braun, G. Carle, S. Fahmy, Y. Koucheryavy (Eds.), Wired/Wireless Internet Communications. XIV, 350 pages. 2006.

Vol. 3968: K.P. Fishkin, B. Schiele, P. Nixon, A. Quigley (Eds.), Pervasive Computing. XV, 402 pages. 2006.

Vol. 3967: D. Grigoriev, J. Harrison, E.A. Hirsch (Eds.), Computer Science – Theory and Applications. XVI, 684 pages. 2006.

Vol. 3966: Q. Wang, D. Pfahl, D.M. Raffo, P. Wernick (Eds.), Software Process Change. XIV, 356 pages. 2006.

Vol. 3965: M. Bernardo, A. Cimatti (Eds.), Formal Methods for Hardware Verification. VII, 243 pages. 2006.

Vol. 3964: M. Ü. Uyar, A.Y. Duale, M.A. Fecko (Eds.), Testing of Communicating Systems. XI, 373 pages. 2006.

Vol. 3963: O. Dikenelli, M.-P. Gleizes, A. Ricci (Eds.), Engineering Societies in the Agents World VI. X, 303 pages. 2006. (Sublibrary LNAI).

Vol. 3962: W. IJsselsteijn, Y. de Kort, C. Midden, B. Eggen, E. van den Hoven (Eds.), Persuasive Technology. XII, 216 pages. 2006.

Vol. 3960: R. Vieira, P. Quaresma, M.d.G.V. Nunes, N.J. Mamede, C. Oliveira, M.C. Dias (Eds.), Computational Processing of the Portuguese Language. XII, 274 pages. 2006. (Sublibrary LNAI).

Vol. 3959: J.-Y. Cai, S. B. Cooper, A. Li (Eds.), Theory and Applications of Models of Computation. XV, 794 pages. 2006.

Vol. 3958: M. Yung, Y. Dodis, A. Kiayias, T. Malkin (Eds.), Public Key Cryptography - PKC 2006. XIV, 543 pages. 2006.

Vol. 3956: G. Barthe, B. Grégoire, M. Huisman, J.-L. Lanet (Eds.), Construction and Analysis of Safe, Secure, and Interoperable Smart Devices. IX, 175 pages. 2006.

Vol. 3955: G. Antoniou, G. Potamias, C. Spyropoulos, D. Plexousakis (Eds.), Advances in Artificial Intelligence. XVII, 611 pages. 2006. (Sublibrary LNAI).

Vol. 3954: A. Leonardis, H. Bischof, A. Pinz (Eds.), Computer Vision – ECCV 2006, Part IV. XVII, 613 pages. 2006.

Vol. 3953: A. Leonardis, H. Bischof, A. Pinz (Eds.), Computer Vision – ECCV 2006, Part III. XVII, 649 pages. 2006.

Vol. 3952: A. Leonardis, H. Bischof, A. Pinz (Eds.), Computer Vision – ECCV 2006, Part II. XVII, 661 pages. 2006.

Vol. 3951: A. Leonardis, H. Bischof, A. Pinz (Eds.), Computer Vision – ECCV 2006, Part I. XXXV, 639 pages. 2006.

Vol. 3950: J.P. Müller, F. Zambonelli (Eds.), Agent-Oriented Software Engineering VI. XVI, 249 pages. 2006.

Vol. 3947: Y.-C. Chung, J.E. Moreira (Eds.), Advances in Grid and Pervasive Computing. XXI, 667 pages. 2006.

Vol. 3946: T.R. Roth-Berghofer, S. Schulz, D.B. Leake (Eds.), Modeling and Retrieval of Context. XI, 149 pages. 2006. (Sublibrary LNAI).

Vol. 3945: M. Hagiya, P. Wadler (Eds.), Functional and Logic Programming. X, 295 pages. 2006.

Vol. 3944: J. Quiñonero-Candela, I. Dagan, B. Magnini, F. d'Alché-Buc (Eds.), Machine Learning Challenges. XIII, 462 pages. 2006. (Sublibrary LNAI).

Vol. 3943: N. Guelfi, A. Savidis (Eds.), Rapid Integration of Software Engineering Techniques. X, 289 pages. 2006.

Vol. 3942: Z. Pan, R. Aylett, H. Diener, X. Jin, S. Göbel, L. Li (Eds.), Technologies for E-Learning and Digital Entertainment. XXV, 1396 pages. 2006.

Vol. 3941: S.W. Gilroy, M.D. Harrison (Eds.), Interactive Systems. XI, 267 pages. 2006.

Vol. 3940: C. Saunders, M. Grobelnik, S. Gunn, J. Shawe-Taylor (Eds.), Subspace, Latent Structure and Feature Selection. X, 209 pages. 2006.

Vol. 3939: C. Priami, L. Cardelli, S. Emmott (Eds.), Transactions on Computational Systems Biology IV. VII, 141 pages. 2006. (Sublibrary LNBI).

Vol. 3936: M. Lalmas, A. MacFarlane, S. Rüger, A. Tombros, T. Tsikrika, A. Yavlinsky (Eds.), Advances in Information Retrieval. XIX, 584 pages. 2006.

Vol. 3935: D. Won, S. Kim (Eds.), Information Security and Cryptology - ICISC 2005. XIV, 458 pages. 2006.

Vol. 3934: J.A. Clark, R.F. Paige, F.A. C. Polack, P.J. Brooke (Eds.), Security in Pervasive Computing. X, 243 pages. 2006.

Vol. 3933: F. Bonchi, J.-F. Boulicaut (Eds.), Knowledge Discovery in Inductive Databases. VIII, 251 pages. 2006.

Vol. 3931: B. Apolloni, M. Marinaro, G. Nicosia, R. Tagliaferri (Eds.), Neural Nets. XIII, 370 pages. 2006.

Vol. 3930: D.S. Yeung, Z.-Q. Liu, X.-Z. Wang, H. Yan (Eds.), Advances in Machine Learning and Cybernetics. XXI, 1110 pages. 2006. (Sublibrary LNAI).

Vol. 3929: W. MacCaull, M. Winter, I. Düntsch (Eds.), Relational Methods in Computer Science. VIII, 263 pages. 2006.

Vol. 3928: J. Domingo-Ferrer, J. Posegga, D. Schreckling (Eds.), Smart Card Research and Advanced Applications. XI, 359 pages. 2006.

Vol. 3927: J. Hespanha, A. Tiwari (Eds.), Hybrid Systems: Computation and Control. XII, 584 pages. 2006.

Vol. 3925: A. Valmari (Ed.), Model Checking Software. X, 307 pages. 2006.

Vol. 3924: P. Sestoft (Ed.), Programming Languages and Systems. XII, 343 pages. 2006.

Vol. 3923: A. Mycroft, A. Zeller (Eds.), Compiler Construction. XIII, 277 pages. 2006.

Vol. 3922: L. Baresi, R. Heckel (Eds.), Fundamental Approaches to Software Engineering. XIII, 427 pages. 2006.

Vol. 3921: L. Aceto, A. Ingólfsdóttir (Eds.), Foundations of Software Science and Computation Structures. XV, 447 pages. 2006.

Vol. 3920: H. Hermanns, J. Palsberg (Eds.), Tools and Algorithms for the Construction and Analysis of Systems. XIV, 506 pages. 2006.

Vol. 3918: W.K. Ng, M. Kitsuregawa, J. Li, K. Chang (Eds.), Advances in Knowledge Discovery and Data Mining. XXIV, 879 pages. 2006. (Sublibrary LNAI).

Vol. 3917: H. Chen, F.-Y. Wang, C.C. Yang, D. Zeng, M. Chau, K. Chang (Eds.), Intelligence and Security Informatics. XII, 186 pages. 2006.

Vol. 3916: J. Li, Q. Yang, A.-H. Tan (Eds.), Data Mining for Biomedical Applications. VIII, 155 pages. 2006. (Sublibrary LNBI).